P. E. Doyle

BREAK-
THROUG

BREAK-
THROUGHS!

P. Ranganath Nayak, Ph.D.

and

John M. Ketteringham, Ph.D.

RAWSON ASSOCIATES: New York

Copyright © 1986 by Arthur D. Little, Inc.
All rights reserved
Published simultaneously in Canada by Collier Macmillan Canada, Inc.
Packaged by Rapid Transcript, a division of March Tenth, Inc.
Composition by Folio Graphics Co., Inc.
Printed and bound by Fairfield Graphics, Fairfield, Pennsylvania
Designed by Jacques Chazaud
First Edition

Library of Congress Cataloging-in-Publication Data

Nayak, P. Ranganath.
  Breakthroughs!

  Includes index.
  1. New products. 2. Inventions. 3. Creative
ability in business. I. Ketteringham, John M.
II. Title.
HF5415.153.K48 1986   306'.42   85-42858
ISBN 0-89256-294-3

Contents

Acknowledgments

From its earliest incarnation, this book has been the result of many people working together, most of them fitting this uncommon project into a normal schedule already crowded with other tasks. *Breakthroughs* never would have been born without the commitment of Alma Triner, Arthur D. Little vice-president of Public Relations. Alma Triner believed that it's possible to harness the varied talents of Arthur D. Little's professional staff long enough to draw from them a readable book. From the very first words of this book, writer David Benjamin immersed himself in this project and prodded both the corporation and the principal chapter investigators through the long months of research, travel, discussion, and composition.

There are many more within Arthur D. Little, Inc., who contributed some measure of themselves to the success of this effort. At the very highest level, Chief Executive Officer John Magee deemed *Breakthroughs* an appropriate project to mark Arthur D. Little's one-hundredth year of operation, and thus gave the book an irreversible impetus. Senior Vice-President Alfred E. Wechsler and Vice-President Karl Klaussen lent their moral and material support, maintaining a constant interest in the project without a hint of interference.

The most important individual in the initial development of this project was research assistant Kathy Carlson, who handled the intricacies of Nexus and the tedium of roaming through volumes of the *Business Periodicals Index* to compile background on our broad spectrum of topics.

A series of stalwart secretaries added to their workload to contribute pieces to the arduous production of drafts, redrafts, edits, revisions, and thousands of photocopies of the manuscript. The lead secretaries of this group were Hans Sachdeva and Robin Lewis. But the job never could have been done without Jane Reehl, Ruth Hergenrother, Ann Swartz, Ann Marie Gattuso, Anne Flaherty, Roseanne DeVito, Joanne Ashe, Sandy Murray, Doris McDermott, Nancy Gray, Cindy Gray, Mildred Brown, Patricia Mayo, and Karyn Powers.

Several key people within Arthur D. Little stepped in during moments of organizational crisis to steer the project back onto course. The concern, competence, and unselfishness of Kathryn Graf, Ann Laynor, and Helen Taverna were invaluable.

Without the assistance of a team of Arthur D. Little professionals in our Tokyo office, the substantial Japanese presence in *Breakthroughs* would be impossible. The head of Arthur D. Little's Tokyo operation, Yoshimichi Yamashita, was most critical in this assistance, but hardly more than his brilliant aide Makiko Yoshimoto. Contacts with a host of Japanese firms were expedited ably by Yoshikatsu Sawada and Hiroyuki Sakemi.

We must add special thanks to Arthur D. Little board member Charles Robinson, without whose intercession the Nike story might have been cancelled, Mason Irving, an Arthur D. Little chemist without whom the Tagamet story might have been incomprehensible, and Janet Parenteau, a manager at Delphi Associates, Inc., an Arthur D. Little subsidiary, who guided us to a crucial element of the Nautilus tale.

We owe thanks that cannot be repaid to the "witnesses" of our stories, participants in the breakthrough events who gave to us their time and candor and contributed to these chapters whatever vividness they contain. Many of their names are included in the chapters that follow, but others worked in anonymity. In every company we visited, we felt welcome, and free to carry out lengthy interviews, because of the people who helped behind the scenes. We offer our gratitude, and admiration, to the following helpers and friends.

At the Victor Company of Japan, Toshihiro Kikuchi and his public relations staff, including Shuji Kurita, Masayuki Murakami, Makoto Nakamura, and Junko Yoshida; additional thanks to John Egawa of JVC-America and to Tadahiro Sakao, who lent so much insight.

At RCA, William E. Boss (vice-president of Distributor and Commercial Relations), Frank McCann, and Paul Harding.

At 3M Corporation, Donald Fischer and Judy Borowski of Public Relations, Julianne H. Prager, Lester C. Krogh (vice-president of Research and Development), and Jerry Partington.

At ChemLawn, Chairman Jack Van Fossen, who personally conducted us to everyone we needed to know.

At Montedison, besides the ubiquitous Dr. Paolo Galli, Dr. Camillo Barbe, Dr. Tonino Simonazzi, and Dr. George Oppenlander.

At Mitsui Petrochemical, Akio Iwatsubo, Kei Uda, Dr. Norio Kashiwa, and Dr. Hideo Mineshima.

At Sony Corporation, Haruyuki Machida, head of Public Relations, and "Walkman Team" members Kunio Shimizu, Shizuo Takashino, Katsuya Nakagawa, and Takichi Tezuka.

At Thorn-EMI, Colin Woodley (head of Public Relations) and Robert Froggatt.

At Raytheon Corporation, Newell Garden and Jeffrey Charney of Public Relations, Arthur Friedman, and John Osepchuk.

At Amana Refrigeration, advertising chief Fred Streicher, Ann Collins of Public Relations, and engineer Louis Blackburn.

At New Japan Radio Corporation, Chokichiro Shibata, head of Research.

At Toshiba Corporation, Masaki Mikura of the Public Relations office, Tadashi Seino and Keiji Noda of the Kitchen Appliance and Refrigerator Division.

At SmithKline Beckman, Gustave Gumpert and Billie Rorres of the Public Relations office, James Geddes, Donald van Roden, Dr. Leon C. Greene and Alan J. Dalby; and in London, Frank W. Hodson. Also, at the Welwyn Research Institute, Research Director Roger Brimblecombe and chemist Dr. Graham Durant.

At Nike, Mary E. Marckx of the Public Relations office, Kenya Palmer, Pamela Magee, and Del Hayes.

At Nautilus, Mark Crone (head of Public Relations), Theresa Nulph, June Cramer, and Harry Lafconski.

At Toyota Motor Works, Tokio Horigome and Hiroshi Gankhoji of the Research and Communications office.

At Federal Express, Nancy Neal of Public Relations and Chief Executive Officer James Barksdale.

Also, our Japanese research was illuminated by the work of four gifted translators, Yoshiko Takeyama and Mari Kurihara of Sansei International, Toyko; Kei Uda at Mitsui Petrochemical; and Junko Yoshida at JVC.

Finally, we owe thanks to one vital member of the Arthur D. Little family who defused several potential explosions and added love to the breakthrough equation, Jean Poskel.

BREAK-THROUGHS!

Innovators, Inventors, and Facilitators

When a handpicked group of Arthur D. Little consultants began the process of choosing topics to be included in a book about great commercial breakthroughs and how they grew, we were professionally curious. For one hundred years, Arthur D. Little, Inc. has been helping companies devise new products, new technologies, and new methods, and in this role we have helped hundreds of enterprises to be born or reborn. With such a heritage, it's compulsive for us to want to dissect successful concepts.

But the drive to proceed with this book, which has involved a substantial investment of the company's time and money, also sprang from a need to examine the heart of the process we so often have accelerated. In 1886, a chemist named Arthur D. Little made a breakthrough by establishing the first business anywhere to devote its full energy to contract research, applying scientific inquiry to the needs of industry and government. From that beginning, contract research has become a multi-billion-dollar industry with hundreds of profitable participants worldwide.

After Dr. Little's entrepreneurial breakthrough, Dr. Little's company turned its attention to other people's breakthrough ideas, lending to them technology, imagination, and direction. For one hundred years, the growing family of Arthur D. Little consultants has served as a touchstone to other inventors' ideas; we have been facilitators to breakthroughs. It seemed fitting to us that, after a century of such service, we return to our own origins as curious, objective researchers. We thought we should explore some breakthroughs that we had not assisted. We thought that this exploration might tell us whether we were still teaching the right things after all these years, whether there might yet be more that we could learn and pass on to our clients. We already knew that when we helped a client solve a problem that was holding back a good idea, we were gaining as much new knowledge from the experience as our client gained in commercial success.

When, for example, in 1939 the Cream of Wheat Company saw the world passing their cereal by, they came to Arthur D. Little, and we devised the first instant fully enriched hot cereal—transforming breakfast for millions of Americans. When in 1942 the government of Puerto Rico sought our help in creating jobs for their people, Arthur D. Little invented the first multi-faceted industrial development project, called Operation Bootstrap, creating an international model for economic recovery projects. In 1945 Merck and Company came to Arthur D. Little to find out if a certain chemical could be used safely to enhance the flavor of food. The resulting Arthur D. Little development was called "Accent," and it rapidly became the generic term for all brands of monosodium glutamate. In 1961 the Husky Oil Company asked Arthur D. Little if we could make a smokefree barbecue fuel from lignite. The outcome was the first charcoal briquet, and it helped make cooking-out a painless and convenient experience.

We have helped companies to break through in far less evident ways—in the development of industrial processes, restructuring of management, mapping out distribution and communications systems, and more recently, in such fields as managing information systems and exploring artificial intelligence.

Sometime in 1984, the concept of exploring the creativity that is at the heart of breakthroughs occupied a small group of Arthur D. Little consultants. The discussion, as usual, ranged far and wide. Two of the members of that discussion group concluded that the best way to examine the issue of our creativity would be to examine companies for whom the breakthrough experience was newer than one hundred years old. Ten years, they decided, would provide a fresher perspective. And rather than focusing presumptively on the qualities that characterize a breakthrough company, these two curious consultants, P. Ranganath Nayak and John Ketteringham, said, "Let's choose a number of products, services, and industrial processes that are widely acknowledged as breakthroughs. Let's make sure they represent a broad spectrum of industries and interests, and let's be sure these breakthroughs reach as far into the corners of the world as possible."

Nayak and Ketteringham, who became the coauthors of this book, assembled a team of a dozen people. The task for each of these team members was to serve as principal investigator into one or two breakthrough stories, then return to the group to tell the tale and relate his or her new knowledge to the findings gathered by the others. Ideally, each principal investigator possessed an in-depth knowledge of the technologies, market dynamics, and business culture of the field in which the breakthrough occurred. But if we were to succeed in pursuit of insights into this hoary topic of invention, we had to apply more than just a technical specialist's insight into our final analyses.

John Ketteringham is the leader of Arthur D. Little's international health care and research planning practices. He took on the investigation of the development of the CT scanning X-ray machine at EMI (chapter 7).

P. Ranganath Nayak, manager of Arthur D. Little's operations management group, led research on the development of the Walkman portable cassette player at Sony Corporation (chapter 6) and the creation of the Toyota Production System (chapter 9).

David Fishman, a management consultant with a background in the entertainment industry, broadcasting, and consumer electronics, led the investigation into the triumph of the VHS-format video cassette recorder (VCR) at JVC, Inc., in Japan, and RCA in the United States (chapter 2).

Derek Till, director of Arthur D. Little's product technology laboratories, and an expert in adhesives, surface coatings, and paper and textile technology, undertook the investigation of 3M Corporation's Post-it Note Pads™ (chapter 3), otherwise known as "those little yellow sticky pads."

Elliott Wilbur, head of Arthur D. Little's resource consulting practice and an expert on the unique dynamics of large-scale service industries, led the examination of ChemLawn Corporation's birth and growth (chapter 4) as America's first national lawn care provider.

Amram Shapiro, leader of our practice in the strategic management of technology, led the research on the discovery and marketing of Tagamet (chapter 5) by Smith Kline & French, Inc. Tagamet, which heals ulcers in the human gastrointestinal tract, became the most successful prescription drug in history.

Richard F. Topping, a senior staff engineer familiar with the appliance industry, also had to visit a number of companies, Raytheon and Amana Refrigeration in the United States and New Japan Radio Corporation in Japan, to explore the breakthrough of the microwave oven (chapter 8).

Ellen Curtiss, one of the leaders of Arthur D. Little Decision Resources, which examines the impact of economic change on industry, led the research effort on the explosive growth of Nike, Inc. (chapter 10) and its distinctive athletic footwear.

David Benjamin, the writer charged with assembling the varied investigations into a cohesive storybook, assisted in research on each chapter, but also took as his own the examination of Nautilus, Inc., (chapter 11) and the exercise machine boom that it launched.

Philip Roussel, a twenty-seven-year veteran of the DuPont Corporation before coming to Arthur D. Little as a consultant to the chemical industries, examined the emergence of a revolutionary high-yield catalyst for the ubiquitous plastic known in the industry as polypropylene (chapter 12). Roussel's research embraced two companies who joined in the dramatic research effort, Montedison SpA. of Italy and Mitsui Petrochemical of Japan.

Richard Norris, a logistics expert, undertook the investigation of Federal Express (chapter 13), researching its beginnings as a company and its creation of the overnight delivery industry in the United States.

In each investigation, principal investigators returned to the *Breakthroughs* team explaining that they had learned more than they expected and had found out facts that defied their expectations. Almost always we realized that the conventional wisdom about innovation diverged dramatically from our real stories of innovation.

In the stories we investigated, we were able to learn more than many others who had researched before us, because we talked to the troops as well as to the executives. And in doing so, we reinforced a healthy disrespect for overly tidy tales of spectacular success. Articles in scientific and business journals tend to depict discovery as a smooth progression, but the actual course of research inevitably is marked by detours, halts and fits of pique that are excised in the retelling. *Because we regard these detours, halts, and fits of pique as often vital to the outcome, we have retained them in our retelling of each story,* many related here for the first time, as they really happened.

1 | Stalking the Breakthrough: We Begin Our Journeys

This is a book about breakthroughs—breakthroughs that are social, medical, technological, and commercial, but mostly commercial. This book is expressly devoted to things that sell . . . and sell . . . and keep on selling. This means we have disregarded compelling tales of courageous researchers working in obscurity on orphan inventions. This is a book about crackpot notions that broke the bank.

It's about whole industries and markets that changed because someone figured out how to get it there faster or make it better or probe deeper without even rippling the surface.

It's about instant mail, instant health, instant food, instant lawns, and instant fortunes. It's about dreams come true. It's about itches scratched. It's about us.

These are stories about the individuals and companies who found big needs and little openings—and filled them.

These stories are an inside look at the creativity and ingenuity, the persistence and conflict, the politics and publicity, the determination and dumb luck that took twelve significant commercial breakthroughs of the past two decades from their conception to domination of markets that in some cases hadn't even existed before.

It's about things that people start taking for granted almost as soon as they notice them at all. For instance, when did you notice that there were Toyotas everywhere? When did they start popping up? And why is it so hard to recall the *first* Toyota you ever saw?

For that matter, where did all those health clubs come from? And those video stores? And who can remember when the only "athletic footwear" anybody owned was a pair of standard-issue, canvas-topped, flat-bottomed, solid-white sneakers?

This is a book about the little changes in our habits that don't seem very important, but if we think about going back to the way it was before, we can't imagine it. Each in its own way, these stories chronicle a heightening of our perception of "the quality of life."

For instance, go to the beach and listen. What *don't* you hear? The answer: transistor radios and "boom boxes" beside every beach blanket—blending Van Cliburn and Van Halen into a hundred private sets of ears, drowning out the sound of the ocean and the cries of the gulls. Why, seemingly overnight, this uncivilized silence? It's quiet because one day a senior executive (who was supposed to be retired) wandered through a research lab and heard music, not on the radio but on a tape recorder that couldn't record anything; it was a failed prototype. But something twinkled in the old man's eye—if someone were to hook that machine up to a pair of earphones he'd seen in a different laboratory, he could significantly reduce the little machine's energy drain and then fit the recording function *back in!* That retired executive happened to be one of the founders of the Sony Corporation, and he happened to be completely wrong about the purpose of those earphones. But never mind. The result of that twinkle in his eye was the Walkman, which has stilled the din, enriched arid stretches of routine boredom, turned joggers into traffic hazards, exposed the philistine to high fidelity sound, and thereby affected irreversibly the quality of millions of lives.

This is a book of similar human stories that serve, in a shrinking world, as the adventures of our time—the intellectual and financial expeditions into the unknown that must precede every commercial breakthrough.

For many readers, the chapters that follow will have value because of the adventure of "discovery." They'll be worth their weight in vicarious satisfaction. But if telling these stories were this book's only purpose, someone else would have written it. The authors are professional consultants in management and technology. The challenge we assumed in researching these events was to find the patterns, the common threads that might emerge in a variety of commercial breakthroughs in a range of disparate fields. Our purpose, bravely conceived, was to link the pieces, to see if we could create from them a recognizable jigsaw picture, a coherent, repeatable process.

We thought we could. After all, Arthur D. Little consultants have invented a host of new products and obtained hundreds of patents; helped other companies redesign their inventions into workable, marketable prototypes; devised manufacturing processes and marketing strategies for thousands of clients around the world. We've been in this business for a hundred years, and during that time, we've conveyed our know-how to generation after generation of scientists, technologists, inventors, managers, corporations, and governments.

We are not the first thoughtful team to tackle the secrets of the commercial breakthrough. Because people, since the invention of currency, have regarded invention as the road to wealth and recognition, it is one of civilization's most discussed, studied, analyzed, and belabored subjects of discourse. This fascination has given birth to countless nostrums ("Early to bed, early to rise. . . ."; "Build a better mousetrap. . . .") and libraries full of earnest (and mostly unread) dissertations. Most of us have come up with an idea that's going to make us rich as soon as we can figure out how to make it work. And American business writing today is immersed in a frenzy of discussion about "entrepreneurialism," "intrapreneurship," and the "management of innovation."

John Jewkes, author of *The Sources of Invention* and probably history's most eloquent commentator on the topic of the commercial breakthrough, summed up the dilemma of all his predecessors and successors.

> . . . The writings on invention, whilst vast and ever increasing, are of extraordinarily mixed quality. There seems to be no subject in which traditional and uncritical stories, casual rumours, sweeping generalizations, myths and conflicting records more widely abound, in which every man seems to be interested and in which, perhaps because miracles seem to be the natural order, skepticism is at a discount. Perhaps no one can hope entirely to escape the mild mesmerizing influence of the subject.

Certainly the first reason this book became a growing obsession among a group of Arthur D. Little professionals was the "mild mesmerizing influence of the subject." As we began our discussion of breakthrough ideas, our team of consultants transformed almost immediately into a tiny band of storytellers. We shared a barrage of anecdotes and oddities. We talked about Archimedes' bathtub and

Newton's apple, Galvani's frogs, Gutenberg's press, Fleming's mold, Land's camera, De Forest's vacuum tube, Shockley's transistor, and Diners Club's plastic card. We had to make a point of distinguishing the lasting breakthroughs from the fads—so we talked about 3-D movies, Silly Putty, mood rings, Peter Max, Pet Rocks, and "Space Invaders."

Robert Fraser, a program systems specialist who had helped several states develop lotteries, told about the company that "invented" orange juice concentrate. The original goal was instant powdered orange juice for use by the armed forces, but their result was "glop" which refused to dry. The scientists, after one long and fruitless day, put a batch of their glop into the refrigerator and went home. Overnight, the glop coagulated. When they added water and stirred, it regained all the qualities of orange juice—including flavor. Shortly thereafter followed the idea that, whether or not the infantry ever got its powdered orange juice, you could stop with the glop, freeze that, and make orange juice a lot easier for *nonmilitary* personnel. The brand name of the historic product that emerged was Minute Maid.

And as we told stories, we sought key elements that would connect all breakthroughs and show us our pattern. But we also realized how easy it is to find a story that breaks the rules. Management consultant David Fishman insisted he could tell the story of a commercial breakthrough that violates every assumption—a breakthrough that did not break new technological ground, which had no apparent champion fighting for it against all odds, which enjoyed no miraculous accidental elevation to public awareness, which was literally left to wither and die *in spite of* overwhelming public enthusiasm.

Talking movies, said Fishman, which burst on the scene—according to legend—with Al Jolson's *The Jazz Singer* in 1927, had been technologically feasible since Thomas Edison had synchronized motion pictures with sound in 1911. But, with the exception of a few experimental short subjects, "Edison's Talking Pictures" languished for eighteen years. The company that had the franchise, Vitagraph, never exercised it and felt no pressure for change from a secure industry that had built its prosperity on silent pictures. It felt no pressure from the public, because the public didn't know what it was missing. When Warner Brothers finally tried one all-talking picture *(The Lights of New York)* in 1928, the public response was immensely favorable. Movie houses worked feverishly to equip themselves with sound, spending dollars they could ill afford as the Great Depression took hold. The end of the Silent Era eventually took four years, a very slow transition for a very trend-conscious industry. The movie studios' resistance to sound is one of the odd chapters in the history of film.

Both in our discussions and in the literature search that began with this project, we observed a confusion—among ourselves as well as among our forebears—between a breakthrough's origins and its process. Too often, people have hastened to state a how-to-do-it formula before understanding the intricacies of how a breakthrough really happened. Too often, commentators have been willing to accept the second-hand version of a breakthrough story. But we have a professional mistrust of tidy stories and a deep-seated aversion to serving food that we haven't tasted ourselves.

This book is a book of discovery, not prescription. The many intangible elements that affect a breakthrough make it impossible to extrapolate a sure-fire success formula. We have tried to avoid the process obsession of the many innovation experts who have preceded us with their hidebound theses. Many of these writers have been right, to some extent, in what they formulate for general emulation. But they often are wrong. And when they are not outright wrong, they frequently are misinformed by sources too far removed from what really happened.

As we prepared for our field work, we collected scrapbooks full of invention, innovation, and entrepreneurial assertions. These assertions compose a vast and fluid mythology. We can only offer here a sampling of these myths, but these are some of the most firmly and erroneously cherished.

THE MYTH: Commercial breakthroughs come from ideas that nobody had before.

THE REALITY: The old saying is "There's nothing new under the sun." Very often, what seems new is something that others before have devised but never quite figured out how to do. Before Sir James Black discovered the second histamine receptor in the human body—which led to the development of a drug called Tagamet, which heals ulcers (chapter 5), he had read about the same concept in scientific journals. But the articles he read were written by people who had given up on the idea.

And Sir Godfrey Hounsfield—who invented the CAT scan machine (chapter 7)—was not the first scientist to imagine an X ray that produces three-dimensional scans of the human body. What both Black and Hounsfield had, that others lacked, was what we have come to describe as the "elegant concept," a mental picture on the part of the inventor in which the breakthrough appears virtually whole. Though in both cases the journey from that concept to its realization was long and difficult, both men knew exactly what they were looking for as soon as they had begun.

Fred Smith, founder of Federal Express, also had seen examples of his concept. The hub-and-spokes transportation system that makes Federal Express work was a feature of at least three air freight services as early as the 1930s. What was new in Fred Smith's concept was the enormous scale of Federal Express. From the beginning, Smith had seen something very big. It was an old concept turned "elegant" in the mind of the breakthrough individual.

THE MYTH: Inventors make breakthroughs.

THE REALITY: Ingenuity is a step, not an end in itself. Inventors, more accurately, have greater power than anyone to trigger breakthroughs, but once invented, a concept must be manufacturable, marketable, and competitive. Inventors need help. So do clever marketers. Eventually, to be commercially successful, a concept requires a measure of organizational cohesion—*teamwork*.

Sometimes, it requires the contributions of a series of people in a series of organizations. The microwave oven (chapter 8) very likely never would have existed without the imagination of Raytheon Corporation's Percy Spencer, who is credited as its inventor. But the microwave oven's breakthrough into the eventual marketplace occurred twenty years after Spencer's invention, and it required redesign by a second inventive genius, Keishi Ogura of New Japan Radio Corporation, and it needed, finally, the help of a relentless marketing genius, George Foerstner of Amana.

THE MYTH: If you build a better mousetrap, the world will beat a path to your doorstep.

THE REALITY: Ideally, any time you can dramatically improve an existing technology (the mousetrap), you should have a breakthrough product that makes you the dominant force in that marketplace. But a fast-moving competitor with a better understanding of the market and an ability to match your technological ingenuity may succeed in paving the path to *his* door more quickly.

In the development of the video cassette recorder (VCR) (chapter 2) using half-inch video tape, Sony got to the market first with the Beta format. But a smaller company, JVC Corporation, not only produced a comparable technology a few months later (in an entirely independent research effort), but they enlisted the collaboration of the majority of consumer electronics companies in Japan to help them manufacture and market the new VHS format. In the end, because JVC used better bait for the same mousetrap, the smaller company got most of the mice.

THE MYTH: All the great ideas come from little guys.

THE REALITY: Certain innovations, especially those that require relatively small investments of capital but a large commitment of individual labor, tend to come from independent entrepreneurs. But innovations that require substantial financial investment and teamwork often emerge within big organizations. In our collection of breakthroughs, the big/small ratio splits almost evenly. If there is a grain of truth in this myth, it lies in the fact that when a breakthrough emerges from a big company, it tends to begin within a not-very-cooperative handful of people whose greatest pleasure is to break off small branches of the big corporate tree and bend them to their own will.

The amazing ulcer-healing drug Tagamet emerged at Smith Kline & French, a large Philadelphia pharmaceuticals company, partly because a gang of obstinate Britons and Scotsmen refused to stop working on the project in the company's small and frugal English research laboratory. But the drug went to market because, once aware of the breakthrough that was brewing in Britain, the Philadelphia management reversed directions, built a $4 million chemical plant, and assembled an international distribution network that gave the company the sales capacity to turn Tagamet from a mere success into an explosion.

THE MYTH: Big success requires big resources.

THE REALITY: At each stage in the process of development, a concept requires a balance of human commitment and financial resources. That balance depends to a great extent on the concept itself. The key is not big resources, but the right resources at the right time. Sometimes the right resources must be large—as was eventually the case in the capitalization of Federal Express. But often—as was true in Sony's tight-fisted approach to the Walkman (chapter 6)—money is almost a forbidden element.

By the same token, we found in our research that the value of "bootlegging" (a popular but ill-defined term that refers to the illicit expropriation of money, within a large company, to carry on unauthorized research) has been significantly overstated. We uncovered only two or three arguable instances of bootlegging among our breakthrough companies, and we saw little indication that a shortage or secrecy of funds provides any more encouragement to committed innovation than does budgeted money and corporate approval. We have, however, uncovered several instances of companies assigning money to their research group for the stated purpose of "bootlegging." Paving a shortcut is an excellent way to scare away the people who blazed it.

THE MYTH: The commercial breakthrough requires a special sort of environment.

THE REALITY: As a rule, it is apparent that employees are happier and more productive working in organizations that follow certain guidelines to create an "environment for creativity." Not so apparent is the idea that this environment can somehow nurture the latent ingenuity in its researchers. Also widely believed is that "corporate culture" can either generate or stifle the innovative spirit within the organization. The stories in this book do not support the idea that certain sorts of organizational environments encourage or discourage breakthroughs. The variety, complexity, and flexibility of *people* and organizations composed of *people* dwarf our ability to reduce them to categories.

In our research, we have opened ourselves to an astounding range of breakthrough environments: a compartmentalized Japanese corporation that seems to discourage interdepartmental communication by emphasizing group solidarity and keeping different groups away from each other; a small town in Ohio; a demoralized research center scheduled for imminent phase-out, in northern Italy; a rotting porch in Lake Helen, Florida; a reconnaissance plane somewhere over the jungles of Vietnam; an understaffed electronics lab in Tokyo where researchers could work only part-time, because they were required to spend part of every week doing field repairs; a large, structured corporation in Minnesota, which requires that each new idea be "sold" by its inventor to the manufacturing and marketing staffs in a network of separate divisions.

THE MYTH: Breakthroughs always respond to an unfulfilled need.

THE REALITY: It is true that no breakthrough becomes commercial unless the people developing it see a market for it. But it is flatly wrong—though we have encountered this assertion frequently—to say that the bulk of successful commercial innovation results from "market pull" rather than "technology push." That is a topsy-turvy analysis—it expresses the *outcome* of a new idea as its *origin*.

In discussions with sixteen companies involved in getting a dozen commercial breakthroughs under way, we asked specifically what was the motivating force—what *really* got the idea going at the very beginning. We focused not on the beginning of product development, but on the *concept* that preceded development. In every case, in all sixteen, it was "technology push"—more accurately, it was the *curiosity* within the originating person—that lit the fire. Neither financial need nor market intelligence played a major role in these exceptional beginnings.

What experts reveal when they assert the predominance of some notion like "market pull" is that they identify more with the administrators of research than with the creators of it. Part of our act of discovery in the research for this book—and a great pleasure besides—was to descend from the upper echelons and venture into the dungeons of research, to explore the sometimes remarkably humble and irrational beginnings of the eventual breakthrough. What we found in the dungeons were people best described as "problem-solvers." Sometimes the new thing they devised solved a technical problem that had been itching at their cortex for a long time. Sometimes the new thing was the solution for a personal problem, a need unfulfilled that bears an interesting similarity to the creative impulse of the artist. Sometimes the problem was a mixture of technological curiosity and creative need. But it always was a *problem to be solved,* not a fortune to be made, not a market to be exploited.

Certainly, the search for a market often followed quickly on the heels of the problem-solver's drive. In some cases it was a parallel phenomenon. *But we found no instance of the market demanding a breakthrough before the inventor had found it lurking in the depths of his febrile semiconsciousness.*

Our opening definition of a breakthrough—to launch us on our research—was that it must be something that visibly, dramatically changed the way people, society, or an industry behaves. After much research, we confidently added to this our conviction that breakthroughs must begin with the urge to solve a problem. But clearly it isn't enough to say that the impulse to solve is sufficient to the solution. It must be expressed properly. In many of our cases we found that the proper *statement* of the problem was embodied in the idea of the "elegant concept." Godfrey Hounsfield, whose first CT scanning machine (chapter 7) was truly an elegant concept, got it together virtually whole in his mind before he set to work on his prototype. He did not see the concept in a flash of inspiration.

Hounsfield typified what philosopher/psychologist Arthur Koestler, in *The Act of Creation,* calls the "bisociative" thinker. Once presented with a problem, Hounsfield could not rid himself of it. It followed him wherever he went and plagued him most persistently when other distractions receded from his consciousness. Koestler's example of this "bisociative" thinker is Archimedes, who was told to weigh the gold in the king's crown without melting the crown and separating the different metals. Archimedes also fretted constantly with his problem and found it most intrusive in times of repose—as when he was taking a bath.

Archimedes, unable to let go of his mental picture of Hiero's crown, finally looked down to notice his own physical volume displacing the water in his tub and shouted, "Eureka!" He had discovered the law of displacement of solids literally surrounding him. In the same way, Hounsfield, living perpetually with his incomplete image of the scanner, finally saw it, built it, and it worked. There was, for both, that "flash of insight," but one that had been arduously cultivated by incessant, obsessive contemplation of the problem.

Koestler defines bisociation as "an escape—from boredom, stagnation, intellectual predicaments, and emotional frustration . . . it is signalled by the spontaneous flash of insight which shows a familiar situation or event in a new light, and elicits a new response to it. The bisociative act connects previously unconnected matrices of experience; it makes us understand what it is . . . 'to be living on several planes at once.' "

In our research, we realized that not everyone can think the way that Archimedes and Hounsfield did. As many management analysts vaguely state, there is a certain type of person who behaves innovatively. Jewkes describes this person as "isolated; because he is engrossed with ideas that he believes to be new and therefore mark him out from other men . . . the world is against him, for it is normally against change and he is against the world. . . ." Management expert Peter Drucker says that no breakthrough happens without the involvement of a "monomaniac with a mission."

Once, trying to firm up these subjective analyses a little bit, Bell Laboratories tried to isolate and quantify the individual qualities of the so-called "creative type." Among all the creative people they selected and studied, they found only two characteristics that correlated clearly enough to indicate a trend. Creative people, Bell Labs concluded, have an exceptional tolerance for living with messy work environments, and they have a well-developed sense of humor.

According to Koestler, humor is the most basic form of bisociative thinking. An effective joke leads the listener along a particular plane of reference and then surprises him, at the punch line, by shifting the plane of reference—virtually standing listeners' perceptions on their ear.

The story of the boastful Texan vacationing in Maine provides a succinct example. The Texan, surveying the puny landholdings of a local farmer, explains that back home on the range, he can get into his car and drive all day without ever crossing his own property line. The Mainer pauses a moment to digest this thought, shifts his toothpick, and replies, "Ayuh. Had a car like that myself once."

The farmer, in this story, is the "bisociater." At the point where the two lines of thinking—property and cars—meet, the farmer *creates* a whole new perception of events, by following the less obvious direction. The farmer, more creative than the Texan, sees a connection in dissimilar things, associates them—or "bisociates"—and produces something new. In this case, bisociation is funny. More seriously, as a *metaphor,* a bringing together of the likeness of the dissimilar, the bisociative vision can be profound.

Thomas P. Hughes, writing recently about the "inventive"

personality, referred to that "certain sort of person" as a "meta-phor-maker." Aristotle wrote that the mastery of metaphor "is a sign of genius, since a good metaphor implies an intuitive perception of the similarity of the dissimilar."[1]

In this light, clearly, the concepts of bisociation and metaphor are nearly identical. Hughes says, "The inventor needs the intuition of the metaphor-maker, some of the insight of Newton, the imagination of the poet, and, perhaps, a touch of the irrational obsession of the schizophrenic. The myth of the inventor as mad genius is not without content."[2]

Perhaps metaphor-making is only a piece of what we were looking for as we undertook this book. But add this to the impulse of the problem-solver and suddenly there are clues that help us to understand that "monomaniac with a mission." This compelling perception about metaphorical thinking underscored an idea that had attracted us from the outset—that the central element in the breakthrough is people. But these are not just good people, not just "persistent" people. These are exceptional people, very difficult to characterize or identify before their emergence as heroes of the breakthrough.

It was some private quality, not even as tangible as bisociative or metaphorical thinking, that motivated Spencer Silver, the man who discovered the adhesive that eventually was applied to 3M Corporation's Post-it Note Pads, "those little yellow sticky pads" (chapter 3). Silver was not the problem-solver who figured out what to do with the adhesive, nor did he see the necessary metaphor. But he knew there was something special about the stuff, and he shopped his little vials of glue around the corporation for five years. People took turns at turning him down, and everybody got a chance—until he finally caught the attention of the right person, the "bisociater" Arthur Fry.

Silver's motivation for persisting had little to do with market potential for the odd adhesive, nor was it a drive for power, which is implicit in many depictions of the "intrapreneur." According to his own admission, Silver kept shopping his idea around an indifferent 3M Corporation because it was "my baby." He had created something, and he would not readily abandon the evidence of his paternity until a use was found for it.

1. Thomas P. Hughes, "How Did the Heroic Inventors Do It?" *American Heritage of Invention and Technology,* fall 1985, page 22.
2. Hughes, page 22.

No one in his right mind would have predicted that Arthur Jones, a social recluse with a bizarre fondness for crocodiles, would give birth to one of the most revolutionary recreational (and social) devices—the Nautilus machine (chapter 11)—in modern times. No one could have identified Percy Spencer, prowling among the radar-builders of Raytheon in 1943, as the man who would change the cooking and eating habits of America—by discovering that he could cook popcorn in front of a microwave guide.

It is the unlikeliness of heroes like these, and in some cases the number of heroes in any of these stories, that makes the breakthrough such a delight to explore and such a quandary to classify. In each of these stories, perhaps the connection is this: that in each one there is at least one person for whom the normal rewards of life—making a living, doing a good job, raising a family, earning the respect of his peers and community—were insufficient. In each story here, there is someone who needed to leave behind to posterity some sign that he had lived and died and made his mark, to give birth to some product or service or enterprise or creation that would live beyond him. In each story, consider the fact that there is someone who might be called a legacy-builder, someone whose desire for a measure of immortality kept him searching for ways to express that desire—beyond reason—and beyond the patience of the average human being.

In our research, we became fascinated with *feelings* like this in people like Spencer Silver at 3M, Dick Duke at ChemLawn, Arthur Jones at Nautilus, and Yuma Shiraishi at JVC. The emergence of the breakthrough came not just in these individuals' outward behavior, but from their hearts, from their spirit. We think the drive from conception to breakthrough is fundamentally fueled by some spirit within individuals. As far as we can determine, this deep-seated personal feeling—manifested in behavior that includes a man looking at a vial of glue and calling it "my baby"—is not the sort of thing an organization can instill in people in order to generate breakthroughs of its own. But whether or not these extraordinary successes can be replicated, we suspect that getting closer to the people who made them happen gets us closer to the how-to-do-it answers that everybody wants.

For Arthur D. Little, the issue of replication is foremost among all our considerations. We want to generate guidelines useful for companies eager to make their own breakthroughs. A host of widely held perceptions never survived our research. We did not find a magic bullet for commercial breakthroughs. They happen in many ways. And the elements that many of these breakthroughs share form a frequently flawed, often confusing, but provocative pattern.

Throughout these stories, we have tried to find and emphasize the similarities that connect one with another, and perhaps with several others. Some of our connections are very tenuous, but that's as it should be. In the end, this investigation was more meaningful to us with lingering questions than it would have been with a pat answer. You will find in these stories no certain elements that assure commercial breakthrough, but we have identified a number of elements without which a breakthrough is almost certainly impossible.

This is a book, then, that will narrow your margin of error—but won't close it. Those who read simply for the pleasure of sharing these adventures probably will have the best time. Those who *gain* the most will be those who, though they begin by seeking the one true key to the great commercial breakthrough, emerge satisfied with knowing where to find the lock.

2 JVC and the VCR Miracle: "You Should Be Very Polite and Gentle"

I n 1926, when inventor Kenjiro Takayanagi formed the trembling image of the Japanese *katakana* ideogram for the letter "e" inside a cathode tube, he created one of the world's first television shows. It was the beginning of an industry that would be born again in other nations at other times and that, within thirty years, would become the most pervasive entertainment medium in human history.

But in the early 1950s, when Takayanagi looked back at those thirty years, he did not see an entirely perfect view of great accomplishment and social good. For one thing, his company, the Victor Company of Japan, Ltd., or JVC, had not exploited or profited much from the emergence of television as a worldwide industry after World War II. For years after 1953, when it became an independent subsidiary of the giant Matsushita Electric Industrial Company, Ltd., JVC's main business was phonograph records and hi-fi sets.

When, in the 1950s, Takayanagi looked at television's impact, he saw a remarkable commercial and technological breakthrough changing the very nature of family life throughout the world, transforming news and information into instantaneous awareness. But he also saw a medium controlled by a handful of broadcast networks, each identified by three initials (CBS, NHK, BBC, ZDF, etc.), each holding almost unchecked sway over whole nations of people. In television, Takayanagi saw a mass medium that too often seemed satisfied with being only mediocre. Between moments of transcendent creativity and journalistic brilliance, it spent vast blocks of time being intellectually barren, artistically crude, and commercially shrill. Worst of all, even as networks proliferated, the networks became imitative of each other, reducing choices just as choice seemed prevalent.

The job, Takayanagi knew, was not finished. Takayanagi dreamed that television might someday be an individual medium, one that not only provided its user with a vast array of program choices but one in which the user could actually make his own television images. Takayanagi's dream was to share with everyone the thrill of that magic, impossible moment when he'd seen that *katakana* "e" flicker to life three decades before.

Even in the early 1950s, Takayanagi's dream was shared by laboratory researchers in many electronics companies throughout the world. Within JVC, where Takayanagi was already a legendary leader, he came to share this vision with a number of young engineers—among them a soft-spoken, bright man named Yuma Shiraishi—who might be young enough to carry the dream to its fruition many years later. The technology they must devise was an awesome challenge—because, as Shiraishi noted early in the search, the only practical way to store images in the way Takayanagi had imagined was on some form of magnetic material, probably tape. But the tape would have to be very wide—much wider than the tape used for sound recording—and the electronic machinery to transfer the images from tape to picture tube would be immense and very costly. How could you make this equipment so small and inexpensive that any family could use it to make their own TV programs? And how would JVC compete against such competitors as Matsushita, a corporation ten times the size of JVC, and Sony, a company whose reputation for research and innovation had made it a household word on three continents?

It seemed a task no ordinary human could achieve.

Indeed, the three JVC leaders who carried the baton forward, despite overwhelming competition from far bigger Japanese electronics companies, even in spite of the resistance of their own top management, were hardly ordinary. Kenjiro Takayanagi was a famous man in Japan, even outside JVC, because of his pioneering discoveries in television. Yuma Shiraishi was gifted not just as an electronics engineer but as a conceptual thinker. But the key member of the group might have been Shizuo Takano, another engineer and also a bundle of energy with a talent for taking risks and for rallying people to a common cause so passionately that they lost their fear of the risks. JVC assigned Takano to work with Shiraishi, making them perhaps the oddest couple in Japanese industry. The commitment they came to share to Takayanagi's vision gave them a union with one another that would have been impossible in normal circumstances.

Nevertheless, the objective—a workable home video tape machine—seemed a task especially unattainable for a company so small and ordinary as JVC. JVC had *not* been one of the companies to profit from Takayanagi's television breakthrough. In the 1950s, as the postwar Japanese incarnation of Victor Talking Machines Company, U.S.A., JVC was mainly a record company with a certain reputation for making decent phonograph machines. It seemed certain that the giant corporations, companies with stables of technological wizards—not JVC—would eventually devise a home-use video tape recorder (VTR).

The first hint that the dream of video tape could come true at all had appeared in America in 1954, when six engineers at Ampex Corporation, Charles E. Anderson, Ray Dolby, Alex Maxey, Shelby Henderson, Charles Ginsburg, and Fred Pfost, built the first magnetic tape machine that recorded not only sound but *pictures*. The Ampex machine was a spectacular breakthrough, and its impact on the broadcast industry was epochal. The day those six engineers finished work on the first video tape recorder (VTR) was the day live television began to decline as a unique communications media. Before long TV shows performed on the East Coast would not have to be shown—live—simultaneously (three hours "earlier") on the West Coast. Network affiliates could tape live shows and then schedule them on prime time across the country.

The Ampex development also made the dream of a home video recorder possible as a reality. Ampex's machine was a monster, a behemoth the size of a vintage jukebox. It ran a two-inch-wide tape from reel to reel rather than within the cassettes that are common today. It employed four heads, the sensors that transfer sound and image to the human eye and ear. It was an amazing, buzzing, whirring hulk, jammed with vacuum tubes and so expensive only large organizations could afford it.

Almost immediately aware of the Ampex breakthrough, Takayanagi at JVC set his engineers, including Yuma Shiraishi, to work on devising a smaller, simpler video recorder (one that used two-inch tape but had only two heads). Five years later, JVC had built its first studio-quality two-head, two-inch VTR. But by then Ampex's four-head hulk was installed in studios all over the world, and a Sony version of the Ampex machine, introduced in 1958, had already claimed a major share of the Japanese market. So the JVC rival failed to sell. JVC had created a simpler technology than its competitors, but it was incompatible with the industry standard Ampex had established.

For JVC, that first experience was both the beginning of a love affair with the home-use video machine and a lesson. Shizuo Takano, who was appointed leader of the video recorder team at JVC, points to that failure as the last time that JVC entered the market without meeting technological standards that were shared by a number of original equipment manufacturers (OEM). It was a lesson that would work to JVC's advantage almost two decades later, when the battle of standards between Beta (Sony) and VHS (JVC) began in Tokyo and swiftly swept the globe.

Through the 1960s, JVC was an active participant in the video tape machine industry, such as it was. The improvement from two-inch to one-inch VTR was inevitable, but the equipment remained the tool of broadcast professionals. Although VTRs shrank dramatically, neither the equipment nor the price shrank far enough to fit into the living room or budget of the average household.

The situation promised dramatic change in 1970, with the appearance in Japan—at three companies—of ³/₄-inch VTR prototypes. The companies were Matsushita, a true giant in consumer electronics in Japan and the world; Sony, a medium-sized but aggressive young company led by one of Japan's most outspoken entrepreneurs, Akio Morita; and JVC.

That year, at a trade show in Osaka, Japan, the three companies had a meeting. Although the representatives of all three companies treated the meeting as happenstance, it was, in fact, long-awaited and carefully orchestrated. Japanese electronics companies, although they are intensely competitive, maintain an informal network of communication about the progress of each other's new product research. At that 1970 Osaka meeting, Matsushita, Sony, and JVC knew where they all stood. They knew that taken separately, the path to a marketable ³/₄-inch VTR would be long and winding. But if they could agree to pool their findings, a shortcut that helped all three companies might be possible.

In the history of the video cassette recorder, that meeting was pivotal. Sony brought to the meeting a prototype of its "U-Matic" tape cassette.

Although all three companies had been working on a "container" for magnetic tape since the first audio tape cassettes were introduced in 1964, Sony, Matsushita, and JVC all had trouble with certain technical features of their cassettes. Since Sony's U-Matic cassette seemed the most promising of the three technologies, the engineers from all three companies collaborated to iron out the kinks in it. The result was a significant breakthrough.

Magnetic tape was no longer confined to loose, separate reels that had to be threaded through the heads of a tape machine. The self-contained cassette held a full hour of ¾-inch tape, as well as the two spools that played out and reeled in the tape as it went through the machine. The U-Matic technology, eventually patented by Nobutoshi Kihara of Sony, placed the home-use video cassette recorder, at last, within reach of the inventors at Sony, Matsushita, and JVC. That U-Matic cassette was so well devised, in fact, that it is still standard for many professional broadcast uses, in which the wide tape and big cassette provide higher image quality.

History was also made at that 1970 conference when the three participants signed a cross-licensing agreement that gave Sony, Matsushita, and JVC free access to all the technical innovations each created throughout their research in video tape recorders. None of the three companies would have to pay for use of another's VTR-related patents. Also understood as part of the cross-licensing agreement was a sharing of future innovations.

As a result of that agreement, the three companies gained access to each other's patented technologies for the ¾-inch VCR technology of the 1970s and also for the enormously lucrative ½-inch home-use VCR technology that emerged at Sony, and then at JVC, in the mid-1970s. Because of the high stakes involved in the newer technology, all three companies ceased—shortly after 1970—to collaborate on VTR research in what Sony continues to call "the spirit of the cross-licensing agreement." After 1970, Matsushita, Sony, and JVC went back to treating each other more as competitors than colleagues. And Sony was the first to gain a competitive advantage.

The three participants in the agreement did not benefit equally. For all of them, the effort to sell a ³/₄-inch product to the home-use market failed dismally. The machine was still too large, heavy, complicated, and expensive (more than $2500 in U.S. dollars) to sell to consumers. The market that bought enough machines to make them profitable was institutional—corporate communications departments and schools—where Sony had always been a more popular supplier than Matsushita and JVC. Sony made a modest profit on the ³/₄-inch VCR; the other two participants in the standards agreement lost money.

Four years later, history seemed to be repeating itself. In December 1974, Shizuo Takano and Yuma Shiraishi were invited to another meeting. Sony was the host and Sony would announce to the two JVC engineers, and demonstrate, a home VCR that consumers at last would buy. This was state of the art, and Sony—just like before—was there first!

In fact, Sony should have been alone in the market by 1974. Their product, called Betamax, was a sophisticated offspring of their ³/₄-inch VTR. It was a ¹/₂-inch, two-head video cassette recorder. It was small, light, and inexpensive enough to sell to consumers. Sony showed Betamax to the two Japanese manufacturers who had joined in the cross-licensing agreement on ³/₄-inch video in 1970, Matsushita and JVC. But they had brought Betamax to Matsushita and JVC after they had unsuccessfully tried to sell it to RCA in the United States.[1]

That little JVC was included in Sony's short list of significant sought-after collaborators was slightly ironic. The ³/₄-inch defeat in 1970 should have discouraged JVC from pursuing the dream any further. In fact, after 1971, JVC's corporate leadership had pulled most of its support away from the effort to develop a home VCR. Only the small team led by Shiraishi and Takano had hung on. The team's four-year struggle from 1971 to 1974 to keep pace with Sony, Matsushita, and the other big competitors was a blend of tenacity, deception, and luck.

In 1971, JVC's failure with the ³/₄-inch VCR as a home-use product had been a bitter disappointment to Yuma Shiraishi and Shizuo Takano. By then, Takayanagi's vision of the home VCR had become a near obsession for both of them. Their disappointment was not merely that the ³/₄-inch VCR was a sales failure for JVC,

1. As reported in *TV Digest*, December 2, 1974.

but that none of the three companies involved had made something that people could use in their everyday lives.

"We had made a very strong commitment to making a machine that could be used in the home. And a ¾-inch was the original target," said Takano. "But then, when we agreed on standards and started manufacture of ¾-inch, we realized that this can't be a home machine. That was the time in 1971 when we started to look back and ask ourselves what we had done wrong."

Takano explained, "Looking back on all the failures, we decided to start out from scratch. All the work of the past was forgotten. The outcome of this new outlook, to give one example, was our decision to require two hours' worth of tape on the cassette. Since Sony's developmental concept was always based on ¾-inch, they never asked whether one hour was enough."

Yuma Shiraishi added, "Sony was working faster than we were, which might explain why they didn't examine more closely the issue of whether the cassette should play for one hour or two. But that wasn't the only technical difference between the concepts. Our first VCR was much lighter than Sony's first VCR—thirteen kilograms compared to twenty-one kilograms—and it fulfilled a goal that was very important to the companies who adopted our format: It was much easier to manufacture."

JVC's engineers discarded all assumptions. They ignored the existing technology and stopped thinking like engineers.

Referring to the idea of *improving* ¾-inch, Shiraishi said, "That was perceived from a purely engineering point of view. If you compare all the previous VTR machines, each one was a big improvement. But none ever became home-use equipment. We began to realize there might be some kind of conditions that had to be incorporated into a *home-use machine* that we hadn't thought of before. Because we had never met those conditions, we were never able to make equipment that people would want in their homes. So we sat down and started to think: 'What are those conditions?' "

Guided by this question, the JVC engineers started thinking like inventors. The JVC research and development group was led by Yuma Shiraishi and included three loyal and talented engineers, Akira Hirota, Yoshihiko Ohta, and Hiroyuki Umeda. They began to think of everything that had to be included in the home-use VCR.

"It wasn't such a formal discussion. We talked to each other," said Shiraishi. "We complained to each other. We were sharing things we didn't usually share."

Instead of asking themselves what might be technically possible, they started asking one another what people would want from a machine like this—engineers, assemblers, retailers, repairmen, customers . . . everyone.

Perhaps unintentionally, Shiraishi's group of brainstorming engineers were acting out what Thomas Edison once described as the essence of invention: ". . . all parts of the system must be constructed with reference to all other parts . . . the failure of one part to cooperate properly with the other parts disorganizes the whole and renders it inoperative for the purpose intended."

When, in 1971, Yuma Shiraishi and his JVC team developed a list of twelve interconnected *goals* that came to be known simply as "the matrix," they intuitively applied Edison's credo to the creation of a video tape machine that people around the world would use to record birthdays and bar mitzvahs and the cherry blossoms in Kyoto in April. From that moment in 1971, they never really were stumped. Every time they encountered an unexpected problem, they found the answer—not far away. It was all there, in "the matrix." Everything.

JVC's research and development organization would not deliver the first VHS VCR, regardless of their management's impatience, until they had fulfilled each of twelve requirements.

For the VCR
- It should be connectable to an ordinary television.
- It should be able to reproduce in quality the same image and sound as an ordinary television receiver.
- It should have a minimum recording time of *two hours*.
- It should be compatible with other manufacturers' VCRs so that the tape is interchangeable.
- It should have a wide range of functions (use with prerecorded software and a video camera should be possible).

For use in private homes
- It should not be too expensive.
- It should be easy to operate.
- Running cost (tape, etc.) should be low.

For the manufacturer
- It should be reasonably easy to produce.

- It should be designed so that parts can be used in a number of models.
- It should be easy to service.

For society
- The VCR should serve as the transmitter of information and culture.

Behind this list of rules was Yuma Shiraishi's intuition. He had seen a new concept of the VCR *three-dimensionally*—as a device that must, in its design, be responsive to the people who have to make it, the people who will buy it, and the people who have to fix it when it breaks. Even before Shiraishi had assembled his engineers to write these rules, this matrix—the basic principles of an elegant concept—had already formed in his mind.

Shiraishi already had done the hardest thing. He had "gone back to scratch" after the failures with home-use 3/4-inch recording. He wasn't so deeply disappointed that the 3/4-inch machine had not *sold*. He was saddened that it was *wrong*, that it hadn't done what he wanted it to do. To set aside all your previous work (almost twenty years of it) is almost impossible for any person. But Yuma Shiraishi realized what he had to do if JVC was to move forward. When he gathered his colleagues to "start from scratch," Shiraishi emptied JVC's workbench. He summoned the courage to trust his creativity and his colleagues' skill to find a path they had not seen before.

In opening his mind, Shiraishi tore away the film of past experience. He saw something as simple as the fact that JVC must change not just the *width* of the video tape, but also its *length!* And he saw the most important thing of all—that this new device must be an *active* medium, not just a better sort of passive television. The reason that the JVC matrix formed an "elegant concept" was that it was uncluttered by preconceptions. The entire horizon of challenges was seen as a whole *before* the researchers began their work.

When the work began in earnest, Yuma Shiraishi was the inventor, Shizuo Takano was the enforcer. In personality, they must have seemed to those around them as different as *yin* and *yang*, but one common element kept them in harmony with one another. One of their colleagues at JVC, Tadahiro Sakao, general manager of the company's Video Disc Division, described their harmony in simple terms: "People like Mr. Takano and Mr. Shiraishi are romantic. They dream, and they stick to the project."

Yuma Shiraishi, now in his fifties, is a reedy, scholarly man who would seem almost painfully shy except for the fact that his vibrant intellect seems to have taken over his vocal cords and will not let him retire quietly into the background. His manner is as honest and lucid as it is self-effacing.

Takano, senior managing director of JVC's Video Products Division and the man in charge of the VCR project for much of its twenty-year gestation at JVC, is a striking contrast. He is small and gray-haired, square-shouldered, and piercingly direct. At first glance he has a military bearing, but this impression fades with the discovery in him of a lurking sense of mischief and a rasping laugh that seems suddenly to take hold of him and bend him forward in merriment. It was his sense of humor that helped Takano endure repeated management suggestions to give up on home VCRs in a decade when television itself seemed to have stopped its technological march and become a static household commodity like refrigerators and flypaper.

Typical of Shizuo Takano's boldness was his opening, in 1977, of the VCR market in Europe. He literally went door to door with a team of engineers and a steamer trunk full of video equipment to the most important national brands of consumer electronics in Western Europe, showing each of them the VHS format. No one at JVC today is entirely sure whether anyone ever authorized Takano to make successive visits to a half dozen European manufacturers. His first two visits, to Dutch giant Philips and to the number one German company, Grundig, were disappointing. But Takano kept moving and succeeded in establishing an impressive VHS network of manufacturers in Europe—Thomson in France, Telefunken in Germany, and Thorn in the United Kingdom.

The determination of Shizuo Takano (and the inventive meticulousness of Yuma Shiraishi) eventually proved to a host of Japanese television manufacturers that there were, indeed, new things possible in their industry. Shizuo Takano recalled, "Many opinion leaders said that video is never going to make it. Post-color television [they said] will be color television. Headquarters in many companies did not have much interest in any sort of video any longer. But I had personal friends in many companies with whom I had shared the dream that video was going to be a good thing, going to change people's lives. We kept in touch, we discussed our research among each other. Since headquarters in each company didn't pay much attention, we were able to pretty much do what we wanted to do within the industry."

By communicating through this "engineer grapevine" with other companies, Shizuo Takano stayed several steps ahead of his own top management for four years. Engineers in many companies believed in the great potential of ½-inch home VCRs, and they were exerting major efforts in this area. Knowing this gave Takano hope. And hope was vital to Takano, Shiraishi, and their team, because there was strong pressure against the VCR project within the company. The pressure began to build after JVC's ¾-inch market failure. Suddenly corporate JVC reduced company expectations— the home video industry was not going to become the multi-billion-yen industry they had once predicted. So in 1971, management cut the team of VCR researchers from ninety people to ten. Many of the survivors could only devote part of their time to Shiraishi's and Takano's dream machine.

Most dramatically, however, the company created a Video Products Division. This organizational change might seem positive at first glance. But at that time, 1971–1972, the only "product" in the new division was a ¾-inch VTR that was selling sluggishly, if at all. The main purpose of separating the Video Products Division from the company's central research and development laboratories was to isolate its budget. Separate divisions at JVC have to be self-supporting, and the Video Products Division's ¾-inch white elephant didn't have the ability to support even a small division.

"Management told us that we didn't need anyone for research and development," said Yuma Shiraishi. "All we need is a division that makes profit, in terms of marketing ¾-inch equipment. So we made it seem that, within the company, the Video Products Division was not doing any development with the VCR. We did it, but we did it in a very secret way. To other company people looking at the Video Products Division, we had [no research department]. No engineers. Marketing people within our division were very busy trying to turn the red ink to black. So they didn't care very much what we were doing either."

In the midst of a culture that, to the West, has always seemed dedicated to obedience and uniformity, a gentle spirit named Yuma Shiraishi and a bantamweight named Shizuo Takano were resolutely defying corporate policies that made it clear that they should run themselves into red ink, drown, and never be heard from again.

"When we were a large group doing research and development on VTR at the main research and development laboratories, we had been constantly told to meet such-and-such goals within such-and-such period, because we were going to have an announcement on such-and-such a date. There was constant pressure on us. And, of course, top management always had deep interest and concern about us," said Shiraishi. "Then they had lots to tell us, lots to drive us. However, when we moved into the Video Products Division, since we were an invisible team, nobody told us to do anything. We didn't have any pressure. No top management had any complaints, because they didn't know we were doing things like this. . . . We did have a hard time finding the money. But all in all, it was a good environment."

Eventually, the red ink might have drowned Takano and Shiraishi and their handful of freedom fighters. But an ill wind struck Japan—the Arab oil embargo (known in Japan simply as "the oil shock")—and it blew money into the Video Products Division.

The oil embargo was a shock to Japan, because it brought an almost unprecedented phenomenon to the island nation: double-digit inflation. Prices skyrocketed. Costs of consumer and professional electronics, hit hard by inflation, went up. The marketing people in JVC's Video Products Division looked around, and what did they see but a large, dusty inventory of 3/4-inch VCRs, priced at pre–oil embargo rates.

While Sony and Matsushita raised prices on their *new* 3/4-inch equipment, JVC held the line by keeping the *old* prices on their old machines. Video Products Division marketing people even claimed they were being patriotic by holding the line on price in the face of Middle Eastern blackmail. By undercutting the competition dramatically, JVC cleared out their inventory in a matter of months. Suddenly the Video Products Division was the apple of JVC's eye.

The lucky breeze from the Mideast was a vital force in preserving the division and saving the VCR research project at JVC, but the division still might not have survived without the support of some very imposing figures within JVC. One of them was the grand old man, Kenjiro Takayanagi. If there was a grander old man in the organization, it was probably Konosuke Matsushita, the chairman of JVC's parent company. One day Konosuke Matsushita (who had already seen a Sony prototype of the Betamax VCR) visited the Video Products Division R&D facility in Yokohama and happened upon a fairly well advanced ½-inch VCR prototype.

Shizuo Takano and Yuma Shiraishi met Matsushita in the executive reception room in the Yokohama plant and showed him their video cassette recorder prototype; it was compact, 45 centimeters wide, 35 centimeters deep, and 15 centimeters high. Matsushita watched a tape that Takano had prepared for him. After all the technical nuances had been explained to him, Matsushita smiled. Then, he leaned over, pressed his cheek against the recorder, and said, "It's marvelous. You have made something very nice."

Konosuke Matsushita never issued a directive or stated in any way his official support of the VCR development project, but in a company as familial as JVC, that fleeting incident was soon known to everyone in the organization.

Shizuo Takano and Yuma Shiraishi had maintained a low profile for their project, never confronting management when their research budget was eliminated, not complaining when their research engineers were told to spend time "in the field" as retail salespeople, equipment repairmen, and maintenance trouble-shooters. No indignity was too great to deter the team.

And the team *felt* like a team. Many of the members of that team were significantly younger than Shizuo Takano, and he was sensitive to the risks they were taking. In Japanese companies, the employee involved in a major failure almost never gets fired. But the assignments that follow failure often land him in outlying offices and dead-end positions, with little advancement, small salary raises, and negligible prestige.

"Big companies, much bigger giants, were doing video developments. Not only myself, but everybody in our division, two hundred fifty people, felt threatened," recalled Takano. "It was such a bold decision to make, to go with our own system in direct competition with those giants. But we had such a wonderful product! One day, I called all the managers in our division into one room. I asked them how they feel about doing the project, if they are prepared to commit suicide with me. We may not succeed, I told them, but if everybody agrees with going, then we go. If there is anybody who feels uneasy about it, please say so; you can leave."

The result of that discussion was that one member of the team decided to depart. Everybody else agreed to "commit suicide" with Takano. "At that moment," said Takano, "I felt the greatest satisfaction. Without that moment, I don't think VHS could have succeeded."

There was also an opportunity for Takano to commit suicide all by himself. It came dramatically in late 1974. The day he got the call from Sony, inviting him and Yuma Shiraishi to come over and look at Sony's new Betamax VCR, which was ready to hit the domestic market early the next year, he knew that JVC's format, called VHS (Video Home System), was still at least eighteen months from market readiness.

If JVC could not work out a competitive advantage of their technology over Sony's machine, Takano and Shiraishi realized, there was no point in introducing VHS as a separate, competitive format. No one but a handful of JVC's engineers would ever see the beautiful machine they had fashioned. JVC would have to face some tough choices.

One choice would be to concede Sony's victory, turn over the JVC technology, and join Sony as a minor partner in the opening of the home VCR market. Another would be to step up development to a panic pace and try to hit the market, if not simultaneously with Sony, at least within a few months of Sony. This choice would mean postponing development of a video camera, an item both Takano and Shiraishi considered an inseparable element of the VCR concept. The third option would have been just to quit and concede Sony's triumph, a course that might have pleased many in JVC management but was unthinkable to the combative Shizuo Takano and his proud cohort, Yuma Shiraishi.

When the meeting at Sony's Tokyo headquarters started, the Sony people demonstrated to the JVC representatives a VCR tape deck that was strikingly similar to prototypes JVC had built in its own laboratories. It had two heads and a cunningly small half-inch tape cassette with a tape duration of one hour.

Only one hour?

For a scant second, Shiraishi and Takano caught each other's eye. It was the most significant glance in either of their careers. It was a look of revelation, relief, and renewed ambition. Sony was indeed opening the door to the market, but they had no way yet to close the door behind them.

Sony suggested to JVC that the two companies join in a mutual effort to build and market this appealing device as the first home-use VCR in the world. They were offering standardization, but at the same time it seemed to Takano and Shiraishi that Sony was offering JVC and Matsushita a fixed package: Take it or leave it.

During the demonstrations, a JVC engineer asked a Sony representative if Sony was planning another "engineers meeting," like the ¾-inch VTR collaboration of 1970, when the three companies' engineers had joined to devise and standardize video tape technology. Shiraishi recalled Sony's reply. " 'This time,' Sony said, 'We're not going to do things like that.' "

For their own part, neither JVC nor Matsushita had any plans to "do things like that" either.

Yuma Shiraishi and Shizuo Takano bowed graciously to the Sony representatives. "Thank you very much," they said. "This was a wonderful presentation, and you have a lovely machine with which we wish you the very best of luck." And they left.

The only sign that they were triumphantly unimpressed with Betamax might have been an extra spring in Takano's departing step and an inner calm that seemed to beam from Shiraishi's eyes.

Although both men knew that little JVC still faced many hurdles en route to the establishment of the VHS standard, they knew at least that Sony would not overwhelm them technologically, nor would Sony attain a quick domination of the market. From JVC's point of view, Sony's prototype was big where it should have been small, and small where it should have been big. The Betamax VCR deck that Takano and Shiraishi saw actually was bigger than the VHS prototype then under development in the JVC Video Products Division, and, most important, the one-hour tape inside Sony's cassette ran only half as long as JVC's!

Having seen Beta, Takano said, "Based on what we saw, what they were thinking at Sony was very much different from what we were doing. We also wondered if that kind of approach, shown in the prototype, could actually succeed as a home-use machine."

The JVC managers felt reassured that they were still in the running, and though they must move with all due haste, they could hold to a schedule that would get them to the market by 1976.

"We didn't feel any hurry for a development, especially when we looked at their machine and saw that it didn't answer the conditions in our matrix," said Takano. "It had to have that minimum two-hour recording and playback." Takano had seen in

Betamax a product that could not fulfill what JVC regarded as a basic consumer need: You had to be able to use it to save your favorite feature-length movie when it came around on television.

After that Sony Betamax demonstration in December 1974, Sony persisted in seeking vital partnerships. They extended to JVC and Matsushita an invitation to inspect the production facilities they had already prepared for the manufacture of the Betamax VCR. The JVC official who received the invitation was then the head of VTR research at JVC and the boss of Shiraishi and Takano; his name was Hirobumi Tokumitsu. He refused the invitation and told Sony that since JVC intended to proceed alone in its VCR development, it would be unfair to see any more of Sony's technology.

But two Matsushita representatives, one of them the venerable Konosuke Matsushita, went along on the inspection in January 1975, viewing all the manufacturing machinery Sony had already put in place to make Betamax VCRs. Sony wanted the giant Matsushita as a partner to command the public's interest and confidence. But Matsushita was unconvinced that a one-hour tape could succeed in the marketplace and dismayed that Sony had committed itself to that limitation before asking Matsushita's opinion. Konosuke Matsushita withheld his company's participation in Sony's "standard," and left the field open for its own researchers and for those of JVC. Sony was left to go it alone.[2]

JVC had time to refine its own technology.

The VHS video cassette recorder that JVC introduced in September 1976 was a sophisticated package, complete because it had not been rushed to market and complete because Yuma Shiraishi's engineers had framed a full vision of what they needed *before* they embarked on solving the problem of the ½-inch VCR.

Even in the early days that Yuma Shiraishi was working with his engineers to form a fresh vision of the video cassette recorder, Shizuo Takano was turning his eyes elsewhere. He was looking within JVC and outward at JVC's relationship to the world. The job of reconciling the JVC style with that of the intensely competitive consumer electronics marketplace was no simple task. In terms of

---

2. As reported in *Clash: Sony vs. Matsushita,* published by Nihon Keizai Shimbun, Tokyo, 1979.

size, prestige, and video experience, JVC was perhaps the least likely company in Japan to win the VCR race.

JVC had no record for creating markets in new technologies, and it had one of the smallest networks of company-owned retail outlets in Japan (one-tenth as many as Matsushita), a consideration that is all-important in new product introductions in Japan. There was also the problem of style. Even today JVC's outlook on the world seems to face in the opposite direction from Madison Avenue. There is a sense of family that emerges even in a brief encounter at JVC's headquarters in Tokyo or at their production facility in Yokohama. People seem to know each other and tolerate one another in ways that family members understand other family members. And, like a family, JVC seems in some ways more comfortable with its own patterns of thought and action than with those of the world outside. They welcome strangers into the *uchi* ("my company") with charm, assurance, and warmth. But their ventures out into the commercial world, notwithstanding Shizuo Takano's extraordinary storming of Western Europe, tend to have an air of polite timorousness. JVC is a company better known for its friendship than its salesmanship.

Takano sensed, though, that this apparent weakness could be a strength. He knew that many companies in both Japan and America were struggling to devise an economically priced home-use VCR. His grapevine had told him this much. And he knew the deep lack of self-confidence prevalent in the industry. If Takano could present before the leading manufacturers the VHS format as a working model for development—and if he could make that presentation humbly, as a friend—he could, in one gesture, flatter their pride and reduce their risk. And he might convince them to adopt VHS rather than continue an expensive race to hit an uncertain market with a wave of different formats.

Intuitively, between the meeting with Sony in 1974 and the introduction of VHS in 1976, Takano found an entry into the market. An engineer who knew very little about conventional ways to market a new product, he simply followed his instincts and saw a way to the maximum rewards of commercial success that other companies in the VCR race had not seen. Sony's approach, starting with its 1974 meetings with RCA, Matsushita, and JVC, had been to reach the market first and establish Beta as the standard so quickly and powerfully that no other format, arriving late, would have a chance. Indeed, there was a certain wisdom in Sony's handing out its technical information, because they reasonably expected every-body to adopt their format eventually anyway.

But by late 1976, that strategy had not made Sony's Beta format an invincible standard in the marketplace. Beta sales were encour-aging but unspectacular. There was still room for another format. Takano was ready to take that other format, VHS, out into the world. His approach to the market would be far different from Sony's. He would try humility.

Humility seems an incongruous marketing tool, but Shizuo Takano had the skill to use it like a scalpel, and he had long worked among people at JVC whose humility was a source of pride.

To Takano and JVC, market domination was a concept that was neither practical nor rational. "Our basic policy was to spread the information as well as to spread the technology and the format," said Takano. "The market is large enough to hold everybody. So we don't have to worry about that. Japan does not have to monopo-lize the video market or video production. One single company does not have to monopolize the whole profit."

Early in 1976, when JVC was ready with a VHS prototype, Takano's challenge was to convince at least four manufacturers—all of them larger than JVC—to abandon their own research and development efforts in the area and join up with JVC.

JVC could not succeed without collaborators, because JVC's production and retail forces simply were too small to handle the consumer demand if response to the VHS format was strong. JVC then had only one factory capable of making 10,000 to 20,000 VCRs a year. A first-year demand of even 25,000 machines could be a disaster. Without help, JVC was a village that could be destroyed by its own success.

Sony meanwhile was developing relationships with Toshiba and Sanyo in Japan and Zenith in the United States. Sony hit both of those markets with Betamax in 1975. But they made little penetra-tion into Europe. In the eighteen months that passed between the introduction of Betamax and the introduction of VHS, Sony's VCR sales did not reach 200,000 units worldwide.

JVC's approach to interesting a number of Japanese consumer electronics companies who had not committed to Sony was a series of VHS demonstrations, first in private, at JVC's research facility, and then with press coverage, at the Okura Hotel in Tokyo on

September 9, 1976. The presentation was made in typical JVC style.

By way of trying to explain the "JVC style," Tadahiro Sakao, general manager of JVC's Video Disc Division, recalled the day Kokichi Matsuno took over as president of JVC in 1975. Sakao credits Matsuno and his successor, Ichiro Shinji, with instilling a more aggressive and risk-taking attitude into the company. But it was not aggressiveness that Matsuno stressed in his first remarks to his employees.

What he said, especially to the Western ear, was extraordinary. Imagine a new CEO of a major U.S. corporation standing before his management team for the first time and saying to them, "The most important value for the people in our company is that you should be very polite and gentle." The belief in gentleness as a business value, virtually unknown to the West, has begun to falter in Japan, but this was Matsuno's foremost message to his employees.

Matsuno believed in a Japanese ethic that is most often applied to relationships between friends, lovers, and spouses—that each member of a relationship should strive to sense the other's feelings, even if the other person cannot or will not articulate them. Matsuno, said Sakao, told his workers that "a JVC person should be one who can understand what your business partner is thinking."

Realizing that it would not be easy for proud companies like Matsushita and Hitachi to concede a technological breakthrough to a minor company like JVC, Shizuo Takano and Yuma Shiraishi appeared before them not as victors but as supplicants.

Shiraishi recalled the typical VHS demonstration. "When we made a demonstration, Mr. Takano was always there. He said, 'Our dream has always been that each home has a video tape recorder, and we certainly believe that the video tape recorder will make our life much more enjoyable. This is our top priority in introducing this equipment.' He showed the VHS prototype and told the other manufacturers, 'Well, JVC has been able to come up with this prototype, but I am sure everyone else in this room has also developed some sort of prototype by now. I don't really care which company's equipment or which format we go for, but let's go for the best system that we all are working on,' " said Shiraishi.

In every presentation Takano emphasized to other manufacturers the importance of having a standard. He was emphatic in telling a series of Japanese consumer electronics giants in succession that little JVC would gladly stand aside and commit itself to another company's VCR standard if theirs was better than JVC's. For all of his humility, Takano sensed with fiery (but unseen) assurance that no one else could top this wonderful product, embodied in VHS. And he knew above all that no one had answered all the aspects of the VCR problem as assiduously as Yuma Shiraishi had with his matrix of requirements.

Takano said, "We never tried to monopolize the technology we developed. If the quality of our technology was good, then we believed we should share it. But not with everybody. To maintain compatability, we had to choose companies that would maintain certain standards that our format requires."

Takano was, as Matsuno emphasized, polite and gentle, but he was also as crafty as a fox at a poultry fair. The JVC policy of very delicately bringing competitors into their confidence and then inviting them to help build, sell, and refine VHS technology was the stroke of humility that finally standardized a format for the home-use video cassette recorder and opened the marketplace—first in Japan. By early 1977, JVC was stretched beyond its own production capacity in manufacturing VCR decks, and partners like Matsushita, Hitachi, and Mitsubishi were hurrying to set up their production facilities under JVC's liberal licensing agreement.

At the same time that JVC was showing VHS to other Japanese manufacturers in 1976, the VHS format had to clear one very tall hurdle. The Japanese Ministry of International Trade and Industry (MITI), which wields substantial influence over issues like product standards in Japan, met with JVC in mid-1976 to suggest the abandonment of the VHS format in favor of a single national standard that was already on the market—Beta. Part of MITI's request was based on the rather arguable contention that picture quality was better with Beta than with VHS. JVC countered with their assertion that VHS would offer comparable picture quality, a more convenient tape duration, and a fully functional video camera.

JVC and Sony engineers to this day argue over which company's format has the better picture. Each company has its impartial technical advocates, but more important, the difference in picture quality between Beta and VHS is so slight that it is not noticeable to the naked eye. To most consumers choosing a VCR, this is a difference that has always been irrelevant.

But this was not really a technological discussion. It was political. MITI had to be convinced that there was sufficient economic might behind this late-to-the-market VHS format to make it viable. If JVC could not show the government that it had formed alliances with major manufacturers, MITI would use all its considerable influence to force JVC to abandon VHS, providing some compensation for its financial losses.

Takano's negotiations with other Japanese consumer electronics manufacturers already had been focused on that inevitable challenge from MITI. So by the time JVC faced MITI to get permission to compete with Betamax, Shizuo Takano had all his ducks in a row. He made all the technological arguments and then, very humbly, trotted out his political allies: Matsushita, Hitachi, Mitsubishi, and Sharp—four powerful manufacturers who were in the course of committing to VHS and who represented a substantial percentage of Japan's gross national product. When this coalition was arrayed against Sony's allies, Toshiba and Sanyo, the balance was clear. The argument was over and MITI bowed out of the VCR standards discussion. This, MITI said graciously, is one of those decisions that we can leave to the marketplace.

On September 9, 1976, more than fifty years after Takayanagi had first had his dream, Shizuo Takano and Yuma Shiraishi stood before a curious group of manufacturers and journalists in Tokyo's Okura Hotel to present to them a machine called VHS (Video Home System), a video cassette recorder (VCR) so simple, small, and inexpensive that almost any family could possess one, take control of their video amusement, and create their own television programming. The humblest company of them all, launched by Takayanagi's dream into a sea of unimaginable troubles, had finally reached the other side—almost.

In Japan, one more crisis remained for the VHS format. Within a year after JVC and its partners had filled their stores with VCRs and had placed their ads, sales fell to a trickle. They had sold their equipment to all the gadget-conscious buyers who had to be the first on the block with a new gadget. It was much harder to sell the average, cautious, conservative consumer a product costing a thousand dollars or more. Such consumers had only a vague idea of what this machine was and what they could *do* with it.

Like salespeople in most small companies, JVC's sales force was accustomed to losing battles to the big companies, especially since the larger manufacturers could afford to cut their prices farther and for longer periods than JVC could. As a result, it didn't take long for JVC's retailers to panic. Sales for VHS equipment began to level off in early 1977, only six months after the equipment had been introduced, and Shizuo Takano faced a gathering of his sales force who were unanimous on one point: In order to compete with Sony, JVC had to cut prices!

Takano didn't give an inch. Instead, to the salespeople's surprise, he flew into a rage. Takano threatened to go back to his development team, add features to the original VCR, and *raise* the price. Faced with this crafty irrationality, the retailers went back to their stores, beat the bushes harder, and eventually found at their fingertips the answer to the VCR marketing problem.

As with all things extraordinarily new, as Sony had realized with Beta, the marketing problem was really an education problem. How could JVC teach the consumers the value of the VCR?

The answer lay in Yuma Shiraishi's matrix, but for a while nobody focused on it. It was an unspoken demand that had existed from the first day of the project. Ten days after introducing the VHS tape deck in 1976, JVC had announced, with somewhat less emphasis, the first complete video camera for making VHS movies. Its cost, when combined with the tape deck, created a prohibitive price barrier. But for Yuma Shiraishi and Shizuo Takano the camera was vital.

Since the beginning of the research, their dream had focused on the idea that the VCR was an *individual* medium, capable of recording the ideas and memories of each of its users in a unique style. "It could touch people's hearts," said Takano. In that sense it was different from every other television product ever invented. It was active rather than passive. And the one ingredient that made it a truly individual medium was the camera. It was as much a piece of the whole concept as the tape deck, and for Takano and Shiraishi the concept could not be broken down into components.

Nevertheless, the video camera began its existence as an irrelevant appendage of the VCR tape deck. Its main purpose came in demonstrations that JVC salespeople conducted when they went out to canvass neighborhoods and show people their brand-new technology. Normally, the salesperson simply posed the family, taped them, then replayed this vignette on the tape deck. But one day, a salesman in Osaka was doing a demonstration in an apartment that was literally so small he couldn't back up far enough to take a picture. Casting about for alternatives, he seized the family photo album from the coffee table, spread out a number of family snapshots, and quickly panned through the photos. The effect he created—by zooming in and out, halting at each picture, and then quickly moving on—was a kinetic enhancement of the family's memory book. In the makeshift approach devised on the spot by that desperate salesperson, memories had sprung to life.

"Suddenly," said Yuma Shiraishi, "they realized that they could make the old times alive. The customers could see themselves back in the 1940s and 1950s. They were actually moving, smiling. It all came back."

A similar incident occurred in the city of Kawasaki, but the retailer added a flourish. "He realized there was no sound," said Shiraishi. "So he brought out his own photo album and taped the album, and at the same time he taped the music he associated with the time the photo was shown to him. After he made his tape he was very touched. He thought this was wonderful."

The Kawasaki retailer followed up by contacting his thirty best customers, methodically gathering from each of them a collection of family photos and lists of their favorite popular songs. Then he set his staff to work editing and mixing these family memories into what he began to call a "video album." When all thirty tapes were complete, he invited these customers to the store "to have a big party." In true JVC style, he told the salesmen, "This is the day when we ought to thank our customers. So none of us should tell the customers to buy this video equipment. We keep our mouths shut. We just show the tape we made for them."

Whether he meant to or not, that Kawasaki retailer got sales from more than a third of those customers, who suddenly needed tape decks to play their lovely family video albums. The retailer had a month's sales in one day. "And that," said Yuma Shiraishi, "was the beginning of the organized sales promotion that we call the Video Album."

Only months later, in August 1977, RCA introduced the VHS tape deck in the United States in a dramatic national announcement. RCA, worried that the market for television in the United States was on the decline, had moved very cautiously toward that VHS introduction in America. They had first declined Betamax, and they had avoided any commitment to manufacture video cassette recorders in the United States. RCA opened the VHS market in the United States by agreeing to sell only VCRs that were made by their Japanese OEM supplier, Matsushita.

Jack Sauter, the RCA marketing executive credited with launching the VHS format in the United States market, noted that while the television/video market was stirring very slowly in Japan, it had come to almost a total halt in America, in the long span from 1969 to 1975. "The industry as a whole was in deep sleep," said Sauter. "It was an industry conclusion as early as 1969 that color television was at the point of maturity and all we had to deal with was a replacement market, and we had to recognize that the life of an average television set was between seven and eleven years. Therefore, what future was there in this business other than just being a commodity supplier?"

A further reason for RCA to be cautious about adopting *any* VCR format was that the United States' television industry did not exactly spring to wakefulness when Sony introduced the Betamax. Said Sauter, "We had looked at the Sony [Betamax], because that's all we had to look at. They were the first on the market. But we did not see a product that would capture the minds of the American consumer. And yet, instinctively, we had to say we've always believed in home recording as far back as 1966 . . . we knew that it had definite consumer possibilities."

As a businessman, Sauter had an even more practical reason to turn away from the Beta format. RCA's brand name was too proud to serve as bridesmaid to another big name brand name, Sony.

Eventually, early in 1977, RCA went to Japan to get a license to market VCRs in the United States. Their first visit was to JVC, but Victor simply didn't have the production capacity to meet the figures suggested by RCA. Matsushita, JVC's parent company and a partner with JVC in the introduction of VHS throughout Japan, was big enough to handle RCA's initial order of 40,000 VCRs for the first year (which ballooned to 60,000). But even with that commitment, Sauter was edgy. Betamax had slowed down in the American market, partly because of licensing problems between Sony and their American partner, Zenith.

In addition, another technology was emerging almost simultaneously with the VCR. RCA had something they called Selecta-Vision—a video disc. It was prerecorded video on a disc, as simple as a record album, less expensive than a VCR, and the visual quality of its prerecorded image was breathtaking.

So when RCA Chief Executive Officer Edgar Griffiths committed his company to Matsushita and VHS in 1977, he was playing it safe. VCRs were, after all, a moderate success in Japan. Video discs might be the technology of tomorrow, but in the meantime, 40,000 VCRs didn't seem too big an inventory in a nation three times the size of Japan. Actually, RCA played it *very* safe. Licensed only to market, not manufacture VCRs, they would suffer the minimum loss in the case of a disaster.

RCA enjoyed spectacular early sales, through the Christmas season that year and through part of January 1978. Then it appeared that disaster had struck. "In February," said Sauter, "we thought someone had declared it illegal. Sales literally stopped. Our distributors panicked!"

Sauter, the marketing chief responsible for selling those 60,000 initial VCRs from Matsushita, followed in his own fashion a marketing program reminiscent of the JVC recovery in Japan. The first step was to visit retailers and find out why customers had stopped buying the VCRs. Sauter found out two things. One was that the VCR was a "big city" product going to "young, affluent" professional people with a fondness for technology and a need to shift the times of television programs in order to fit their personal schedules. The VCR was not yet a family-oriented, small-town item. The second thing he found out was that the market needed education. Somehow, RCA's retailers had to move the VCR market from the first-on-the-block experimenters in New York City to the average family in Dubuque. Sauter's idea: "What we decided is, why don't we put on a good front? We'll just go out and tell the world it's a fabulous product."

The "good front" put up by RCA was called SPRINT '78 (which stood, rather ridiculously, for Selling Programs, Retail and Institutional, to Nudge store Traffic). The program actually was a triumph of *chutzpah.* Its centerpiece was a booklet of promotional schemes designed to educate and excite consumers about VCRs. Implicit in it was a message of confidence from RCA.

Just as JVC's market in Japan had grown from a grass roots educational effort, so did RCA's. The American giant threw parties and made movies from people's snapshot albums. Takano, Shiraishi, and Sauter, each in his own time and place, had an intuitive perception that no market researcher could have given them. All three realized that the VCR was something that had to be presented individually to regular people, face-to-face, so that each person could place his or her own value upon this unique medium. The

VCR, as Shiraishi noted, is a device with the power to "touch your heart." Discovering this was a phenomenon as gradual and remarkable to the salesperson as it was to the customer.

For JVC and its Japanese partners, RCA's contribution to the breakthrough of VHS was enormous. As big and enthusiastic as the Japanese market was, it was the immense, affluent American market that sent the VCR into the commercial stratosphere and launched the proliferation of manufacturers, hardware features, software makers, retail and rental options, and a multi-billion dollar network of industries that—by most experts' analysis—has yet to reach *half* its annual potential for making money.

Working through a network of powerful partners gently cultivated, JVC was able to make VHS equal to Beta in a remarkably short time, and then VHS dramatically surpassed Sony's format in the early 1980s. By 1985, the VHS format accounted for more than 80 percent of all VCR sales in the world, and the U.S. Beta owner looking for blank tapes and software prerecorded in his format was relegated to the status of a disadvantaged minority.

Also by 1985, the VCR (largely in VHS format) had become a worldwide phenomenon that was rapidly cutting across all social classes and demonstrating more and more functions. In the United States and Britain especially, the emergence of the rental industry, in tape players, prerecorded tapes, and even video cameras, spread the VCR fever among people who couldn't yet afford to purchase a unit of their own. Jane Fonda's famous exercise tape became the most obvious example of the educational potential of the VCR, a function which has swept through schools, colleges, and corporations, replacing the more expensive and less convenient use of 8mm and 16mm film.

From humble and very uncertain beginnings, the VCR now numbers more than 100 million units throughout the world. Many experts believe it will approach the same sort of "necessity" status in Western society as the color television set and the refrigerator. This has become possible largely because the VHS format video cassette recorder not only worked dependably but responded almost intuitively to the needs of users. JVC succeeded because, before they introduced their format, they tried a little harder to understand the subtleties of both the device and the consumer.

The swift proliferation of VCRs throughout the world resulted from the early creation of a standard format that solved every possible problem inherent in the concept. An uncanny harmony—cutting across nations, cultures, and industries—took hold. What should have happened, according to the usual business script, was a war among format inventors, eventually leading to suicidal escalations of competition, total consumer confusion, and a market fragmented and disillusioned for at least a decade. But the Great War of the VCR Formats was over before anybody could get it started.

This exceptional peace was born in 1971 because Shizuo Takano and Yuma Shiraishi realized that the problem of the home VCR was not just one of technological improvement; it was a problem of fundamental concept. In order to solve the problem, they discarded everything they and others had done, even disregarding for the moment the miracle at Ampex and the genius of their mentor, Kenjiro Takayanagi. They joined with their fellow engineers and asked every question they could think of. They prepared themselves for every unexpected reversal of fortune. They changed identities at each stage in their imagined course, from conceptualization to consumption. The concept they developed was so finely examined that it contained within a dozen simple goals the answers to questions they hadn't even asked.

Politely, gently, the JVC people stepped outside their own experience and tried to "understand what your business partner [and your customer] is thinking." In doing so, they gave to their beloved teacher, Kenjiro Takayanagi, the fulfillment, in his lifetime, of a fifty-year vision. And they gave people all over the world a precious gift: the sights and sounds they cherish most, easily at hand and instantly recalled.

3 | 3M's Little Yellow Note Pads: "Never Mind. I'll Do It Myself."

Near the end of 1978, the bleak reports came back to corporate headquarters at Minnesota Mining & Manufacturing (3M) Corporation in St. Paul. The news from the four-city test market was that this "Post-it™ Note Pads" idea was a real stinker. These reports came as no surprise, of course, to a large number of 3M's most astute observers of new product ideas; this one had smelled funny to them right from the beginning!

From its earliest days, Post-it brand adhesive had to be one of the most neglected product notions in company history. The company had ignored it before it was a note pad, when the product-to-be was just an adhesive that didn't adhere very well. The first product to reach the marketplace was a sticky bulletin board whose sales were less than exciting to a company like 3M.

But why was it still around? For five years, beginning before 1970, just when a few reluctant mourners should have been burying it and saying words over it, this odd material kept coming around like a bad penny, always rattling in the pocket of Spencer Silver, the chemist who had mixed it up in the first place. Even after the adhesive had evolved into a stickum-covered bulletin board, and then into note pad glue, there were manufacturing people who said they couldn't mass-produce the pads. The 3M marketing crew also got in their two cents' worth. They said you could only sell these things if you gave them away free, because who's going to pay a dollar for scratch paper?

So by 1978, when the reports came in from the test market, it seemed everyone who'd said disparaging things about the Post-it Note Pad was right after all. 3M was finally going to do the merciful thing and cremate the remains. At that critical moment, it was only one last try by two highly placed executives, Geoffrey Nicholson and Joseph Ramey, that kept "those little yellow sticky pads" from going the way of the woolly mammoth and the bossa nova.

Nicholson and Ramey knew the 3M marketing and distribution network well—its strengths and its weaknesses—and they were curious as to why a product that to them had obvious appeal had bombed. Had 3M's conventional marketing approach victimized an unconventional product? They were dubious enough about that trial to get onto an airplane and fly to one of the cities in the market test—Richmond, Virginia.

If Nicholson and Ramey hadn't gone to Richmond, 3M almost certainly would have ceased pilot production of Post-it notes, retired the strange machinery they'd designed for the job, and let the supplies slowly dwindle into dusty inventory. 3M had always been a company very skilled at developing new variations from old products and then expanding their range of activities as a result of such developments. But the Post-it Note Pad was unique, a product entirely unrelated to anything that had ever been sold by 3M. Because Nicholson and Ramey recognized the unique properties of the Post-it note and conveyed this touch of magic to a few people in Richmond, there are today "little yellow sticky pads" proliferating like hamsters in offices everywhere. They seem to breed in desk drawers. They bristle from the margin of half-written reports, speckle the broad surface of spreadsheet printouts, cling to telephone receivers, and insinuate reminders from walls and typewriters, desk tops, bookcases, coffee cups, in-baskets and out-baskets, framed photos of the wife and kids, phone books and Rolodexes, computer screens, and copying machines. They seem to have a special affinity for the soles of shoes. They're everywhere!

Post-it notes, spawned by Spence Silver, refined by two quiet scientists named Henry Courtney and Roger Merrill, nurtured from embryo to offspring by Arthur Fry, and sold by Nicholson and Ramey, are now a ubiquitous presence in modern business because they do something no product ever did before. They convey messages in the exact spot where people want the messages, and then they leave no telltale sign that the message was ever there at all. They stick to pages of manuscript without removing part of the manuscript along with the message, and they leave no adhesive behind. They don't make paper clip dents or staple holes. They can even move from place to place if you want them to, and their adhesive never gets tired. They're adaptable to the message-sender's purpose; they come in various sizes—for short, emphatic messages or long, contemplative ones, and they can even be strung together like an analytical choo-choo train chuffing across a snowy plane of inadequate prose. Their variety of sizes and their mobility make them precise. A tiny Post-it note can be stuck down with understated reproach beside the tiniest error, and a big Post-it note can sprawl across the very center of the perfect report, celebrating it in a single, boldly lettered word of praise without ever sullying the pristine surface beneath.

The Post-it note is a breakthrough because it is a tangible tool that allows the business person—from clerk to CEO—to do something always desired but rarely attained in the modern corporation: to be critical and equivocal at the same time. To have your words and eat them, too!

Until they engineered the market reversal in Richmond, it was Nicholson and Ramey who would have had to eat their words, and several hundred thousand note pads besides. The reason they made the extra effort was that they had both used Post-it notes. They knew how clever and irresistible they were. They also knew that their own marketing people had approached the market tests in the four cities of Tulsa, Denver, Richmond, and Tampa in a traditional style that made them an exercise in futility. These were tests that relied heavily on advertising to generate enthusiasm in distributors who did not themselves use Post-it notes and who saw little sense in exerting sales efforts on a scratch pad that represented both an exorbitant price and a dubious profit margin. Nicholson and Ramey took to Richmond a bit of knowledge that had apparently eluded all the marketers and distributors: Post-it notes were just something you had to *use* in order to appreciate.

Since Nicholson and Ramey were ultimately responsible for the success or failure of Post-it notes, they took a logical step. They stopped depending on the organization. They went out and did it themselves. In doing so, they returned to the two things that had already "sold" Post-it notes more than once. First, like Spencer Silver shuffling from 3M division to 3M division with his queer adhesive, Nicholson and Ramey went door to door. Second, they gave away the product, just as Nicholson and Fry had been doing within 3M for more than a year.

Up and down the business district of Richmond, Virginia, Nicholson and Ramey introduced themselves into banks and offices, handed out little sticky pads of Post-it notes, and said, "Here, try this." And they watched as people—secretaries and receptionists, programmers, middle managers, and vice-presidents—did just that. They tested Post-it notes in the flesh with their own little hands.

Nicholson and Ramey saw and empathized as the flush of addiction crept inexorably over these first-time users. People started sticking them everywhere—papers, desks, phones, books, lapels, faces. In one day of personal contacts in Richmond, Nicholson and Ramey obtained vivid assurance not only that people liked these things but that they wanted more of them and were going to tell their friends about them. That night in Richmond, they knew that dozens of people would greet their spouses after a long day's work by saying, "Here, try this!" As was later proven more scientifically, first in a massive marketing/giveaway program in Idaho (immortalized in 3M song and legend as "The Boise Blitz") and then in the U.S. market as a whole, people loved the Post-it notes they got free at first, and if getting more meant they had to pay a dollar a pad, the pads were cheap at the price.

Post-it notes literally spoil office people forever. (Nicholson and Ramey knew this from experience.) Once you've used Post-it notes, you can't go back to staples and paper clips.

The Boise Blitz was unusual but not unique at 3M. The company had saturated test markets before with products and ads, but had restricted the number of employees involved. Besides spending a small fortune on advertising, promotions, and free Post-it notes, 3M diverted most of its Office Supply Division sales force and a battalion of temporary employees to the city of Boise, a medium-sized Western state capital. The blitz confirmed the appeal of the Post-it notes, revealing that Post-it note sales inevitably follow the distribution of free samples. Reorders come in at a rate of 90 percent—double the rate of any other wildly successful office product. This might be partly because Post-it notes possess an uncanny characteristic previously unique to cheap plastic pens—they always get lost before they get used up (until they're replaced, of course; then they reappear).

But Boise notwithstanding, the real key to the market breakthrough for Post-it notes was that first effort, in Richmond, when Nicholson and Ramey did what 3M sales representatives had been trained to do since the early days when sandpaper was their only product; they talked directly to the end-user, and then they showed distributors and retailers the results.

Recalling the trip to Richmond, Nicholson called it an "accident" and "an act of desperation." Neither he nor Ramey were hopeful that they could rejuvenate a doomed product by an impulsive flight to Richmond to knock on strange doors. "What made me go out into the market was the enthusiasm of Geoff Nicholson, and Art Fry," said Ramey. "I just figured that for their morale I should get out and find out whether we ought to kill it once and for all. . . . My reaction when I first went out into those markets was that we probably had a dead duck on our hands. . . . I didn't frankly think that it was a product that people would buy."[1]

Nicholson described the Richmond revelation as the last in a series of accidents. "I really think a lot of the things were accidents," said Nicholson. "The initial invention [of adhesive technology] was accidental, by Spence Silver. Even the invention of the Post-it note was somewhat accidental, by Art [Fry]. He was around the adhesive, and he had a problem and he solved the problem. But if he had not been in an environment where people were playing around with that [adhesive], he would not have come up with it."

There is an irony in Nicholson's description of this "series of accidents." Although he believes that the 3M breakthrough with Post-it notes is not a model of innovation for other companies, the development of Post-it notes has become one of the most studied and analyzed paradigms of the environment for innovation in modern business. It's a legend in its own time. Companies that want product breakthroughs are counseled to read about what 3M did with Post-it notes and do the same thing.

Retrospective writings about Post-it notes refer effusively to the encouragement provided to "creative people"—namely Arthur Fry—by "champions" and patrons in 3M management. Nicholson, who's been anointed by most analysts as the primary champion in Post-its technology development, wondered aloud one day where all that management encouragement was during the first five years of Spence Silver's struggle to be heard.

The 3M organization does, in fact, provide interesting soil for

1. George Dixon, "Sticking It Out: How 3M Almost Scotched Its Best-Selling Office Product," *Minnesota Corporate Report,* July 1984, page 51.

new ideas to grow, but until Nicholson listened to a presentation one day in 1973 by Silver and his colleague, Robert Oliveira, management at 3M had given no hint of support for what eventually became the Post-it notes project. Until then, the flame was borne entirely by middle and lower echelon troops acting largely in solitude and, occasionally, in defiance of the organization's implicit desires. Silver's adhesive (and the sticky bulletin board it spawned) lasted out a half decade of cold shoulders only because the company has a tradition of "internal selling." Anyone with a product idea at 3M can carry it around to the company's many divisions and seek support—both spiritual and fiscal—to develop the product for market. This means that inventors never really get *stopped* at 3M. There isn't any central overseer to say, "Cut that out and get back to work!" Instead, laboring in his spare time, the inventor experiences a mounting series of rejections from a legion of middle management functionaries, most of whom have neither the imagination nor the budget to take a serious look at his idea. Product ideas die at 3M—just like other places—but the death tends to be slow and lingering.

Spence Silver's job was as a chemist, working in 3M's central research and development laboratories. His particular sidekick was Robert Oliveira. They were among a host of fellow chemists whose job it is to develop variations in 3M chemical products. Like the other chemists, he worked within specific programs set out by 3M to attain certain results, but he had some encouragement to follow up on interesting, unexpected results—within reason, of course!

According to 3M, "3M scientists use up to 15 percent of their time pursuing interests outside their primary assignment. Their patrons on these projects are the successive layers of management to whom they report, from laboratory management up through the CEO. While review of individual lab notebooks and oral presentations may not be met with wild enthusiasm, rarely do inventors get stopped."

This 15 percent rule is policy in many companies involved in active research and development, and 3M is regarded as one of its originators. But when asked who keeps track of 3M researchers' use of the 15 percent rule, and how this is done, the answer is that no one really keeps track. In fact, 3M managers are wise *not* to monitor very carefully their scientists' use of this symbolic 15 percent rule. It's a policy which, if it were enforced rigidly, would undermine its intent and inhibit the creative energy of researchers such as Silver and Oliveira.

Spencer Silver kept the Post-it adhesive alive for a remarkably long time—beyond reason—partly because he also kept busy with other research tasks assigned by the company and didn't devote his entire energy to his funny adhesive, and partly because of an amazing tolerance for rejection. Silver is a man of infinite cheer and disarming goodwill.

An almost forgotten point is that Spence Silver's adhesive was, until Fry thought of a use for it, a really oddball idea. His adhesive was something that made little sense, either scientifically or commercially. The 3M system had the strength and good reasons to kill it. Post-it adhesive might have died also because it had no obsessed, fanatical advocates. Silver was a model citizen of the corporation. He rarely raised his voice, never asked for his office to be repainted, scrimped on equipment and chemicals when the budget was tight, and he had never—not once—ever grabbed his boss by the lapels to talk about his new invention and shake sense into him. Silver's sidekick, Oliveira, was more aggressive, but his most demonstrative moments were not the sort of tempests that could sway the sturdy bastion of 3M's indifference.

But the worst thing about this unsticky adhesive was that, for five years, it had no perceptible *application*. It was a solution looking for a problem.

Of all ways to devise new products, probably the most inefficient is to invent some substance with novel properties and then cast about for ways to use it—especially when the ultimate goal is a product people have to pay for.

Faced with an irrational commercial challenge, Spence Silver applied an unnatural irrationality to the Post-it adhesive. To understand his persistence, it's necessary to go back to his moment of discovery.

Silver's role in the development of Post-it Note Pads began in 1964 with a "Polymers for Adhesives" program in 3M's Central Research Laboratories. Since the time of William L. McKnight, a 3M salesman who interviewed furniture makers in 1912 in order to find ways for the company to make better sandpaper, 3M has had a tradition of periodically reexamining its own products, inside-out, to look for ways to improve them. Sometimes this policy turns into a problem of not seeing the forest for the trees, and sometimes it results in 3M "fixing" something that "ain't broke." But it's a tradition that, at its best, results in incremental "innovations" that occasionally lead to new markets, new technologies, even whole new product lines. "Every so many years," said Silver, "they would put together a bunch of people who looked like they might be productive in developing new types of adhesives."

In the course of that "Polymers for Adhesives" research program, which went on for four years, Silver found out about a new family of monomers developed by Archer-Daniels Midland, Inc., which he thought contained potential as ingredients for polymer-based adhesives. He received a number of samples from ADM and began to work with them, with the full approval of 3M. This was an open-ended research effort, and Silver's acquisition of the Archer-Daniels Midland monomers was the sort of exploration the company encouraged.

"As long as you were producing new things, everybody was happy," said Silver. "Of course, they had to be new molecules, new patentable molecules."

Silver went on, "In the course of this exploration, I tried an experiment with one of the monomers in which I wanted to see what would happen if I put a lot of it into the reaction mixture. Before, we had used amounts that would correspond to conventional wisdom." Silver had no expectation whatsoever of what might occur if he did this. He just thought it might be interesting to find out.

Already, Silver was venturing into the realm of the irrational. In polymerization catalysis, scientists usually control the amounts of interacting ingredients to very tightly defined proportions, in accordance with prevailing theory and experience.

Silver said with a certain measure of glee, "The key to the Post-it adhesive was doing the experiment. If I had sat down and factored it out beforehand, and thought about it, I wouldn't have done the experiment. If I had really seriously cracked the books and gone through the literature, I would have stopped. The literature was full of examples that said you can't do this."

Reliable, published experts could have told Spence Silver there was no point in doing what he did. But there is a charm in Spence Silver that supplied him both with indefatigable good spirits and, eventually, an irrational loyalty to his odd adhesive. He understood that science is one part meticulous calculation and one part "fooling around."

"People like myself," said Silver, "get excited about looking for new properties in materials. I find that very satisfying, to perturb the structure slightly and just see what happens. I have a hard time talking people into doing that—people who are more highly trained. It's been my experience that people are reluctant just to *try*, to experiment—just to see what will happen!"

When Silver went ahead with the "wrong" proportions of the ADM monomers, "just to see what would happen," he got a reaction that departed from the predictions of theory. It was like an extra flash in the fireworks display. It's what Nicholson calls an "accident" and what Silver called a "Eureka moment."

What Silver experienced with the appearance of what would become the Post-it adhesive polymer was the moment for which all scientists become scientists—the emergence of a unique, unexpected, previously unobserved and reliable scientific phenomenon—reliable because it is natural. Each time Silver put those things together, they fell into the same pattern—every time.

"It's one of those things you look at and you say, 'This has got to be useful! You're not forcing materials into a situation to make them work.' It wanted to do this. It wanted to make Post-it adhesive," Silver said.

Technically the material was what the research program called for, a new polymer with adhesive properties. But in examining it, Silver noticed among its other curious properties that this material was not "aggressively" adhesive. It would create what 3M scientists call "tack" between two surfaces, but it would not bond tightly to them. Also—and this was a problem not solved for years—this material was more "cohesive" than it was "adhesive." It clung to its own molecules better than it clung to any other molecules. So if you sprayed it on a surface (it was sprayable, another property that attracted Silver) and then slapped a piece of paper on the sprayed surface, you could remove all or none of the adhesive when you lifted the paper. It might "prefer" one surface to another, but not stick well to either. Someone would have to invent a new coating for paper if 3M were to use this as an adhesive for pieces of paper. But paper? Not very likely, thought Silver— and on this point, at least, everyone agreed with him.

What Silver had done was more than a synthesis—which was the usual procedure in 3M's labs; it was a discovery—the sort of thing a scientist can put his name on. When he watched the reaction, Silver was achieving fatherhood, and he was falling in love. He knew he might never again be responsible for so pure and simple a phenomenon.

Almost instantly, he personified this viscous goo: It "wanted" to do this, he said. And soon he came to call the stuff "my baby." It may not have been very sticky, but Spence Silver got very attached to it.

Silver started presenting this discovery to people who shared none of his perceptions about the beauty of his glue. Interested in practical applications, they had only a passing appreciation for the science embodied in Silver's adhesive. More significantly, they were "trapped by the metaphor" that insists that the ultimate adhesive is one that forms an unbreakable bond. The whole world in which they lived was looking for a better glue, not a worse glue. And like any other sensible adhesives manufacturer, 3M's sights had never wavered from a progressive course of developing stronger and stronger adhesives. Suddenly, here was Spence Silver, circulating among the devotees of constancy, touting the virtues of promiscuity.

He couldn't say exactly what it was good for. "But it has to be good for something," he would tell them. Aren't there times, Silver would ask people, when you want a glue to hold something for a while but not forever? Let's think about those situations. Let's see if we can turn this adhesive into a product that will hold tight as long as people need it to hold but then let go when people want it to let go.

From 1968 through 1973, company support systematically slipped away from him. First, the Polymers for Adhesives Program disappeared. 3M had given its researchers a specified time and a limited budget to conduct that program. When the time and money were used up, the researchers were reassigned. Some, like Silver, had got personally involved and were just starting to have fun.

"The adhesives program died a natural death," Silver recalled. "The company's business went off, and in the usual cycle of things, the longer-range research programs were cut. So the emphasis was diminished and we still had some interesting materials that we wanted to push—being the inventors of these things."

The members of the Polymers for Adhesives group—the other "inventors"—were assigned to new research projects. Left as a team, they might have fought together to keep alive a number of their odd little discoveries. But all those discoveries were shelved—with Silver's one glaring exception—and he got little assistance from his teammates in promoting the survival of his oddball adhesive. So he did what seems to happen frequently at 3M. He shrugged at the organization and he did it himself. He had to wage a battle to get the money just to patent his unique polymer. 3M eventually spent the minimum money possible. Post-it adhesive was patented *only* in the United States.

"We really had to fight to get a patent," said Silver, "because there was no commercial product readily apparent. It's kind of a shame. I wish it would change. If you commit yourself [3M] to hundreds of thousands of dollars for research, you ought to follow it up with a $10,000 patent."

People at 3M, when they fight for something, seem to do it with an understated grace, a politeness that conceals their tenacity. This is true of Silver, who quietly began the arduous struggle to capture the imagination of his colleagues and superiors. Silver's only advantage was that he was, after all, in love.

"I was just absolutely convinced that this had some potential," Silver said. "There are some things that have a little spark to them—that are worth pursuing.

"You have to be almost a zealot at times in order to keep interest alive, because it will die off. It seems like the pattern always goes like this: In the fat times, these groups appear and we do a lot of interesting research. And then the lean times come just about at the point when you've developed your first goody, your gizmo. And then you've got to go out and try to sell it. Well, everybody in the divisions is so busy that they don't want to touch it. They don't have time to look at new product ideas with no end-product already in mind."

Silver went door-to-door to every division at 3M that might be able to think up an application for an adhesive with the curious charm of hanging around without making a commitment. The organization never protested his search. When he sought slots of time at in-house technical seminars, he always got a segment to show off his now-it-works, now-it-doesn't adhesive. At every seminar, some people left, some people stayed. Most of them said, "What can you do with a glue that doesn't glue?" But *no one* said to Silver, "Don't try. Stop wasting our time."

In fact, it would have violated some very deeply felt principles of the 3M Company to have killed Silver's pet project. Much is made of 3M's "environment for innovation," but 3M's environment is, more accurately, an environment of nonintervention—of expecting people to fulfill their day's responsibilities, every day, without discernible pressure from above. Silver, no matter how much time he spent fooling around with the Post-it adhesive, never failed in his other duties, and so, at 3M, there was no reason whatsoever to overtly discourage his extracurricular activities.

The positive side of this corporate ethic is the feeling of independence each worker experiences in doing his job. The disadvantage is that, when you have a good idea that requires more than one person to share the work and get the credit, it can be hard to convince people to postpone their chores and help with yours.

As Silver pursued his lonely quest, his best inspiration for applying his adhesive was a sticky bulletin board—a product that wasn't especially stimulating even to its inventor. He got 3M to manufacture a number of them—through a fairly low-tech and inexpensive process—and they were sent out to the company's distribution and retail network. The outcome was predictable. 3M sold a few, but it was a slow-moving item in a sleepy market niche.

Silver knew there had to be a better idea. "At times I was angry because this stuff is so obviously unique," said Silver. "I said to myself, 'Why can't you think of a product? It's your job!' "

Although Silver had overcome the metaphorical trap of always striving for stickier stickum, he, too, at the next stage of development for his adhesive, became trapped by the metaphor. The bulletin board, the only product he could think of, was coated with adhesive—it was sticky everywhere. The metaphor said that some thing is either sticky or not sticky. Something *partly sticky* did not occur to him.

More intellectually seductive was the fact that, until Silver's adhesive made it possible, there was no such thing as a self-adhesive piece of note paper. Note paper was cheap and trivial, and the valuable elements in the conveyance of these bits of paper were their durable fasteners. The world is an ocean of pins, tacks, tapes, and clips—so Silver was immersed in an organization whose lifeblood was tape—Scotch brand tapes, like cellophane tape, duct tape, masking tape, electrical tape, caulking tape, security tape, diaper tape, and surgical tape—to name a few. In this atmosphere, imagining a piece of paper that eliminates the need for tape is an almost unthinkable leap into the void.

*　　*　　*

In the early 1970s, 3M transferred Silver to its System Research group—still in the Central Research laboratories. There he met Oliveira, a biochemist, who shared Silver's fascination with things that did things you didn't think they could do. Silver and Oliveira, keeping each other from getting discouraged, were the team who eventually showed the adhesive to Geoff Nicholson.

Nicholson, who has emphasized the accidental nature of what he calls the "series of breakthroughs" in Post-it technology, might have been the biggest accident of all. He was, in 1973, appointed the leader of a new venture team in the Commercial Tape Division laboratory. New venture teams are open-ended research and development groups formed, when funds are available, to explore new directions in one of 3M's many lines of business and technology. Nicholson had been given a fresh budget and a free hand to develop new products in the company's Commercial Tape Division, whose new product development had grown sluggish. It is a standing policy at 3M that each division must generate 25 percent of its annual revenue from products developed in the last five years, a tall order for any division, especially those in the old, established product lines, and one on which Commercial Tape consistently had been coming up short.

Silver had been to see the people in Commercial Tape at least twice before. Both times they had rejected his adhesive. Two days before Nicholson arrived in Commercial Tape, Silver and Oliveira had been around again, trying to sell the idea to the division's technical director, James Irwin. Irwin sidestepped them by saying there would be a new guy running research projects there in a couple of days.

Two days later, Silver and Oliveira were almost the first people in Nicholson's new office. "Here I am, brand-new to the division, and I don't know a lot about adhesives. And here they were talking to me about adhesives," Nicholson recalled. "I'm ripe for something new, different, and exciting. Most anybody who had walked in the door, I would have put my arms around them."

Silver explained his adhesive, his discovery, his Eureka moment for the umpteenth time, and Nicholson, who didn't understand half of what he was saying, loved it. "It sure sounded different and unique to me," said Nicholson. "I was ripe for the plucking."

Finally, Silver's unloved, uncommitted adhesive had a home. Nicholson went about recruiting people for the new venture team;

Silver hoped that one of those people would arrive with a *problem* to match his five-year-old *solution*. The one who had the problem was a chemist, choir director, and amateur mechanic named Arthur Fry.

Arthur Fry's benign exterior belies the playground of curiosity that capers within him. He is the person who took the baton from Silver's weary grasp, infused the quest with substance, and carried it over a jumble of discouraging hurdles. Fry, unlike Silver, had support from above, from Nicholson, but the technological problems he dealt with were far more daunting than Silver's.

Even before joining the new venture team in Commercial Tape, Fry had seen Spence Silver show off his adhesive. Like Archimedes pondering the tyrant's crown, Fry kept the idea turnng slowly in the back of his mind. He agreed with Silver that this adhesive was special, but he wondered what to do with it.

"Then one day in 1974, while I was singing in the choir of the North Presbyterian Church in north St. Paul, I had one of those creative moments," Fry explained. "To make it easier to find the songs we were going to sing at each Sunday's service, I used to mark the places with little slips of paper."

Inevitably, when everyone in the church stood up, or when Fry had to communicate—through gestures—with other members of the choir, he would divert his attention from the placement of his array of bookmarks. One unguarded move, and they fluttered to the floor or sank into the deep crack of the hymnal's binding. Suddenly, while Fry leafed frantically for his place in the book, the North Presbyterian Church was gripped with a moment of sweaty anticipation. "I thought, 'Gee, if I had a little adhesive on these bookmarks, that would be just the ticket,' " said Fry. "So I decided to check into that idea the next week at work. What I had in mind, of course, was Silver's adhesive."

What had happened in Fry's ever-searching curiosity was what Arthur Koestler called a "bisociation," the association, at once, of two unrelated ideas. After Fry went to 3M, mixed up some adhesive and paper, and tried different concentrations, he had invented what he called "the better bookmark."

By then, certainly encouraged by Silver's enthusiasm and the Nicholson push for new products, Fry began to realize the magnitude of his "creative moment."

"I knew I had made a much bigger discovery than that," said

Fry. "I also now realized that the primary application for Silver's adhesive was not to put it on a fixed surface, like the bulletin boards. That was a secondary application. The primary application concerned paper to paper. I realized that immediately."

What Silver and the rest of 3M had not realized in five years, Fry realized in a flash. It was one of those ideas that contemplation doesn't seem to generate: It either pops into one's head or it doesn't happen at all. For Arthur Fry, that moment of insight has had effects more extensive than the success of Post-it notes. Through a sort of conspiracy among journalists, business analysts, and 3M executives, Fry has been ordained as the Post-it notes champion, a title which, in ensuing years, has imposed some unusual burdens on him. Today, rather than working side-by-side in a lab with old friends like Silver and Oliveira, Art Fry is ensconced in his own laboratory. To a chemist, this is the equivalent of the corporate corner office, lofty among the echelons of the organization. According to 3M, "The thrust of his day-to-day corporate activity is far-ranging across many 3M laboratories." Being "far-ranging" appears to be a lonely job.

On the other hand, Fry is often freed from the splendid isolation of his private lab. He often speaks to large groups of businessmen about the climate for creativity at 3M. When he's doing his bit as company spokesman, Fry presents a long prepared speech (which 3M's public relations people unconvincingly insist Art Fry wrote himself), and an accompanying slide show. Interviews by business writers invariably quote him saying, "A lot of people in major corporations can make names for themselves by killing projects." Fry has been quoted so often saying this because apparently it is the clinching statement that pegs him as the Post-it notes product champion (he knew the enemy and he prevailed). Still, the cynical tone of this quote seems out of character for Fry, whose mood seems so much brighter and more optimistic. Fry has also had to suffer from business writers' depictions of him as "ornery," "unpredictable," and "simmering."[2] Yet he has an almost saintly absence of orneriness.

With Fry trapped under labels like that, it's easy to see why Spence Silver seemed relieved and grateful at the comparatively short shrift given to his role in the Post-it story. Silver is still in

2. Dixon, page 52.

3M's basement, working out of a cramped, windowless office in a large, open, multi-hood laboratory—a place where experimental ferment still seems to seep from the grouting of the cinderblock walls.

In Silver, the scientific playfulness that gave birth to the Post-it adhesive still seems intact. In fact, without much prompting, he will find, somewhere jammed in an overflowing drawer, a glass cylinder filled with the old Post-it polymer. He holds it up, showing it in its restful state. It is milky white in color. But then he squeezes the polymer with a plunger and, under pressure, the contents become—magically—crystal clear. Silver releases the pressure and the adhesive becomes opaque again!

Silver doesn't know why it does that. "Isn't that wonderful?" he says. "There must be some way you can *use* that!"

In 1974, after Silver had been making the same exclamation for years already, Fry provided the first truly affirmative response. But with the "Eureka moment" at the North Presbyterian Church came an immediate problem. On the bulletin board, Silver's adhesive was attached to a favorable "substrate." It stuck to the bulletin board better than anything else. Move it to paper, though, and it peeled off onto everything it touched. If you couldn't change this property, you still couldn't make a future for Silver's Post-it adhesive.

The two members of the Nicholson team who invented a paper coating that made the Post-it adhesive work were named Henry Courtney and Roger Merrill.

Silver said, "Those guys actually made one of the most important contributions to the whole project, and they haven't got a lot of credit for it. The Post-it adhesive was always interesting to people, but if you put it down on something and pulled it apart, it could stay with either side. It had no memory of where it should be. It was difficult to figure out a way to prime the substrate, to get it to stick to the surface you originally put it on. Roger and Hank [invented] a way to stick the Post-it adhesive down. And they're the ones who really made the breakthrough discovery, because once you've learned that, you can apply it to all sorts of different surfaces."

Courtney and Merrill's contribution was the first in a series of actions that definitely were not accidents. Although there was still organizational resistance after early 1974 and Fry's choir book epiphany, every action thenceforth—including Courtney and Merrill's research—was directed toward the development, production, and market success of the Post-it note. Fry was a tenacious advocate of the product through all phases from development to production scale-up.

While Silver's task had been simply to convince his corporation that his glue was not just a footnote in the obscure history of adhesives, the job Fry assumed when he joined in the fatherhood of the Post-it note was to help his division manufacture something that was (a) not sticky at all on one side, (b) only sticky on part of the other side, and (c) wasn't actually *very* sticky anywhere. It had to be produced in big sheets, not in rolls, and then the big sheets had to be laid together and cut into smaller sizes. This might sound hard, but what added to the difficulty was the natural resistance of people. The engineers in 3M's Commercial Tape Division were accustomed to tape—which is sticky all over on one side and then gets packaged into rolls. To apply glue selectively to one side of the paper, and to move the product from rolls to sheets, the engineers would have to invent at least two entirely unique machines.

In war and politics, the best strategy is divide and conquer. In production engineering, the reverse seems to be true. Fry brought together the production people, designers, mechanical engineers, product foremen, and machine operators and let them describe the many reasons why something like that could not be done. He encouraged them to speculate on ways that they might accomplish the impossible. A lifelong gadgeteer, Fry found himself offering his own suggestions. "Problems are wonderful things to have, especially early in the game, when you really should be looking for problems," said Fry.

Inevitably, from these discussions people started thinking of places around 3M where they'd seen machines and parts they could use to piece together the impossible machines they needed to build. And they thought of people who could help. "In a small company, if you had an idea that would incorporate a variety of technologies and you had to go out and buy the equipment to put those together, you probably couldn't afford it, or you'd have to go as inexpensively—or as small—as possible," said Fry. "At 3M, we've got so many different types of technology operating and so many experts—guys that really know all about any subject you want—oh, and so much equipment scattered here and there, that we can piece things together when we're starting off. We can go to this place and do Step A on a product, and we can make the adhesive and some of the raw materials here, and do one part over here, and another part there, and convert a space there and make a few things that aren't available."

And then there was Arthur Fry's basement. He had had arguments with several mechanical engineers about a difficult phase of production, applying adhesive to paper in a continuous roll. He said it could be done; they said it couldn't. He assembled a small-scale basic machine in his basement, then adapted it until he'd solved the problem. The machine worked, and it would work even better once the mechanical engineers had a chance to refine it. But the next problem Fry had was worse—the new machine was too big to fit through his basement door. If he couldn't get it out of his cellar, he couldn't show it off to the engineers.

Fry accepted the consequences of his genius and did what he had to do. He bashed a hole through his basement wall and delivered his machine by caesarean section.

Within two years, Fry and 3M's mechanical engineers had tinkered their way to a series of machines that, among other things, coated the yellow paper with its "substrate," applied adhesive, and cut the sticky paper into little square and rectangular note pads. All of the machines are unique, proprietary to the company (and secret)—and they are the key to the Post-it notes' marvelous consistency and dependability. The immense difficulty of duplicating 3M's machinery—without the slightest notion of what Fry and the Commercial Tape Division engineers did—is part of the reason few competitors have made it to the market with Post-it note imitations.

Fry and the engineers worked on their unique machines and mass production methods in a pilot plant in the Commercial Tape lab. They produced more than enough Post-it note prototypes to supply all the company's offices. All the sticky pads went to Nicholson's office. From there his secretary carried out a program of providing every office at 3M with Post-it notes. Early in the program, secretaries on the fourteenth floor, where the senior managers work, all received Post-it notes and became hooked. Jack Wilkins, the Commercial Tape Division's marketing director at the time, described the process of discovery that hit people the first time they encountered the Post-it notes.

"Once people started using them it was like handing them marijuana," said Wilkins. "Once you start using it you can't stop."

But strangely, the personal enthusiasm of secretaries and marketing people like Wilkins did not impress the people responsible for putting Post-it notes into the market. For the division's marketing organization, fear of the unfamiliar repeatedly raised its unsightly head and threatened to scuttle the program. The marketing department had got out of the habit of dealing directly with consumers. This is ironic, because that 3M ancient warrior, William L. McKnight, had established a tradition of direct contact with consumers in 1914. That year, as the company's brand-new national sales manager, the first act performed by the twenty-four-year-old McKnight was to visit furniture factories in Rockford, Illinois, and find out from laborers what was wrong with 3M's mediocre sandpaper—which was then the company's only product. That trip to Rockford was the first instance of an executive from 3M walking in the door, approaching a worker, and saying, "Here! Try this! Tell me what you think!"

By 1978 the Commercial Tape Division's marketing department was involved in the introduction of half a dozen new products that met easily identified needs for clearly defined markets—products like book binding tape for libraries and PMA adhesives for the art market. The Post-it note was just another new product, and not a high-priority product at that. While the company's marketing people had become mesmerized by Post-it notes in their own offices, they couldn't imagine that other people would feel the same way.

Although most of the marketing group had used Post-it notes, when they created marketing materials to present the new product they included no samples. Instead they wrote brochures describing the note pads, then sent boxes of samples separately—which people would open only if they got excited by the brochures.

The 3M marketing group was trapped, just as Spence Silver had been trapped by the metaphor of the adhesive bulletin board and could not envision his adhesive going onto paper instead. As marketing experts, it was their job to explain products, not to demonstrate them. And as explainers, they had no words to overcome the "scratch paper" metaphor. If they couldn't explain them, they couldn't sell them.

Nicholson, who had spread Post-it notes like an infection within 3M, only had limited power to push them outside the company. When the four-city test failed, he might not have had the influence alone to keep the product alive. But by this time Nicholson had a heavyweight ally in Joe Ramey, general sales manager of the Commercial Tape Division and Nicholson's boss. Ramey was a marketing troubleshooter. He knew that some market problems are too far advanced to be saved. He had gone to Richmond because he liked Nicholson, not because he liked Post-it notes' chances.

But the reactions, face-to-face, when people in Richmond started "playing" with Post-it notes, were so dramatic that Ramey had all the evidence he needed to throw all the artillery into Boise. It was a moment when Nicholson and Ramey must have felt a little like William McKnight among the furniture makers of Rockford.

It's remarkable that two of the company's greatest breakthroughs, sixty-six years apart, grew out of a similar style and faith in the wisdom of sitting down with customers and asking questions—without any of the trappings of corporate protocol. It could be just a coincidence, but according to most business analysts, Post-it notes finally succeeded because 3M's corporate culture creates a positive environment for innovation. Although *corporate culture* is one of those fragments of business jargon that eventually will pass from the English language without ever being defined, suffice it to say that there is something in 3M's style that tends to encourage a measure of individual ingenuity among its workers.

One of 3M's corporate strengths for more than fifty years has been its perpetual efforts to improve the product line. The development of cellophane tape in the 1930s was a breakthrough that came from 3M's work on developing insulation for railroad cars. From that point, 3M sustained its interest in tape, improving cellophane tape constantly, always devising an improved product that left their imitators behind, culminating (most recently) in the Scotch brand Magic Tape revolution in the 1960s.

Whenever 3M's constant search for improvement led in a slightly different direction, the company let a few people follow that direction. If the detour resulted in a product line, even of modest profitability, 3M allowed the effort to proceed.

"3M . . . operates on a simple principle," *Forbes* magazine once said, "that no market, no end product is so small as to be scorned; that with the proper organization, a myriad of small products can be as profitable, if not more so, than a few big ones. More firmly than most, 3M management appreciates that the beach is composed of grains of sand, the ocean of drops of water."[3]

3. Quoted in *Our Story, So Far: Notes from the First 75 Years of the 3M Company*, St. Paul: Minnesota Mining & Manufacturing Company, 1977.

This tolerance of the small-scale certainly helped Spence Silver, and then Art Fry, to keep the company from stomping on the Post-it notes project before the project had developed a life of its own. But there was also the benefit of bigness. Over the years, 3M has grown into a loosely integrated cluster of divisions, with senior management in the St. Paul corporate headquarters. One of the results of this corporate sprawl is that it permits the clever researcher to hide in the crevices and carry out his own version of the "15 percent principle." Silver benefitted more from this "neglect of magnitude" than from anyone overtly encouraging him to innovate. Fry also enjoyed this dispensation from scrutiny as he fostered the Post-it project through the touchy and costly labor of product development.

A more provocative issue, though, is why people at 3M enjoy such unchecked opportunity to "get away with things." A hasty judgment—often delivered both within the company and outside—is that the company's senior management has consciously decided to foster an orderly chaos as the rich plankton of innovative growth. But there is plenty of evidence to challenge this assertion. The company tends to cast its most successful creative people in bronze—investing them into a living frieze called the Carlton Society or, as in the case of Fry, installing them in private laboratories. After each unexpected invention emerges at 3M, the company tends to follow up by creating new programs for innovation (the latest is called Genesis) and new honors to motivate inventors. Yet there seems to have been no desire for trophies in any of the Post-it project principals nor in any of 3M's prior inventors. They were people obsessed with problems, not rewards, and they usually invented their own program in order to get a problem solved.

Incentives aren't why 3M gets creativity from its Silvers and Frys. There might be a more credible explanation in the company's origins. Since moving from Duluth in 1910, 3M has been inextricably linked with the city of St. Paul. Some 80 percent of its employees are drawn from the upper Midwest. For seventy-five years, St. Paul has been the company town for 3M, and 3M has been St. Paul's town company. One of the striking characteristics of community-linked Midwestern companies like 3M is that company and community have grown up together, and they like to think they know what to expect from each other. This bond among town, corporate management, and workers creates trust, and with trust comes an air of amiability. The ease and unpretentiousness of the highest officials at 3M is different from the formality and status sensitivity of managements in other regions, especially in the East. Nicholson and Ramey, for example, did not need to overcome a lot of deep-seated conditioning in order to go out on the streets and behave like peddlers.

At 3M, it is simply not good form for management to watch too closely over the shoulders of its veteran employees. It is equally bad form for employees to violate the trust placed in them by a less than vigilant management. There is an honor system, and it works.

The source of this heartland ethos is in the farms that surround St. Paul. This pioneer farming region, stretching almost changelessly from the Dakotas east to Detroit, is a place where—for more than a century—the lactation cycle of the Guernsey cow has had more effect on people's lives than the daily fluctuations of the Dow Jones industrials. This is not to say that people think about cows at 3M, but the ethic that has governed the farms around St. Paul has some very explicit effects on 3M's company style. It can be found similarly in other Midwestern companies—very often companies that are close to their communities but distant from their competition. There is a streak of stubborn independence in the management of these companies—and their managers tend to get that attitude from their employees, rather than giving it to them.

A Midwestern American farm is a place where—for generations—each worker has been expected to complete his daily chores before sitting down to supper. Nobody ever watches him do his chores; if he doesn't do them, the disastrous evidence will become apparent by the next day's dawn. Nobody ever asks him if he did his chores, because he wouldn't be eating if he hadn't. The Midwest is a place where two or more separate farms (or "business development units") have traditionally joined forces to do a job that's too big for any single household to handle—such as threshing the harvest of oats or rebuilding a windmill. Although this pioneer spirit has begun to disappear from the increasingly mechanized farms of the Midwest, the frame of mind and the ways of perceiving the world that grew from that spirit still hold on tenaciously within the people who live there.

People carry on without permission at 3M because they're trustworthy. And they're trustworthy because trust is a part of the larger culture that has surrounded and affected 3M for eighty-five years.

Even 3M's sprawling divisional structure has the aspect of a series of small towns spread throughout one of Minnesota's big, lake-strewn counties—each town (or division) fiercely independent yet alert to what is happening in every neighboring community. A sophisticated analysis of 3M structure might say that management created radical decentralization in order to spread the entrepreneurial spirit. A simpler outlook might simply view 3M as having grown according to the natural contours of its geography and its people.

But one thing 3M has proven is that when it gets self-conscious about managing its innovation, it doesn't innovate any better than any other company. As Nicholson said, Post-it notes came from accidents, not calculations.

The Post-it note accidents were Spence Silver's polymer discovery, Arthur Fry's bookmark epiphany, and Geoff Nicholson's dragging Joe Ramey off to Richmond. Each accident occurred after one person took an entirely independent course of action from the one assigned by the corporation. Each time, the individual got frustrated either by the indifference or the resistance of the organization.

Similar accidents had occurred in the past. In 1956 a researcher spilled a tube full of totally useless fluorocarbon compound on her shoes—and from that accident, chemists Patsy Sherman and Sam Smith created Scotchgard fabric protector. In 1950, after three polite 3M requests to stop wasting money, researcher Alvin W. Boese squeezed synthetic fibers mixed with wood pulp through a makeshift comb and created one of the most successful types of nonwoven decorative ribbon ever devised.

These accidents happened because when the organization—or management—discouraged people from doing something, the cancellation orders didn't carry much conviction. Ego is not popular at 3M, and it is clear that the people thinking up things often have more room to express their egos than the people who are supposed to be running things. If there is an organizational key to breakthrough at 3M, a significant element of corporate culture, it is in the fact that people there don't believe in placing the values of the corporation above the values of the individual. People keep the organization vital by not taking the organization very seriously. As a result, when the creative people, Silver and Fry and Nicholson, inevitably ran into the resistance of the organization, they felt the freedom to say, "Well, okay. Never mind. I'll do it myself." The organization simply did not have an equal measure of persistence in response. 3M gives in to people who are sure of themselves.

Just as important, everybody at 3M knows that if someone's pet project blows up in his face, it isn't the end of the world. If Silver, Fry, or Nicholson had failed, they wouldn't have been dismissed or disgraced. As long as they had their chores done, they would always have a place at the table.

4 | ChemLawn: Dick Duke's Lonely Battle

I n the spring of 1969, in the village of Troy, Ohio, the few employees of a new company called ChemLawn harbored in their bosoms no grand schemes, no great expectations. In those days ChemLawn was composed of a small band of men whose long-term ambitions, thus far, had usually extended no farther than the weekend. They had got little from life and expected little. This new company seemed to promise slightly more than they ever had received—at least as long as it lasted.

These were common people but uncommon in that they possessed the rare humility to describe themselves as common. "We were all pretty uncomplicated people who, having had a farm life background, were on our own all the time. You saw something that had to be done—you did it. There wasn't anybody else around to do it," explained Richard C. Lyons, one of that first ChemLawn crew and now a vice-president of what has become the largest lawn service company in the world.

ChemLawn became the largest corporation in its industry by inventing the industry. Until the first ChemLawn tank trucks began to venture boldly forth from Troy, Ohio, in 1968, lawn care had been—to quote ChemLawn's own promotional copy—the province of a "shabby unskilled lawn worker with a dirty pickup truck." This description, with the deletion of the word *shabby,* for some twenty years would have fit Richard L. Duke, who, with his father, Paul, founded ChemLawn. Paul and Dick Duke began business in

1949 as proprietors of the Duke Garden Center of Troy, Ohio. That business served as the family livelihood until 1968, and its only successful expansion was the purchase of a sod farm in the early 1960s. The sod farm added a little to the family income and a great deal to the hard work the Dukes had to do to make ends meet.

ChemLawn became possible (just barely) with the sale of the Duke Garden Center and sod farm in summer 1968. The sale netted a total of $40,000, barely enough to outfit a pair of trucks designed (on the kitchen table at Dick's house) to spray liquid lawn food four times a year on the yard of anyone who signed up for it. Crucial to this concept, besides the truck and the lawn food, were hoses that Duke and sidekick Thomas Grapner had designed and at least one employee per truck, whom they decided to title a "lawn care specialist." The ChemLawn idea was to free the suburbanites of America from one of the most difficult and mysterious tasks associated with the care and feeding of their realty—lawn care. It became successful beyond the wildest dreams of Paul or Dick or any of the fuzzy-faced crew that originally set out from Troy at the crack of dawn each rainless day with those two trucks and their array of makeshift spraying gear. In every city that ChemLawn entered—and Duke entered cities the way Napoleon devoured western Europe—ChemLawn invariably attained, within a year, a customer base in the thousands and a customary profit margin of slightly more than 20 percent. Within thirty months of that $40,000 investment, Richard L. Duke was entertaining a buyout offer from ITT that would have made him—and his original crew of five "lawn care specialists"—a personal fortune in excess of $1 million.

In 1969, Richard Lyons was fresh from a tour in Vietnam. His credentials consisted of a high school diploma and an honorable discharge from the army. For his position at ChemLawn as a "lawn care specialist," he had quit a job in neighboring Piqua, Ohio, as the ad-taker in the local newspaper office. The $180-a-week ChemLawn job represented a $70-a-week raise for Lyons.

Tom Grapner had been working with Dick Duke longer than any of that first crew. He had signed on as a manual laborer, to help Paul and Dick handle the humble tedium of the Duke Garden Center's sod-laying operation. Grapner had taken a job with the Dukes that barely supported his family; but his choice, he recalled, lay in assurances—from other folks—that the Dukes took pride in their work and took good care of anyone who worked for them.

Grapner, who didn't anticipate much from life, placed a great deal of stock in an employer who would help him watch over his family if he got hurt or sick. He eventually became the president of ChemLawn, and he retired still a young man, amazed at his good fortune, to a sleepy, picturesque cattle ranch in Georgia.

John Wright eventually became one of three group vice-presidents of the ChemLawn Corporation. But in 1969, the ChemLawn job marked his entry into a whole new social stratum. As operator of his own landscaping business in Union City, Indiana—a job that involved a lot of lawn mowing, shrub trimming, and bug control—he only recently had begun to grant himself a weekly take-home stipend of $70 a week. ChemLawn was a real improvement for Wright, both in pay and working conditions, but he admitted that it did not look much more promising than anything else he'd seen so far in his eminently unpromising life. He said that if he had felt any serious faith in the ChemLawn experiment, he would have sold off all his landscaping gear the year before. But in the spring of 1969, Wright still had all that stuff tucked safely away in his garage—just in case.

For Lyons, the enigma of ChemLawn's future was solved by not thinking about it. "I never asked the question," said Lyons one day as he sat in his spacious office at ChemLawn's Columbus, Ohio, headquarters. "We all thought the guy was going to have money coming in. From where, we didn't know. But everything worked out that way. Of course, as I look back now, I think, Boy! Was that risky!"

"The guy" was Richard L. Duke, co-founder of ChemLawn and recent proprietor of the Duke Garden Center of Troy, Ohio. What Duke expected from Lyons and Wright was the even application, on customers' lawns, of a rather ingenious liquid blend of fertilizer, weed killer, and bug killer. This mixture, usually applied when the homeowner was not there (making it seem all the more magical), had the captivating effect of making a lawn uniformly green and healthy—very quickly. The ChemLawn truck, a custom-designed six-wheel tanker with a huge lawn-green logo splashed across its sides, would come and go while the residents were at work and at school. The only sign of its passing was a notice on the door reminding people not to roll around in the grass until the chemicals had had a chance to dry (about an hour).

The treatment didn't cost very much and—under orders from Duke—the lawn care specialists were expected to be extremely friendly to customers. The last part wasn't hard to do. The lawn care specialists were a pretty friendly bunch. They were friendlier, in fact, than the boss, who was nice to the paying public but a little tough, now and then, on friends, family, and employees. But if there seemed to be a vaguely threatening air about Duke, there was also an electric intensity that stirred his emotions constantly. It was that voltage, and Duke's unreasonable self-confidence, that compelled far more timid souls like Wright to join up with this unlikely lawn-spraying outfit.

Wright didn't worry about believing in the company. He had believed, for several years, in Dick Duke. Before spraying lawns, one of the things Duke did was raise sod. Wright used sod in his landscaping business, and he often made the short trip from Union City to Troy to pick up a load. While Wright and the Dukes—Dick and his father, Paul—loaded Wright's pickup truck, the conversation would range into aspirations that were—to John Wright—both alluring and unattainable.

"I often told people that what was fascinating about the whole process was that loading a small amount of sod is a very simple job," said Wright. "It should take three men about twenty minutes. But I would invariably spend at least half a day when I'd go there, because Dick would start talking about this idea he had for an organization. The focus was going to be on the *people* of the organization. That attracted me. And I found we had a lot of things in common philosophically. I guess we had a lot in common in reality, too. We both worked hard and we were starving to death, and we were sure that there had to be a better way to succeed."

The newborn ChemLawn Corporation took its first brazen steps in midsummer 1968, when Dick and Paul Duke, Tom Grapner, and later John Wright plunged full-time into the novel occupation of liquid lawn care. Nobody had ever done the unwelcome job of fertilizing the yard quite in that manner before. By late spring the next year, the ChemLawn crew was beginning to sense just how unusual this lawn-spraying idea was. At first, they were just a few men doing their jobs. But one by one they looked up from the grass and began to see untold possibilities.

"Well, for one thing, all the checks cashed," Wright recalled. "When that is twice as much money as you've ever made in your life, and those checks do cash, that's a tremendous source of motivation. And the thing that really pulled the trigger was going down and talking to the people and closing eight out of ten sales. I'd never been in a business like that. I'd been fighting for every dollar and here these people were signing up for $50, $100 a year—bingo!''

Unexpectedly to even the irrepressible Duke, who kept pumping his people with the assurance that "anything is possible," the ChemLawn concept—all those suddenly green, lush, rampant, dandelion-free lawns glistening in the neighborhood like emeralds among the zircons—had struck a resounding chord with the homeowners of Troy and Piqua and Dayton—and pretty soon, even Columbus!

"Saturday was a big sale day. More than once, we'd park in a cul-de-sac, and people would come to line up at the truck and sign up for the service. You'd see them walking from blocks away to the truck," recalled Lyons. "You'd stand there and you wouldn't get any lawns sprayed. And you'd go back and they'd say, 'How come you didn't get any lawns sprayed?' 'That's because I got these twelve new customers!' They'd be lined up at the truck and you'd be filling out paperwork and saying, 'I'll be down there as quick as I can.' And they'd say, 'I don't care what it costs. Just come and do it.' And that was *routine*."

In that first year, the growth of ChemLawn was extraordinary. A company that had recorded little discernible revenue in 1968 was en route to $218,000 in sales in 1969. That might not sound like much, but with a work force of five guys, an original fleet of two trucks, and with a price structure that topped out at $100 for a very big lawn, the workload was sometimes overwhelming. Grapner, Wright, Lyons, Russell C. "Bus" Favorite, and James Sackett—the first crew—often worked from dawn until the late-falling summer darkness, then found Dick Duke waiting back at the office with a case of beer.

The beer and the lingering conversations in the parking lot were a soothing experience, but they were also a way for Dick Duke to push his people. He never stopped pushing. He knew that the lines forming around his trucks on Saturday mornings would not last forever. He knew he had to push to develop ChemLawn and spread it beyond Ohio—and push even harder to keep those homeowners coming back, paying for their greenery year in and year out. Duke was still the only person in the company whose vision habitually extended beyond the weekend.

"He said we were going to be a multimillion-dollar company," said Lyons. "I think I, probably, inside, laughed at him. I'd never seen a million dollars. I wouldn't know how to deal with that. He started talking about all the cities we'd be in."

Within two years, ChemLawn was virtually a million-dollar company. From year to year, the growth was exponential: $981,000 in sales in 1970, $2.3 million in 1971, $4.9 million in 1972, $141 million by 1980, and in 1985 well over $300 million in sales. Not only has growth been spectacular at ChemLawn, but the company's profitability (23 percent return on equity, 1982–84) has consistently been almost twice as strong as Standard & Poor's listing of the 400 most profitable companies in the United States.

No one with any experience in or near the ChemLawn Corporation credits the company's phenomenal success curve—and the accompanying loyalty of hundreds of thousands of customers throughout the United States—to anything but the personal qualities of Richard L. Duke—his magnetism, his enthusiasm, his perfectionism and, above all, his almost fanatic devotion to his employees. Success gave Dick Duke an opportunity to take care of a great number of people. His employees felt Duke's devotion, and for many of them he became a personal idol.

"Dick was the leader," said Wright. "He was my personal mentor. Dick inspired people. I mean, it was a fire burning all the time. There was something going on: Get in front! Get out of the road! But do something! If Dick could think of it, the chances were we could probably do it. We didn't know how all the time, but there was an attitude, particularly among the original group of people, which was—I have since found out—not terribly common in society. A lot of people look at things in terms of what's in it for them; how much security can you give me in return for this effort you want me to put forth? I don't know if it was ignorance or integrity, but we weren't smart enough to ask that. We just went out and tried to do the best we knew how to do."

For the people who joined ChemLawn in those first days, when Duke was recruiting his small group of zealots, he conveyed a quality that was virtually messianic. Lyons, for example, was not simply hired away from the Piqua newspaper; he was rescued.

"There was something about him," recalled Lyons. "He had an air of confidence, that I thought, 'I'm not sure what I want to do, and this guy just acts like he knows what he's going to do, and this is going to be a success.' I was pretty much convinced that he had no doubt—you could *believe* in the guy."

Even the one person in his life who knew him best of all, his wife, Opal, found in Richard L. Duke a presence that seemed, when he called upon it, to make him larger than life. "He was very good at coming into a room and planting an idea in people," she said. "And everybody would start talking and they'd think *they* came up with the idea. He was a master of doing that."

But besides charisma, Duke also started in 1968 with a business concept that was virtually complete, fully developed before ChemLawn's first day of operation. The elements of that concept had synthesized—almost unconsciously—in Duke's mind over a span of twenty years, most of it in the very unromantic occupations of backyard horticulture and sod farming.

Among the elements of this synthesis was his experience with every possible chemical and combination of chemicals that can be used to nurture healthy, verdant expanses of grass. Because he didn't like big companies (and because he knew he was smarter than they were), Duke devised a service that provided an alternative to bagged premixed products sold by big lawn food suppliers like O. M. Scott and Ortho.

Duke also advanced a fairly new concept in the application of lawn fertilizer. Liquid fertilizer application, in agricultural uses, had become a common practice in the United States by the 1960s. The Dukes had found it a very efficient way to get a uniform application of fertilizer on their tracts of sod. At the same time, Dick had gradually developed a small clientele of local lawn care customers for whom he was applying fertilizer. For a long time, he did that by the old method—running a cart full of dry fertilizer across the lawn. But it was no great leap of imagination for Dick to connect the speed and efficiency of liquid application on the farm to the same practice on people's lawns. Developing equipment such as tanks, spray nozzles, and chemical-resistant hoses represented a relatively small technological obstacle for two inveterate thinkers like Duke and Tom Grapner.

A third, even more important element was Duke's realization that the market for this service was ripe and eager. By the mid-1960s, the post–World War II housing boom was settling down. The tracts of houses that had burgeoned across America were now the dwellings of affluent, middle-class people with a growing consciousness of their "image" in the neighborhood. To some extent, the quality of construction in the average raised ranch home with Georgian gables, Greek columns, and a small herd of plaster deer in the front yard was less important to the householder than how the house looked to passersby. "Curb appeal" had come into its own and Dick Duke had seen this market developing in Troy.

Since the Duke Garden Center's beginning in 1949, people kept coming in saying they had trouble getting fertilizer evenly distributed. Should they put it down just before it rains, just after, or what? And how much did the average lawn need? What time of year? How many times a year? Faced with questions like these and possessed by an uncontrollable urge to help out, to do more, to *grow,* it was an inevitable compulsion for Dick Duke to offer to do the job *for* people—to sell the stuff and then spread it for, say, an extra dollar a bag. From that notion, the next step was to realize that by buying the basic ingredients of commercial "lawn food," mixing them himself, and applying the mixture for the customer, he could earn as much money as he did by selling the premixed, marked-up brand-name material over the counter.

Combine the desire for people to keep up with the Joneses with this simple element of extra effort—which Dick Duke eventually did—and you have a potential service that responds to a very deep and persistent need. People weren't spending any more money, they didn't have to do *any work,* and suddenly they had the best-looking yard on the block. The neighbors could eat their hearts out!

In such an analysis, ChemLawn is a marvelous exploitation of the competitive spirit of the American suburbanite. But there was always more than that to the ChemLawn idea. The real product of a service industry is not so much what emerges at the end of the line; it is the intangible feeling of being cared for. More important than its green grass, ChemLawn provided good care to people. It was the same sort of care that had kept customers of the Duke Garden Center lingering at the counter after they had already paid for their bag of fertilizer. If you judge ChemLawn only by the product, you reveal only part of the story. But if you judge ChemLawn by its behavior, you reveal something more deep-seated and emotional in a customer who—in most of his or her daily life—feels a little lonely and forgotten by an impersonal society.

But ChemLawn was hardly the first company in the lawn care business. People like John Wright had scratched out a living in the trade for generations. For something really big—like today's ChemLawn Corporation—an already big company like O. M. Scott seems like the most logical entrepreneur. But neither small companies nor big companies—either before Dick Duke's success or since Duke's success—have succeeded like Dick Duke. ChemLawn has been imitated in a dozen styles in a dozen locales, but ChemLawn stands alone in the yard. The presence of the man Richard L. Duke in those first nine formative years was the irreplaceable ingredient.

To "believers" like Grapner, the Duke magic that summoned strength from ordinary people was something best left alone, as a felicitous mystery. Perhaps only recently has Grapner found a way to express that mystery. "I never second-guessed Dick. No matter how close a friend you were, you couldn't know everything that was going on in his mind," said Grapner. "A true entrepreneurial person is going to get way beyond you so fast that you tune out certain parts of it. You don't dare to get too far out there."

Tom Grapner, though he eventually served for a while as president of ChemLawn Corporation, couldn't "get too far out there." He didn't think he had the ability. In a way, he represents, in microcosm, the attainment of Richard L. Duke—to literally build people up. Not a concept. Not a business. Not an enterprise. But the people of whom the enterprise would eventually consist. In that building process, the ChemLawn founder could seem brutal.

Opal Duke Abbink (his now remarried widow) described Dick Duke's relationship to Grapner. "He could tear Tom Grapner apart. He could really come down hard on a guy. But when he got done, the thing that always came out, he never held a grudge, because he was fair. And you'd go right back and work harder than ever for him, because you knew he was fair. I've seen him be so hard on Tom. He gave Tom Grapner responsibility that he didn't have the capacity to do. He would hit him hard, but yet he would come around again and be very compassionate. And Tom idolized him."

Grapner speaks of Duke the way a recruit, having completed basic training and a tour of combat duty, speaks of the drill sergeant who harshly instilled in him the tools of survival. "He was tough but fair. And he would listen to you—even when he was dressing you down, he never left you feeling smaller," said Grapner. "He always built you up. He might totally take you to the bone, but he would build you up."

* * *

Dick Duke died suddenly of a heart attack in 1977, at the age of forty-eight. By then ChemLawn was a company with annual sales of $49 million—built on that capital of $40,000 which Paul and Dick Duke had netted from the combined sale of their sod farm and garden store nine years before. For people who had grown personally dependent on Duke's leadership, the death of their mentor was like a blow to the head. Many were uncertain whether they could cope with this loss and go on. For Duke's company, crisis seemed inevitable.

"When Dick died, for the immediate time afterward, I felt I was totally leaderless," said Lyons. "All of a sudden, there's this light that goes out and you say, 'What the hell happened?' "

No management crisis ever materialized after the founder's death. Duke is credited with instilling in his company's succeeding leaders an enormous measure of self-sufficiency and business savvy. It seems clear that the ChemLawn management group had learned how to get along without Dick Duke long before he died. To a significant extent, Dick Duke's sudden physical departure came seven or eight years after his mental departure. Perhaps, as his widow suggests, he was never really totally present.

"Dick Duke didn't want to be president [of ChemLawn] because he didn't like to go to work day in and day out," said Opal. "He didn't work good that way. He worked better if he was on his own, and like worked 'til two o'clock in the morning one day, or he might be sitting on the beach—that's the way Dick worked the best. He could not stand to keep regular hours."

It seems incredible that Dick Duke's day-to-day interest in ChemLawn seemed to wax and wane with his biorhythms—even as early as 1970–1971, when the company's success still faced long odds. In 1970, he abruptly moved his family from Ohio to Georgia and told his officers that he would run the company from there. This seems amazing in light of the fact that ChemLawn was a personal creation—a company that still bears Dick Duke's stamp. It seems impossible that Duke could be so inconstant—at least in his outward behavior. But it's true that his air of inspirational fellowship—a magnetism that filled his people with boundless enthusiasm—was only half of the personality that Richard L. Duke somehow harnessed in order to create ChemLawn.

Certainly the aspect of Duke that he conveyed instantly and forcefully to people was a powerful self-confidence. But asked how deep that went, Opal said simply that it was a quality reserved for presentation to the world. It existed, she said, "in business, not in his personal life."

Opal's portrait of her husband is that of a man driven, but not always by bright forces such as confidence, optimism, and the entrepreneurial spirit. In private, he was a moody, often intimidating man who sometimes made his family walk on eggs until they could figure out his frame of mind. "I used to say the girls and I would get along fine when he'd be gone a week, but when he'd come in we'd all be [tense]," said Opal. "You just never knew what that mood was going to be."

There were times in the life of the company when Duke seemed to disappear from the face of the earth. ChemLawn was facing the daily operations crises of starting from scratch and then dealing with growth that was literally doubling, tripling, quadrupling annually. But often it had to face these crises without any counsel from its founder, chairman, and chief executive officer. Grapner said that Duke's disappearances were a strategy to force his subordinates to "think on your own two feet." William Copeland, ChemLawn's first chief financial officer, characterizes Duke's mercurial wanderings as a master plan to decentralize the company and "delegate responsibility to the branch managers." But the fact is that Duke was impulsive. Many times, instead of "delegating" responsibility to branch managers, he was out in the field, interrogating lawn care specialists and then grilling their branch managers about his workers' complaints. Duke tended to trust the word of a rank-and-file worker over that of a branch manager. It didn't matter to him if the branch manager had just been promoted—on Duke's recommendation—from the rank-and-file a month or two before. In Dick Duke's eyes, people changed when they became "management," and it was not a change for the better.

Jack Van Fossen, the man whom Duke chose to succeed himself as the leader of ChemLawn and now the chairman of the board, said, "The last thing he would put up with was somebody abusing those who he called 'the real people of the company,' the lawn care specialists who made contact with the customers. His approach was that the customer comes right after the people in the company. In some respects, he didn't consider management to be people."

If any quality typified Dick Duke as a social creature, it was his emotional belief, which only grew stronger as he grew older, in the integrity of the working man. This was why, when he started his company, he placed such enthusiastic faith in people as initially unpromising as Grapner, Wright, and Lyons. This is why, when he saw the need to hire a chief executive officer to handle the administration of a company literally bursting at its seams, he chose Van Fossen, a man who possessed all the tools but not a shred of the pretensions of an educated business executive. (He had had another business executive who possessed those pretensions but, after only six weeks of complaints about the man from his rank-and-file lawn care specialists, "fired the son of a bitch.") And this is why, nine years after his death, Dick Duke's company still conveys an unearthly air of simplicity, fellowship, and common purpose—a dedication to employee (first) and customer (second) welfare that gives it the air of a Midwestern religious community.

"It's been our credo," explained Paul Duke, "if you take care of the people and then you take care of the customers, nothing's going to happen to the business but good. Our people first, our customers next, and the thing will work." There is no clearer expression of the essence of an excellent service company. However, Paul left one thing out of his formula. As the family elder, Paul Duke often had spoken this philosophy, but he had not built the business in which he could have used it. The added ingredient was a burning desire—and this came from Dick—to make a business, *apply* this creed, and prove that it would work.

Before the beginnings of ChemLawn, long before Lyons and Wright had experienced an epiphany in the charismatic presence of Dick Duke, the idea of Paul or Dick Duke starting up any sort of going concern was not merely unlikely, it was actually silly. The consensus around Troy about the Dukes was that they wouldn't amount to much. They were good people and you could count on them to do a good job, but that's all. Everyone knew it. In a small town like Troy, a person's limitations come to be pretty well known and pretty well accepted fairly early in life.

Dick Duke's limitations were embodied in his business, the Duke Garden Center, in his so-called career, in his history, and in his debts. He was a poor person in a small town. In a sense, that's the best way to be poor, because a person can always count on the community, the neighborhood, to rally 'round and help him somehow through the worst of times. "It was hand-to-mouth," said Opal. "That's the way we lived for quite a while. No salaries and, you know, we lived in a small town and nobody ever lost a penny on us. I look back now and I can hardly believe it. But it was like the milkman would wait, and the groceryman would wait, and when the season came in, we would pay all that back. But they knew us."

But the other side of small-town poverty haunted Dick Duke. It wasn't just a social condition; it was a personal trait, and it couldn't be altered. Even after ChemLawn had passed its millionth dollar in revenue and was fast closing on its ten millionth, Dick Duke's fortune could not transcend his image. One reason that ChemLawn headquarters is in Columbus is that Duke could not convince a contractor in Troy that he could afford to put up a building.

Dick Duke had been tied to the Duke Garden Center since 1949—the year he dropped out of college. The store had provided a living for the family—Dick and Opal, the three girls, and Dick's parents—but it put no money in the bank. When gardening got impractical in Ohio, from September 'til April, things got tight among the Dukes. Christmas tree sales barely extended their income into January. When, in the 1960s, the family branched off into sod farming, the work got harder but the money didn't get any more abundant. Dick tried to expand his garden center by opening a branch in Piqua, but that was a financial failure and almost wiped out the rest of the business.

Both of the Dukes' businesses carried with them—besides hard work and a cycle of frightening dry spells—crucial lessons for the future. Dick Duke, for instance, learned to hate banks. One day, in the mid-1960s, after fifteen years in the same garden center business in the same town, Duke went to a local banker he had trusted for years and asked him for a loan extension on the garden store until the weather improved and the garden center business got rolling. The banker turned him down, not very diplomatically.

"The day he was turned down for a loan, he said he rode around for two hours. He didn't know whether to go down to the bridge and jump in the Miami River, or what to do," recalled Opal. "He had hit rock bottom. Normally, I never saw that in Dick. And I don't think I really saw it then. But, you know, as he rode around, he thought, 'Well, by God, I'll show 'em.' " This was the sort of thing Dick Duke said frequently. It was part of his reputation in Troy. Even though he had never ceased to regard himself as a creative spirit and entrepreneur, among the businessmen of Troy he was more commonly regarded as a "big talker," the guy down at the garden shop who had lots of dreams but nothing to back them.

Having a reputation as a blowhard is fairly commonplace among entrepreneurs; it is easily overcome if and when the entrepreneur can put his money where his mouth is. But Dick Duke had no money, and the entrepreneur who walks into banks with a chip on his shoulder usually can look forward to a brief business history. Duke turned that conventional wisdom around and made it work to his advantage. His distrust of banks forced him to think of ways to manage without them.

Van Fossen became the lawyer for the ChemLawn Corporation years before Duke hired him as president of the company. He recalled the first major effort at capitalization in 1969. It started when a young banker from Dayton, unaware of Duke's unique hostility to the banking community, dropped by the ChemLawn offices in Troy, where people were working almost around the clock in order to keep pace with demand. "The young banker," said Van Fossen, "had seen a truck or two in Dayton. He called on Dick and said, 'Anything I can do for you?' Dick said, 'Yeah, how much money you got?' The banker looked at the financial statements and said, 'We're sorry, but if you'll put $150,000 in capital into this business, then we'll match it with a $150,000 line of credit.' Well, Dick didn't have $150,000 in capital, so he just said, 'Well, there's only one thing to do. I'll just sell some stock.' So he put together an intrastate offering circular and went out and sold the stock door-to-door to customers and employees of the company. They oversubscribed the issue, raised $150,000, and said to the bank, 'We don't need your line of credit. We'll be back next year.' So that basically established the borrowing relationship for the company. And except for stock sold to employees of the company under stock option plans, that was the only outside equity put into the company until 1981."

For most entrepreneurs, doing it without banks would be very satisfying. For Dick Duke, it was revenge. Life had taught him to hate banks; it also had taught him to believe that most people were truly good, basically trustworthy. He eventually gambled his future on that belief. In doing so, Duke instilled in his company the bond that a good service company must share with its customers.

Opal explained the evolution of that principle. "We lived right there and you never got a minute's peace, and if Dick would take a day off, he wouldn't let anybody see him. He wouldn't answer the door. He would just go away." But every day that Dick escaped, the garden center didn't do any business. "Finally he said, 'Just take what you want, and you can pay me later,' " Opal recalled. "He put a lot of trust in people and it really would work.

"The same way with our Christmas trees. We used to rent a spot there at the fairgrounds and it was very cold. Dick tried sleeping in the car so people wouldn't steal our trees. He couldn't exist that way. The temperature that year had gone to eighteen below zero. Finally, he just decided, well, if they steal, they steal. And it was funny, people would come and take a tree and leave a note, and then come and look him up later and pay. We were just amazed at the honesty of people."

What had begun as a matter of self-preservation became a matter of conviction. Dick Duke challenged people to cheat him. For all his apparent toughness, he placed himself in a position from which he could not retaliate. This ingenuous, practical trust accomplished an unplanned purpose, instilling a reciprocal feeling in the customer. As a matter of principle, Dick Duke expected people to live up to their best instincts.

This ethic posed a problem for Jack Van Fossen in the early 1970s when he signed up as the corporate attorney for the infant ChemLawn company. The first thing a lawyer does for a new client, Van Fossen thought, is start to draw up contracts.

"[Dick Duke] said to me, 'We don't have any contracts,' " Van Fossen recalled. "I said, 'You've got to have contracts.' He said, 'Why do I have to have contracts with my customers?' I told him everybody has contracts. 'I don't need a contract,' he said. 'The customer and I agree that I'm going to do the job, and if I don't do the job the customer can cancel me. If I've got a contract, it isn't going to make any difference. Why do I need a contract if a customer, any time he's not satisfied with me, he can quit?' And I said, 'But if you had a contract, you could sue him.' He said, 'Yeah, but who wants to sue his customer? I don't need a contract.' So I said, 'How are you going to be sure you get paid?' He said, 'Ninety-nine point nine percent of the people in the world will pay their bill. That other percentage—there's nothing you can do about them anyway. So, those people we just won't service anymore. Most customers you can trust.' "

Another service company entrepreneur who appears in this book is Fred Smith, who studied business at Yale (see chapter 13). Dick Duke didn't study business anywhere. Both learned the value of understanding and trusting their customers and employees not through study, but through experience. Smith's lessons came in Vietnam; Duke's in Troy. For both, the idea of trust became more than just a concept. It was a passion.

The experience of Richard L. Duke before he had taken the first step toward the formation of the ChemLawn Corporation and of Frederick W. Smith prior to his initial efforts to create Federal Express bear a resemblance. Both men developed and refined the dominant value of their companies in times of personal crisis, literally at the level of survival. Both men, Duke in more than fifteen years of "hand to mouth" existence as proprietor of a local garden store, and Smith in three years of "life and death" as an officer in Vietnam, were forced to place an extraordinary measure of their lives and livelihoods into the hands of people who just happened to be around them. These were not people selected—as in a corporate organization—to serve in "support roles" commensurate with their qualifications. Both men had to depend for everything on a totally random group. For Duke, these were customers, salesmen, acquaintances, strangers who bought Christmas trees, patient creditors, farmers. For Smith, these were draftees, noncommissioned officers, reconnaissance pilots, medics, peasants, and courageous enemies. Both men brought to these experiences an implicit faith in people. Dependability was the test. Not all the people passed the test, but both Duke and Smith found the least "complicated" people the most reliable. Both men had the idealism to emerge from the darkest episodes of personal experience, not with a negative outlook based on the worst in people, but with a deeper idealism—a greater faith in "ordinary people," based on their proven honesty, their sensibilities, their intelligence.

Both men built organizations that were incredibly nonselective in their choice of employees. They literally took people off the streets to work at ChemLawn and Federal. In a way, both men— perhaps at the expense of their immediate family and friends (certainly this was true for Duke)—used their companies to demonstrate a completely noncommercial principle in which they both believed passionately: that the majority of people are diligent, resourceful, and exceptionally trustworthy. Duke and Smith had learned that leadership begins with trust and that the almost inevitable response to that is tireless effort and intense loyalty. Perhaps this is a lesson that can be learned in the abstract, but neither Duke nor Smith had to learn it that way. They had both done their time in the trenches.

While Smith's ordeal was more dangerous, Duke's could very well have lasted a lifetime. Throughout the 1950s and 1960s, there was no visible evidence that the Duke family would ever manage to venture far from the trenches where they had begun. From the opening of the Duke Garden Center, almost two decades passed with no indication that Dick Duke had a single worthwhile idea in his head. For every inspiration, there was a misgiving. His desk was full of diagrams and plans that "only need $500 of capital." Even when he had the $500, he would think twice, think again, and in a while the money would be spent and the latest plan would be at the back of the drawer.

William Copeland remembers a dreamy, restless Dick Duke in those days who would spend hours in the back room of his garden store, sketching ads and diagrams for new lawn care equipment. Tom Grapner remembers a Dick Duke who would drive away in his pickup truck to hide at the airport in Vandalia, where he would sit by the runway and watch the planes going out, leaving Ohio—and all of its struggles—behind.

And of all possible times, 1968 had to be the least likely year for Dick Duke to give birth to an empire called ChemLawn. The first thing he had to do that year was close down that crummy store in Piqua—which was steadily leading the Duke family toward bankruptcy. Giving it up was a bitter pill for Dick, and Opal had to cajole him.

"You know, a lot of times when you're in something, even though the public is out there whispering about you, it hurts your pride to say you've failed," said Opal. She saw Dick hesitate to give up the Piqua store because it would be further proof to his neighbors in Troy that Dick Duke was a legend in his own mind. Opal pressed Dick to give it up before it drained away all their money.

"So we closed the Piqua store," said Opal. "I don't want to take credit for that, but sometimes when you're a husband and you're out making a living, maybe your living isn't successful and you don't want to fail in the eyes of your family. And it was just like he needed the support of his family."

But also by 1968, all the pieces of the ChemLawn Corporation had come together. Dick Duke, with Grapner's help, had devised methods and equipment to deliver lawn food in solution. Duke had become a master of the psychology of his customers, and he had developed a service clientele that numbered 400 households. The economics of a potential lawn care business had become not just a concept, but an obsession. He talked to people about it all the time.

A strange fact emerges, though. The first time that he had

envisioned this business and described it to people was in 1964. The idea had already formed in Dick Duke's mind, but he didn't follow through. After countless hat-in-hand trips to the bank, after the shutdown in Piqua, after four years of developing a lawn care concept and the basic technology to make it work, Dick Duke, now almost forty years old, still hesitated. Like Hamlet "sicklied o'er with the pale cast of thought," Duke clung to his two dying businesses.

Opal recalled a man who went to work for the Dukes in the summer of 1968, "a sociology major—I don't remember his name." This man had to listen, every day on the sod truck, to Dick talking ceaselessly about the great potential for the liquid application lawn care business. "And this guy said, 'Well, you know, if you really love the idea, why don't you do it?' " Opal went on, "So then he [Dick] and Tom and Pat [Dick's sister] were here one time, sitting in the dining room, and we really started talking about it—we've got the one truck; we can take old Gertrude and get her all done over; we could have her painted up. Dick came up with the brochure. We had all the marketing ideas and Dick came up with the logo."

From that moment of commitment, ChemLawn grew from what John Wright eloquently described as "the available resources." One of those resources was Dick Duke's well-thought-out concept, which was whole before the company had even begun. Another vital resource was a one-man sales force—Paul Duke—who was uniquely suited to the marketplace. His contribution was as poetic as it was essential.

Almost eighty years old now, Paul Duke conveys the manner of a man who would have been satisfied if he had lived, talked to a lot of folks, paid his bills, made friends, and worked until the day he died. In the early days of ChemLawn, he was suddenly dispossessed of his main source of income (the Garden Center) at what would have been beyond retirement age for most people. Without thinking twice, Paul went out and started hitting the neighborhoods as the ChemLawn company salesman. His salesmanship appeared to lack polish, a trait that made it perfect for Dayton. Passing the time of day shooting the breeze with older people is still a respected activity in the Midwest. Paul Duke is a kitchen-table, back-fence, driveway conversationalist, the kind of person who'll get you through a tough morning's leaf raking, because he'll delay you for forty-five minutes between the front yard and the back.

As Paul described it, the birth of ChemLawn had a lyrical simplicity. However, it should be remembered that ChemLawn had only about half a summer's time to turn their capital into enough revenue to support three families through the long Ohio winter. They had spent the $40,000 they had on a truck and lawn spraying equipment. The first half summer of ChemLawn was do or die. They would do by "branching out."

"The fact that Dick and Tom agreed wholeheartedly on the idea of branching out sold me as much as anything else," said Paul. "I liked the idea. The boys had just one truck. They started out to do the spraying, and I started out to do the selling. The [first] five hundred customers were within a ten-mile range from here—here and West Milton and Covington and Piqua, and whatever. We branched out immediately, into some of the better neighborhoods in Dayton, and came up with a brochure that we distributed ahead of time. And we got response to it. We picked the exact right time, I think, to get into this thing. I went out and 'Pappy Duke' sold to beat the devil. I had a good time and put in hours you wouldn't believe. So many people had to work during the day, and I had to make evening calls, you know. My gosh, I sold remarkably well, I thought. And the boys then would follow up with the spraying, and inevitably they picked up customers while they were out doing that. The neighbor would say, 'Hey, do you want to do my lawn while you're here?' The thing just mushroomed."

Several things dramatically facilitated that mushroom effect. One important decision by Dick Duke was the 1969 hiring of Bill Copeland, who turned out to be a talented financial manager. Copeland's skill combined nicely with Duke's own budgeting abilities, which were as disciplined as his office hours were undisciplined. ChemLawn became a model of a small company that understood the value of growing as fast as possible, and it grew as close to the brink of its growth potential as Dick Duke dared to go—which was always further than Copeland would have gone.

Eighteen months after Paul Duke's first foray into Covington, ChemLawn's territory included all the communities in the Troy vicinity, plus Dayton, Columbus, Louisville, and Indianapolis. Cincinnati was on the drawing board.

Still, the foremost reason for the unhesitating growth of ChemLawn was the independence and commitment of the lawn care specialists whom Dick Duke put into trucks and set loose into the neighborhoods of the Midwest. These people were expected to get involved with their customers, listen to their problems, and do something about them. The lawn care specialist didn't stop working on a customer's lawn until the customer was satisfied. If a lawn care specialist did something wrong, he corrected it, replaced it, paid for it, or gave the customer his money back. Each lawn care specialist was expected to be his own salesperson, expanding his customer base even as he served his existing customers. He delivered the service, billed for it, maintained his truck, mixed his own chemicals, scheduled and ran his own route every day. He was expected to understand lawn problems on the spot and prescribe for them, or find someone else who could. He was expected to be a public relations expert, too, to keep himself clean, neat, shaven, and professional in his behavior all the time.

The lawn care specialist was rarely watched over, because he was always alone and on the move. Companies like O. M. Scott, which had been in the lawn food business for decades, had always hesitated to enter the service end of the business because they could think of no way to control all those truck drivers. Dick Duke's method of approach was unfathomable to that kind of thinking. He never tried to control anybody.

The importance of the individual lawn care specialists—their sense of responsibility, loyalty, and raw energy—can't really be emphasized strongly enough. They took it upon themselves to make Dick Duke's aspirations their own aspirations and never challenged the reasoning (if there was any) that Duke used to justify all their hard work. If anything characterized the first two years of ChemLawn's existence, it was a prevalence of people like Dick Lyons who "never asked a question." They didn't look around to see what anyone else might think about the prospects for this crazy business. They didn't even reflect on whether—or why—anybody would allow strangers to spray chemicals on their property while nobody was home.

Van Fossen described the ChemLawn approach to estimating the potential market. "You drive to the marketplace, look around, and see whether people are taking care of their lawns. If people had attractive lawns, that indicated that they had the interest. We figured we had a market there. That was our very sophisticated market research." And, as Wright noted, it became bad form—very early—to ask, "What's in it for me?" Wright recalled a meeting held at ChemLawn's first office, a rented space at the Miami

Savings & Loan building in Troy. The meeting was held because it was raining outside and nobody could spray.

"We resolved a lot of issues that day. One was our growth plan. Our growth plan was to go as far and fast as we possibly could and keep this thing barely glued together," said Wright. "The second thing we covered was our benefits plan. It was . . . well, first Dick made it clear that we couldn't afford it. So the benefit plan was going to be that if anything happened to any of us, the rest of us would take care of the wives and families. Everybody said okay."

By 1970 the ChemLawn growth curve had begun its precipitous upward progress. A few minor complications in operations barely slowed it. The 1973–1974 Arab oil embargo and an accompanying fertilizer shortage forced Duke to halt his Napoleonic campaign of city-by-city expansion, but he made up for lost time the next year, annexing nineteen cities in 1975. Earlier, when ChemLawn invaded Texas, they did so—literally—with a "scorched earth" policy, "burning" dozens of lawns before realizing that soil and climate conditions in Texas require substantially different lawn food formulations than those used in Ohio. In typical ChemLawn style, the company resodded every damaged lawn and gave the customers all their money back. And in typical ChemLawn customer style, many of those "burnt" patrons stuck with ChemLawn for lawn care.

Certainly, by 1970, even though ChemLawn was only in its second full year of operation, the Dukes had breathing room for the first time in their lives. ChemLawn was making strides toward becoming a structured corporation. The question was, could Dick Duke transform himself from entrepreneurial free spirit to manager? The answer seemed evident in what Dick Duke did late that summer.

Suddenly he packed wife and children into the family car and disappeared on a pilgrimage across the southern United States. When it was over, he announced to his ragtag management team that he and Opal and the girls were moving to Lake Lanier, Georgia. Dick had thought of moving ChemLawn headquarters, lock, stock, and barrel, to Atlanta but this idea had been firmly discouraged by his father. However, it certainly appeared as though ChemLawn had got too big and Dick Duke had lost interest.

Back in Columbus, there wasn't a soul who knew how to run a corporation. For that matter, nobody really knew if Dick could run a corporation, but he was the one most willing to try. Nobody could figure out how he was going to run it from a lake in Georgia.

"Dick Duke," said Copeland, "was a true Confederate. He hated the north and everything to do with the north—particularly the snow." A strange explanation! A man struggles for twenty years, finally founds a promising business, and then throws it all into jeopardy because he doesn't like the weather in Ohio!

There are at least two logical explanations for Dick Duke's swift exodus. The first is that, finally, the Dukes could afford to flee Troy, Ohio, a town that held little for them but the reminders of their twenty years of struggle and humiliation. The other is that, by moving to Atlanta, Duke was doing something that made it easier for him to manage ChemLawn. If he had stayed in Ohio, he would have faced the necessity of showing up at the office every day at the same time, sitting in the same place, saying "good morning" to the same people. For him, that sort of routine would have been intolerable. It might, indeed, have dulled his enthusiasm for the management of his company.

But the mobility and unpredictability that had characterized his career before ChemLawn continued in his next incarnation. Instead of getting in his pickup truck and going off, Duke started to make frequent flights between Atlanta and Columbus. And even though he had moved from Ohio, he had lost none of the passion he felt for the people in his organization. Not long after he moved to Lake Lanier, he proposed buying a marina on the lake that was in the process of going broke. He wanted to convert it into a recreation center—a free vacation resort—for the exclusive use of ChemLawn employees. Copeland and Grapner and a few others spent about ten minutes reviewing the operating expenses of the marina and hurried to Lake Lanier and talked Dick out of the purchase.

Not much later, Duke turned up in Florida, where he found a lovely little motel, with a beach on the Atlantic shore. "How about buying *this* as an employee resort?" he said to his management team. Another flight followed, this time to Florida. Again, they talked Dick out of the idea. But Duke did buy a luxury houseboat for use by vacationing ChemLawn employees. And when a number of lawn care specialists won a sales contest, Duke chartered a Boeing 727 and flew them all to Washington, D.C., for a party.

Copeland, who enjoyed giving in to Duke's impulses more than he enjoyed talking him out of them, loved the idea of chartering the jet. "I was writing the checks at that time, and I wasn't sure whether I was going to be able to cover that one. But what he did with that one impulsive act was worth it. The enthusiasm that he created was incredible. Most of those people—well, they'd never been on a plane before. You should have seen their faces," said Copeland.

"He never gave a thought to how much it was costing him to charter a 727," said Van Fossen. "He always figured he'd get it back."

If Duke had genuinely felt a waning of enthusiasm for his rapidly enlarging company, he had a golden opportunity to step away from it as a very rich man. In 1971 several companies offered to absorb the fledgling lawn care company, at a price that would have returned to the founder about $175 for every dollar he originally had invested.

"At that point, Dick could have taken the offer and walked away with $1 to $2 million—on an original investment, two years before, of $40,000. But he just had no concept of doing that," said Van Fossen. "He thought he could be a force in making this company grow a lot more. And besides, he didn't like those big company bastards."

As a manager, Dick Duke surrendered a great deal of responsibility very early in the company's life. But he scrupulously oversaw the annual budget process (a throwback to the penny-pinching days at the garden store). And he watched relentlessly over the morale of his work force. Everything he did circled back to his sensitivity to the people who worked. His personnel decisions reflected that sensitivity. With a few tempestuous exceptions, he scouted administrative talent well, bringing in very good people to assume the white-collar duties he found distasteful. He demanded from these people an unqualified respect for "the real people of the company," the lawn care specialists. And he operated on what John Wright calls "management by bombshell." Just as complacency threatened to take over the executive offices, a memo would arrive from Lake Lanier, something like the 1971 message lovingly unearthed by Wright and excepted below.

That memo began as an orderly presentation of a number of pressing management issues, then mounted (by the middle of its second page) into polemic. Up to that point, Duke's rambling dissertation progressed coherently without the use of an exclama-

tion point. The remainder of the memo contains twenty-six exclamation points—usually in combinations of three.

> It is the responsibility of every man receiving this letter to recog-
> nize a problem promptly and openly! Next, it is equally important to
> analyze the problem—to find the cause, to the best of your, or our
> ability. We solve nothing and we satisfy no one by waiting, by deferring
> action, by hesitating until we can arrive at a consensus. There are
> times when a consensus of one is the best consensus—even though it
> gets lonely for that one man. Then, after analysis, it's time to act!!! Do
> something!!! Call somebody!!! But stop this incessant stalling and
> buckpassing!!! If it's a problem today, take some action today!!!

The memo's next point of contention was "the insect problem in
Cincinnati." Duke suddenly had leaped into the situation himself
and "taken some action today."

> You felt that it was a rash action, Well, maybe it was a rash action—
> but for as much as six weeks, you people sat looking at this problem, all
> of you, [and] customers' lawns were being ruined. Customers were
> getting pissed off and the morale in our branch was shot! It's easy to
> point the finger at John [Wright]. It was a service problem and John's in
> charge of service. John wants to point the finger at Bill [Copeland]
> because Bill is too tight with the money. I want to point the finger at
> every damned one of you—because you didn't have the guts to stand
> up and be counted. And then you want to complain that my decision
> was rash? Bullshit!!!

Balancing bombast with guilt, in a sort of instinctive rhythm,
Duke continued thus:

> There's a lot of privilege and reward involved with being an officer
> or key manager in this company—but there's also a high degree of
> responsibility involved. Up to this point, I've heard a lot of discussion
> concerning the delegation of authority—but I've seen little willingness
> to accept responsibility in such a manner and to such a degree that
> authority comes naturally.

One of the things that Opal pointed out about Richard L. Duke
was that he expected everyone in the company to want to be in
charge as much as he wanted it. He assumed that hunger for
leadership was part of everyone's makeup. Duke was disappointed
when he realized, years after that 1971 memo was written, that
some people are satisfied with mediocrity. When Duke told his
employees that every person has the talent to "reach for the sun,"
he truly believed it—and he made them believe it.

The memo went on:

> And while I'm chewing, let's clear up another matter. I've heard
> several reports that indicated that our coordinators were afraid, and
> that you all are afraid, to take a hard line with a poorly performing
> employee—because I might get mad and fire the coordinator or one of
> you. Once again, Bullshit!!! I have fired only one man in this com-
> pany—and at least three of you were directly involved in the long
> series of discussions leading to the rotten bastard's dismissal.

As unequivocal as these words are, Opal recalled that she spent
several weeks convincing her husband to fire that employee—who
went back almost to the beginning of ChemLawn. Within a family,
almost all transgressions are forgivable, and Dick Duke—for whom
his company was family—groped for weeks for some way to
forgive.

There is a temptation to characterize ChemLawn's breakthrough as "self-expression via entrepreneurism," because there is
so much of Richard L. Duke in the company, even today. There is
reason also to explain ChemLawn as the brainchild of a creative
artist. But Dick Duke's creative talents remain articulated mainly
by those who loved him deeply; and his creative vision was twenty
years in working its way to the top of his mind.

Persistently, in those who shared the birth of ChemLawn with
Dick Duke, there emerges the magnified sense of personal responsibility that Duke first, and then his successors to leadership of the
company, felt for the well-being of the people in the company. This
is from a ChemLawn promotional tape recorded by Duke in about
1976: "If you will concern yourselves with improving the people
with whom you work, if you'll be concerned about their welfare,
their benefits, their advancement, to the almost total exclusion of
your own, you'll almost inevitably advance."

Though this reads like a hackneyed revision of the Golden Rule,
designed to keep employees in line and labor unions at bay, it
tends—among the thousands of ChemLawn people who understand
its origins—to bring a tear to the eye. Dick Duke, first in small ways
at his garden store, applied to his dealings with customers a childish
ideal of trust and concern. His customers responded in kind,
reinforcing in him a faith he knew to be perilous in a predatory
world but one he wanted to sustain. He formed from this experience a belief that you could make a living, maybe even make a

business—maybe even a big business—out of *taking care of people*. But the only way it would work would be to take care of everybody, employees and customers, with a tireless and unambiguous devotion. You had to be good to people, and *mean it*—not just say it.

"Dick said these things, and he sounded like a goddamn hick who wouldn't last ten minutes in business," said Wright. "But he meant every word. And that's why it worked."

Somehow Duke knew also that the only way to keep it working—even if it got bigger than he ever imagined—was to keep taking care and never, ever give more attention to the business than to the people.

Opal recalled a celebration at the Duke house in Troy to mark the official launch of ChemLawn as a corporation. "He said, 'My God, what have we done? Where are we? We've got five families.' And he took that responsibility very seriously," said Opal. "That's the only time in my whole association with Dick that I ever saw that little bit of weakness. I never saw it again."

Dick Lyons and Dick Duke's father, Paul, repeated an almost identical theme, Paul with a deep sense of gratification. "Along with those meetings I'd have sometimes for a week at a time with Dick, we would look at each other, and one or the other of us would say, 'Hey, do you know that we're responsible for the welfare of hundreds of people on the payroll right now?' " said Paul. "Right now, I understand it's something over five thousand people. To be responsible and concerned with the welfare of that many families, how much more satisfaction could you have in this world?"

It seems that, for Dick Duke, the creation of ChemLawn was not only an act of free enterprise, it was parenthood. This helps to explain why his people so readily forgave his tendency to manage by bombshell.

Again, from the 1971 memo:

> Finally, I want to make this point: for the balance of this year and continuing through 1972, we're going to supply this company with the hard-hitting, decisive, and positive leadership it deserves. That doesn't mean that we will stop being concerned about people or that we will abandon the philosophy and motives that we have held. It simply means that we will do whatever needs to be done— and that we are not going to be concerned about hurt feelings or tender toes, especially among this management group. I've already been accused, probably

by one of you, of blowing smoke up some asses. Well, let me assure you that I'm prepared to do a lot more of that, if necessary, to keep this company moving.

The reason John Wright saved this memo with such delight and pride is that he saw, beneath its seeming petulance, the hyperbole that a father uses to frighten his sons into behaving like gentlemen. Beneath Dick Duke's roar—and everyone near him knew that—there was love.

Dick Duke's patriarchal influence held sway over business meetings in Lake Lanier, in the days of the company's critical growth. Opal remembered, "I've seen business meetings where the officers would come and they'd all be going at each other. He wouldn't be saying a word. Finally, after this had gone on for a couple hours, he would just make a statement: 'This is the way I see it.' And everything would just stop. It was just amazing. It seemed that it would just evolve. He would really listen and think and then come out with a decision—the course we'll take. He had a lot of charisma. He really believed in his people."

It was Dick Duke's talent for presenting himself genuinely as father to a group of disparate employees that, more than anything else, lends to the atmosphere of the ChemLawn Corporation even today a strangely noncorporate air of communion and reverence to the founder—even religiosity.

"I've tried to discern how much of the feelings I have now—values, priorities—particularly in regard to people—how much of that was there all along and how much of that developed as a result of Dick Duke and the ChemLawn experience," explained John Wright. "I feel reasonably sure that the desire to believe that was there. It was inherent to my growing up; it was instilled in me. Dick is the guy who lit the match. We all want to believe in people, right? We want to believe that good overcomes evil, and all those lofty things that we're taught. Dick was the guy who made that happen. I remember one guy who came into the organization in the mid-1970s. I don't remember what big company he came from. I just remember he was a three-piece suiter when those guys weren't too common around our offices, and therefore they got a lot of attention. He was particularly interested in how this organization could expand the way it was expanding. And we told this guy, 'Well, it's real simple. You decide what city you're going to open up. You call the guy you want to open it. You tell him to get a Ryder truck and be there Monday morning.' His point of view was, 'No, you can't do that. You see, you have to plan this. You have to do market research.' This guy's conclusion, after talking to eight or ten of us, was that this wasn't a company. This was actually a religion. Because that was not the way you manage a business; that was the way you had religion."

Whether this unworldly air of loving grace will prevail at ChemLawn into the next century is impossible to predict. ChemLawn is still growing rapidly, and with increased age has come increased structure. Clearly though, if ChemLawn loses its still-thriving belief in people as its most important asset, it will have lost touch with its breakthrough.

Lyons stated the same point. "It's a simple business," he said. "It's the people difference that makes us what we are. Every company that's tried to copy us is not even close to success of our size, simply because their philosophy is a very different philosophy from ours. Unless that core is built or started by someone as dynamic as Dick, you can't buy it, you can't rent it, you can't copy it."

It might not be quite so simple. Certainly, the values that Dick Duke instilled in the company were a remarkable source of solidarity—*family*—that made the work easier to bear and made the vision seem possible. Dick Duke, in his unembarrassed style of promotional overstatement, called it "reaching for the sun." But all the cherished values would have been little more than personal moral convictions if that simple idea of mixing water with fertilizer and hauling it around Troy on the back of a flatbed truck had not finally come to light in his overwrought brain.

And the idea might have lingered unpursued in Duke's mind if, like his father, he had been a little more content with his life in the little hamlet of Troy. If Dick Duke hadn't wanted a ride out of Troy, he wouldn't have needed a ChemLawn truck.

5 | Tagamet: Repairing Ulcers Without Surgery

I n 1963, when Dr. Edward Paget hired a former colleague, Dr. James Black, to take over the position as chief of pharmacology at the Welwyn Research Institute, in Welwyn Garden City, England, Paget quietly set in motion a fourteen-year research effort that eventually would bring to market the most successful prescription drug in history. The drug, which was developed at Welwyn for Smith Kline & French Laboratories (SK&F), a Philadelphia-based pharmaceutical firm, is called Tagamet, and it has changed forever the way people, and doctors, cope with stomach distress. Tagamet is the drug that heals ulcers quickly, simply, and painlessly.

Tagamet became the first billion-dollar drug in pharmaceutical history, and it changed SK&F from what one source called "the senior citizen of the drug business" into a diversified international giant with the world's most modern pharmaceutical research and development facilities.

The idea for what eventually became Tagamet stirred for years in James Black's mind. It was an idea unique to Black's vision and scientific persistence. In all likelihood, Tagamet never would have appeared in pharmaceutical research if Black had not conceived it and fought for it and if Paget had not given Black three necessities: a laboratory at Welwyn, a free hand to create a research team and spend SK&F's money, and a defender named Bill Duncan.

Dr. William Duncan, following Paget and then Black, was the third member of a trio of key individuals who left Imperial Chemical Industries in Manchester, England, one of the world's great chemical and drug houses, to take up jobs at the SK&F Welwyn Research Institute. For Paget, who began the exodus from ICI, the change was logical. The chance to be managing director of the Welwyn Research Institute was an advancement in Paget's career, even if it meant going to work for a second-tier company.

In those days, Smith Kline & French, the parent company of the Welwyn facility (later to become SmithKline Beckman), was widely regarded as an also-ran among the world's pharmaceutical companies. Part of the reason Paget had been brought to Welwyn was to upgrade the company's research reputation. By hiring Black, Paget instantly succeeded in that goal. Although Paget might be expected to do a little discreet raiding of talent from his old firm, getting Black to come over was the unlikeliest of thefts. Dr. Black was one of ICI's stars. Only recently, James Black had made history in the pharmaceutical world by synthesizing drugs called "beta blockers." He did so by building what might be called "false messengers" to infiltrate the messenger/receptor mechanism in human cells that triggers the release of adrenaline, thus calming the hearts of people who suffer from high blood pressure. Beta blockers were not just a new drug. They represented a new *class* of drug and a revolutionary approach to pharmaceutical research. In the world of prescription drug development, Black was a celebrity. Bringing him to a research facility as insignificant as Welwyn was the equivalent of getting Baryshnikov to dance with the Teheran Ballet.

But Paget had several aces in the hole. The first was an exceptionally free hand to refurbish the whole research organization at Welwyn. His second ace was James Black's restlessness. Black had told Paget and the leadership of ICI that his beta blocker work was just the first in a series of potential discoveries that involved not merely *finding* new drugs in the conventional "hunt-and-peck" style of pharmaceutical research, but actually *designing drugs according to a specific goal.*

What Black was proposing to the senior management of ICI was revolution. He was also proposing to beat the odds. ICI knew that major scientific breakthroughs are a once-in-a-lifetime event. With beta blockers, Black had used up his quota. He had earned the chance to occupy a big desk and *administer* research, rather than continue to get his hands dirty doing it. But neither Black nor a handful of his confederates in the beta blockers research—including Paget and William Duncan—were interested in taking a breather. Beta blockers had got them excited!

Commenting years later, Paget said, "We had just come through a most exciting period [at ICI] when Dr. James Black . . . headed a team that had discovered the beta-androgenic receptor-blocking agents. It was a very elegant piece of creative thinking on Jim's part. We had all gotten quite wrapped up in it. But the great creative urge that we had shared and had all joined in on—the enormous fun we had—was dying away."

Black, in fact, did not share many common interests with ICI— or with most of the pharmaceutical companies in the world. The company was interested in making drugs. Black was interested in proving a theory. The best way for him to prove his concept was to make drugs, but this remained simply the commercial justification that supported his greater goal. Black's whole loyalty was to his concept; if another company was more willing to support him in his conceptual pursuit, Black would leave ICI in a flash.

As a follow-up to the development of beta blockers, Black proposed to ICI that he could use the same method of research to develop something he called "H_2 antagonist" drugs, which would virtually wipe out most of the peptic ulcers suffered by mankind by penetrating to the very source of the problem.

ICI said no, and Black did not hesitate. He took Paget's offer to move to Welwyn. Suddenly Welwyn was a different place. Until Paget's advent, Welwyn had consisted of a contented little group of Britons working frugally in their labs in the tranquil verdure of Hertfordshire, minding their own business and faithfully obeying the occasional note that bobbed their way from the SK&F headquarters in Philadelphia. Suddenly Black was rampant on the scene, throwing together his "H_2 team" with virtually no regard for existing practices and seniority.

Duncan, a biochemist who had worked with Black on beta blockers and who quickly followed when Black departed ICI for Welwyn, was accustomed to Black's aggressive manner. He knew that the people at Welwyn would need some help in adjusting; from the moment he arrived at Welwyn, William Duncan served to soften the impact of Black's personality on both the corporation far away in Philadelphia and on the small group at hand in Hertfordshire.

Nevertheless, there were bruised egos and hurt feelings among the veteran staff at Welwyn. Black drafted a number of his former

ICI team members into his new "H$_2$ team," and he pointedly excluded several people formerly regarded as stars at the Research Institute. Among the slighted researchers was a clever and forthright chemist named Dr. Robin Ganellin. Ganellin nearly departed Welwyn when he was not invited to join Black's research group. As with Black and Duncan, Ganellin's participation turned out to be mandatory. If he had not been welcomed back into the fold a little later, the Tagamet breakthrough might have been crucially delayed or even killed.

"He [James Black] had difficulty finding the right people to work with," said Ganellin, who eventually became the head chemist on Black's team. "A lot of the senior people left because they couldn't understand what he was after.

"He's a very vexing man," Ganellin went on. "He wants you to work in a particular way and he won't suffer fools. He always makes rather quick judgments. . . . He has a problem looking at people and making judgments about them."

Meanwhile, in Philadelphia, all this activity was viewed with a certain approval. After years of scientific dormancy, SK&F had a world-renowned scientist of the first rank, and he obviously was making things hop in Welwyn. Also, Paget and Duncan made certain that Philadelphia knew relatively little about Black's research plans.

Philadelphia knew, for instance, that Black would be seeking a drug that would inhibit the flow of excess gastric acid in the human gastrointestinal (GI) tract, a problem that causes ulcers. This was perhaps not the most promising line of research in terms of potential profits. Annually, the drug market for anti-ulcer compounds (most of them antacids that coat the stomach lining) was only about $100 million. But it was research to which SK&F was committed; their main research laboratories in Pennsylvania were seeking "anti-secretory" agents—chemicals that might somehow reduce the excess acid secretions that eat holes in people's stomachs.

What Welwyn did not tell Philadelphia was that Black's research was not "anti-secretory." Rather than trying to *find* anything, Black believed he could *create* something unique—a compound that could change the very chemistry of the GI tract. In order to accomplish that, Black had to make some assumptions that no scientist had ever proved. If SK&F in Philadelphia had been allowed a clear explanation of what Black wanted to do, they probably would have followed ICI's example and told him to stop.

He had ideas that no one in the practical world of the pharmaceutical industry could trust. But to people in the laboratory, they were ideas of irresistible appeal—especially as Black described them. "Vexing" in some ways, Black was hypnotic when he talked about science. Paget, like everyone who eventually blended devotedly into the H_2 team at Welwyn, saw in Black's ideas an esthetic quality that touched the senses as well as the mind.

"One of the things that impressed the chemists about Jim Black was his ability to communicate, to direct them, even though he didn't understand all of the mechanics of chemistry," said Paget.

"The essence of it all is scientific taste. It is possible to be a very well-informed, knowledgeable person and lack taste. I believe one can feel about science the way a great artist feels about a painting or a musician feels about a piece of music. I think that's the way most of us felt about those days at the Research Institute."

Perhaps even more appealing than Black's line of research to corporate leadership in Philadelphia was Black's *speed*. The main SK&F laboratories in the United States were working on anti-ulcer compounds, but they couldn't say when they'd find one and get it into development. In the summer of 1964, James Black reported confidently to Philadelphia that he could present them an H_2 compound by Christmas. When Black made that promise, he wasn't kidding. His vision of the compound he wanted was clear; his optimism was infectious.

Everybody believed Black was on the brink of a breakthrough. They believed it because he was such a convincing mentor, and they believed it despite a body of existing data that said Black was wrong. Black's colleagues were also well-versed scientists who knew that other scientists had devised similar theories in the past.

Before Black began his research at Welwyn, three Swedish scientists (named Folkow, Haeger, and Kahlson) had theorized the existence of a second "receptor" for histamine, a common chemical present in the human body. Histamine's most apparent function in the body is to trigger the flow of mucus in the sinuses. The most dramatic symptom of too much histamine in the sinuses is the "stuffed-up nose." Dr. Reuben Jones, of Eli Lilly & Company, had done practical experiments to determine whether there might be a different kind of histamine receptor in the GI tract that triggers the flow of gastric acid. Jones's research proved to the satisfaction of most that you couldn't stop gastric acid by stopping histamine. Black disagreed, and he didn't care what Jones or anybody said.

"You had to ask yourself, how does somebody like Black have the nerve to go over the same ground?" said Ganellin. "Why does he think he's got something different? It was not that the idea was totally new, but that he felt that it hadn't been explored sufficiently well. There was an opportunity to look again."

When he looked, Black hoped to see a way to interfere with the messenger/receptor mechanism that exists in the relationship between molecules of histamine and cells in the GI tract that release acid into the stomach. He hoped to see the GI tract operating the way the sinuses operate. In the sinuses, histamine carries a "message" to cells in the sinuses to release mucus, which coats the passages of the sinuses, nose, and throat and protects them from drying out. These messages can be conveyed to the cells only through "receptor sites" located on the cells. These act almost the way a lock acts in a door. Molecules of histamine, acting as keys, enter the receptor locks, turn the locks, and open the door of the cell to the flow of mucus. All of this works very nicely, except when an imbalance in the chemistry of the body unnecessarily increases the level of histamine in the sinuses. Suddenly every receptor in every cell is flooded with histamine, mucus pours from every door, and the human host is afflicted with "congestion." Enter *antihistamine*.

Antihistamine is an engineered chemical compound. It was invented in a laboratory to look like histamine. It is the same size, the same shape, almost exactly the same composition—*it fits into the lock* on the receptor site. The only thing it cannot do is turn the lock and open the door. So when antihistamine is added to the sinuses' messenger/receptor mucus system, it competes for receptor sites with the real messengers, the real histamine. Histamine wins some; antihistamine wins some. As a result, the body still gets enough mucus, but not too much. Congestion is relieved.

James Black, at ICI, advanced messenger/receptor chemistry significantly when he developed beta blockers. These are "phony messengers" that interfere with the body's release of adrenaline. An excess of adrenaline can cause something worse than congestion—it can cause heart failure.

Based on his work in beta blockers, Black believed the next logical site for engineering precise chemical compounds to control out-of-control messenger/receptor systems in the body was in the GI tract and with histamine. To succeed, Black had *to prove* that the GI tract operates on a messenger/receptor mechanism. But, in order to prove that, he had to prove that his thus far imaginary second sort of histamine was the messenger. And in order to prove *that,* he had to *make* something to antagonize the second sort of histamine. In essence, Black set up a challenge more suited to a riverboat gambler than an industrial researcher. He could not proceed in gradual stages to unveil proofs of his theory. He had to start with the hardest part—invent a way to stop something from happening when nobody really knew if it was happening at all.

Perhaps Black's most unnerving quality—in light of established procedures within the pharmaceutical world—was that he was adding an entirely new direction for research. Until Black changed the "imagery" of drug research with beta blockers, and then with Tagamet, the word that motivated people in the laboratory was the *hunt.* The "microbe hunter" would spot a new bug in the view-finder of his microscope and then, largely through trial and error, search out a weapon that would kill—or at least *affect*—the microbe.

Now, here was James Black suggesting that researchers change from hunters to engineers—rational drug discoverers who build novel compounds—combining atoms in ways that nature hadn't thought of. The problem James Black faced in proposing this new method of research at the Welwyn Research Institute was one of magnitude. The total number of possible combinations on the route to what eventually would become Tagamet was 30 billion different compounds. If SK&F in Philadelphia was willing to support Black's research for as long as four years, Black and his handful of researchers would synthesize several hundred of these possibilities. To explore *every one* of the possible combinations and do it in only four years would have required the efforts of 18 million scientists.

Given these odds, it was very important to James Black's research that his parent organization was very far away and that they didn't really understand what he was doing. In a major internal reorganization not long after the H_2 search began, Welwyn research director Edward Paget decided to choose William Duncan—over Black—as deputy director of research, which meant Duncan would run Welwyn when Paget relocated to Philadelphia. It was a crucial choice, because it kept Black in the laboratory, where he belonged, and elevated Duncan to a position where he could battle indefinitely against the nervous purseholders in Philadelphia.

As time wore on, it became more and more important that Duncan insert himself into every attempt by Philadelphia to determine how the H_2 project was progressing at Welwyn. Christmas 1964 had been the original deadline. Two more Christmases came and went, and still SK&F headquarters received no word that James Black had discovered the breakthrough compound. The budget for H_2 research, even though it averaged $2.5 million a year from 1964 through 1968, kept shrinking.

One of the major problems at Welwyn, as the research ground forward through some 700 unsuccessful experiments, was to sustain optimism. Duncan had to keep people believing both in the goal of the research project and in his ability to keep Philadelphia from giving up on it.

One of the compounds the researchers in Welwyn synthesized, for example, turned out to be an anti-ulcer anti-secretory—just the thing that the Philadelphia research group was looking for. But Duncan knew that anti-secretory compounds could only be a partial solution. He feared that if Philadelphia knew Welwyn had found one, they might be satisfied and call off any further exploration for an H_2 antagonist. Duncan simply cut Philadelphia off from any knowledge of Welwyn's discovery. For years after, none of the corporate leaders in the United States knew of the anti-secretory agent that had been engineered at Welwyn.

In 1966 three of Black's team, chemists John Emmett and Graham Durant and pharmacologist Michael Parsons, succeeded in synthesizing two separate compounds that stimulated acid flow at two different receptor sites. They were looking for a compound that did the opposite: *inhibited* acid flow. But this was still a good sign. Seeing the effect of these engineered compounds strengthened the belief that the GI tract was a messenger/receptor mechanism. "This selectivity of action confirmed that we were on the right track and spurred us to go on," said Duncan.

Still, after two years and millions of dollars, such results were only vague hints of possible success, and they offered precious little encouragement for the corporation, which had assumed that this experiment would end at Christmas two years before. And even when the group in Welwyn made a few halting steps of progress, Duncan didn't send much of the "good" news to the United States.

Ganellin was one of the troops at Welwyn who appreciated the irony of having to sneak around behind Philadelphia's back. "It's very interesting when an organization invests in research because it wants the value of a different approach," said Ganellin. "That's why you've got a major company in one country that bothers to go abroad at all—to get a different group of scientists working with a different type of approach, in the hope that they will come up with something. And then you start pressuring them as much as you can to *conform*. You go over there at the start because you want to be different—and then you start worrying about some of the differences."

Duncan, however, was not just romancing the brass in Philadelphia into tolerating the continued work on Welwyn's dubious histamine project. He had changed priorities within the Welwyn research organization. Husbanding the trickle of resources from Philadelphia, he pushed the H_2 hunt to the top of Welwyn's agenda, forcing a number of other projects there either into limbo or death. Duncan and Parsons, writing in retrospect in 1979, said that this maneuver "produced trauma" within the organization. Ganellin recalled that the more accurate term might have been *war*. But Duncan had the upper hand as research director—as well as a talent for politics, something lacking in the vast majority of research scientists. So Welwyn followed where Duncan pointed his sword.

"These were not happy times," Duncan wrote in 1979, "although every effort was made to isolate the scientists from the political and financial hardships of a company undergoing major reorganization and a new-product famine."

Still, in the midst of all this opposition, Welwyn staffers like Duncan and Ganellin—who perceived the political maelstrom that swirled about them—might have been in the minority. Michael Parsons confessed to being rather oblivious of the whole mess. "When I was essentially a new Ph.D. at that point, working with somebody inspirational, toward a goal which I thought was achievable and certainly desirable, there was a kind of tunnel vision," said Parsons. "I was less aware of the political and financial pressures."

Black, for his part, accepted Duncan's protection and rarely looked up to see what might be going on around his project. He had envisioned an idea, and for ten years his only interest was to prove that idea was the truth. His intensity became infectious.

"The best research is done by people who are really deeply committed to it," said Paget, "who are passionately interested in the outcome. They believe in their ideas enough to be rude to you if you don't agree with them. They'll try to argue you down if you have opposing views. They'll defend their own points of view tooth and nail. It could also be frustrating as hell. When I was in charge, there were times when we were jammed up with one backlog or another, and the chemists would come in and say, 'We cannot work with him [Black] any longer.' And I would laugh. And then we all would go on."

"The extent of emotion was phenomenal," said Ganellin. "Feelings were running very high—for many reasons. It was a very messy situation. It wasn't just the U.S. versus the U.K. There were a lot of differences in the team on science. Some of the research team . . . didn't see the value of Black's proposal. He found people he could not get on with. He's an emotional man and he generates emotion. I suspect that that's what's required to achieve something. If you don't have emotion, you probably just don't react. Nothing happens."

Eventually, the team that composed the H_2 antagonist program sifted down to a core of five: pharmacologists Black and Parsons and chemists Ganellin, Durant, and Emmett—each of whom provided significant breakthroughs along the way. As Ganellin admitted, these five scientists succeeded because they were able to narrow themselves to an almost fanatical focus. "One gets on this scientific high, and you just do it," he said. "You can become very narrow, but you get wrapped up and believe in what you're doing. You feel it's important and worthwhile."

The value of that obsessive outlook—the sheer emotion at Welwyn—came home to Duncan in a conversation several years later with Dr. Heinz Schild, one of the great pharmacologists of this century and Black's revered predecessor as professor of pharmacology at King's College, London. Schild brought home to Duncan that the object of this furious activity at Welwyn was thoroughly illogical. Said Duncan, "I was talking to him [Schild] one day about some data or other, and he suddenly looked up and said, 'It's amazing.' 'Oh, yes,' I said, 'these results surprised me as well.' 'Oh, I didn't mean that,' he said. 'I'm amazed that the H_2 program ever amounted to anything.' "

Schild should have been right. By 1968 the Welwyn team had made 700 different compounds and they had got nothing. No end was in sight. Only a faint glimmer of hope had shone. This slight hope lay in the fact that Michael Parsons, who assisted Black with all the pharmacological tests, noticed that he had been making the same basic mistake in his test assays for four years. He realized that this might not be an important mistake, but it was worth correcting—to see what might happen.

Michael Parsons had been seasoned by repeated testing of compounds that showed no antagonism at all to histamine. Four years of fruitless effort enabled him at last to recognize his oversight. Every time he had tested a compound, he had introduced into the test medium much less histamine than might occur in a real stomach. His levels of histamine were only 30 to 40 percent of the maximum possible in real life. He did this because that was the way he was supposed to work. He was going by the book, following a procedure that had been laid out by—among others—the sainted Dr. Schild. Even Black agreed with this method. But Parsons suddenly realized how simple and blinding the error in this method was. If he was using only 40 percent of the histamine (the agonist) capable of "filling" every receptor in the system and matching that with an equal amount of potential antagonist compound, the receptors were receiving only 80 percent of their capacity. There was, essentially, lots of room for both agonist and antagonist to find receptors, without changing the known level of acid that would enter the system at a 40 percent histamine level. But if Parsons flooded the system with 100 percent of the possible histamine and sent in a possible antagonist candidate to compete, then there might be a change in acid levels. The agonist and antagonist would have to quit *sharing* the receptors and start *fighting* over them.

This meant that everything he had done before—all 700 compounds—hadn't been given the right test! A lesser scientist might have been demoralized, but Parsons was enormously encouraged. The first six compounds that James Black had theorized four years before as possible H_2 antagonists had possessed a logic, an appropriateness, that had excited Parsons at the beginning of his tests. He had been surprised then that none of them had tested positive as an H_2 antagonist. Now, at last, with the right test, they might work. So Parsons jacked up the juice and went back to the beginning, to the first half-dozen compounds Durant had synthesized before Christmas 1964.

And there it was.

The reaction was weak but strong enough to prove the theory. The compound that finally tested "positive" acted as an H_2 *agonist* at lower levels and as an *antagonist* at the maximum level. But the important fact was not what the specific reactions were, *but that there was a reaction at all.* The proof was there; Jim Black was right. He had been right in 1964, and he had even proposed the right compounds to synthesize.

With Parsons' discovery, things changed dramatically at the SK&F Research Institute. Duncan informed Philadelphia of the news that Black's theory had been proved correct. The GI tract was unquestionably a second site for histamine receptors. And this meant that there might be a compound, and then a drug, that changed the way the GI tract secretes gastric acid. This could be a drug that didn't just clog up the secretion of gastric acid, which was the way everybody had been treating hyperacidity, but one that could make the GI tract behave differently!

Philadelphia's attitude began to change, but gradually. At first, management remained unenthusiastic. The discovery of that timid compound by Parsons was hardly the culmination of the research project. If a drug was going to emerge, it would still mean the creation of a much stronger H_2 antagonist in the form of a stable compound that inhibited gastric acid without halting it entirely. Most important, it had to be a compound that *only* inhibited acid and had no other side effects on the human body.

The search for an H_2 antagonist, after all, required the engineering of molecules unknown to nature. No one would know this compound's effects on people until it had been used on people. After the identification of a lead compound, the clinical testing procedure would require hundreds of doctors, thousands of patients, and years of use under strict controls.

Parsons' discovery of his little mistake in 1968 might have seemed like the end of the road to many people at the Research Institute, but it was barely a beginning for Smith Kline & French. The company's leaders still had ample reason to be pessimistic.

SK&F in the late 1960s was a pharmaceutical company in an advanced stage of recession. Its most successful product, a psychotropic drug called Thorazine (a tranquilizing agent that calmed even the most violent manifestations of mental illness), was in decline and about to lose its patent protection. There were no new products on the immediate horizon, and however hopeful this H_2 project might seem to people at Welwyn, it was no quick cure for the company's troubles. Thomas M. Rauch, president and chief executive officer of SK&F in those dark days, recalled, "I was convinced things couldn't get any worse. We were at rock bottom."

It was that sense of desperation, according to Rauch, that gave
SK&F "the courage to take risks. Without that, the days of Smith
Kline as an independent company were just about over." But what
was there to take a risk on? SK&F's leaders were ready to grasp at
straws, but there were barely any straws.

Among those leaders was Henry Wendt. Today, he is chief
executive officer of SmithKline Beckman, reigning over the corporation from an immense corner office in SmithKline's new office
tower in downtown Philadelphia. In the late 1960s, Wendt com-
manded a much less lofty outlook, as chief of commercial drug
development for SK&F's modest international division. Wendt was
one of the first to carry the news back to Philadelphia that a new
product emerging at Welwyn might be worth a major investment.
He started to get good feelings about the H_2 project on a visit to
Great Britain in 1969.

Wendt was in attendance at a research and development seminar conducted at the Welwyn Research Institute to inform corporate leadership of ongoing projects. William Duncan, leading the
presentation, came to the subject of H_2 antagonists. Wendt recalled, "I sat next to the medical director for our international
division, Dr. David Ovedoff. Suddenly, he grabbed me by the
elbow and said, 'You've got to watch this one! This is the main
chance!' I probably didn't understand much else of what was being
said, but I certainly understood that." Dr. Ovedoff was a confirmed
skeptic. Wendt trusted him to look at new ideas with cold-blooded
realism. To see such excitement in Ovedoff was, to Wendt, an
unusual experience and a sign that the H_2 project held great
potential.

Wendt carried back to Philadelphia Ovedoff's sense of excitement. Wendt conveyed to then SK&F's chief operating officer,
Robert Dee (now chairman of the board), that this H_2 notion might
be the main chance for a big drug in the 1970s. SK&F had not had a
big drug since the beginning of the 1950s, when they introduced
Thorazine.

The idea that an H_2 antagonist could be as big a drug as
Thorazine was an odd notion. The numbers simply did not support
the idea. Market estimates were critical to a decision to invest big
money in an H_2 antagonist, but throughout the early 1970s, no one
at SK&F could demonstrate that there would be a big market—or
even a medium-sized market. Even years later, after Smith Kline

had committed millions to priming the market for Tagamet, there was no solid sense of how much of this product they could sell.

While Philadelphia was pondering the mysteries of the GI market, the H_2 team in Welwyn was piecing together a compound. Because of Parsons' critical assay, the group was able to focus its chemistry on a few promising molecular configurations. "Those were exciting days," Ganellin recalled. "We saw each other every day. We had very few formal meetings. Every lunchtime became a conversation about chemistry."

Those constant conversations led to the synthesis and testing of new compounds. The team was close, but they still had nothing more than their faintly antagonistic, useless lead compound. But the nearness of the goal created an intensity of feeling that was both exhilarating and exhausting. The slightest intrusion created spasms of frustration among team members, and then spurred them on to even longer hours and harder work.

From 1968 to 1970 Black's team synthesized compounds that competed aggressively and selectively with histamine. Philadelphia, eager now to get out of the laboratory and start the drug development process, pressured Duncan repeatedly to move one of these compounds along for human studies. But the sense of the chemists was that they had not yet found a compound that would be safe in a human system. So they kept looking for two more years. And they still had to keep selling delay to the uneasy leaders in Philadelphia.

Robert Dee recalled, "In 1969, things looked bleak and there were a lot of dry holes. Black came over to the United States and made an impassioned plea with us to continue the program. Tom Rauch was CEO at the time; I was chief operating officer. After discussing the matter with Black, we finally decided he was so imbued with the correctness of his theory—he almost had a religious fervor—that we gave him another year."

Finally, in 1970, Black determined that a compound called *burimamide* was pharmacologically clean enough to test in humans. It had some drawbacks, including the fact that it would not be very potent if taken in any oral form, but it was a major step on the way to Tagamet. Burimamide was the first H_2 compound that could legitimately be called a drug. Within minutes of Black's decision that burimamide was relatively safe, Duncan was contacting hospitals to see if they'd be interested in testing the compound and seeking volunteers within Welwyn to be the first guinea pigs. Ganellin and Duncan himself were the first two volunteers in line. When they tested their own stomachs and found a reduction in gastric acid activity, they shouted with triumph. Their lonely search was over.

From that point, the researchers would be working closely with corporate headquarters and with a network of clinicians throughout the United Kingdom.

Duncan noted that the reaction from Philadelphia, when he informed them that *burimamide* had tested positive on himself, Ganellin, and several other eager guinea pigs, was restrained. SK&F headquarters replied with a memo asking, "Did you check with corporate personnel about the insurance before you did it?"

Duncan's response was unprintable.

Within a year of the burimamide discovery, burimamide was an obsolete lead compound. It had acted only as a transition. The researchers had subsequently synthesized and distributed to every clinician who wanted it a much more promising compound called *metiamide*. This compound was pharmacologically spotless, had no discernible side effects, and was strong enough to use in oral applications, either as a pill or a liquid. Metiamide was the drug SK&F had been waiting for.

As metiamide was emerging, Duncan was reversing the secretive style that had shielded the H_2 project. For years he had kept his researchers concealed from view, even from the company headquarters that was paying the bills. But with the identification of burimamide, the H_2 project was ready for the world to see. Duncan went out of his way to seize the attention of the scientific and medical communities. In April 1972, the scientific journal *Nature* published a complete description of burimamide, written by Black, Duncan, Durant, *et al*.

It was highly unusual for a research facility to release information in such meticulous detail while a compound was still in relatively early stages of development. But Duncan's strategy of full disclosure served two important purposes. First, it gave fair warning to other researchers that Welwyn did indeed have a huge head start (and a patent) in a field of inquiry that most scientists had theretofore viewed as a dry hole. Second, it piqued the curiosity of clinicians, who began to clamor for samples of burimamide—and then metiamide—to test on their ulcer patients. With full disclosure, SK&F carried out one of the most effective premarketing campaigns in the history of the pharmaceutical industry. Moreover, the flood of voluntary clinical tests provided volumes of information for the research team at Welwyn. By sharing some very prolonged and painstaking test procedures with hundreds of clinicians, the Welwyn team prevented countless mistakes and side trips and hastened the development of Tagamet.

Sometime in the period between 1968 and 1972, the emphasis of the research shifted subtly from pharmacology to chemistry, and then it began to move even farther afield to clinical experimentation and to the dynamics of pharmaceutical market development. All of this activity held little charm for James Black. He was a theorist whose theory had been proven true. Jim Black was getting restless again.

Thus, in 1972, even before metiamide had begun its clinical tests, even before Smith Kline had begun clinical work on another compound called *cimetidine,* Black was gone. With the Tagamet job literally half finished, Black said good-bye to his research team and his company and went off to London to take the prestigious position of professor of pharmacology at University Hospital, King's College.

According to Bryce Douglas, a fellow Scotsman and Smith Kline's former vice-president of Corporate Science and Technology, Black left to attain the intellectual respect to which few industrial researchers in England ever dare aspire. "Here you have a guy who's in industry in the U.K. . . . . In the academic world in the U.K. it was almost a dirty thing to be working in industry," Douglas said. "[It was] absolutely remarkable for an academic institution of preeminence in histamine pharmacology [King's College School of Medicine] to call a Jim Black to be the next professor of pharmacology—the very chair for which all his work had been done. How could you resist a thing like that?"

An easy conclusion from this surprising departure might be that Black is, as Douglas called him, "a disorderly fellow," able to focus now and then on some great vision that might someday bring glory down upon his shoulders, but otherwise a sort of bumbling, blustering, lovable chap wandering quixotically among the great institutions of British medical research—an absent-minded professor.

But rather than being a disorderly fellow at all, Black's thinking had been marked by a clarity and orderliness greater than anyone else's. He knew precisely what he hoped to find. He knew precisely how to recognize it when he found it. He had a vision of the unseen and a certainty of that vision that somehow, without a shred of evidence, kept a stubborn group in England and an impatient American corporation committed to it, beyond reason, for four years.

One thing that Black, the visionary of the lab, rarely ever saw— or cared to see—was the international pharmaceuticals market. But as the Welwyn team worked toward the synthesis of burimamide and then the exciting promise of metiamide, Smith Kline & French's Philadelphia marketing organization struggled to assess how much they could sell of a genuine anti-ulcer compound. Prevailing over every discussion was a conflict between the vision held by a few people and realistic probabilities. Again, the visions won out.

In those first few years of the 1970s, while the Welwyn team was still synthesizing new compounds, SK&F's senior management made a do-or-die commitment to the results of the H_2 project. Several elements triggered the commitment. Perhaps the most important of these was wishful thinking. The senior executives of the 1970s in Smith Kline had been the Thorazine salesmen of the 1950s. They had felt the explosive excitement of selling a drug that improved human lives almost miraculously. They had seen mental institutions transformed from zoos to treatment centers. They had felt the salesman's rare thrill of hearing people clamor for their product. But people like Henry Wendt and Robert Dee had also seen SK&F carry out a disorganized marketing program for Thorazine. One of their standard laments was, "Well, we did well with Thorazine, but if we'd been *ready,* we could have done a lot better."

Since the Thorazine days, those former salesmen—grown up into executives—had been waiting and wishing for another main chance like Thorazine. When they started to hear from their researchers and medical staff that the H_2 compound had the same dramatic medical potential as Thorazine, statistical measurements of the market faded among their considerations. They wanted a chance to do it again; they wanted to be *ready* the way they had not been ready before.

There was also a hint of desperation in SK&F's leadership in

Philadelphia. The company's research wing, both in the United States and in the United Kingdom, had generated very few promising drugs in two decades of effort. Tagamet represented a low risk for Smith Kline's leaders. Even if they poured resources into Tagamet and failed, they would feel vindicated by an all-out effort to halt the company's decline. If they went down, they would at least go down fighting!

Something else, though, drew SK&F into the Tagamet commitment. And this was the thing that kept coming up in conversations. More than a decade after Tagamet's breakthrough, SmithKline Beckman executives looked back and described themselves as a group of risk-takers who were willing to bet the company's future on one roll of the dice. Looking back, Wendt said, "We're a home run company. We strike out a lot, but when we make contact, we make it big!" But in truth, in 1970 probably no one in Philadelphia had yet conceived of a corporate home run philosophy to justify big risk decisions. No one dared admit the company was desperate. But when they considered the H_2 project, many at SK&F shared an intuition that there were more people in the world coping with ulcers than antacid sales, hospital admissions, or prescription totals ever had revealed. Thomas Collins, the head of Tagamet's United States marketing effort, recalled the intuition that lurked in the back of his mind. He had a vision of patients "coming out of the woodwork." The SK&F marketing machinery geared up to unprecedented intensity to sell Jim Black's brainchild because of—as much as any other influence—Tom Collins's success-driven, hyperacidic friends.

"In my age group," said Collins, "I can remember all sorts of people with ulcers. But they weren't under active treatment. They did whatever they had to. They stopped drinking. They stopped whatever it was that agitated them. But they didn't change the environment at all. So, from my point of view, I always said, I don't think anybody knows what the hell the size of this market is. This is the 'woodwork factor.' They're my friends.

"How many would take something like this if it were available? How many would at last go to their physician and say, 'I haven't been feeling that well. Would *this* drug help me?' What was the so-called pull-through factor of this product?"

Collins couldn't answer that question. Neither could Robert Dee. But based on a collection of misgivings and hunches, Dee decided very early in Tagamet's evolution to take the chance. By 1970 he had set in motion a series of acquisitions and expansions that changed forever the face of Smith Kline & French.

Before Tagamet, SK&F did not own a major fine chemicals plant. To manufacture enough drug to match the necessary marketing push, Dee committed the company to the construction of a chemical plant in Cork, Ireland, later to be known as Penn Chemical Corporation. It represented a major risk for SK&F. It was a $10 million item in 1973, when SK&F had a total capital investment budget of only $16 million.

The most dramatic sign of the company's commitment to Tagamet was that costly chemical plant in Cork. But probably more significant was that SK&F, notwithstanding a certain fiscal shakiness, was using the potential of that drug to create something it never had before—a company-controlled international sales organization. Dee saw Tagamet as a world drug, and a world drug couldn't be sold by a domestic pill company.

"We began systematically to build the infrastructure outside the United States because our international marketing apparatus was inadequate," said Wendt. SK&F acquired drug companies in Germany and France, just for starters. Those companies were intended as forces to expedite the swift distribution of SK&F's next big drug. SK&F signed a joint agreement with Fujisawa, Ltd., in Japan, for distribution of the new drug there, and eventually the company created a network that would allow a remarkably fast rollout of Tagamet, beginning in Britain in 1976, reaching sixty countries by 1978.

By 1974 the full extent of SK&F's preparations to launch Tagamet into an international market had become irreversible. While Dee and the organization in Philadelphia were opening distribution and sales organizations in a dozen new places throughout the world, the Welwyn staff was flooding its own network of hospitals and clinics with samples of metiamide. But all this momentum, and the tremendous buildup of optimism in SK&F, stopped suddenly in 1974, when metiamide crashed.

In June 1974 clinical studies revealed a case of a patient with agranulocytosis (a loss of infection-fighting white blood cells) directly connected with metiamide. One such incident might have been overlooked, but this was the second occurrence. Agranulocytosis is a rare condition to which only a few patients are susceptible, but Britain's Committee on Safety in Medicine (CSM) was extraordinarily swift and harsh in response. It halted all clinical tests with metiamide on June 14 and, with that decision, buried metiamide as a potential H_2 antagonist. The next month, the CSM reinstated metiamide for limited use on seriously ill patients showing no sign of reduced blood count. But the message to SK&F was ringingly clear: If you don't have an H_2 antagonist that avoids this problem, you don't have an H_2 antagonist.

The news went through SK&F like a knife.

"Bill [Duncan] called me into his office," recalled Ganellin. "He told me, 'Work has got to stop.' I had an enormous reaction. It was as if the ground had opened up—like I was falling down through a rushing hole."

James Geddes, who has been product manager for Tagamet since 1974, was in Amsterdam the day of the metiamide crash, attending a meeting in which all SK&F's international marketing leaders were building excitement and strategies for the metiamide launch. "The second day of the meetings," Geddes recalled, "we got this phone call. They said metiamide had been suspended . . . Well, God! I mean, we had to walk hand in hand over the bridges in Amsterdam because of the fear somebody might jump. Everybody was very depressed."

"It was very depressing," recalled Michael Parsons. "We could not be sure it was not a consequence of H_2 receptor blocking. We had faith that it was not. But clearly, that had to be depressing, although we had other compounds in the pipeline—thank God for that!"

Looking at the metiamide failure from the laboratory point of view, Parsons was correct when he said that Welwyn had "other compounds in the pipeline." But most of those compounds were inferior to metiamide in most respects. There was only one compound in the pipeline that held nearly as much promise as metiamide. It had just been synthesized. It was so new that it barely had a name: *cimetidine*. Philadelphia, whose wishful thinking had been reinforced by millions of dollars in investment, was irreversibly committed to cimetidine—even though the leaders in Philadelphia barely knew it existed, or whether it was any good.

Wendt recalled, "We reviewed proposals to commence construction at Cork, to produce metiamide—almost exactly at the same time metiamide was dead. Cimetidine wasn't up yet, although it was a prospect. And we said, 'Look, one of these things is going to work—one of these compounds. Odds are we're going to be able to make it in this plant. If we don't have the plant, we're going to wish we did. If we do have the plant but don't have the compounds, we'll think of something else. We'd better build it.' So we built the plant. And along came cimetidine."

In 1973 Dee, in Philadelphia, had noticed the agranulocytosis problem in laboratory animals and had asked Duncan to look for a compound to back up metiamide.

William Duncan had added cimetidine to the pipeline just to be on the safe side. Metiamide was a compound that contained something called a "thiourea group." Duncan always had concerns about the presence of thiourea, so he insisted researchers begin developing a non-thiourea compound, even as SK&F was shouting "Metiamide!" from the rooftops.

To provide some measure of how critical the success of cimetidine was, it should be noted that in the decade that followed the synthesis of cimetidine, only one other effective H_2 antagonist—a compound called ranitidine (Zantac), discovered by Glaxo Pharmaceuticals of Great Britain, was synthesized and approved by *anyone*, including SK&F Welwyn. Parsons might not have realized it in 1974 but, at that point, for SK&F it was cimetidine or *nothing*.

As soon as the shock had passed from the metiamide failure, SK&F moved aggressively to begin clinical development of cimetidine. But the first clinical trial came almost too soon.

Dr. William Burland had joined the Clinical Investigation Group at Welwyn shortly before the metiamide crash. In the second half of 1974, with the CSM metiamide suspension still a fresh sore, a clinician phoned Welwyn demanding cimetidine for a critically ill patient who had developed agranulocytosis in metiamide treatment. "Clearly, if you have the first compound of a new class in the clinic, where it appears to be effective, and its usefulness is suddenly limited by discovery of untoward effects, then any second agent has to be even more intensely scrutinized. A single mistake could result in a decision to kill the whole program," explained Burland. In other words, Burland would have been crazy to send cimetidine to the doctor.

But when the call demanding cimetidine came in from Dr. Duncan Colin-Jones at Southampton Hospital in Great Britain, Burland was in favor of helping the patient. When he tracked down Duncan in the United States—en route with SK&F's international clinical director, Leon Greene, to a medical conference in New Orleans—he received a concurring opinion.

Colin-Jones got the cimetidine, and the patient not only got better from his ulcer, he got better from his agranulocytosis. In very short order—too fast—SK&F had some tantalizing evidence that they could make H_2 antagonists that didn't kill white blood cells.

Something happened in this incident that almost has been lost in the Tagamet story. If Burland had not been able to reach Duncan in the United States, he admitted, he probably would have given Colin-Jones the medicine he wanted anyway, and he would have done so without informing Philadelphia. The risk was that the patient would die, primarily because of metiamide's effect. But if he died, the innocent compound (cimetidine) would be indistinguishable from the guilty one (metiamide). Both might well be banned forever from human use. It was obvious to Burland that, whatever the danger inherent in turning over an untested drug to a doctor with a critically ill patient, there was a corresponding opportunity—to find out immediately whether cimetidine possessed the same tragic flaw as metiamide. It was an all-or-nothing step in which corporate headquarters would likely see only the "nothing" and none of the "all." Subjected to the usual hours of organizational hesitation, the opportunity might be lost. With that in mind, Burland, Duncan, and Welwyn were ready to hand out their mystery vial of cimetidine. What the boss didn't know wouldn't hurt him.

Throughout the advance of Tagamet, there appears a series of these critical decisions, made not by corporate chiefs measuring their options, but by middle managers close to the "action" who trusted the quality of their peers' work and carefully regulated the amount of information that reached the company's senior management.

In Tagamet's history, there is an unmistakable pattern of unheralded players making critical, independent decisions without the obligatory by-your-leave from higher authority. The honor roll obviously includes Burland and Duncan, but it also includes Paget, whose motives in hiring Black at the outset were partly concealed from Philadelphia. Even Michael Parsons, when he changed the proportions of histamine in the assay, violated the authority of the greatest living pharmacologist in Great Britain, Heinz Schild. None of these unauthorized decisions were carried out in defiance. They were made, in fact, by men who believed they knew better what was good for the company in a special situation than the people who were supposed to be running the company.

In 1976, twelve years after Black promised an H_2 antagonist by Christmas and four years after Black's departure from the SK&F Research Institute, Smith Kline launched Tagamet in Great Britain. The careful market preparation engineered by Duncan and controlled by Alan Dalby and Donald van Roden, then SK&F's top marketing executives, resulted in immediate sales success and intensified interest in Tagamet throughout countries that could not yet get it. The United States and world launch came in 1977—as soon as the U.S. Food and Drug Administration had found Tagamet to be without serious side effects in the treatment of duodenal ulcers. Since then Tagamet has been prescribed by doctors for a host of other ailments, including prevention of hangovers—but its FDA approvals still cover only a few "official" human ills.

Within a year, Tagamet had sold more in the United States than the company's wildly optimistic peak forecast of $68 million. It was steaming past the $100 million plateau. Tagamet's sales astounded even the most experienced marketing people at SK&F. They surprised even Collins, who had never imagined the "woodwork factor" to be that big. The intense worldwide demand for Tagamet occurred even though the tablets cost a then astonishing amount, almost $20 for a bottle of one hundred.

Doctors and patients were buying Tagamet ravenously. Doctors were calling up SK&F drug salesmen and insisting on more of this stuff. Strangers were approaching officials of SK&F and thanking them for their wonderful, expensive drug. SK&F was trying to figure out ways to make four times as much Tagamet as they had ever thought they would sell.

Tagamet burst so spectacularly onto the scene largely because it was such a dramatic improvement over the ulcer treatment approaches at that time. The available therapies worked poorly, and even when they did work rarely had lasting effects. Furthermore, they were unpleasant to use and avoided by patients. Antacids, the most commonly available remedy, are inexpensive, foul-tasting chalky substances that work by coating the stomach lining and preventing it from being attacked by its own secretions. The other anti-secretory drugs available at the time, also quite inexpensive, caused dry mouth.

Like any drug, anti-secretories work only when patients take them. When people don't take the remedy, the result is more severe: life-threatening ulcers and eventually surgery. In the 1970s ulcer surgery itself cost thousands of dollars along with days—or weeks—of hospitalization, physician visits, and income loss. Ulcers were costing people a fortune.

Tagamet was the magic bullet. It healed ulcers—little ulcers and big ulcers. It did not just replace Tums; it replaced scalpels. People finally could get better from one of the most widespread, uncomfortable, and dangerous ills of modern life without drinking chalk or getting cut open. So it didn't matter that the pills cost $20. If they were ten times as much, they still beat surgery.

The unexpected popularity of Tagamet hit hard at SK&F headquarters in Philadelphia. But it hit even harder in Cork. For two years, between 1978 and 1980, Penn Chemical plant manager Declan Scott lived and worked on the brink of catastrophe. For those two years, he was in charge of the only manufacturing source for the fastest-growing prescription drug on earth. When SK&F's leaders had decided, several years before, to build the chemical plant in Cork, it had seemed huge. Most of them wondered how they would ever sell enough drugs to justify the staggering capital investment. The issue of whether the plant in Cork might not be big enough to meet demand was, at that time, absurd. No one even brought it up.

But by 1978 the absurdity of five years before had become Declan Scott's and Henry Wendt's reality.

Back in Philadelphia, Henry Wendt was then SK&F's chief operating officer. He found himself trapped in his office, thrilled by the popularity of Tagamet and terrified by the fact that the only place in the world where it could be made was that little chemical plant in Cork being run by an Irishman named Scott.

Almost every day for two years, Wendt looked into one of his desk drawers at a list of countries that would stop getting shipments of Tagamet if Declan Scott couldn't sustain production in Cork. Each time Wendt contemplated the idea of rationing Tagamet, his blood ran cold.

To suddenly mar the dream-come-true by denying treatment to whole nations of people, favoring one country while ostracizing another, would permanently stain SK&F's image and probably damage its business. Wendt lived in fear that a failure in the flow of cimetidine supply would label his "home run" company permanently as a minor league operation, unworthy of the magnitude of its greatest drug discovery.

Every week, Wendt called Scott three or four times. He checked to see if a consignment of the ingredients of cimetidine had arrived from Switzerland, or America, or the Bahamas. Scott and Wendt carried on an exceptional communication throughout this period. "Here was the chief operating officer calling me from Philadelphia," Scott recalled, "asking me about individual shipments of drug. 'Has it arrived yet?' 'How soon can you get it processed?' Believe me, I haven't got many calls from Philadelphia since then!"

In Ireland, Declan Scott treated the entire crisis as a pleasant surprise that provided him with a ceaseless round of entertainment. He was expected, with a workforce of about 200 people (all of whom went onto twelve-hour shifts early in 1978) to generate in Penn Chemical twice the amount of cimetidine (350 tons a year) that the plant was designed to produce. SK&F's next production facility, in Puerto Rico, would not be in full operation for a year or more.

Wendt's instructions to Scott were remarkable. " 'Money is no issue,' he told me," recalled Scott. " 'Make as much as you can. As much as you can!' "

At the same time that Scott was reciting precise production levels and exact arrival and departure times for shipments of chemical, he was consciously soft-pedaling to Wendt a crisis that repeatedly threatened to shut down Penn Chemical at the peak of its production. In cimetidine, Scott was producing a chemical whose very nature had yet to be understood by almost everyone in the world. Normally, when a new drug goes from laboratory to chemical plant, it passes through a pilot plant stage, where production people find out if the chemical has any strange qualities that only emerge when a lot of it is synthesized. But cimetidine had been pushed straight from the lab to the big time, without going through a pilot plant. The result was a smell that drifted unpleasantly outward from Penn Chemical into several of the nicer neighborhoods of Cork. It turned out that when you make lots of cimetidine, it smells awful.

Cork is one of Ireland's industrial centers, and people there are accustomed to an occasional whiff of industrial effluvium. But with cimetidine, Penn Chemical and Declan Scott strained the limits of Cork's tolerance. Tagamet was good for the economy but bad for the atmosphere.

As Scott assiduously applied his engineers to the solution of the odor problem, he found himself meeting ever more frequently with the two local governing councils, for both the City and County of Cork, to explain his progress—if any—in shutting off the stench entirely. The less patient and more powerful of these bodies was the county council, and in 1979 Scott entered a council meeting under threat of a court injunction (brought by a strident neighborhood activist) and possible immediate cessation of industrial activity. In the meantime, Scott had soothed Wendt with the news that he was making swift progress in the solution of Penn Chemical's minor environmental problem.

When Scott went into that critical county council meeting, he did so with barely any of the legal support that Philadelphia might have marshalled on his behalf. Scott's only card was one that—he knew—had higher value in Cork than anything Smith Kline could deal from across the Atlantic. He went into the council meeting as a fellow citizen and businessman in Cork, and he reminded them that he shared their hopes and concerns for the revival of a city that had slipped into a prolonged economic recession. Scott presented to the council a plan that would result in a steady, gradual clean-up of the Tagamet pollution problem without staunching the critical flow of chemicals from the plant. Scott, as only a fellow citizen can do, impressed the council with the realization that they, the City and County of Cork, for a brief period of history, were the vital link in a commercial breakthrough that reached around the world and touched the lives of millions of people. Through the guileless, neighborly appeal of Declan Scott, the council understood the importance of Penn Chemical's product to the marketplace and the importance of a livable Cork to the leadership of Penn Chemical.

Scott's negotiations with the county council were a face-saving *tour de force*. The council was able to impose upon Penn Chemical a series of strict deadlines for environmental compliance (all of them proposed by Scott), and Scott was able to go back to work.

Scott's tap dance with the county council was one more spontaneous decision in the pattern that kept several Tagamet crises safely in the hands of a few wise mediators who knew the territory.

However, to characterize the breakthrough at SK&F solely as the crafty work of a series of middle management mediators is to minimize the importance of the series of courageous moves by Robert Dee to drastically enlarge SK&F in anticipation of the emergence of Tagamet, putting his company onto the world stage. Scott performed heroically in squeezing double production from Penn Chemical and in keeping it open in the local political crisis, but it was Philadelphia that had the foresight to build Penn Chemical. And the enormous demand for Tagamet, right from the start, was the product of masterful marketing planning by Collins in Philadelphia and by Alan Dalby in Brussels.

For the world at large, the most dramatic implications of the Tagamet discovery at SK&F are not in the exceptional interplay that emerged between top management and the "underground" of key players. Nor is it most important that SK&F gave to the world a drug that spares people from surgery. In the longest possible term, the most profound impact of the Tagamet story is in the concept conceived by James Black and brought to full term by the Welwyn, Philadelphia, and Cork organizations.

The "house that Black built" is not merely a huge, reborn pharmaceuticals company in Philadelphia. Nor is it the new state-of-the-art SmithKline Beckman research complex in Upper Merion, Pennsylvania. The "house that Black built" encompasses the entire community of pharmaceuticals research. In proving the truth of his H_2 concept, James Black changed permanently the way scientists seek new drugs. He opened the doors, in his house, to the limits of human possibility.

The importance of the H_2 accomplishment at SK&F is that all three compounds that led to a final product called Tagamet were substances that do not exist naturally. Burimamide first, then metiamide, and then cimetidine—all were created by chemists who assembled them from atoms. Black imagined and then built a molecule that ameliorates a destructive effect within a natural system *but doesn't change anything else in the system*. Because of the huge impact of Tagamet on the practice of medicine and on the course of human lives, Black's concept revealed on a grand scale the potential of what is now known as bio-engineering.

Before James Black, pharmaceutical researchers labored doggedly among a tangle of nameless solutions in hopes of matching one of them, sooner or later, to an important problem. Scientists today still blend chemicals like the medieval herbalists who made potions from different combinations of leaves and tested them on human subjects. But because of Black, science is now moving away from that wasteful level of trial and error. Pharmaceutical researchers can now, without fear of being laughed at or fired, specify the problem they wish to solve and design the combination of atoms they believe will solve it.

Now problems that through guesswork might have taken centuries to solve will perhaps take only decades; and problems otherwise still decades from solution will be conquered in years.

This promise lies today at the fingertips of most scientists largely because James Black, in defiance of the stated interests of most of the institutions for whom he worked, pressed on stubbornly with his unique view of life and its subtle mechanisms. But Black could not have moved science forward so dramatically on his own. The world's medical and scientific establishment would not have so swiftly embraced, or even noticed, Black's vision if not for a handful of Smith Kline baton-carriers who barely missed a beat after their mentor had proven his point and ascended to academia. Quietly, diligently, they picked up Black's conception from the place where he had set it aside, and turned it into a simple, friendly presence on the medicine shelf.

6 Walkman: From "Dumb Product" to the Headphone Culture

They had been disappointed at first, but it wasn't something that was going to keep them awake nights. Mitsuro Ida and a group of electronics engineers in Sony Corporation's Tape Recorder Division in Tokyo had tried to redesign a small, portable tape recorder, called "Pressman," so that it gave out stereophonic sounds. A year or so before, Ida and his group had been responsible for inventing the first Pressman, a wonderfully compact machine—ideal for use by journalists—which had sold very well.

But the sound in that tape machine was monaural. The next challenge for Sony's tape recorder engineers was to make a portable machine just as small, but with stereophonic sound. The very first stereo Pressman they made, in the last few months of 1978, didn't succeed. When Ida and his colleagues got the stereo circuits into the Pressman chassis (5.25 inches by 3.46 inches, and only 1.14 inches deep), they didn't have any space left to fit in the recording mechanism. They had made a stereophonic tape recorder that couldn't record anything. Ida regarded this as a good first try but a useless product. But he didn't throw it away. The stereo Pressman was a nice little music machine. So the engineers found a few favorite music cassettes and played them while they worked.

Meanwhile, Mitsuro Ida went back to the drawing board, looking for a way to fit *both* stereo playback and stereo recording into the tiny box. Ida and his fellow engineers were tape recorder engineers, and the device they had just made could *not* record. So in their eyes, it really didn't work.

However, a year later, Kozo Ohsone, the general manager for Sony Corporation's Tape Recorder Division, became the unwitting heir to Ida's "failed" music box. Ohsone was charged with transforming Bonson Electric's production facility (Sony's electronic product division) in Saitama so that it could manufacture millions of these things.

Sony suddenly needed millions of these things because the unthinkable had happened. By early 1980 the new devices, hastily dubbed Walkman by Sony's marketing people, were the most explosively popular magnetic tape machine in history. Everybody seemed to want one. Electronics stores throughout Japan could not stock them fast enough. Tourists and business travelers from the United States and Europe were buying them by the armful and smuggling them through Customs to give (and sell) to friends and associates at home. A half dozen Japanese electronics competitors were pouring resources into production of their own little music machines.

The reason Ida's machine became the best-selling electronic device in the world for several years, and surprised everyone at Sony, was one simple addition to the design: *headphones*.

But these were not just any headphones, certainly not the immense headphones of the 1970s that tied stereophiles, like dogs on leashes, to hi-fi sets. Walkman headphones were comfortable, weightless, loose-fitting things that pumped hypnotically vivid sound directly into the human brain.

Today, because of those friendly headphones, most people know what a Walkman is—and how it *sounds!* Walkman has become a staple item of modern life; most households have one. Many people own portable cassette players made by Sony's competitors, but even though Walkman is Sony's trade name for their product, many people call *all* personal portable stereo players Walkmans. The name was coined in discussions at Sony, at first rejected by chairman Akio Morita, and then, in a strategic change of mind, forced upon the company's distribution network by the same Morita.

But in 1978 and throughout much of 1979, few people at Sony saw or imagined any potential in this accidental product. When the Walkman I was introduced in July of 1979, senior management and the leaders of the Tape Recorder Division had made sure the minimum of money and manpower went into the product launch. Sony started Walkman's existence by thinking of it as a toy, designed to occupy the minds of young people and exploit their impulsive spending habits.

Sony was rather perplexed by Walkman, especially in its first generation. The product expressed little of the technological sophistication that is intrinsic to much of the company's product line. Even today, ambivalence about Walkman exists in the company. When Sony chairman Akio Morita arrived in a conference room one day in 1985 for an interview on Walkman's genesis, he diverted the conversation to a newer, higher technology. "You should be asking me about compact disks," Morita said. "Now this is the true breakthrough! A great technology developed here at Sony!"

Regardless of his disclaimer, Walkman is a source of great pride for Morita, who justly claims a major role in fostering its development. The company circulates colored glossy 8" x 10" photos of the twelve-member "Walkman Team," with Morita prominent in the center of the group. And indisputably, Sony's emergence from the postwar struggle of the Japanese electronics industry was forged partly by its manufacture of little things that respond to simple personal needs. The first product that the newly formed Sony Corporation (then called the Tokyo Telecommunications Engineering Corporation) introduced after its founding in 1946 was a rice cooker that proved not only unsuccessful but dangerous. The first *successful* product was a tape recorder, introduced in 1950, the first in a long line of Sony innovations in tape recording technology.

Sony, in 1954, was the first and best company to find a simple use for Bell Laboratories' astounding invention of the transistor. Sony was the company which—through its tiny, blaring, ubiquitous transistor radios—made the word *transistor* common to a dozen languages. Like the transistor radio, Walkman conceals technological sophistication within its outward simplicity. It's possible, for a few thousand dollars, to get extraordinary stereophonic music by carefully refining and assembling many electronic components in a room acoustically designed for such a purpose, organizing an array of high-fidelity speakers in perfect juxtaposition to a stationary listener seated in a special chair. It's possible to achieve the same goal by strapping on a $100 Walkman and flipping the switch.

Analogously, a nuclear submarine and a minnow both maneuver under water and contain, in their design, a breathtaking sophistication. One awes us with its complexity; the other captivates us with its darting grace and its utter simplicity.

Walkman and the transistor radio, deceptively simple machines, have fulfilled a simple, eternal need in human culture. Morita explained that Sony Corporation attained preeminence in the consumer electronics industry by originating and promoting, better than anyone else, the idea of personal entertainment. Transistor radios were the first generation of the idea that everybody could carry around in his hip pocket a separate world of sound and sensation both far away and closer to the listener than anything immediately near. Walkman is the latest generation of this pervasive social need.

The Walkman is a minimal item of apparel, silent and barely noticeable. Yet it envelopes the user in a cocoon, closing off the sounds and distractions that swirl about him in a crowded, hurrying, tense human environment. Walkman is an urban pacifier. It extends personal privacy into a new dimension; it accomplishes something that previously only drugs, Zen, and mental illness could achieve—it separates the individual from his surroundings without physically removing him to another place. Morita's realization was that besides its power to take people *away* from civilization, Walkman can bring the blessings of civilization to places that civilized people never have reached.

"Years ago, when I went to Hong Kong," said Morita, "I saw that many people had a small boat. That was their home. They had no entertainment—but each boat had a transistor radio. The transistor radio was their first chance to get outside entertainment. I hope to put Walkman into the jungle, so that people there can enjoy stereo."

Even to reach Morita's attention, however, Walkman had to catch the eye of the other highest authority at Sony—Honorary Chairman Masaru Ibuka, founder of Sony in 1946. It was Ibuka who discovered the first Walkman prototype, made and then rejected by Ida's team of researchers working under Kozo Ohsone in the Tape Recorder Division.

After Ida and his fellow designers had turned their nonrecording tape recorder into background music, they didn't entirely ignore it. They had frequent discussions about how to fit the stereo function and the recording mechanism into that overly small space. It was not an easy problem to solve, and because of that it was all the more fascinating and attractive to Ida and his group of inveterate problem-solvers. Their focus on the problem of the stereo Pressman blinded them to the solution—to a different problem—that was in their hands.

"And then one day," said Takichi Tezuka, manager of product planning for the Tape Recorder Division, "into our room came Mr. Ibuka, our honorary chairman. He just popped into the room, saw us listening to this, and thought it was very interesting."

It is the province of honorary chairmen everywhere, because their status is almost invariably ceremonial, to potter about the plant looking in on this group and that group, nodding over the latest incomprehensible gadget. To this mundane task, Masaru Ibuka brought an undiminished intelligence and an active imagination. When he happened into the Tape Recorder Division and saw Ida's incomplete tape recorder, he admired the quality of its stereophonic sound. He also remembered an entirely unrelated project going on elsewhere in the building, where an engineer named Yoshiyuki Kamon was working to develop lightweight portable headphones.

What if you combined them? asked Ibuka. At the very least, he said, the headphones would use battery power much more efficiently than stereo speakers. Reduce power requirements and you can reduce battery consumption. But another idea began to form in his mind. If you added the headphones, wouldn't you dramatically increase the quality of what the listener hears? Could you leave out the recorder entirely and make a successful product that just plays music?

In the world of tape recorders, Ibuka's thought was heresy. He was mixing up functions. Headphones traditionally were supposed to extend the usefulness of tape recorders, not be essential to their success. This idea was so well established that if Ibuka had not made an association between a defective tape recorder design and an unfinished headphone design, Walkman may well have remained a little byway in musical history. Design groups within Sony tend to be very close-knit and remain focused on short-term task completion. Even when things were less busy, there was no reason for tape recorder people ever to communicate with headphone people. They had nothing to do with each other. Tezuka, the man who later was described as "the secretariat of the Walkman project," said, "No one dreamed that a headphone would ever come in a package with a tape recorder. We're not very interested in what they do in the Headphone Division."

But, even without this insularity, there is no assurance that someone else at Sony would have made the connection that Ibuka made. To people today, the relationship between a cassette player and a set of headphones is self-evident. But to people at Sony, and at virtually every consumer electronics company, that connection was invisible in 1978.

Ibuka got a predictable response from the researchers in the electronics lab and from others in the Tape Recorder and Headphone divisions. They were painfully polite but noncommittal. Ibuka might be right that the headphones would improve Pressman's efficiency, but nobody could guess how much of an improvement that would be. No one wanted to tell Ibuka that the idea of removing the speaker in favor of headphones was crazy. But it was! What if the owner of the device wanted to play back a tape so that more than one person could listen?

When Ibuka ventured further into illogic by suggesting a playback machine with *no speaker* and *no recorder,* he lost everybody. Who would want to buy such a thing? Who in Sony Corporation would support even ten minutes of development on such a harebrained scheme?

In a way, they were right and Ibuka was wrong. This was an idea that violated most industries' well-established criteria for judging the natural increments of product development. It only makes sense that a new product prototype should be better than the previous generation of product. Ida's nonrecording prototype seemed *worse.* The idea had no support from the people who eventually would be responsible for funding its development, carrying out the research, and trying to sell it to a consumer market. The idea should have been killed. The system made sense and the people who worked within the system were making sense.

For Honorary Chairman Ibuka, the handwriting was on the wall. Even though he was a revered man at Sony, he had no authority to order such a project undertaken against the wishes of the division's leaders. It was clear that the only way to sell a bad idea to a group of cautious, reasonable businessmen was to find an ally. So, in his enthusiasm, his next step was straight to the office of his partner and friend, Akio Morita. The interplay between Honorary Chairman Ibuka and Chairman Morita was a fascinating drama and a critical step in the survival of the idea that eventually would be called Walkman.

Ibuka was taking advantage of a fundamental quirk in Morita's personality. Morita loves new gadgets, and he often exercises dubious judgment about which gadgets have solid commercial potential and which ones don't. Among the worst mistakes commercialized by Morita was "Morning Toaster," a tape player (with a clock) designed in the shape of a toaster, brought to Morita by an engineer who burst into the chairman's office equipped with a Morning Toaster prototype and an excess of enthusiasm. The rule around Sony is that anyone with the nerve to barge into Morita's office with a strange idea has a good chance of selling it.

One other impulse, however, also motivated Ibuka's visit to Morita with this odd notion of a tape recorder with headphones but no recorder. The two men had shared, together in the same workshops, offices, and laboratories, for more than thirty years, a common purpose. They had formed Sony from the rubble of Tokyo, after World War II, and they granted to each other a trust that springs not from logic but from love. In expressing that passion, Morita has said, "Even to this day, Sony is a company of compatriots gathered together for the sole purpose of realizing Masaru Ibuka's dreams."

Even then, Morita might have bowed and thanked his friend profusely and then slipped the idea into a bottom drawer—some dreams are more worthy of respect than capital investment. But Ibuka had gone in prepared for this possibility. He said, "Let's put together one of these things and try it. Let's see how it *sounds*." This was a harmless request. The ingredients were available. So, Ida's machine was combined with a set of conventional, heavy headphones.

According to popular legend, Morita and Ibuka then went out into the world to test the infant Walkman. They wore it, it is said, in airports, on helicopters, on tennis courts, and on golf courses. The story is nice but not credible. Morita smiles mischievously at the fabric of legends he has created among gullible journalists. "There were many stories that came out. Many rumors spread. All these couldn't have occurred. It was a promotion," said Morita. "A journalist would say, 'You developed the Walkman for playing tennis.' I would say, 'Yes, that's right.' A journalist would say, 'You developed Walkman for playing golf.' I would say, 'Yes.' Such an interesting story is good for the promotion."

The most important result of his trial was Morita's discovery of sounds he had never heard before. The stereo that burst from that little box was wonderful. He and Ibuka had done what none of the more sensible folks in the Tape Recorder Division had done. They had *tried* it.

And they loved it.

Morita's decision, to push the development of a nonrecording cassette playback tape recorder, was immediate. It shocked the people in the Tape Recorder Division. How could the honorary chairman and now Chairman Morita *both* support this departure from rational product *development?*

For Sony, partly because of the personality of its chairman, the idea of being the market creator is far more important than it is for most Japanese companies. Sony's philosophy of success, as explained by Takichi Tezuka, sounds, in fact, more American than Japanese.

"It's a Sony policy," Tezuka said, "that we should be the leader in the very beginning, from technology development to marketing. We should always advance the product ahead of everyone else."

The philosophy is that of Ibuka, who wrote the company charter, and Morita, who enforces it: "Do what others have not done." Virtually alone among chief executives in Japan, Morita is outspoken, and provocative. Opposite to the quiet, self-effacing style expected of the Japanese company executive, Morita charges into the public eye, makes bold predictions, and challenges his industry's conventional ideas. But he also provides enormous entertainment to a journalistic community bored by the standard Japanese corporate style. Morita stands up bravely to his failures, justly claims more victories than defeats, and enjoys the limelight's glow. Walkman provided Morita with another possibility—however remote—of creating a market.

Morita's passion is to assure that Sony is the first with the newest. Whenever possible he lends an air of impulsiveness to some of the company's decisions. And he creates the impression that Sony's employees are helpless captives of a leader who is both quixotic and autocratic. In fact, Morita is only one member of a management group at Sony that shares the task of making major decisions, routinely challenges his judgment, and gains the maximum publicity for the company from the chairman's remarkable personal style.

If there is resentment of Morita's rule, it is not the divisive anger employees might feel for a corporate tyrant; it is, more accurately, the token resistance one offers to a dominating but benevolent father.

The Japanese word *uchi* can be used interchangeably to mean "my company" or "my home." For many Japanese, especially men, one's relationships with colleagues at work are the focus and the purpose of life; the company is home. In the rapid cultural change that is now constant in Japanese society, this unusual relationship between home and work may erode. However, Morita has used this cultural phenomenon with the generation now on the job to create a remarkably efficient organization.

Morita not only said, "Let's try this"; he also said that he would be watching this project closely. The last part was extremely important. If the people in the Tape Recorder Division had sensed for a moment that Morita was not taking this product seriously, they might have set it aside. In the spring and summer of 1979, the Walkman project was for them mainly a drain on the division's money and manpower.

In that period, there was little feeling of pressure. Even though it had been ordered as early as February that the product must be developed, priced, advertised, manufactured, and introduced by the middle of the summer, nobody felt concerned. There was a prevailing devil-may-care attitude about the creation of Walkman I. Part of that stemmed from the belief that it would fail; it was a crazy adventure. Another reason was the influence of Yasuo Kuroki, director of Consumer Product Design, to whom Morita had given the responsibility of shepherding Walkman through its development.

Watching Yasuo Kuroki is a little bit like watching a man who seems permanently in the midst of a Dick Van Dyke comedy routine. Kuroki is a laughing, gangling, animated man who can seem simultaneously overwhelmed and delighted by any situation, and totally unable to control his physical expression of those feelings. His presence on the Walkman scene lent a lighthearted air to the anxiety that began to flow in increasing intensity from Morita's office. No one else in the group was as merry as Kuroki. Kozo Ohsone, general manager of the Tape Recorder Division at Sony and Kuroki's cohort in the production of Walkman, was calm and less animated.

Of course, according to most reports, it was neither Yasuo Kuroki nor Kozo Ohsone who served as product manager for Walkman. Morita adopted this project as his very own and drove it through the system with constant attention and unstinting energy. Yasuo Kuroki smiles at this suggestion and implies that if you believe that, he's got a bridge in Brooklyn you might like to buy. "Mr. Morita, as he claimed, was the project manager," said Kuroki, his eyebrows dancing with ambiguity. "That's the way he liked to think of himself. But what do you think? On something like this, do you really think the chairman of the board would be able to serve as the project boss?"

Appropriately, Morita left the day-to-day details to Yasuo Kuroki and Kozo Ohsone. But he understood one thing very clearly: Everybody working on Walkman had to believe that this was Morita's pet project.

Common to all the members of the team Kuroki assembled to design and build Morita's pet project was a marked lack of enthusiasm. No one had yet convinced them that a nonrecording tape recorder made any sense. Nevertheless, they followed orders and began gingerly to move things around in the maddeningly small space inside the body of the Pressman.

Although Sony's promotional lore insists that the builder of the unintentional Walkman prototype is unknown, Mitsuro Ida's role as its primary creator is quietly acknowledged by his coworkers. Ida is a problem-solver. Behind his round and bashful face, there is a brain that focuses tirelessly on the minute details of his work. He has the rare capacity to see, without the aid of tools or pictures, the contours of a mechanical problem and the myriad changes in configuration that might finally represent the solution. He has confessed that he cultivates this flow of possibilities while he is eating, sleeping, vacationing, or just roaming a corridor. He finds his hours in a bar not far from Sony most fruitful. There, he and his coworkers retire frequently after work, extending their workday several hours, talking shop, engaging in a uniquely Japanese activity: bonding to their immediate fellow workers and their company more intimately than they ever will bond to their families and their private lives. When Ida says bluntly, "I like to drink," he implies a great deal more than fluid ingestion.

Late in February 1979, a friendly truce prevailed among the designers, and a few prototypes had been built. The Tape Recorder Division, which had been handed the Walkman project for better or worse, had a mixed reaction. Division executives knew they couldn't afford to launch this new product, regardless of its good design, unless it could make money. At Sony, each division bears the cost of its risks. To the Tape Recorder Division, it looked as though they had a loser, a nonrecording tape recorder that, with headphones, would retail for at least ¥50,000 ($249). This was more than people were paying for tape recorders that *recorded*.

The marketing people at the Tape Recorder Division were blunt in their assessment of the Walkman. "This is a dumb product," they said.

With this sort of attitude prevalent in the division, project leader Yasuo Kuroki decided it was time for a pep rally. He arranged a meeting in February 1979 between the "young engineers" and Morita, in Morita's office. This literally was the first time these engineers ever had faced the chairman without being in trouble.

"To be invited to the chairman's room is something extraordinary," Takashino recalled. "For most of us it's a once-in-a-lifetime experience."

Aware of the nervousness that a visit to Morita's office could instill, Kuroki gave the young engineers a briefing—which backfired. "I told them, please, if you disagree with Mr. Morita, feel free to say, 'No,' " said Kuroki. "But they were so obedient to my words that when the meeting started they kept saying, 'No. No.' Toward the end of the meeting, I was very much troubled, and I regretted my words."

The meeting failed because the representatives of the Tape Recorder Division would not give in to Morita on the issue of price. "The division has a right to refuse," said Kuroki. The gap between a price that would attract youthful buyers (about ¥35,000 or $170) and the Tape Recorder Division's break-even price (¥49,800, or $249) was huge. Based on that irreconcilable difference, Morita had to respect the division's right to refuse.

But he didn't. Morita had visualized the market for this playback-only device, and he wanted to explore it. Morita was able to express a perception of consumer desires that supported his faith. He began to promote the idea, within Sony, that this playback/headphone machine was not a tape recorder but a new concept in entertainment, one that dovetailed with the growing market in prerecorded cassettes. It was a concept that, Morita believed, would strike an immediate chord with teenagers, a social group that "can't live without music."

Morita observed correctly that teenagers carry music to school, to the beach, to athletic events, even to musical performances. To teenagers Walkman would mean that they could easily carry their music virtually anywhere—to the library, to church! Walkman, said Morita, would break down the last barriers.

The result of Morita's eagerness was that Kuroki had to call another meeting to change the minds of the young engineers. "It was not because the chairman instructed us," Kuroki insisted. "It was not a command, an order. We were very aware of the enthusiasm, the emotion in Mr. Morita. We responded emotionally. We sympathized."

In this meeting, Morita and the Tape Recorder Division haggled over the price. The division's engineers conceded that, by trimming a few costs and praying for incredible sales, they could justify a price somewhere around ¥40,000 ($200). Given an inch, Morita declared that the price would be ¥33,000 ($165). The number coincided with Sony Corporation's thirty-third anniversary that year. It was also a price that was conceivably affordable for a Japanese youth. Morita also used the occasion to set a product launch date of July 1, 1979—four months hence.

For many companies, a four-month deadline would have been absurd. But for the design and engineering staff of Sony's Tape Recorder Division, the pressure was barely noticeable. Outwardly, Sony's structure is rigid, so orderly and specialized that tape recorder researchers can't imagine communicating with headphone researchers. Yet, sparked suddenly by the chairman's whim, a team formed—led by Yasuo Kuroki, Takichi Tezuka, and Kozo Ohsone—to respond to the challenge. Morita, as lofty and imperious as any chairman in Japan, knew not only that he had people able to follow his orders creatively, but also knew exactly where to look them up. He had more than the technological pieces to put together a Walkman; he had an entire network of people who thrived on doing odd jobs on the spur of the moment.

For this spontaneous network of people, the biggest immediate problem was Morita's crazy price. At $165, the Tape Recorder Division could sell out the entire first production run of 60,000 Walkman units, which most people regarded as a wildly optimistic outlook, and still lose $35 on each unit sale. "There was no profit," said Tezuka. "The more we produced, the more we lost."

Kozo Ohsone was production chief for the Tape Recorder

Division in 1979. He could see that a tape recorder that could not record might easily linger into the future as a stain on his reputation. The division had already spent about $100,000 for injection molding equipment to manufacture Walkman when Yasuo Kuroki told Kozo Ohsone to prepare an initial production run of 60,000 units, which was the most optimistic sales forecast anyone could imagine. Ohsone, a pragmatist, made a deal. He would acquire from his vendors enough parts for 60,000 Walkmans, but he would *make* only 30,000. If he saw that the first batch was selling briskly, he would have time to produce the remainder with little or no delay. And if the first batch died on the market, Sony would be spared the expense of making 30,000 additional unwanted Walkmans. Kuroki and Ohsone cut this deal—and made sure Morita didn't know a thing about it.

Ohsone's production scale-up budget for Walkman I was frugal, but it was lavish compared to the money given the Tape Recorder Division's marketing group. They received $100,000 earmarked for advertising; for promotion, they got almost no money at all. Most of their "budget" consisted of Walkman samples. They used this resource creatively. Aiming their efforts at the youth market, they got the maximum promotion for the minimum yen. Their free samples all went to celebrities in the music and show business industries—several of them to pop stars from America and Europe who were touring Japan that summer. The Walkman press announcement went out on cassettes rather than on paper. And the day of the product release, Sony bused the members of the press (each of them wearing a brand-new Walkman) to Yoyogi Park in Tokyo, where a throng of teenagers of both sexes, all of them listening to Walkmans and shimmying to the beat, roller-skated circles around the press.

The Japanese press found this introduction delightful and gave it extraordinary coverage the next day and throughout the ensuing weeks. The Tape Recorder Division seemingly had taken a risk with an unconventional market introduction, and they had succeeded.

But while the press had got excited, they hadn't been able to infect Japan's youth with that excitement. Teenagers didn't buy Walkman in numbers that even approached Sony's expectations. Indeed, through the month of July, *nobody* bought Walkman.

Why hadn't these young people, who supposedly couldn't live without music, eagerly bought this novel way to listen to their music? Part of the explanation lies in the intrinsic conformity of adolescents. Both Japanese and American cultures give teenagers a lot of credit as a source of fashion trends. But teenagers aren't leaders; they are among the most lockstep trend-followers in consumer societies. They will consume almost anything, but they wait until they see other people consuming it first.

After weeks, and with very little response from teenagers, Walkman sales finally began to pick up. August was a good sales month for Walkman. And then suddenly sales exploded. By the first week in September, supplies of Walkman in Japan had dried up. There wasn't a Walkman to be found in any retail outlet.

Chairman Morita fumed. He asked why supplies had run out at 30,000 units, when the production level had been established at 60,000. Ohsone was in trouble for holding back on the second 30,000 units; it wouldn't be until almost October before Walkman would be back on the market. But Yasuo Kuroki stepped in between Morita and Ohsone and took some of the responsibility for the decision, reminding Morita that Ohsone's caution was a justified decision, based on the original dubious outlook for a product that didn't make much sense to experienced people in the tape recorder business.

But the market didn't make much sense either. Who was buying Walkman? Without a teenage market, the marketing group in the Tape Recorder Division wondered why Walkman was selling at all.

Later market studies showed that Sony had discovered, before the official designation existed, the demographic group that has come to be known as young urban professionals, or "yuppies." Walkman was an ideal accessory for members of the young professional middle class (average age: twenty-eight), whose lives are affluent and active. For this group, recorded music has been a pervasive presence all their lives. Most of these people already owned other cassette-playing devices and lots of prerecorded cassettes. The price of Walkman, designed to fit into most teenagers' tight budgets, presented no cost barrier at all to older, wealthier members of the young professional class, who enjoy their role as conspicuous consumers and are not self-conscious about breaking new ground in society. Now they could drive, jog, commute on the subway, play golf, and all the while enjoy perfect stereophonic sound. Sony, to its credit, quickly recognized this market and identified the buyers as "heavy users." They aimed ensuing advertising and marketing campaigns at these heavy users, concentrating on issues such as life-style, quality of sound, and technological innovation. It wasn't until February 1981, eighteen months after that teen-oriented launch at Yoyogi Park, that Sony was able to determine that Walkman finally had penetrated the youth market.

With Walkman I and that basic core group of heavy users, Sony had a fad on their hands. Other consumer electronics companies quickly began to make authentic copies. To stay ahead of the competition, Sony had to make a better Walkman. But also, to raise Walkman beyond its status as a fad, Sony still had to have another breakthrough. The new breakthrough effort began almost before the first 60,000 Walkmans were sold. Walkman II was on the drawing board by October of 1979.

October 1979 also spawned a small marketing crisis that eventually took seven months to solve. At an international sales meeting in Tokyo, Morita introduced Walkman to Sony sales representatives from America, Europe, Australia, and other outposts of consumer culture. Within two months, Walkman was introduced in the United States under the name "Soundabout." Two months later, it was on sale in the United Kingdom under the name "Stowaway." Sony in Japan had consented to the name changes because their English-speaking marketing groups had told them the name Walkman sounded funny in English. Nevertheless, with Western tourists importing Walkmans from Japan and spreading the original name faster than any advertising agency could have done it, Walkman became the name most people used when they asked for a Soundabout or a Stowaway in a retail store. Sony was losing Walkman sales because they had three different names for the same thing. That crisis was solved suddenly by Morita in May 1980, at Sony's United States national sales convention. He simply declared that, funny or not, Walkman was the name everybody had to use.

However, regardless of what they called it, Sony had to follow Walkman I with Walkman II quickly or lose the advantage of introducing a product that was both exceptionally new and exceptionally easy for other manufacturers to imitate.

Walkman II was the reason the "headphone culture" took root in our lives. With the decision at last to put the company's commitment behind Walkman, Sony did a number of extraordinary things. A first critical step was to reduce the size of the Walkman dramatically, to only slightly larger than the tape cassette itself. With this reduction in size came improvements in stereo function, headphone design, and energy use.

The design was not the only breakthrough. Morita and Kuroki, discussing the next step, knew that they had to match the moment of worldwide interest in Walkman with a flood of products. If within a year they could not manufacture enormous numbers of the Walkman, the magic moment might either go by or be seized by competing manufacturers. Suddenly, the mood went from devil-may-care to deadly serious. And with that change in atmosphere, the job of orchestration went from Kuroki to Ohsone's main production group at Bonson Electric.

Kozo Ohsone is a man of exceptional outward tranquility. His soft-spoken manner conceals an iron focus on getting things done the right way and on time. Defined by the Western stereotype, Ohsone seems the archetypal Japanese manager. He seems to have moved upward in management by virtue of his conformity, by acquiescence to the homogeneous norm. But his intuitive awareness of people's feelings—especially their frustrations—and capabilities has made him an exceptional leader. His quiet style is a mark not of submissiveness, but of strength. He needed all that strength to deal with Morita's fast-growing expectations for Walkman II.

The task was frightening. Sony had reached the production peak of a little over 30,000 units of Walkman I per month in the first months of 1980. But by October 1979 it was already Morita's plan to make Walkman I obsolete within eight months and to replace it with Walkman II. The production target for Walkman II, by mid-year 1980, was 200,000 units a month.

Ohsone smiles when he is asked whether that goal made him feel pressured. Like Kuroki, Ohsone responds obediently to the expectations of Sony's chairman, but he also has learned the difference between Morita's bark and Morita's bite. "Ask a woman to give birth in three months. Does she feel pressure?" said Ohsone. "No, because she knows it's impossible."

In fact, before the Walkman II project was under way, a new target date of January 1, 1981, had already been set.

Kozo Ohsone knew that the most important contribution he could make to the success of the team assembled for the development and scale-up to Walkman II would be to select the right people for the group. "This team consisted of individuals who are rare. They had to be cohesive, because this was a challenge that was like mountain climbing. Teamwork is critical. Some only go as far as the base camp. Some go to the peak, but they would not get there without the support of the others," explained Ohsone.

Ohsone went about the task of forming his team by interrogating managers in Sony's Tape Recorder and Headphone divisions about their people. He wanted to know how well they had responded to working with another division, and he judged how well they might interact with one another.

After he had formed the team, Ohsone stood back and did his best to protect the team from Morita's demands. One of his most important decisions was the selection of production engineer Kenji Sano as the man to implement the Walkman II scale-up.

Sano's job was overwhelming. Pointing to his silvery hair, he said, "Before Walkman II, my hair was black!"

The touch of humor in Kenji Sano is quiet but constant, punctuated by the irrepressible twinkle in his eye. More than anything else, the prolonged warmth of his handshake—two hands enveloping one hand of his interviewer—expresses a fellowship that must have made it easier for him to push a design crew of harried engineers, mechanics, assembly trainees, and a host of outside suppliers through the ordeal of setting up in months a production system that reasonably should have taken years.

Sano was the person with hands-on responsibility for the whole production project. There were times when the place he most wanted his hands was on the throat of Mitsuro Ida. The challenge of completely restructuring the mechanics and electronics of Walkman II to fit into a space little more than half the size of Walkman I required cunning solutions, many coming from the fertile brain of Ida.

"The problem with Mr. Ida is that his ideas are so creative," said Sano. "He would give me designs that nobody knows how to manufacture, and they are so clever that nobody—including Mr. Ida—knows how to modify them. This was one of the worst years of my life."

Besides dealing with internal issues, Sano coped with suppliers of parts, some of them members of Sony's "family" of companies, some outside that family, none of whom, at the beginning of 1980, could turn out parts at a rate of almost a quarter of a million a month.

At the breaking point, Kozo Ohsone would appear, as though from nowhere, as though he had felt the building frustration in the Walkman team. He would supply the team members with bottles of *sake* and whiskey and dispatch them to the beach for a few days. For two days, they would relax; on the third day, they would begin to feel uneasy about taking time off in the middle of the crisis. On the fourth day, Ohsone would show up and say, "So, got any ideas how we can do this?"

Kozo Ohsone's ploys were never subtle, but they were always welcome. Besides providing rest and recreation, Ohsone kept the chemistry of the Walkman team under control. It bubbled away at a furious rate, under tremendous pressure, but never popped.

By November 1980 Bonson's production line was ready to run. With a blend of manual and automatic assembly, Walkman II went into production. By February 1981 inventory of Walkman II was large enough for Sony to begin selling the new product. Sano's fully automated assembly line was in operation that month. Production levels reached 200,000 per month by spring of 1981 and 250,000 in November 1981. Sano had earned the right to plant the flag atop his Everest.

Sano's attainment is acknowledged throughout the Sony organization. He receives a measure of special respect from those aware of his two-year ordeal. Yet his role has been lost in the abbreviated Walkman story that has circulated among the journals of the business press. Absent also are such key players as designer Mitsuro Ida and Kiyomasa Iwasaki and production chief Ohsone. "Product Manager" Morita is the simplified hero of these popular stories. However, this emphasis on Morita's idiosyncratic leadership is not entirely misplaced, because it was his personal interest that gave Walkman a special glow within Sony's organization. The Sony Corporation is, after all, a busy place where people tend to concentrate on well-defined assignments. They are reluctant to divert their attention toward notions that are less concrete than the task at hand. They need a good reason to break outside the familiar circle of a few intimate coworkers.

Morita's involvement in Walkman, from the very beginning, made it possible and psychologically acceptable for engineers from two separate divisions to communicate and invent together.

In this light, it is clear that the Walkman breakthrough at Sony was attained substantially through the intervention of Akio Morita. It also seems likely that normal organizational inertia might prevent any similar breakthrough unless Morita intervenes again.

But that may not be so. It wasn't Morita, after all, who transformed the Pressman into Walkman I. It wasn't Morita who made

the critical link between the cassette player and lightweight headphones. Nor was it Morita's negotiating magic that compelled the
Tape Recorder Division to risk a major financial loss on an unproven device they had disliked from the beginning. Nor did Morita
personally create the extraordinary Walkman team or the awesome
production capacity that emerged at Bonson Electric. In fact, when
the need arose within Sony for people to overcome the company's
customary structure and complete an extraordinary project, a
network of special people emerged: Ida, the inventor; Kuroki, the
negotiator; Ohsone, the psychologist; Sano, the builder. All of the
key people were long-established Sony people. None seemed troubled by the unstructured style of the Walkman project; each
adapted quickly, naturally, to the flying-squad approach to product
development. Nor were Kuroki, Ohsone, or Sano visibly awed by
Chairman Morita.

From the heart of a company which to the world appears as a
tightly ordered series of cubicles where drones meekly labor away
for the common good under a charismatic leader, a host of unique
performances suddenly burst forth and guided Sony to an exceptional success. Akio Morita, that charismatic leader, injected the
initial energy that the Walkman project needed, but the sudden
turns and spot decisions that followed in unerring succession were
too quick and intuitive to await the approval of the chairman. The
most exceptional feature, among all the exceptions that forged the
Walkman breakthrough at Sony, was its speed. While it is safe to
say that the majority of significant, lasting commercial breakthroughs are years in the making, Sony's breakthrough ran its full
course—from concept to market fireworks—in less than a year.

This is true partly because of Walkman's technical heritage.
Sony had all the necessary technology present and warmed up
when the Walkman opportunity emerged. It helped that Walkman
was a relatively simple product concept. But these driving forces
cannot explain the clockwork coordination within the Sony organism that transformed Chairman Ibuka's lucky discovery into the
headphone culture in less than a year.

Somehow, exactly when the need arose, the special skills,
talent, and ingenuity needed for the project emerged from within
Sony. A similar phenomenon occurred, though much more slowly,
in the emergence of the Post-it breakthrough at 3M. There, also, a
series of seemingly ordinary people emerged from the small circle
of colleagues and contributed in escalating sequence to an extraor-

dinary product. This process happened faster at Sony for a very important reason. At 3M, in a sprawling network of divisions, the members of the Post-it group had to hunt each other out; they formed their team by volunteer enlistment. At Sony, the right people for the Walkman team got drafted. Project leaders Yasuo Kuroki, Kozo Ohsone, and Takichi Tezuka had an intimate knowledge of the personal qualities of a vast number of people in several departments who might be able to contribute to Walkman.

In the Japanese industrial ideal of lifetime employment, a great deal of experimentation goes on. Employees are moved around, sometimes arbitrarily, among a number of jobs and departments. That is why a law school graduate like Katsuya Kakagawa found himself on the Walkman marketing team. The purpose of this shuffling is to allow managers to discover an individual worker's range of talents and at best to fit him into the spot in the company where he eventually will remain and contribute the most of his potential. When this system of shifting people is abused or misused, it turns the worker into chattel, demeaned and down-sized. It provides no benefit to the company and gives play to the worst impulses of manipulative managers. But in the hands of good managers it identifies the special talents of the people who work for them. Kuroki and Ohsone at Sony—and Geoff Nicholson at 3M— perceive their pool of stable "lifetime" workers as a wealth of diversity and creativity. They don't worry about finding special creative types, because they have learned the special qualities within the people whom they see and supervise every day. When a rare opportunity emerged with Walkman, Kozo Ohsone knew how and where to find the rare individuals to respond to the unusual challenge.

When Walkman became his responsibility, Ohsone had a free hand. He knew that the most intensive task he faced was the selection of his working group. It was a moment calling upon all of his experience and judgment. If he chose the right people within Sony, their talent and personal character would carry the effort forward. Sony is, after all, a delicately (and not accidentally) balanced organization. Within a year it could muster true teamwork to turn a raw concept into a popular necessity in the consumer society. It is especially remarkable that this happened without a clearly discernible hero—one person who kicked the organization off its tracks in order to make it move and then kept pushing, with unreasonable passion, all the way through the process. Rather than heroes, there was a series of quiet leaders who passed the baton gracefully because they understood each other's needs and style as clearly as they understood the expectations of the chairman.

Peter Drucker once said that every major entrepreneurial breakthrough requires the presence of a "monomaniac with a mission," one person who must battle fanatically to drive his idea through the brick-and-mortar resistance of the layers of corporate organization. But this wasn't so with Walkman. The standard story identifies Morita as that apparent maniacal force, but that emerges as a piece of melodrama manufactured in retrospect. Not coincidentally, the story of Post-it at 3M was also dramatized afterward for outside consumption. One lesson that emerges from both Sony and 3M is that an organization can do new things without the outward appearance of creative ferment. To do so, it must, with genuine compassion, provide its employees with longevity, security, and an appreciation for their individual talents. Somehow it must recognize and cherish its vital role players.

There weren't any monomaniacs at Sony—not even Akio Morita. Although he recognized the team's need for his involvement, Morita also understood how important it was that the company's highest officer stand slightly removed from the action—to do his other work and to shield from a possible failure the corporate prestige that had become so closely attached to Morita himself. What Sony had—far more important than the watchfulness of Morita—was *intimacy*. Weaving down through the structure of the company, in and through and among those permeable departments and divisions, was an unbroken fabric of people who trusted one another. They knew one another intimately and humanly, so that when a great opportunity emerged and cried out for rare individuals, they were easy to find. They had been there all along. They were willing to help—and perfectly willing to let Akio Morita finish the climb and stand on the mountaintop.

7 "Problems! We've Got to Have Problems!"

The scene at the Rochester, Minnesota, airport one warm day in 1971 might have been staged by film director Mel Brooks as part of a sequel to *Young Frankenstein*. At the routine security checkpoint, guards halted a man carrying a suspicious-looking container. When the container had passed through the security X-ray machine, the unmistakable contours of a human skull had been visible on the display screen.

When the security staff opened the container, they saw that this really *was* someone's head. It was not a skull, nor was it a preserved head, redolent of formalin and discolored by years of immersion in a chemical bath. This head was recently severed. The removal of the head from the container, in front of a growing crowd of curious passengers, was a memorable event in Rochester aviation history. Women blanched. Children gaped.

For the discoverers of this grisly luggage, this was the first time they had ever apprehended anyone trying to transport a detached head across state lines. But what to do with him? The man said he was on his way to London. He said he wanted the head for "scanning." What did he mean by that? They let him make an international phone call, to somebody in England named Hounsfield.

"Godfrey," the man said, "I'm at the airport in Rochester. The head went through the X-ray machine!"

The negotiations that followed were touchy. The man with the head, with some help from the voice of Mr. Hounsfield in England (it was a very dignified-sounding voice), explained that the head had been obtained legitimately at the Mayo Clinic in Rochester. A call to the Mayo confirmed this. Clinic spokesmen assured the people at the airport that the head's original owner was finished with it. The head was intended for medical research, to be subjected to a new type of X ray at the laboratories of EMI, Ltd., in Hayes, Middlesex, England. Airport officials eventually released *both* prisoners, with a stern warning that they would not again permit this sort of thing unless someone first called ahead to warn them.

Godfrey Hounsfield was the spirit behind this scene. Hounsfield, unlike Frankenstein, was not a Hollywood-style mad scientist, even though many in his parent company and in the medical community—and even a few people at the Rochester airport—certainly regarded him for a long time as pretty odd.

Hounsfield is the inventor who in 1972 presented to a skeptical medical community, and then to the world at large, the CT scanner (also often referred to as the CAT scanner), a device intricate in conception and execution but compellingly simple in its results. Hounsfield's computerized tomographic (CT) scanning technology has allowed radiologists to take pictures inside the human body of much greater clarity than is possible through traditional X-ray photography. Hounsfield thought of a way to look inside people to see tissues that are too soft for an X ray to show, and to overcome the obscuring effect of dense materials—like bone—that in conventional X-ray pictures mask system tissues lying behind them. Hounsfield's concept meant that exploratory surgery into people's brains and bodies often could be replaced by a swift, painless, and safe computerized probe. Through Hounsfield's efforts in the Central Research Laboratories of EMI, between 1968 and 1975, the science of "medical imaging" moved permanently from the limited technology of photographic film to the boundless possibilities of computer science.

In light of the fact that Hounsfield did indeed launch a revolution in radiology, surgery, and computer technology, one would expect that vast resources and legions of well-trained technicians were the arsenal of his breakthrough. But Hounsfield invented the CT scanner with a grant of less than $15,000 from the British

Department of Health and Social Security (DHSS). His staff was composed of two research assistants who were still completing their training. He built a prototype within that budget, substantially by himself, including computer software no one previously had imagined. The prototype was based on a lathe bed of the sort more often used for putting threads on the ends of gas pipes and used a gear borrowed from a German-made overhead crane. That prototype, still on display at EMI's Central Research Laboratories in Hayes, has an appearance that most kindly might be referred to as rustic. It was the simplest possible device created to perform the most sophisticated possible function. And for many reasons, the primitive approach (including the carrying through Customs of sample human heads) was the only way it could have been done. Hounsfield, after all, had an idea that was unworthy of any sort of financial investment because, by a wide consensus, it was regarded as impossible.

Hounsfield himself came across the idea of computerized tomography by pure chance. He was an electrical engineer who had moved up from earlier occupations as cinema operator, radio repairman, and builders' draftsman. He had been torn from that mundane life by World War II, in which he became a skilled radar technician in the Royal Air Force (RAF). He finished his formal education shortly after the war, under the British equivalent of the GI Bill. EMI (originally Electric and Musical Industries, Ltd.) had been his only postgraduate employer. EMI, a pioneer in entertainment technologies, including television, high-fidelity phonographs, and records, was by the 1960s mostly a manufacturer of records, equipment to play records, and television and radio sets. However, the company also maintained an active interest in new electronic technologies, and it was in this area where Hounsfield exercised his creativity. Having transferred from designing computers to the EMI Research Laboratories, he proved himself a brilliant innovator in the newborn specialty of computer memory storage, discovering ways to keep huge amounts of information on terribly small bits of magnetized nickel iron for immediate access by a computer.

But EMI decided not to support development of this breakthrough by Hounsfield. The company's early interest in computers diminished when management saw the intense competition that had emerged very quickly. EMI didn't want to take on IBM and a crowd of IBM imitators. This frustrated Hounsfield, but it served him well in the long run. His intellectual energy at least had gained recognition in EMI Central Research Laboratories (CRL). CRL director Dr. Leonard Broadway realized that Hounsfield needed no prompting or pressure to tackle new problems and explore new areas of development. Hounsfield was capable of stirring up his own research projects and was practical enough to make them adaptable to commercial development by EMI. Dr. Broadway offered Hounsfield condolences for the death of the memory storage idea and told him to cast about for another new idea.

"I was told to go away and see what I could think of to do," said Hounsfield. "So I was stuck in a corner, thinking of all the various ideas I'd thought of in the past. There were about four or five things I'd been thinking of, and CT was one of them. . . . I was talking to somebody . . . about computing. . . . We made the observation that if you were to take readings which could detect the presence of material from all angles through a box, in three dimensions, then you would have enough information, without opening the box, to tell what was inside."

The field of Hounsfield's contemplation is called pattern recognition, a highly theoretical science at that time. People with advanced degrees in math and engineering thought of ways for computers to recognize and identify images as swiftly and efficiently as the human eye and brain and then perform work in response to that recognition. (The simplest form of pattern recognition is the recognition and digital translation by machines of characters like the alphabet.)

For some reason, Hounsfield's mind hopped into another universe. He envisioned a sort of mathematical puzzle so vast in its complexity that it was beyond the scope of human persistence to solve it. He kept thinking of that unknown object inside the box. How could you identify the object without opening the box? he wondered. If the object were reduced to "picture points" (the tiny dots that compose the elements of a photograph), then all the picture points could be assigned a mathematical value. Each view through the box could be regarded as the result of a mathematical equation. If you could collect all the individual equations outside the box and teach a computer how to put them back together just as they had been arranged inside the box, you could display the reconstructed object on a computer screen and see what's inside.

The idea was pure science fiction. Hounsfield was proposing a real-life application of the phenomenon called "beaming" in the popular television series "Star Trek." In the television series, a person stood under a "transporter beam," which reduced all the matter in his body to a stream of *molecules,* directed the stream at a distant point, and then reassembled the molecules at the person's desired destination, presumably losing no parts in transit. In essence, Hounsfield's notion was to *take a picture of each molecule,* "transport" those pictures on an X ray into a computer memory, then have the computer reassemble all the little pictures on a monitor screen in exactly their original order.

Hounsfield doesn't remember when he stopped thinking about boxes and started thinking about human bodies. But suddenly his thoughts had intersected on two hitherto unrelated planes, associating his knowledge of computerized pattern recognition and that of medical radiology. Hounsfield didn't even consider as yet the immense task of assembling and reassembling all the picture points in the human body in three dimensions. What occurred to him was that he could make pictures of "slices" of the human body. Instead of spraying the body with a blast of X rays as in conventional radiography and then catching those rays on the other side of the body on a photo plate, thought Hounsfield, you needed to penetrate a specific point on the body with a slender shaft of radiation. What you would capture on the other side would be a quantity of X rays, the intensity of which would give information about the tissue in the plane that the shaft had passed through inside the body. This could be accurately recorded. Then you could send through another slender shaft and record information about another part of the same plane. Eventually, by repeatedly irradiating this plane, or slice, through the body, you would have sufficient information about all points in the slice to reassemble all the information and create an image of that slice of human tissue, the object in the box.

It was a wonderful theory, the physicists told him. But he would need a mechanism that would uniformly obtain all those pieces of information, and capture them quickly. Live humans move and breathe; their hearts beat and their fluids flow—and all these things tend to make computer photos blur just the way regular photos blur when people move. Moreover, Hounsfield would need a medium to collect and reproduce all the thousands and thousands of mathematical photo points. And besides that, he would need some sort of algorithm—a problem-solving software code—to unscramble all the little narrow snapshots.

Hounsfield was undaunted by the formidable practical implications of his concept. As soon as the idea occurred to him, it made such vivid sense to him that he knew it would work. However, he couldn't be certain of the value of his idea to medical science—he admits cheerily that he knew nothing about medicine. But he had a practical understanding of radiology, and he was intimate with the ability of a computer to perform the vast, complicated, and tedious task of information storage, assembly, and reassembly. In an interview in 1979 with Dr. Charles Susskind of the University of California, a physician who has exhaustively researched the history of computed tomography, Hounsfield revealed that his confidence, even as he began to devise his CT scanner, was unassailable. "It became rather obvious," said Hounsfield, "that X rays were the thing. . . . Once I realized that my method was considerably more efficient, I hoped to see things that conventional X rays could not possibly see. I must win in the end, was my general feeling."[1]

While Hounsfield was thus making these random associations, he had no idea whether medicine would want or need the device whose contours had already formed in his mind. He only thought doctors might like to have it.

Almost a decade earlier, the need for some sort of tomographic X-ray machine was urgently expressed by Dr. William H. Olden-dorf, a neurologist and psychiatrist at the University of California and one of the first real pioneers to attempt building one. Oldendorf built a model of a tomographic scanner in 1961 and patented it in 1963. He made his models without a knowledge of computers— there were then no computers capable of handling the amount of data that would be generated by a scan.

Oldendorf's model was a truly heroic effort, and he undertook it because of his sense of the profound need in radiology to progress beyond the limited images available in standard X rays. In 1961, after constructing his model, he declared with greater emotion than is customary at a symposium of the Institute of Radio Engineers Transactions on Biomedical Electronics, "As a practicing clinical neurologist I am daily confronted with the necessity of performing these traumatic tests [angiography and ventriculography] because the information obtained is so vital to intelligent case management. These tests were both introduced into clinical medicine between thirty and forty years ago, and neither has changed basically since

1. Charles Susskind, "The History of Computed Tomography," in *History of Technology*, A. R. Hall and N. Smith, editors; London: Mansell Publishing, 1984; page 49.

then. Each time I perform one of these primitive procedures, I wonder why no more pressing need is felt by the clinical neurological world to seek some technique that would yield direct information about brain structure without traumatizing it."[2]

Hounsfield lay the groundwork for his computerized tomographic scanner in 1968 without any knowledge of Oldendorf's work and submitted the idea to his superiors at EMI. They agreed to obtain a patent for "a method and apparatus for examination of a body by radiation such as gamma radiation." Beyond that, EMI was hesitant to attempt any development of Hounsfield's idea. They would be trying to compete with companies in the X-ray industry that had laboratory technology, manufacturing facilities, and vital access to doctors and hospitals.

Dr. Leonard Broadway was Hounsfield's boss for only the first two years of the CT project, but he tilled the soil and planted Hounsfield's seed.

Broadway had a difficult balancing act. He was expected to encourage research that would provide EMI with marketable products in new markets, but he believed that real freedom of inquiry requires researchers to ignore commercial considerations at the outset and just simply explore ideas that provoke their curiosity. Of all his explorers, Hounsfield was Broadway's best, and he indulged Hounsfield as much as he could without incurring the displeasure of EMI's results-oriented management.

Broadway had enough background in the field of radiography to know that Hounsfield's idea had merit—as well as faced a mountain of technological problems. Broadway also knew that Hounsfield, given time and a little money, could weave his dogged, ingenious way through any number of technical problems—Hounsfield is only happy when he has something to solve. "He worked on these problems with enormous dedication, frequently until midnight," Broadway told Charles Susskind. "Eventually I found that he was overdoing things and I instructed him to take a week's holiday. This he refused to do, but I said I would instruct the commissionaire to refuse him admission to the laboratories for a week."[3]

2. W. H. Oldendorf, "Isolated Flying Spot Detection of Radiodensity Discontinuities: Displaying the Internal Structural Pattern of a Complex Object," *Institute of Radio Engineers Transactions on Biomedical Electronics,* Vol. 8, pages 68–72, 1961.

3. Susskind, page 49.

Broadway solved Hounsfield's initial money problem by acquiring an innovative research grant from a fund established by Sir John Read, EMI's chief executive officer. He also provided Hounsfield with two key pieces of technology, a computer terminal for processing equations and a Pantak industrial radiography machine for generating "signals."

Equipment purchases and a few experiments used up the Read grant very quickly, and EMI told Broadway either to prove that Hounsfield could make a machine that does something, a machine EMI could *sell,* or else Hounsfield would have to go on to something else. Internally, the CT scanner project was dead.

Hounsfield's biggest dilemma, after a theory and a technology had been worked out in his mind, was finding an audience that could even partly grasp what he was talking about and also see that it served some necessary purpose. Doctors, who needed this technology, didn't understand it. Physicists, who could understand it, didn't need it.

Physicists were curious when he suggested the possibilities to them, but they weren't interested in practical application for most theories, much less one that proposed to make photographic slices of the human brain! The idea of moving another quantum leap forward from X-ray technology into computerized tomography was unnerving to some and appalling to many in the British medical establishment. Hounsfield recalled, "A colleague and I visited several London hospitals armed with our first laboratory test pictures, to assess likely sales possibilities. Some were mildly interested, but some of the teaching radiological hospitals were very conservative. Possibly because they were wedded to conventional X-ray technologies, some in the medical profession didn't see any advantages in the system, although generally physicists were more imaginative in their reaction. Despite the poor reaction, I maintained that we could sell at least twenty-five machines— because of the greater sensitivity it offered."

Dr. John Alfred Powell, the executive who eventually brought the CT scanner to market, described one not uncommon reaction to his efforts to promote the CT scanner among doctors in Great Britain. "I had a [medical] professor from Birmingham . . . who rang me up and said, 'What's all this computer nonsense you're trying to bring into medicine? I've got no confidence at all in computers and I want nothing whatsoever to do with them! You can't do this!' Well, he was seventy-four years old, retired, and he consulted on technology to several hospitals."

In essence, the resistance to Hounsfield's improbable notion was so pervasive and so deeply felt in some quarters that only a "shoestring and sealing wax" effort, as Hounsfield termed it, could have brought about the very first CT scanner.

The only possible outside source for the continuation of Hounsfield's concept, after EMI's seed money had been used up, was the British Department of Health and Social Security (DHSS), an organization that contained both physicians and physicists. The symbiosis that grew up after Dr. Broadway introduced Godfrey Hounsfield to DHSS was a remarkable union. Dr. James Ambrose, the clinical radiologist at Atkinson Morley's Hospital, who later teamed with Hounsfield to make the first CT scans of the human brain, recalled his astonishment that the DHSS was so generously subsidizing research at a wealthy private corporation such as EMI. Ambrose, like many British doctors, had waged a lifelong war to extract money by the shilling and by the penny from the tightfisted DHSS.

"I was astounded when I heard they were paying EMI fifteen hundred pounds a month to defray the costs of these experiments," said Ambrose. "This was outrageous."

The first step in this outrageous relationship was for Hounsfield to talk to Cliff Gregory, a DHSS official who "kept the gate" on agency spending for experimental medicine. Hounsfield was poorly equipped to "sell" his idea to the skeptical Gregory. He was not a salesman by training or temperament, nor was he impressively pompous and professorial. "To meet him and talk to him, you'd never classify him as a brilliant academic. He'd be the first person to admit it," explained Powell, who ultimately directed the CT project. "He's extremely humble. But he has that certain genius touch about him, a sort of vision, to see problems before they arise. One of the real characteristics of many innovators is that they are loners and have great difficulty communicating with their fellows. It was frequently very difficult to extract all the information from a Godfrey and get it down on paper so that one could communicate effectively with others he needed to communicate with."

However, Hounsfield could communicate with—and enthuse—those with whom he worked closely. The CT project staff eventually grew into a sizable team.

*   *   *

Sometimes apparently detached from the world outside his laboratory, Godfrey Hounsfield is a person who has found within himself an intellectual galaxy that provides an endless program of introspective stargazing. He has little interest in or dependence on the philistine clamor outside his mind.

In November 1972, Dr. James Ambrose of Atkinson Morley's presented a paper on clinical experience with the first head scanner to a rapturous gathering of the Radiological Society of North America (RSNA). The demonstration of the scanner's operation at the exhibition associated with the convention provided EMI with a breakthrough into the huge and wealthy American medical market. The moment was historic for EMI and for the future of medical computing. But for Hounsfield, the necessity of going to Chicago, of all places, was a profound annoyance. Hounsfield intensely dislikes going anywhere that does not keep Greenwich mean time. Powell recalled, "He wouldn't change the time on his watch, especially on a trip of short duration. He wouldn't change his habits. In Chicago, he was seven hours ahead of everyone else."

A few years later, after he had become a Nobel laureate for his CT invention, Hounsfield was in demand as a sort of British monument. He received numerous invitations to hobnob with VIPs at black-tie affairs. He never adjusted to the limelight and "stardom" that his achievement thrust on him, seeming embarrassed by the acclaim.

To characterize Hounsfield as an absent-minded professor is far too simple, however. When he made his presentation to Gregory at DHSS in 1969, he already had formed a theoretical image of his CT concept that was intellectually unassailable. At every turn, from Gregory onward, through the network of medical specialists and physicists assembled by DHSS, Hounsfield had a wealth of precise, articulate responses to every challenge, every question. "Godfrey would look upon a problem from a practical point of view of how to solve it, rather than sitting down with pen and paper and going through a whole series of mathematical processes," said Powell. "That's not to say he didn't know a lot of math. He did. . . . He had what most people don't have, an intuitive, practical mind—which he would apply to problem-solving."

Dr. Frank Doyle, a bone radiology specialist at Hammersmith Hospital in London, was appointed by DHSS to review the Hounsfield concept before the department committed itself to support it. Doyle interrogated Hounsfield, looking for flaws in his theory. He discovered a scientist whose intellect and intuition worked in harmony. Hounsfield seemed to have a sixth sense that told him the difference between advanced conceptualization and seat-of-the-pants fix-ups.

"Godfrey Hounsfield was a knight's move ahead of me at every turn," Doyle told Susskind. "Any objection I raised he had already thought about and had satisfied himself by calculations that it was not a serious problem. To cut a long story short, I was able to report that I could not fault any of Godfrey Hounsfield's ideas and could find no flaw in anything he said. His notion of computerized tomography was very much worth backing."[4]

Each of the DHSS examiners in turn found Hounsfield's idea almost impossible to understand and equally impossible to dismiss. Ambrose said, "Gregory, you know, is the principal physicist at DHSS, a very intelligent chap. But what Hounsfield brought to DHSS was so revolutionary at this stage that I don't think anybody understood what he was talking about. Gregory sent Hounsfield along to [radiologist] Dr. Evan Lennon, and Lennon rang me up and said, 'I don't know what he's talking about. He's either a crackpot or a genius. Will you see him and listen to what he has to say?' "

In the course of his meetings with DHSS and a number of doctors, Hounsfield instilled in everyone a feeling that he *could* make an image much better than an X ray. When Gregory suggested that Hounsfield should first concentrate on the brain, Hounsfield seized on the idea eagerly. The head could be held steady for an indefinite period, and that solved the problem of the extended time exposure needed for the CT scanner series of pictures.

"Hounsfield used to say to me, 'Problems! We've got to have problems! We thrive on problems!' " recalled Ambrose. Perhaps the quality in Hounsfield that inspired first the support of Broadway and then the unlikely backing of DHSS was this dauntless eagerness to tackle tribulation. Even with a destination clearly in view, Hounsfield would not be happy unless he got to travel every inch of every detour along the route.

However, as focused as Hounsfield was when solving technical problems, he really was unaware of the problems that EMI's organization posed for the continuation of his CT research. While

4. Susskind, page 55.

Broadway, his first savior, was still just opening the door for DHSS to underwrite the construction of the first CT machine, Hounsfield actually went ahead with construction—before he got any money from DHSS.

For Hounsfield the theoretical conception of computerized tomography was indivisible from his mechanical vision of how to *make it work*. As he was building a hypothesis on one side of his brain, he was building a gadget on the other side of his brain. But his vision was not of some glistening steel-and-chrome-and-silicon marvel, because he couldn't afford steel, chrome, or silicon. He was limited to available resources, and when he started, those available resources—not counting his ingenuity and his persistence—added up to zero.

Gathering together the basic ingredients of Godfrey Hounsfield's first CT scanning machine had the aspect of a successful expedition to a flea market. As noted, the foundation of Hounsfield's machine was an industrial lathe bed. He removed most of its moving parts. In the center of the lathe bed, he mounted a rotating vise, a ten-inch plastic box. He filled the box with water and placed in the water a number of metal fragments and other junk. On one side of the plastic box he positioned a source of radiation, a sort of ray gun that shot mildly radioactive gamma rays from an isotope called americium. On the other side of the box he positioned a device to "catch" the radioactive rays. The catching device was a simple scintillation counter. Hounsfield then harnessed the simple mechanics of the lathe to move the isotope and scintillation counter backward and forward past the plastic box in tiny steps. The box containing the objects being scanned was rotated one degree each time the radioactive source passed the box. As the scanner moved, one click at a time, the slender shafts of radiation were beamed through the box, giving readings at a succession of different angles.

Every time a gamma ray was released, it was altered by the contents of the box—through which it passed—and that alteration became the reading on the scintillation counter. The counter was hooked into a computer. The computer registered the radiation level that emerged in each "exposure" from the isotope. The gamma radiation was constant, always the same *before* it passed through the plastic box. By reading the radiation level from the scintillation counter, the computer recorded the *change* in radiation. All the readings were stored until there were enough to produce a picture; only then could the computer calculate all the values of the picture matrix and form them into a whole picture. The hoped-for result was a photograph of what the gamma rays had encountered in the box on their way from the isotope to the scintillation counter.

To form the whole picture, Hounsfield's first machine had to make 28,800 "clicks," from which 24,000 picture points could be calculated. The gamma ray was a very weak radiation source, and the machine ran slowly, which meant that each of those 28,800 exposures lasted several seconds. Hounsfield's first scans—from the moment he turned on the juice until the last reading was punched onto a paper tape in digital computer language—took *nine days* each. By comparison, the current generation of scanners can complete more than 115,000 picture points in less than a minute.

That product of Hounsfield's ingenuity possessed a technical eclecticism that bordered on chaos. Somehow Hounsfield had heaped together a system of memory storage and electronic computation (so new that most experts in computers were still catching up to it) with a rotating lathe bed, a vacuum cleaner motor, a box full of assorted objects, and a radioactive squirt gun. It was a laughable contraption which no sensible person would have expected to work. Hounsfield, who had some pretensions to sensibleness himself, kept his own hopes in check.

"It pays to be cautious. From a psychological point of view, you've got to be all the time not expecting success," Hounsfield said. "Then when it doesn't come, you don't get all depressed and in the dumps."

Once the nine days of scanning were over, another two and a half hours passed while the readings, on paper tape, were processed by the computer. Finally the computer "assembled" the readings, as a picture on a monitor screen. A Polaroid photograph of the screen image became a permanent CT scan record. It showed a visual slice of what was inside the box, exactly as Hounsfield had imagined it would. Variations in the density of the contents were shown as varying shades of white, black, and gray. It became clear very early in the experiments that it was possible to see varying densities of shading in objects that would not have been visible in normal X-ray photographs.

If Hounsfield's gamma ray results could be reproduced with X rays, it would be possible for the first time not just to see details of soft tissue inside the brain, but to highlight that tissue with adjustments in exposure.

From that point, as Doyle noted, Hounsfield stayed always "a knight's move ahead." The problems that emerged throughout 1970 had nothing to do with Hounsfield's concept. They were practical. In the plastic box of that early machine, for example, Hounsfield began to scan pig abdomens, and these would decompose over the nine-day period. "Things rather deteriorated. . . . and that changed the picture, of course," said Hounsfield. "But I was satisfied that I hadn't made a mistake."

Throughout 1970 Hounsfield reported exciting results to DHSS and EMI, and he enthusiastically spent the money allocated (it was being carefully controlled and monitored) making his prototype machine better, switching from gamma to X-ray radiation. When he graduated to heads of cattle that had been acquired in a nearby slaughterhouse, Hounsfield was clearly worried. Images of tissue in these samples were almost indistinguishable. There was something wrong. As it turned out, CT scanners learned to insist on kosher cattle. The first sample cattle, obtained from a non-kosher abattoir, had been killed by electric jolts or bullets to the head, and their brains had been scrambled—literally. Once kosher cattle, killed with a knife, were substituted, the brain scans came through vividly.

After Hounsfield's marvelous machine had seen through an array of inanimate objects and various animal brains (both pickled and fresh), and had even reproduced in stunning detail a preserved slice of human brain, the only question that remained was whether it would succeed on a living person.

The location for the test was Atkinson Morley's Hospital in Wimbledon, where Dr. James Ambrose practiced neuroradiology out of a crowded, dimly lit office adjoining a cramped and even more dimly lit examination room, most of which was occupied by a CT scanner. (Ambrose, like Hounsfield, lives in total unconcern about the impression he makes on mankind in general.) An almost instinctive kinship developed between Ambrose and Hounsfield. The construction of an improved CT prototype at Atkinson Morley's gave each the daily opportunities to refine both the engineering and the medical integrity of the machine. In working together, each became a student of the other's specialty. Oblivious and sometimes hostile to the concerns of the world around them, they meshed in focused harmony on their singular invention.

At around this time, Dr. Broadway retired and was succeeded by William Ingham, who had joined EMI as a research engineer in 1946 and after a broad-based career in EMI Electronics that culminated in a position as its chief scientist, transferred to the Central Research Laboratories as assistant director in 1970, taking up the appointment of director in January 1971. He was an enthusiastic supporter of Hounsfield's work and played a crucial role in helping it through the next phases of its evolution.

By the summer of 1971, DHSS was deeply committed to the CT scanner project. The original grant had long been used up, but both DHSS and EMI continued to provide money for the development of the prototype scanner. In 1971, virtually the entire DHSS research and development budget, about a quarter of a million pounds, had gone to Hounsfield and Ambrose. In order to keep the project going—even before the new prototype had been built and tested on a human subject—DHSS agreed to purchase the first five machines if EMI would make a commitment to build them.

If the machines failed, both participants would lose a bundle. EMI, which was then the recording company for a group called the Beatles, could cope with a setback of that magnitude, especially if the company held the line at building five machines by hand in Hounsfield's laboratory. DHSS officials like Gregory and Gordon Higson, who were accountable to politicians and taxpayers, faced far darker consequences if Hounsfield failed.

But Hounsfield was supremely confident. Finally, in the autumn of 1971, he and Ambrose had reduced the scanning time for a human brain to several minutes. They were ready for a patient.

The first CT scanner patient was a woman who had been diagnosed as having a brain tumor. "We hoped to use the image," said Ambrose, "to determine whether the tumor was solid, cystic, necrotic, well-defined or not." To be scanned, the woman had to lie on a flat couch. The circular scanning path of the machine surrounded her head, and her head was immobilized by a water bag through which the X rays could pass without obstruction. A year later, when EMI publicist Colin Woodley was asked to describe this process for the British Broadcasting Corporation's world radio service, it was suggested he compare it to "putting your head inside a washing machine."

Although that first scan took only a few minutes, the processing back at EMI's lab in Hayes consumed the rest of the day and lingered into the night. The transfer of information—from X rays to magnetic tape, then from Atkinson Morley's to Hayes, then from magnetic tape to computer to magnetic tape again, then to Atkinson Morley's tape deck and from that to an oscilloscope screen and finally to Polaroid film—was tedious. (Within a year, the advent of minicomputers dramatically reduced the steps and time required and also brought the information processing technology directly into the hospital beside the scanner.)

When Hounsfield finally returned to Atkinson Morley's with the pictures, for review by Ambrose and an eager group of surgeons, the reaction was explosive. "It was clear!" said Ambrose. "Her set of images told us there was a cystic tumor in the left frontal lobe. We couldn't have known that without going in [with surgery]. You'd have to guess at that. The surgeons were terribly excited!"

Ambrose and Hounsfield ". . . jump[ed] up and down like football players who had just scored a winning goal."

Hounsfield, for his part, was "rather pleased." But the problem-solver in him had already departed for a more worrisome destination. "My first reaction," Hounsfield confessed, "was that I was very worried, because I had this awful feeling—as everybody was jumping around for joy—that we just happened to be lucky with that particular patient."

Although Hounsfield worried then whether the machine ever would work again and immediately thereafter began to worry about the next, *better* CT scanner, actually very little of the basic design of the CT head scanner has been improved since that prototype was built at Atkinson Morley's.

Hounsfield had *imagined* the CT's concept as a whole before even picking up a screwdriver. He had later applied a student's openness to the medical contingencies and an engineer's practicality to the mechanical hitches when he encountered problems in the process of building. When it was built—in just fifteen months—Hounsfield's prototype left very little for him or any successor to fix up. When EMI began to manufacture CT scanners for hospitals throughout the world, they made almost exact copies of that screwed-together, glued-together first machine hunkering among the yellowed files and pasteboard cartons in the dungeon of Atkinson Morley's. The prototype was the paradigm. Hounsfield soon recognized that he couldn't go on to a better head machine, so he switched to a different part of the human subject, the body.

After that fall day in Wimbledon, scans kept getting better and better and it was clear that the five machines ordered by DHSS would do what they had been designed to do. Then Hounsfield expressed the question that lurked in minds at EMI, DHSS, and Atkinson Morley's: "When I got the first view and saw parts of the head you couldn't see in normal X rays, I knew that somebody would want this," he said. "But how many? And who?"

At this point in the history of the CT scanner, EMI might quickly have faded from the scene. That would not have been an uncommon experience for EMI. The company had a sorry record of failing to exploit its own technological breakthroughs. Isaac Shoenberg and Alan Dower Blumlein, two of the charter reseachers at the Central Research Laboratory (CRL) in Hayes, had developed a method for electronic television before World War II, which preceded and was technologically superior to any system in the world. But EMI failed to pursue that technology and profited little from the postwar television explosion. EMI researchers, Hounsfield leading them, built the first large all-transistor computer in 1955, the EMIDEC 1100. It was literally years ahead of any other computer company's technology. EMI built twenty-four large machines selling at £250,000 each. They were very successful, until faster transistors curtailed their design life. However, EMI hestitated to follow through to the next generation and so missed out on the computer explosion of the 1960s and 1970s.

John Powell is a Briton with American attitudes. A physicist trained at Oxford, with wartime experience in the RAF, Powell came to EMI under the powerful wing of CEO Sir John Read. By 1971 Powell had been imprinted with an American style of aggressive management after several years as the director of Northern European Operations for Texas Instruments during a fourteen-year career with them. Powell's mandate at EMI was ambiguous, but it was clear to the people who worked for him that Read had given him authority to make waves. He arrived in Hayes as group technical director for EMI's kaleidoscopic electronics practice and found a wealth of ingenuity outside the mainstream of defense electronics activity that was not really getting anywhere.

"One of my first assignments was to carry out an audit of all the technical resources at EMI and try to form some strategy of what the hell to do with all of it," recalled Powell. "There was a tremendous amount of technology and talent at EMI, but it never went anywhere. It was devoted to too many things and dedicated to too few."

Powell's sense of the problem was that managers at the very top, including men like Leonard Broadway, had indulged the inventors at EMI, especially the truly creative geniuses like Hounsfield, but had carried this indulgence only as far as the completion of a research goal within CRL. When the time came to get a broad corporate commitment to a new idea, the research director had no power to overrule senior managers loath to risk the company's profit margin on an unproven technology. Indeed, if Broadway had not found help outside the company, at DHSS, the CT scanner project would have been a memory by 1971, when Powell arrived at EMI.

"I . . . look back in EMI history and, really, it was strewn with a lot of good ideas that never really got to the marketplace, or from which EMI never really profited," said Powell. "EMI got these bright ideas and it got to a certain stage and then they stopped. They weren't properly supported or resourced, and no one seemed to have the drive, the enthusiasm to push forward."

Powell had something that Dr. Broadway did not have, the clear support of CEO John Read. He also had a philosophy of technology management. Texas Instruments' success in the semiconductor industry, especially early in their history under charismatic leader Pat Haggerty, was Powell's inspiration. In his audit of EMI technology, Powell hoped to find at least one area that was new to the world, one that he could build from obscurity and use as EMI's foundation for technological dominance. The CT scanner, which was then at Atkinson Morley's, was made to order for Powell's master plan, and Hounsfield was the sort of driven personality whom Powell had learned early in his career to admire. Hounsfield was the sort of person he could bet his shirt on.

"I felt that, if the CT scanner was successful, here was an opportunity of building up electronics at EMI," said Powell. "I don't care what it is, medical or what have you, it was an *electronics* business. I was looking for ideas to rejuvenate electronics at EMI."

One of Powell's first perceptions was that the CT market was much larger than anyone at EMI or DHSS imagined. As an American salesman at heart, he knew he could make the market even bigger. Without Powell's aggressive approach to the market, CT technology certainly would have gone over to the other companies much earlier. Because of the potential fortune available in CT technology, competing companies much bigger than EMI would have launched major research efforts and within several years would have had their own machines on the market. It would not matter to them that these might violate Hounsfield's 1968 patent, because by the time all the patent litigation had ended, the competition would have driven EMI from the market. The financial penalty eventually paid for patent infringements would be a pittance compared to the interim financial gain.

Powell was EMI's best and last hope with the scanner. But even Powell might have passed over the technology if he had not seen in it the fulfillment of a personal goal. Hounsfield was the problem-solver in the breakthrough formula; Powell was the legacy-builder. At Texas Instruments, Powell had lived in a beautiful empire. He had been happy there, and he left only because he saw an opportunity to build a new organization in his own image. Powell wanted to leave his mark.

"To be absolutely frank," said Powell, "our management at EMI was appalling. I had come from a company where management was a culture throughout the organization. Texas Instruments was a tremendous company. It still is. They very rarely went outside for management. They bred their own managers. It was a management culture. There was no such thing at EMI. Everybody [at EMI] seemed to be on the defensive, concerned with how to protect what they had, rather than to branch out and make something of what they had. What I tried to do was inculcate the same sort of culture I had seen at TI. I thought the only way to do this was with a new product, building up a management team with that sort of culture, and gradually turn the whole electronics group at EMI. The major evolutionary vehicle was going to be the CT scanner, from which hopefully one could build up a total culture which, in turn, could be spread out into other operations."

Powell succeeded and then failed. "To do what I wanted to do, you need disciples. I didn't have enough disciples."

The resistance of EMI's managers, who were not sympathetic to this Texanized go-getter, left him fending for himself when the CT scanner faced a crisis in the marketplace late in the 1970s. But regardless of the unhappy endings, Powell gave Hounsfield precisely what he needed at the very moment that the machine was emerging from its strikingly successful trial at Atkinson Morley's— someplace to go. That someplace had always been a mystery to the marketing executives in EMI electronics. To the benefit of both Hounsfield and EMI, Powell managed the two functions that EMI typically ruined—marketing and manufacturing.

As research director, Leonard Broadway had proposed a cautious approach to the market. In essence, he said that EMI should take this new technology, spread it among a number of original equipment manufacturers (OEM), and reap the benefits to come from license fees and rapid, widespread production by a number of companies. "I advised the granting of nonexclusive patent licenses to American and other overseas companies such as General Electric, Westinghouse, and Varian Associates," Broadway told Susskind, "since I felt that EMI would find it difficult to compete with the enormous technical and commercial resources available to these companies."[5]

It seemed a sensible course in light of EMI's weak manufacturing base. But this course failed to fulfill a key criterion for Powell: the establishment of EMI's name internationally as a leader in medical electronics. Without that infusion of prestige, Powell's own agenda of assembling disciples and rebuilding the EMI management structure would remain unrealized indefinitely. Powell convinced EMI's board that this was an opportunity too big to ignore. The bigness of EMI's competitors, he maintained, was as much a hindrance to their successful development of the CT scanner as it was an advantage.

"What do these big ones have that gives them this so-called virtue of being able to seize on these breakthroughs and make them commercially successful?" asked Powell. "I say nothing! There's nothing that suggests they will be successful at it. The probability is that the right small company will be far more successful at it. And really, it was the model of past experiences that I had with Texas Instruments that really persuaded me that EMI ought to be able to do this. . . . I sought, too, an opportunity to make electronics at EMI really something, rather than the nondescript activity it was before."

He counseled going it alone, and EMI did what they were

5. Susskind, page 61.

unaccustomed to doing: They took a chance. The financial commitment was an astounding (for EMI) £6 million, about $15 million.

Backed by Read and his own aggressiveness, Powell got his way and sparked grudges at EMI that would haunt him for more than a decade. But in the meantime, his go-it-alone gamble worked, although not as efficiently as he might have imagined it would. The most efficient aspect was the marketing of the CT scanner, which rested on Powell's belief that the British medical establishment's conservatism about new technology would be reversed in the United States, where doctors seize new gadgets with almost indiscriminate eagerness, always confident that private medical insurers will foot the bill.

To his credit, Powell understood America. Of the first five scanners ordered by DHSS, which were hand-built in Hounsfield's laboratory, Powell made certain two went to the United States, to two prestigious American hospitals, the Mayo Clinic in Rochester, Minnesota, and Massachusetts General Hospital in Boston.

"It was after the scanners had been installed at the Mayo Clinic and Massachusetts General that the message started creeping across the United States of what it was all about, and I went to New York," Powell recalled. "I had a friend who collected a whole bevy of consultants and radiologists. I remember sitting at a table and saying, 'How many of these do you think we could sell in the United States over the next couple of years?' The first guess was five every year. Then someone else said, 'Oh, much more than that!' And the numbers just went up and up and up. In the last guess, it exceeded a thousand per year."

The marketing campaign, neatly managed by the engaging Colin Woodley, head of corporate communications at EMI, began with a press conference at EMI in April 1972, immediately following a presentation by Ambrose and Hounsfield at the British Radiological Society. "They were flabbergasted," said Ambrose.

The combination of the two presentations created an international grapevine tremor among radiologists, so when London neurologist James Bull took Hounsfield to New York in the summer of 1972 for a series of neuroradiology lectures, participants were in a state of tense anticipation. They knew that Hounsfield had astonished the world, but few had seen either his results or the scanners' technical specifications, which Powell and Woodley did not release until August.

Hounsfield was overwhelmed in New York. "I more or less sold a dozen machines that day," recalled Hounsfield, his voice conveying disbelief at receiving such a hero's reception. "The first dozen, just for showing pictures! And then they began coming to the laboratory, all the way to Hayes, to see pictures. . . ."

The stage was set for the biggest radiological event of the year, the Radiological Society of North America's annual meeting in Chicago, in November 1972. The orders for EMI's scanner had begun to proliferate with the publication of the technical specifications. In Chicago, there was a year's worth of clinical experience at Atkinson Morley's to draw on and hundreds of pictures to show—and Woodley's advance publicity work had excited everyone's interest. Ambrose presented his paper on the CT scanner and brought the house down. They cheered; they stood; they applauded; they loved it!

Hospitals throughout North America, as well as in Japan and Germany and a handful of other nations, wanted head scanners as soon as possible. It wasn't easy to get one. EMI, after all, was going to build these things on their own. EMI took orders, demanded big down payments to finance work-in-progress, and told customers to wait six months—none of which deterred them. Meanwhile, back in Hayes, a makeshift assembly operation lurched into being across the street from the CRL. "To make the first five machines, the laboratories had had to become, in part, a factory. It was totally alien to their normal function. But it had to be done that way," said Woodley. "There was still fine-tuning going on. We were still fixing little things here and there."

Powell complains to this day about the shortage of British industrial engineers, which hindered the assembly setup. But the functions of the production plant evolved as a number of assemblers, each of them working on several machines—and with different bugs in each different machine—attained a highly erratic but steady output of products. As more orders came in, more assemblers joined the team, and together, EMI's CT scanner engineers learned by doing. In the midst of all this, Hounsfield ranged about like a fretful teacher at a kindergarten arts and crafts show.

"The plant had to be close to the Central Research Laboratories, so we could tap the brain of Godfrey Hounsfield," said Powell. "Hounsfield was absolutely essential. No one else understood it in its entirety, other than Godfrey. But this unavoidably had its drawbacks. Godfrey could get terribly frustrated when simple mistakes in the work were not immediately spotted and rectified. He'd come to me and complain. I'd say, 'Godfrey, that poor fellow! You've been working on this for several years and you know it inside out. But what about this poor guy? He's never seen one before.' "

Whatever the difficulties, Powell's go-it-alone approach was unquestionably an enormous short-term success. EMI, already rich from John, Paul, George, and Ringo, got richer on Godfrey. In five years the medical electronics group went from a net loss to producing 20 percent of EMI's total £75 million profit for 1977. By itself, from 1972 through 1977, EMI sold 704 CT scanners, at prices between $300,000 and $1 million each. By 1977 there were 1,130 scanners in the world, a proliferation that dumbfounded everyone. "There was a feeling around here that it could not lose money," said Woodley. "But it really would have been beyond peoples' wildest dreams at that time to forecast this sort of success."

Success lasted through much of the 1970s, then shifted dramatically into reverse for EMI and John Powell. In 1975, in Bermuda, in another of his remarkable performances before an audience of awestruck radiologists, Hounsfield showed the first pictures produced in a whole-body CT scan machine. This was the trigger for EMI to begin production of body scan machines, and Powell pushed for production facilities in the United States, where the marketplace for body scanners would be greater than the rest of the world combined.

But Powell's plans ran into a series of troubles, each magnifying the previous one. In five years EMI went from being a profitable manufacturer of CT scanning equipment to a company that was losing so much money on its now considerably broadened medical electronics activities that it had to call a halt, since the funds necessary to continue essential development could not be generated. By a conspiracy of coincidence, a worldwide recession in the recorded music business denied the possibility of succour from that usually buoyant sector of the company's operations.

Many of the problems with the production facility in the United States were beyond Powell's powers of control. A medical cost-containment drive by the administration of President Jimmy Carter used the costly body scanner as a symbolic whipping boy. Also, there were design problems that delayed the start of U.S. production more than a year. Meanwhile, in England, EMI was feeling twin pressures—losses from the drastic downturn in the music industry and the expensive creation of the American CT plant with no projections of when production could finally start. Now EMI was truly alone.

And within EMI, Powell was alone. His U.S. production plan had followed logically on his successful U.S. marketing focus. When he hired his former Texas Instruments mentor, Norman Provost, to supervise the American scale-up, he was sure he had found the ideal leader.

The reversal for EMI and Powell's master plan probably began on a shocking day in May 1976. Powell and Provost were drawing up plans for the U.S. production facility. "We had spent the whole day together, discussing this," said Powell. "I was expecting him in the office the next day at eight o'clock, but I had a call from the hotel saying he was dead. So that really did set us back an awful lot. It took us ages to find anybody with comparable experience and caliber to go forward with the programs we had set out for ourselves."

Provost had been the slim underpinning of a strategy that encompassed North America, and a heart attack had withdrawn him suddenly from Powell's master plan. In his conversations with CT historian Susskind, Powell said, "From that moment onwards, we really suffered many delays, and I could find no way of overcoming them rapidly. You see, the whole growing-up of the scanner business and the scanner organization was a hothouse. It really was. There weren't enough people in EMI to do this, so one had to go outside to recruit, and we were spreading all over the world, all different cultures, different nationalities, because you had to service the things. It was as if one had grown in a hothouse a long slender stalk whose roots were not properly developed, and it was fragile. It was bound to be fragile, in terms of human relationships, organizations, culture—everything. Consequently, a setback like that is pretty devastating."[6]

If the course of a breakthrough can be described as the passing of a baton in a relay, eventually the baton was dropped by EMI. In 1980, after three years of losses—all exacerbated by Powell's ill-fated efforts to set up body scanner production facilities in the United States—EMI announced its withdrawal completely from the

6. Susskind, pages 71–72.

medical electronics industry. All EMI interests outside the United States went to a competitor, General Electric. In the last year of operations, EMI medical electronics activities *lost* £13 million—more than $25 million.

Woodley, who observed the CT phenomenon almost from beginning to end at EMI, expressed the ambivalence of the experience. "I became convinced," he said, "that we were living exponents of a company that had learned at last to manage a breakthrough technology . . . except at the very end, of course."

But another observation by Woodley expresses a more significant result of Hounsfield's accomplishments. It goes back to Oldendorf's ambition for a less traumatic X-ray technology. "Later on, having the opportunity to visit the hospitals and seeing kids at the age that mine were then, diagnosed by a technique that is infinitely less intrusive than would have been the case otherwise, was the greatest satisfaction for me," said Woodley. "One day I hoped I might become involved again in something which is technologically as much a breakthrough, but also one that would have the same terrific social advantage. I'd be very lucky to find that sort of lightning striking again."

In analyzing EMI's dramatic rise and fall with the CT scanner, it is easy to forget the impact of Hounsfield's breakthrough. Hounsfield had turned an almost unbelievable theory into practice, and he had done it on the first try. Others had talked about it, but Hounsfield actually had done it. The theory of tomography—seeing inside the body in two dimensional slices—dated all the way back to 1917 and the work of an Austrian mathematician named Johann Radon. Oldendorf followed with his work in the 1960s, constructing a model of a tomographic scanner, and a decade later, while Hounsfield, in Hayes, was devising his CT scanner, physicist Allan McLod Cormack at Tufts University, in Medford, Massachusetts, was pursuing parallel research. When the 1979 Nobel Prize for Physiology/Medicine was handed out for the CT scanner, two of the three men who thought of it—Hounsfield and Cormack—shared the award.

But James Ambrose was both loyal and correct when he said that Godfrey Hounsfield was the prime mover. The breakthrough for computer tomography was not in the statement of a theory. It was not in the development of mathematical computations that verified the possibilities. The breakthrough was, in Hounsfield's plain word, the creation of a *product,* a thing that worked. Oldendorf had known he must have this *thing* and he had tried to make it himself. "But he didn't have the computer then," said Ambrose. Cormack lacked ingredients, too. One of them might have been Hounsfield's nonacademic appreciation of commerce.

"I had a lot of experience before I came into research, on the practical side," Hounsfield explained. "I was in computers before I came here—designing computers. I'd already got the idea that if you were in research, you're here for eventually producing a product. You may do research to understand things, but you're only going to understand things in order to use the things, but this is wasted commercially if you don't come up with a useful product."

That attitude sets Hounsfield apart from theoreticians who might indeed have understood the idea of tomography better than he does. Hounsfield was neither a physicist nor radiologist. But he was a computer designer more practically advanced in the abstruse realm of pattern recognitions than most people in the world. The creation of the machine itself required, above all, a gifted engineer unhindered by intellectual preconceptions. Hounsfield was expert in mechanical design, electronic design, computer design, the development of complex software algorithms, and in X-ray detection devices. He possessed an ear, a sense, an intuition that led him, with an inexplicable economy of effort, directly to the source of the problem. Because he is also a great mechanic, Hounsfield never seems to feel that a machine is finished. There is always something one can do to make it better. This sense of the unfinished conveys, from Hounsfield, an intensity and a touching humility.

Hounsfield is so unself-consciously humble because he never really believes he is finished. In his mind, everything is incomplete. Both Powell and another CRL cohort of Hounsfield's, Robert Froggatt, were in attendance in Bermuda when Hounsfield hastily presented the first results of his work on a whole body scanner in 1975. They described the occasion as "typical Hounsfield." The presentation was an exercise in self-deprecation. To a large gathering of the world's foremost radiologists, Hounsfield was showing the first CT "slices" in history exposed fast enough to see inside the human body without blurring. The body on display was his own. In order to get these photos, he had lain on a platform, perfectly still, holding his breath and working the scanner's controls. Photo after photo, as the crowd murmured with amazement

at the clarity of the images—even those that had blurred slightly—
Hounsfield kept saying, "Well, this one isn't very good."

Finally, after a series of "not very good" pictures, which
nevertheless awed the radiologists, Hounsfield put his *pièce de
résistance* onto the screen. It was a perfectly exposed, brightly
contrasted portrait of Hounsfield's internal organs, a slice of the
inventor. "Now this one," he said, "I'm rather pleased with."

"Well, it was brilliant!" recalled Powell. "People couldn't control themselves any longer. They stood up and began to cheer."

"He absolutely shattered the place!" said Froggatt. "There was
a burst of applause. People had never seen anything like this. They
had never expected to see anything like this!"

But Hounsfield's self-deprecation, his dissatisfaction with those
imperfect pictures in Bermuda, was genuine. There was too much
yet to do with the body scanner for him to be satisfied. It nagged at
him, an unfinished problem; it turned constantly in his mind,
haunting him. There was always "just one more little thing" before
he could declare the job finished.

Today, Hounsfield is described as semiretired, but he does not
himself accept the description. He continues to spend part of his
time working on a nuclear magnetic resonance (NMR) machine at a
London hospital, and he is also working, again part-time, on a
tunnelling microscope project "for looking at atoms," as he describes it. If perhaps frustrated by EMI's enforced withdrawal from
the medical imaging field, he has certainly not sought to settle into
tranquil, laureled repose.

Some experts feel that NMR will eventually replace CTs for
most diagnostic scanning purposes. But if Hounsfield had not
opened people's eyes to the union of computer pattern recognition
and medical imaging, the leap from X-ray negatives probably still
would be awaiting its birth. In Hounsfield alone were combined
both the mind of a mathematician, the wits of a puzzle-player, and
the hands of a builder.

Woodley noted that "Hounsfield's unique experience" contained all the ingredients necessary to give birth to CT scanner
technology. But to keep it going all the way to the marketplace,
there were two other keys to the breakthrough. One was Powell's
ego, the force that moved the CT scanner from the tight scrutiny of
a handful of researchers and doctors to the broad gaze of the
marketplace. The other element was restlessness. Powell saw a

chronic restlessness in Hounsfield and knew that, however far-fetched the technology might be, here was someone who would hammer on something until it worked. And every time the thing seemed to be working well enough to please most everybody, Hounsfield could always find a reason to keep on hammering.

Woodley recalled the triumphant moment for the theory of computer tomography. EMI had stunned the Radiological Society of North America with Hounsfield's head scan. The company's hospitality suite at their Chicago hotel was a traffic jam. EMI representatives received repeated toasts and tributes from the world's foremost radiologists. In the midst of the cheering, sales were quietly promised, phone numbers exchanged. The successful sound of money rustled through the room. In all the noise and celebration, Woodley hadn't noticed Hounsfield at all.

"Finally, there was a quiet moment," said Woodley. "I found Hounsfield in a corner, scribbling away on the back of an envelope. I asked him what he was up to. He said he was working. I said, 'What in the world could you be working on?' Hounsfield said, 'On the body scanner of course.' "

There was just one more little thing . . . and then Godfrey would be finished.

8 The Microwave Oven: "'Tis Black Magic!"

The last chance for the microwave oven to be seen by the world as an American invention came at a 1965 meeting in the corporate headquarters of Raytheon Company in Lexington, Massachusetts. Virtually unknown to everyone at that meeting was that a number of Japanese companies were on the verge of a dramatic series of breakthroughs that could move the sluggish microwave oven industry from a limited market of restaurants and railroad cars to millions of middle-class kitchens. Despite Raytheon's success, once the Japanese developments gained momentum, no American company could retain any claim to the technology, or a position in the marketplace.

Raytheon had given birth to the microwave oven in 1946, then within a few years had all but orphaned it. The microwave oven, based on a marvelous device called the magnetron, was a consumer product trapped within a company that didn't make consumer products. Raytheon had made its money without resorting to consumers. Raytheon, from World War II onward, was a member in excellent standing of what President Dwight D. Eisenhower called the "military-industrial complex." Its lifeblood was government contracts. Placed next to Raytheon's two proudest offspring, the Hawk and Sparrow guided missiles, the Radarange oven—which warmed up chicken soup and thawed out frozen cakes—was a comic oddity.

179

Appropriately, in that 1965 meeting, the key person was a man who must have seemed a comic oddity on the hoof to the staid managers of Raytheon. George Foerstner, the manager and founder of Amana Refrigeration, Inc., of Amana, Iowa, was a perplexing blend of traits that suggested both Harry Truman and a TV used-car salesman. He scoffed openly at the costly, impractical ways of Raytheon. "This product was really foreign to Raytheon. They were not a consumer products company. They were used to making products for the Pentagon," recalled Foerstner.

Foerstner attended that 1965 meeting only because Raytheon's president, Thomas L. Phillips, had stroked and cajoled him for weeks. The two companies were getting together at last to discuss the takeover of the Radarange oven project by Amana. In a way, Foerstner was a captive audience. Raytheon had recently bought Amana, and one major reason for that purchase was an intention to pump life into the dying potential of the Radarange oven. After almost twenty years of muddling around with microwave ovens at Raytheon, Chairman Charles F. Adams had laid out an ultimatum: "We'd give it one shot," he said, "and if it didn't work, then we'd forget it—put an end to it once and for all."

For Adams, that was a difficult ultimatum. Consumer products, perhaps because they presented such a contrast to Raytheon's general stock-in-trade, held a soft spot in his heart. He wanted a consumer success for Raytheon, but so far all of the company's efforts had failed. "We somehow or another had to prove we knew how to make *something* out of the flow of this technology," said Adams. "It would be nice for people to look at a Raytheon brand on a product and feel good about it." Raytheon had tried time and again to crack the consumer marketplace. But they had failed in the transistor radio business and had failed in the television business, and their microwave oven, with losses, according to Adams, of more than $5 million, threatened to become the biggest consumer failure in their history.

Foerstner had been strongly inclined to put an end to it before he got involved in "one last shot," but he had agreed with Phillips to consider the machine's potential. Palmer Derby, a Raytheon vice-president, remembered Foerstner's galvanizing effect on that 1965 meeting.

"We talked George into taking over the Radarange oven operation," said Derby. "Now came the nitty gritty. What's it going to cost? George says, 'It's no problem. It's about the same size as an air conditioner. It weighs about the same. It should sell for the same. So we'll price it at $499.' Now you think that's silly, but you stop and think about it. Here's a man who really didn't understand the technologies. But there is about the same amount of copper involved, and the same amount of steel as an air conditioner. And these are basic raw materials. It didn't make a hell of a lot of difference how you fit them together to make them work. They're both boxes; they're both made out of sheet metal; and they both require some kind of trim."

Adams, who enjoyed the Foerstner performance more than anyone else, sensed that the Radarange oven had finally found its destiny. In several terse sentences, Foerstner had taken microwave radar, one of the greatest military secrets of World War II and a technology twenty years in development by armies of researchers, and reduced it to the level of an air conditioner. But he had seen what all the researchers had failed to see, and they all knew he was right.

In adopting Raytheon's orphan, Foerstner brought to microwave oven technology an extraordinary force. Part of that was Amana Refrigeration's impeccable reputation for quality in the appliance industry. Equally important was Foerstner's personality. He is one of those rare individuals who have elevated salesmanship to the level of genius. If Foerstner decided to take a product under his wing, whatever it was, it was going to sell. You could bank on it! Amana's Radarange was destined to cook as Raytheon's Radarange had never cooked.

Microwave technology had come to the United States originally from Great Britain. Students of scientific history know that a group of British scientists, led by H. A. H. Boot and J. T. Randall, devised the pulsed-type microwave magnetron for radar use in 1939, and that it was radar that eventually turned the Battle of Britain against Germany.

Until radar began to spot German aircraft crossing the English Channel, the Royal Air Force had to depend on human ground spotters to warn of an attack. When German attacks came at night, the impact was devastating. Without radar to see through the darkness and launch the RAF into an early counterattack, England eventually might have succumbed to Adolf Hitler's *Blitzkrieg*.

Among the American firms invited by the British government in 1940 to help produce the vital and ultra-secret magnetrons was Raytheon.

After the end of World War II, most companies in the magnetron business stopped making them, because of the sudden cutback in military orders. But Raytheon had an old-fashioned inventor in charge of its Power Tube Division. His name was Percy Spencer. While Raytheon was still frantically building and delivering magnetrons for the war effort, Spencer was fooling around with them, thinking of other uses and encouraging fellow engineers like Palmer Derby to fool around, too.

Percy Spencer was presumably the homelier and less ambitious of the two Spencer brothers who worked for Raytheon. When he came to Raytheon, he had no more formal education than the average nomadic laborer looking for a job after World War I. His first college degree came much later—an honorary degree bestowed by the University of Massachusetts in 1950. He had been hired as an inspector at Raytheon by his brother Al, in 1925. Through his whole life, no matter how many times he impressed people with the bursts of brilliant thinking that struck abruptly from within him, each time people would look at him in disbelief. He did not have an aura of genius. Otto Scott, author of *The Creative Ordeal,* recorded a typical Spencer encounter with the academic world.

> One day, while Spencer was lunching with Dr. Ivan Getting and several other Raytheon scientists, a mathematical question arose. Several men, in a familiar reflex, pulled out their slide rules, but before any could complete the equation, Spencer gave the answer.
>
> Dr. Getting was astonished. "How did you do that?" he asked.
>
> "The root," said Spencer shortly. "I learned cube roots and squares by using blocks as a boy. Since then, all I have to do is visualize them placed together."[1]

In a similar way, within a few months of his association with the technology, Spencer's thoughts had seized upon the use of microwaves to cook things.

The "discovery" of microwave cooking is one of the great legends of American industry. It is cluttered by a host of engaging

---

1. Otto J. Scott, *The Creative Ordeal: The Story of Raytheon,* New York: Atheneum, 1974, page 287.

anecdotes, and the whole story likely never will be clarified. Among the certainties, however, is that Percy Spencer was the man responsible for associating radar waves with cooking. The site was Raytheon's power tube plant in Waltham, Massachusetts.

The place was new in 1942, but, like most of the buildings constructed in wartime, it looked lived-in from the first day. It was thoroughly unembellished—little more than a huge room that contained a series of long tables where women with sons and husbands overseas hurriedly assembled magnetrons. There were no offices and only a few desks. Percy Spencer prowled the factory, restless, vigilant, and leonine.

As supervisor of the frantic assembly of magnetrons for the Allied battle against Germany and Japan, the paradox of Percy Spencer was vividly evident. To members of Raytheon management who remembered him in retrospect, he was a cauldron of curiosity, a wild-eyed inventor whose mind always bubbled toward eruptions of mechanical ingenuity. But Spencer also carried with him the insecurity of a rank-and-file worker who had moved into the uneasy echelons of management. Thus, he applied a fanatical intensity to the oversight of his assembly workers, watching their time and their performance religiously. He was always the first person in the plant and one of the last to leave, proving a point to his blue-collar peers that probably few of them appreciated. He wanted them to understand that hard work and personal discipline were more important to advancement than genius, education, or talent. To some extent, his devotion to proving that point led him away from his own talent.

Ultimately, Spencer's bootstrap ascent in the Raytheon organization curtailed his inventive career. By the early 1960s, as a vice-president, he had departed the assembly floor forever, both physically and psychologically. His focus had become leadership of his company in an administrative capacity, and although he often performed brilliantly as a leader, he unquestionably had left behind a greater brilliance.

It's very likely that had Spencer remained closer to the workbench, he would have worked continuously to improve his microwave oven magnetron. But without Spencer in the trenches at Raytheon, the reinvention of the magnetron would have to await the scrutiny of a jigsaw genius named Keishi Ogura, thousands of miles from Waltham.

*   *   *

Raytheon's Waltham plant was a cold place in the winter. Palmer Derby recalled that those early magnetrons didn't generate a continuous flow of microwaves. They pulsed, and because of that, they weren't very powerful. But they performed a service, beyond the war effort overseas, that was highly appreciated in a New England winter. "Their average power was maybe 100, 200 watts—not very much, but it was enough to warm your hands and it was nice, particularly when you came in from outside," said Derby. "That's one of the things I really miss."

Today, given the prevailing concern about the health hazards of microwave radiation and the volumes of Occupational Safety and Health Administration (OSHA) regulations, microwave cooking would never have been envisioned.

"In those days we weren't concerned about microwave radiation," recalled Derby. "Those tubes radiated into space. The result was that if you tested a magnetron, you tested it by holding a neon tube next to it to see how bright the bulb would get. The brighter it got, the more power it had. After a while you got pretty skilled and you could say, 'Well, this one is bright enough to pass.' And if it was bright enough to pass, then you went and got the more sophisticated equipment with which you could make a measurement. In the process of holding the bulb this way, it was quite obvious that your hands got hot. I don't know when Percy really came up with the thought of microwave ovens, but he knew at that time—and this was 1942. He mentioned and talked frequently that this would be a good device for cooking."

In the intense push for magnetron production, the cooking idea could only linger in casual conversation. But it became much more feasible—and tempting—in 1944, when Derby found a way to make a continuous-power magnetron to replace the pulsing magnetron. Then, Spencer knew that cooking with magnetrons was possible, and he broached the idea to Raytheon chairman Laurence K. Marshall. Marshall told Spencer he'd have to wait until the war was over.

But with the end of the war, suddenly the American magnetron industry ceased to exist. "The day the war ended, the factory closed down. Down! Boom! That was it," Derby remembered. "Everybody went home, and the next day I went in, and there was just nobody there."

For Spencer, Derby, William C. Brown, Leslie Vandt, and a few engineers at Raytheon, the overnight disappearance of their industry meant that they finally had time to tinker with this cooking notion that had haunted them for almost five years. They set up a fairly strong power tube (300–500 watts), and one day Vandt had an idea. "Les Vandt went out and bought some popcorn, brought the bag back, and held it in front of the wave guide," said Derby. "And it began to jump all over hell. And it didn't involve the board of directors and all that kind of stuff. All it involved was Les Vandt and the bag of popcorn. Percy came over later to see how it worked."

Spencer and his engineers next tried hanging a pork chop in front of the wave guide. Not only did it cook, but someone even had the courage to eat it. After a few dozen more trips to the corner grocery, it was time to show off the thing to the board of directors. Spencer could have chosen any number of demonstration foods, but he opted for one that would leave an indelible impression: an egg.

"Percy asked the operator to put an egg on the pedestal in front of the wave guide," Derby recalled. "Then, the wave guide pumped a kilowatt of energy into the egg. There's only one thing that could have happened. All over everybody!"

Percy Spencer had won his point. After they cleaned the egg off their faces, suits, and ties, the board of directors agreed to put some money into microwave cooking. It was a pittance compared to the amount the company might spend on a guided missile; even so $5 million over a period of seven to ten years was an exorbitant sum for Raytheon to spend in a consumer market. In a company that made its living as a government contractor, this money was life support for a fish out of water.

From Spencer's first microwave cooking patent in 1949 until 1960, the technology evolved with painful slowness. The Radarange oven made progress, but no one really had an idea where it was going. By 1953, Raytheon had a Radarange oven on the market. By the mid-1950s, Raytheon had licensed the technology to two other companies whose names have since become more closely identified with microwave cooking than Raytheon's, Tappan and Litton. In 1955, Tappan began selling a "home" microwave oven for $1295. There were several models of automobiles that in 1955 could be had for *less* than $1295.

Aside from costing far too much, there were other glaring flaws in those early microwave ovens. Most were almost as large as a refrigerator and weighed as much. Operating at 220 volts, they couldn't be plugged into most wall outlets without the help of an electrician. Besides the electrician, the microwave oven of the 1950s also required a plumber, because the power tube was water-cooled to keep it from overheating. Installation required an entire new set of pipes.

In the fourteen years between 1953 and 1967, fewer than 10,000 microwave ovens were sold in the United States, most of them literally made by hand in Raytheon's chaotic manufacturing plant in Hookset, New Hampshire. Almost all of them went to such institutional users as restaurants and airlines. The biggest individual customer for the big 220-volt microwave ovens was not in America at all. It was the Japanese National Railroad, which installed in its trains 2500 microwave ovens made by Toshiba. Today, almost everyone at Raytheon who remembers that period of time admits that the company's efforts to market microwave cooking in the 1950s were thoroughly incompetent. John M. Osepchuk, a Raytheon physicist who has been a part of microwave development for most of his career, was blunt: "We didn't have the foggiest idea of how to market them and we knew it. We were pouring money into a rat hole."

By the end of the 1950s, Raytheon's continued support of the Radarange project was obviously senseless. Osepchuk said, "If it weren't for Charlie Adams [chairman of the board], the whole microwave oven project might have died at Raytheon. For many years, the microwave oven was never a moneymaker, and yet Charlie Adams kept it alive. If Charlie Adams had let the thing die in the mid-1950s, then in the mid-1960s, would it have been current enough for Tom Phillips to think about it?"

But why had Adams kept it alive? He was a responsible corporate official. As things looked worse and worse for the Radarange oven, he seemed ever more devoted. By the late 1950s, the technology had diverged drastically from Raytheon's mainstream business. The cooking magnetron had become so specialized that it couldn't be adapted to any other use. It was a dead end, and there was a certain oddball quality in this consumer business that clashed with the Raytheon image.

Adams recalled, for instance, an engineer named Bud Haagensen, who worked for Spencer and had designed the Radarange oven door. (The door itself is a brilliant technology, a flawless seal against radiation.) Adams' description of Haagensen is rich with affection.

"Now, Percy was a great disciplinarian, and yet here was Bud Haagensen, working for him. He [Haagensen] would go around with this dreamy look on his face, a cigarette hanging out of his mouth, ashes all over him. He'd come in and work forty-eight hours at a stretch, taking a cat nap or two along the way, and then he'd disappear. I'd say to Percy, 'Where the hell is Bud?' 'I don't know.' 'Why the hell do you keep him around?' And Percy would say, 'He's worth it.' "

While Adams continued to indulge the Radarange oven, a different microwave heating technology, based on a power tube called the klystron, developed by a former Raytheon engineer named John Gunnarson, lived and died without a ripple of interest from industry and the consuming public. Adams failed to heed that warning, too. Meanwhile, microwave research at M.I.T., Columbia, and Bell Laboratories also died out.

But then, in 1960, when microwave cooking made its first appearance in Japan, Raytheon demonstrated a Radarange oven at an international trade show in Japan. Almost immediately, Japanese consumer electronics companies, led by Toshiba and Sanyo, seized on this as a promising area of development. While America slept, the sun was dawning in the East.

In Japan, as in the United States, the main problem for microwave oven development was finding a magnetron source. The only competent suppliers were companies that had made radar units during World War II. By 1960, the only one left was New Japan Radio Company (NJRC). In modest ways, NJRC had made greater progress in developing nonmilitary uses for magnetrons than Raytheon. Since 1945, NJRC had been banned by American occupation laws from any military work. Consequently, the focus of their research was on civilian communications and medical heat therapy (diathermy). Crippling shortages of many basic raw materials, especially metals, had forced them into looking for ways to make magnetrons from cheaper materials.

Almost immediately after that 1960 trade show, Japanese companies began building copies of the large restaurant-model Radarange oven, buying NJRC's magnetrons as the heat source within their ovens. But that original NJRC oven tube was not primarily designed for cooking. Back in the United States, by the early 1960s, Litton had redesigned Spencer's tube for faster warm-up and greater energy efficiency. But the oven was still a water-cooled behemoth. Even a Litton countertop oven introduced in 1964 was unsuitable to the average household.

The problem that everyone had always had, from Raytheon to Litton to NJRC, was the intricacy of that power tube. The technology had moved in fits and starts for more than ten years, but it was handicapped most dramatically by the intimidating complexity of the magnetron. To make one at all was a technological challenge beyond the powers of many electronics laboratories and far beyond the capacity of most consumer electronics companies. To make one *cheaply* was unthinkable.

But New Japan Radio *needed* to do it. Japanese industries were demanding it, and a decade of NJRC experience in nonmilitary magnetrons made it conceivable. Yoshihiko Sato, manager of NJRC's microwave power tube operation, recalled, "We believed that if the size of the microwave oven stayed the same, it would not become prevalent in Japan. It wouldn't be well accepted by the Japanese people. But then Sanyo Electric Company decided to invest in the manufacture of microwave ovens for the Japanese market, and they came to an agreement that we do research here and we develop low-cost magnetrons."

One critical element also accelerated Japanese interest in the microwave oven while it languished in America. The problem was expressed plainly by Adams. "Everyone in the United States wants to eat steak," he said. "And steak was the only thing you couldn't do in a microwave oven."

Tadashi Seino, one of the leaders of Toshiba Corporation's swift (1961) entry into the microwave oven market, noted that by comparison the two staple items of the Japanese diet, rice and sake, are ideally suited to reheating in the microwave oven. If both could be heated perfectly in single servings, without stealing time and cooking surfaces from other more complicated foods, the crowded, hectic nature of Japanese life would be reduced dramatically. Based on those two basic foods, rice and sake, Japanese appliance makers saw that microwave cooking would have an immediate appeal to the Japanese people. When Seino first saw the Radarange oven in 1960, he suffered few of the marked misgivings that had plagued America and Raytheon.

But Toshiba had no more talent available to redesign the Raytheon power tube than any other consumer electronics company in the world. No one knew magnetrons then any better than Raytheon and NJRC, and by 1961 those two companies were linked. In a series of international acquisitions, Adams and Spencer had decided to acquire a one-third interest in NJRC. From this merger, NJRC got complete access to Raytheon's magnetron designs, and Raytheon would eventually reap the genius of Keishi Ogura.

Ogura was the man Sato assigned to the intimidating job of improving Percy Spencer's magnetron. In essence, he had to do what Percy Spencer did in 1940 when he first saw the British version of the magnetron.

The Creative Ordeal relates the day that Spencer met John D. Cockcroft, the technical leader of the British government project to fortify the fragile English coast with radar installations.

> Cockcroft liked Spencer at once. He showed him the magnetron and the American regarded it thoughtfully. He asked questions—very intelligent ones—about how it was produced, and the Britisher answered at length.
>
> Later Spencer wrote, "The technique of making these tubes, as described to us, was awkward and impractical." *Awkward and impractical.* Nobody else dared draw such a judgment about a product of undoubted scientific brilliance, produced and displayed by the leaders of British science.
>
> The conversation took place on a Friday afternoon. As the men talked, shadows began to lengthen, and at some point, Cockcroft later told Carl Gilbert, Spencer looked up.
>
> "I wonder," he asked, "if I could take this home with me over the weekend?"[2]

Cockcroft could never quite explain why he consented. He was, after all, carrying Britain's most valuable secret. It was possible he had been followed by enemy agents. Spencer could have a car accident on the way to or from home, could have a heart attack—anything might arise. In the event of any of these or any other possible problem, Cockcroft would have been hard put to explain why he had allowed the magnetron out of his hands. But at the moment assent seemed natural.

> The following Monday they again met in the laboratory. Spencer was smiling and optimistic. He thought Raytheon could produce magnetrons; he implied that some improvements might be possible in the manner in which they were turned out. He discussed some of these, and Cockcroft, who was himself a notable scientist, grasped their implications immediately. He was surprised but impressed.[3]

2. Scott, pages 112–113.
3. Scott, page 113.

In order to make an affordable cooking magnetron, Ogura had to do to Spencer's design what Spencer had done to Cockcroft's. He must disregard the elements of the past to focus on the functions of the present. He must try to make the first magnetron in history that contained no memory of the Battle of Britain.

Before he began his design, Ogura paused to envision every problem that had been built into the Raytheon magnetron. Most observers had seen these not as *problems* at all, but as "features." Other researchers had seen the Spencer magnetron as a sort of final achievement—to which only incremental improvements might be made. But Keishi Ogura, as he turned the power tube in his hand, saw a web of problems that required him to go back to the very beginning to start fresh.

Osepchuk expressed the importance of Ogura's revolutionary approach to magnetron design. "The magnetron was poorly understood, despite the academics," said Osepchuk. "Most magnetron manufacturers since World War II, even though they had brilliant physicists around, made the things work by hook or by crook. And fairly often, the professors from M.I.T. and Stanford couldn't answer the question, 'What's causing this?' Even at the time that New Japan Radio designed their tube, there were a lot of these problems, and New Japan Radio found ways that minimized these problems. They came up with a design that turned out to be almost ideal, in terms of performance. It definitely was a key point. All microwave ovens today—*all tubes*—still basically have the same design parameters as that Japan Radio tube."

Ogura's accomplishment was another case of "going back to scratch," just as Yuma Shiraishi had done in the redesign of the ½-inch video cassette recorder. Ogura organized the challenge he faced, perceiving the conflicting elements that had been built into the old design. Ogura said, "The design policy we had at that time was to design a low-cost product which was easy to make. So the design had to be as simple as possible and at the same time achieve high efficiency, stable performance. These objectives to some extent may contradict each other. My biggest goal was to try to incorporate all these characteristics, try to fit all these into one system. A lot of trade-offs had to be made."

Instinctively, Ogura responded to Edison's admonition—"All parts of the system must be constructed with reference to all other parts of the system." In one "magnificent design," as Sato calls it,

Ogura accomplished the following. The Ogura design attained:

- higher technical sophistication than ever before
- design simplicity for easy service
- ease of manufacture
- no improvements in technology that would add cost
- a reduction in material costs (because of entirely different materials that were cheaper but better)
- greater performance stability
- longer tube life
- instantaneous heating
- an electric voltage requirement suitable to the average home, both in Japan and in the United States
- much greater energy efficiency

Ogura never wrote down this list of requirements. He shares a special kind of creative perception with—among others—CT scanner inventor Godfrey Hounsfield. Like Hounsfield, he had an immediate awareness that standard practice and accepted theory would be a hindrance to his work, so paid it little attention. Hounsfield, indeed, barely knew that there was a standard practice in computerized technology. Ogura understood his goal and somehow "saw it three-dimensionally," without writing everything down in advance. He resolved the actual details of assembly as he built the prototype. Like Spence Silver at 3M, Ogura "tried it, just to see what it would do." And behind it all, Ogura—like Hounsfield (and Thomas Edison)—dwelled not on understanding how things work, but on the *product* that must emerge from the understanding of how things work.

Sato expressed Ogura's purpose succinctly: "It was understood at that time that this was a sanctuary to the scientist. It was an area of high technology belonging only to the scientist. We, at that time, especially Mr. Ogura, felt strongly that we had to bring the technology down to an ordinary level, in order to popularize microwave ovens."

William C. Brown, who worked side-by-side with Spencer during the frantic war years at Raytheon, stated the same idea: "Our contributions during the war were those of experimentalists and designers rather than theorists."[4]

4. William C. Brown, "The Microwave Magnetron and Its Derivatives," *IEEE Transactions on Electron Devices*, Vol. ED-31, No. 11, November 1984.

Curiously, Ogura's breakthrough was not greeted with shouts of amazement and exultation in the United States. Raytheon had never expressly asked their Japanese partner, NJRC, to work on a new cooking magnetron. It hardly matters, since Sanyo had already got the ball rolling. And by 1964, Ogura's product was finished. Japanese manufacturers began the development process of a compact microwave oven for home use two years before Tom Phillips of Raytheon talked George Foerstner into doing it at Amana. Although no one really knew it, time was running out in the United States.

Technically, Raytheon and Amana were an ideal match. Raytheon brought to the appliance company an advanced technology. They had invented a working oven already tested, proven, and sold, with several remarkable technological elements—such as Bud Haagensen's door—that would never have emerged from an appliance company. In 1965 Raytheon also "discovered" Ogura's NJRC magnetron design and could add it to the concept. Amana provided the military contractor an intimate familiarity with consumer attitudes and a distribution capability foreign to Raytheon. But, culturally, these were two very strange bedfellows.

Raytheon was Eastern establishment. Amana was a Midwestern outsider. And Amana's differences from Raytheon were more than just regional. Founded by George Foerstner in 1934, Amana Refrigeration is the largest employer in a cluster of seven tiny villages in central Iowa, which compose the Amana Colonies. The Amanas were, until 1931, a community entirely controlled by their church. Members of the Amana Colonies belonged to the Society of True Inspiration, a religious sect born in the seventeenth century as a Pietist splinter group of the Lutheran Church. A German carpenter named Christian Metz brought a group of believers to America in 1842, settling first near Buffalo, New York, but moving farther west to Iowa in 1854. The outcome of that move was the Amana Colonies—25,000 acres, seven churches with a village built around each one. The colonists built a seven-mile canal to the Iowa River and became agriculturally and economically self-supporting.

Within the churches, people were expected to worship long and hard every day, aside from doing work dedicated to a fairly doctrinaire communalist ideal. Children were educated to the age of thirteen and then put to work. The theocracy of the Amana Colonies did not substantially erode until the 1930s, when a number of social pressures cracked the isolation of the community. People wanted possessions of their own; they wanted some time away from work and worship. They wanted electricity, and radios! Some wanted advanced education. Some began to chafe for the rights and privileges they observed in the lives of people in nearby communities. Also, with a community debt of almost $500,000, the Amana Colonies were almost broke by 1931. Communalism was changed to socialism. The church elders reduced their control to religious matters only, and Amana edged toward the American mainstream.[5]

What remained was an intense sense of community and purpose. George Foerstner grew up in an atmosphere of purposefulness that defined his character and complemented his irrepressible rebelliousness. While still a teenager, Foerstner was on the road as a salesman for his father's auto accessory business. When traveling, Foerstner exercised his compulsion to tinker with machines, and his interest turned to refrigeration, an almost nonexistent technology in the 1930s. Foerstner quickly realized that rather than *fixing* the iceboxes and beer coolers that he encountered in his travels, he could build a better one from scratch—which is what he did.

By 1934 he was selling his own line of hand-built beer coolers in partnership with a friend, Otto Zuber. That became enough of a business so that, by 1936, Foerstner had sold it to the managers of the Amana Society—who had the infinite good sense to tell Foerstner to just keep on running it. By 1949 the Amana Society had forebodings. They never had owned a $1 million business before. Foerstner and a consortium of eastern Iowa business people, including Howard Hall, head of Iowa Manufacturing in Cedar Rapids, bought the firm from the Amana Society. Fifteen years later, with sales at $25 million, Foerstner had Amana Refrigeration primed for another merger, this time with Raytheon. For Raytheon's new CEO, Thomas Phillips, the central purpose of the Amana purchase was the microwave oven. Foerstner, who knew the oven's pathetic history and was additionally concerned about his company's suitability to manufacture a cooking rather than refrigeration appliance, played hard-to-get. "At first, George didn't want to have anything to do with the damn thing," recalled Charlie Adams afterward.

But oven or no oven, the Raytheon purchase would be good for Amana, and the merger was effected in 1965. History will record

5. Information derived largely from Diane L. Barthel, *Amana: From Pietist Sect to American Community*, Lincoln, Nebraska: University of Nebraska Press, 1984.

that from the moment that Foerstner, "in that dictatorial voice that knew the answer to everything," announced the shape (like an air conditioner) and the price ($500) of the ideal microwave oven, the technology was smoothly shifted from New England to Iowa and the new Radarange oven took shape. But the people involved in magnetron production at Raytheon faced an impossible demand. In order to meet Foerstner's recommended retail price, they needed a magnetron that cost less than $25 to make. Palmer Derby, who was present to hear Foerstner's demand, knew that it couldn't be done. In more than ten years, the cheapest magnetron Raytheon had made cost $125.

Raytheon never found the answer to that enormous cost dilemma. What they did find was Keishi Ogura's new design. Raytheon and Amana bought only enough of the NJRC magnetrons to copy over his design and make their own at the old Waltham plant. Derby (who died suddenly in 1985) lamented the fact that after the NJRC design was adopted and copied at Raytheon and Amana, United States magnetron development continued to trail that of the Japanese. By the 1980s, no American company was making magnetrons for microwave cooking. All were imported from Japan or Korea. Ironically, New Japan Radio also halted cooking magnetron production by 1980—unable to compete with volume producers like Toshiba, who had pulled the price of a magnetron down to as low as $7.

The job of handling the transition of the Radarange oven from Raytheon to Amana went directly to George Foerstner's son, Richard, a gifted mechanical engineer who created an inexpensive, compact chassis. "The plus that we had," recalled Louis Blackburn, an Amana engineer, "was that Dick Foerstner spent a lot of his early years in the manufacturing facility in industrial engineering, and he knew the cost effective ways of putting a unit together."

"For the first time we had an appliance engineer designing it, not an electronics engineer," added John Osepchuk.

Blackburn also recalled that, after working most of his life on the intricacies of refrigeration, this little oven unit was "terrifyingly simple." Again, the key to the exceptionally fast development of the countertop microwave oven at Amana was born out of a sort of mechanic's imperative—which Foerstner shared with Spencer and Ogura, as well as other breakthrough inventors like Hounsfield and

Spence Silver. Making it work was more important than understanding how it worked.

While Richard Foerstner was re-creating the design and the Amana manufacturing facilities were building up to a level of production unknown in their history, George Foerstner was standing atop his hill—where his house imperiously overlooks the Amana Refrigeration plant—looking out at a consumer market that didn't understand or care about microwave cooking. Derby had already expressed to Foerstner his awareness of the real challenge of the Radarange oven.

"I don't give a goddamn how exciting a thing is that you've got technologically. It's not going to sell in the marketplace until you can convince the consumer that he needs it. And if you can't find that market need—if you can't produce that market need—I think you'd better throw the damn thing away," said Foerstner.

But finding that market need was George Foerstner's favorite sport. When he demanded a $500 price ceiling, he didn't know that it was an impossible technological demand, nor did he care. He didn't pay much attention to his son's design work, except to complain about how slow it was. George Foerstner saw the market; he understood it, and he wanted to get at it. There was a fire in his eyes and an itch in his heel.

Two years passed between the meeting in Lexington and the day Amana was ready to test the new Radarange oven in the market. By then, although this was essentially unknown in America, Sharp had introduced, in Japan, the first functional countertop microwave oven for home use. Like the Radarange oven, it was based on Ogura's magnetron design.

If anyone had told Foerstner then about the Sharp oven, he would have said he didn't give a damn. The same answer would have returned to anyone with the temerity to suggest that Amana had no evidence of who and where their market might be. Jack Kammerer, Amana's senior vice-president of Marketing, said, "I think if this project had been given to a very highly structured company from a marketing standpoint that had all the demographics and had spent a year and hundreds of thousands of dollars in market research, they'd have probably thrown it in the wastebasket and never done it. It's only a gut feeling of a couple of individuals that this is the right product at the right time."

George Foerstner, like Akio Morita pushing the Walkman project at Sony Corporation, paid little respect to the science of marketing. Both men operated with the unassailable assurance that they knew "what makes people tick."

Charles Adams said with a smile of admiration, "George is one of the most stubborn men who's ever lived. It's a little hard to talk to George in his field."

From the time Amana consented to develop Raytheon's Radarange oven, the program had relied on George Foerstner's confidence. George knew how to sell. Years before, Amana had pioneered the market for home freezers, eventually wiping out the cold storage locker industry, not by selling freezers—which were big, ugly, dull, and expensive—but by selling wholesale food door-to-door. Once people bought the food, at prices that were cheaper and in amounts that were larger than they'd ever experienced before, they needed something to store it in.

Besides the pure perception of how to approach an untested market, Foerstner appreciated the unmitigated gall that typifies true salesmanship. Foerstner had begun life on the road in the Depression, selling car parts and beer coolers. He knew that sometimes the best approach to the consumer is to make the presentation impossible to ignore. Foerstner's fundamental marketing principle is "First, you get the mule's attention." Wayne Giddings, Amana's senior vice-president of Engineering and Manufacturing and one of the people responsible for the Radarange oven market push in 1967, recalled the early days, when Foerstner was selling freezers.

"In a show," said Giddings, "we were showing the upright freezer, and he shocked everybody on the stage presenting the thing. He said, 'We build 'em strong!' and he walked up to the front and he climbed onto the top of the door—like a ladder. Well, my God, we were afraid the whole unit was going to topple forward and kill him. So we ran over and grabbed it."

With the microwave oven as with those home freezers, Amana was again going to sell a function, not a product. And by 1967, Foerstner's company was better equipped to do this than they had been for the freezer campaign. Still, everyone in Amana knew that it wasn't going to be an easy job. "We knew by talking to our distributors and dealers, even talking to people in the company here, that the educational job we had to do was just absolutely astronomical," said Amana chairman Alex Meyer. "We had to educate people on how to change their way of cooking. And when you go into a home and try to tell a housewife how to change her way of cooking—over twenty years ago—you had a problem. You were messing around with her last stronghold."

Foerstner's answer to the problem was an all-out push in the city of Chicago, as a one-year test market for the Radarange oven. The features of the all-out push were a combination of freezer-climbing, impeccable organization, and relentless education. The first thing Foerstner's troops did was educate the distribution organization—wholesalers and retailers—to the full range of the Radarange oven's capabilities. Everyone who sold one had to be able to demonstrate it. And Foerstner made it clear that if they didn't know how to demonstrate it, they weren't going to sell any of them.

Although Foerstner talks a great deal about housewives, it's clear that they were only a secondary market in the Radarange oven push. The primary market was the appliance distributors themselves. "Distributors," said Foerstner, "are the first line of defense. The secret in obtaining and keeping good distributors is to appeal to their selfishness. A distributor has to be selfish. He must be able to make enough money handling your appliances to abandon everyone else's line and switch to yours. Any other appeal is a waste of time."[6]

What Foerstner's troops told the distributors was that the most important element of their program was to understand housewives, calm their fears, and simplify the instruction manual. "The housewife didn't understand it," said Meyer. "It was too technical for her. She didn't understand that we were stirring these molecules 2450 times per second. She didn't understand that the friction of the molecules was the source of heat. There are no flames. There is no calrod heater. How did that thing really work? It was a little scary. So we had to take out the scary aura and make it very practical—cook a steak and brown a steak, pop popcorn, do the coffee, get a plastic pouch and do a meal, do the vegetables, take it from the freezer to the microwave oven, make it convenient, reheat meals when everybody's in a hurry and eating at three or four different times."

After the distributors had been exhaustively grounded in microwave cooking, in housewives' psychology, and then pep-talked into a mercantile froth, Amana turned up the emotion a notch with an

6. Scott, page 368.

impressive press party—making sure all the distributors, retailers, salesmen, and various hangers-on were in attendance. Demonstrations were perpetual and amusing.

"One of the great things in our later presentations," said Meyer, "was the discovery of popcorn. We kept their attention by giving them popcorn. They would wait for the popcorn to pop. They would watch the popcorn pop. They'd watch the molecular disturbance of the makeup of popcorn and the bursting of the popcorn. They would smell the popcorn popping. They would hear the popcorn popping. *Then,* we'd give them some, and then they'd stand around and look at this crazy thing and say, 'Gosh, this really does work!' "

The *pièce de résistance* for the Chicago introduction was the train. For days, a railroad coach weaved its way through the vast suburban sprawl that fans out westward from Chicago. At each stop, throngs of heavily recruited housewives were ushered onto the train and regaled with cooking demonstrations, food and drink, and homespun Amana, Iowa, *joie de vivre.*

"In Chicago, we rode around in a train and did this," said Meyer. "We picked up the press. We were cooking on the train and we had balloons and we had bands. We did the thing up properly. We had church groups. We gave them coupons to go in and buy the product at a discount. At every stop we had some new group of people."

After sales were consummated, the Foerstner touch was especially evident. George Foerstner is an old-fashioned man, still comfortable with the idea of putting women on a pedestal and still demanding enough to make women stay up there where they've been put. His perception of housewives was that the technology of the microwave oven might not merely be strange; it might be frightening. Even as early as 1967—when *microwave radiation* was a meaningless term to most people—fears about it had already come into circulation.

"Even then, we were worried about safety," said Giddings. "We used to talk about real weird things. They used to be afraid that some kid was going to take the family cat and put him in the microwave and cook it. Gruesome kinds of things! You know, you could take the family cat and put him in the regular oven and cook him, too!"

Foerstner was not going to let fear or housewifely ignorance hinder the march of the microwave. So, with every delivery of a new oven in the Chicago blitz, an Amana home economist, a woman specially trained in microwave oven use, arrived to help the housewife install it in her kitchen, cook her first microwave meal, and learn how to use all three buttons on the front of it. That home economist stayed on twenty-four-hour call for each of her clients, and there was a service man also on call—guaranteed to show up within an hour or so.

Few products have ever been introduced into any market in the world with the level of handholding, babysitting, and fatherly solicitude that George Foerstner applied to the Chicago Radarange oven campaign. That campaign did not die. As Amana rolled the Radarange oven out throughout the nation, George made sure that the distribution network acted as a sort of a Housewife Polytechnic Institute, teaching safe microwave oven use wherever the product was sold.

"One of the basic criteria after a couple of years into this product was that the distributor have a home economist or a qualified person on board to conduct schools," said Meyer. "And we wrote the script. We told them what to cook. We told them what to buy. We told them what their shopping list was. We told them how much money they could spend. We told them how much we would participate—and that was like signing the franchise. They had to do these things, or it wouldn't work. We found that out. If they didn't do the whole thing, *in toto,* it wouldn't work."

In fact, the misgivings that Foerstner applied to housewives were true of all microwave oven customers. It was a strange, new thing, and by concentrating on education, Amana obliterated the cloud of mystery and quickened the time that might otherwise have been needed for America to adapt to the microwave oven. Time had become critical. By 1968, Japanese manufacturers were beginning to export microwave ovens to the United States—at an appealing price. By the 1980s, Japan would have the dominant share of the American market.

There is a small irony in the fact that, in Japan, the microwave oven is the tool of the full-time homemaker. It allows the Japanese housewife to prepare several courses of a meal at once—some of it cold, some of it hot from the stove top, some of it heated in the microwave oven. It is a marvelous addition to the traditional Japanese style of food preparation. In the United States, the microwave actually served a contrasting purpose. It freed housewives from the kitchen, allowed them to work outside the home and prepare meals (or order their husbands to do so!) in much less time than in the traditional kitchen.

Rose Rennekamp, vice-president of Product Planning and Marketing at Amana, summarized the change in her own life. "I really feel that what we've done with the microwave oven has contributed to the quality of people's lives," she said. "We've given them more time to spend with their families. The microwave oven gives me thirty minutes more a day probably to spend with my own kids. And it's given that to every woman who is working in America who's got a microwave oven."

In 1968, following the spectacular success of the Chicago campaign, George Foerstner enjoyed one of the great triumphs of his life, the national introduction of the Radarange oven—"back east" in Raytheon territory. At a dinner held at Anthony's Pier 4, then by far the most prestigious restaurant in Boston, Foerstner was introduced, in front of what he called "that Harvard crowd," as a technological champion. Even then, however, neither Foerstner nor anyone in America—nor any of the Japanese manufacturers— had any conception that they had created a monster of spectacular magnitude. Growth at first was manageable but steady. The break-even point—when profits caught up to the expense of starting up— came in Amana's second year of manufacture. Keishi Ogura, who studied markets as well as technology, had estimated peak production for the Japanese market would come to less than 100,000 units a year. Wayne Giddings, at Amana, estimated the U.S. market would peak at about that amount per year. In less than four years, after the introduction of the pioneering products by Sharp and Amana—and in spite of a dramatic microwave radiation scare in 1968—world sales reached 30,000 units per annum. In 1975, the number was 790,000, dwarfing Ogura's and Giddings' rather generous predictions. In 1984, 7.7 million microwave oven units were sold internationally, and 1985 sales were twice that much. Many experts in the appliance industry believe that, by the turn of the century, the microwave oven will become, like the refrigerator and the kitchen range, a "basic appliance" in kitchens in industrialized nations. Everyone will have one.

In looking back at the history of the microwave oven development, it's easy to identify a number of keys to the breakthrough. The technology, for example, was "sophisticated and simple," which is to say that, though its complexity created the demand for real scientific ingenuity at the stage of invention, it emerged as a very simple device in the hands of the consumer. Foerstner's decisions on design and price were vital to the breakthrough into the American marketplace. Because the microwave oven was something entirely new to the consumer, the emphasis on education was a critical marketing springboard. Also crucial was Amana's concentration on its intermediate market—the distributors. Not coincidentally, Toshiba in Japan followed the same marketing recipe in introducing microwave ovens to their domestic market.

But all these "keys" leave unanswered the question that leaps out from the history of the product. From the moment in the early 1940s when Raytheon's magnetron makers were popping corn and sizzling chops in front of wave guides, the product potential of microwave heat was obvious. It was insistent! It cried out for development! Why did it take so long?

Part of the answer has to lie in the fact that all the companies originally involved in microwave development were technical enclaves working for the government. None were consumer products companies, even in a broad definition of that concept. Raytheon certainly made components that went into consumer products, but their market was composed of manufacturers, not people.

Part of the answer is that microwave technology was terribly unfamiliar and it took years for its developers to find a way to explain it (or realize it doesn't have to be explained!) to people who just want to cook dinner. Raytheon's Charles Adams provided a vivid example of the public education problem. Early in the development, he had turned his kitchen at home into the proving ground for each successive generation of Raytheon microwave ovens. Eventually, the forefront of technology collided with the resistance of culture, as embodied by the Adams family cook. "We had a cook who was a rather old Irish lady," Adams recalled, "who walked into the kitchen while I was experimenting with it. 'Oh!' she said. ' 'Tis black magic!' And she went upstairs and packed her bags, and she never was heard from again."

However, neither the consumer marketing incompetence of technology companies nor the set ways of professional cooks explains adequately a quarter century of failure for a product of such compelling value for the average middle-class household.

Unquestionably, if Raytheon or one of its partners had been able to launch into the market a compact, affordable microwave oven in the 1950s, the success of this product would not have had to wait for George Foerstner to march into Chicago with a locomotive and an army of Betty Crockers. But this was the problem—a fundamental technological flaw. Nobody could make *affordable* the basic element of the microwave oven; nobody could make a cheap magnetron.

Time has clouded the significance of this problem, but it was a crippling flaw. Osepchuk, whose hindsight on microwave cooking technology is irreverently lucid, said it flatly: "They had to be on the countertop, and they had to be under five hundred bucks. As long as Raytheon was selling something for $1500—in the 1950s, that's ridiculous! I don't care if it was a sex machine. They still couldn't sell it!"

Technological perfection doesn't mean a thing if it costs too much. For the sensible middle-class breadwinner, cooking the bread faster is not worth a $1300 to $1500 investment—not today, and certainly not thirty years ago, when the dollar was worth more. Foerstner was right in identifying $500 as the ideal price, but his audience for that statement was a research and development team that had been trying to reduce costs for twenty years, a research team that was the acknowledged world leader in microwave cooking technology. After twenty years, they had yet to get within $1000 of Foerstner's magic number. Everyone assumes that George was expressing a *goal* with that $500 maximum price. But what he might have been doing was stating the impossible. If Raytheon couldn't meet that figure, then Amana could not be expected to pursue development any further. Amana would be saved from the "rat hole" that had already wasted millions of Raytheon's dollars.

In this light, the pertinent question is not why it took so long for someone to make the microwave oven into a successful product. Rather, we should ask why a fatally imperfect technology survived all that time? The magnetron should have suffered through several courageous development generations—all of them grossly expensive—and then fallen under the cold and unsentimental review of Raytheon's corporate leadership. Then, the company's leaders should have made several basic conclusions: (a) this thing is still far too costly to make; (b) we don't know how to mass-produce it, and if we knew, we'd be mass-producing something too expensive for people to buy; (c) besides being too expensive, our end product is something we can't sell to people—we can't even *explain* it.

Someone at Raytheon should have killed this thing. As with a number of other breakthroughs—including the CT scan machine at EMI, 3M's Post-it Note Pad, even Walkman—a rational, sensible system of product review broke down at Raytheon. When Charles Adams says that Raytheon poured $5 million into the Radarange oven between 1949 and 1960, he is providing a rather self-protective underestimate. The figures were larger, and the period of wasting money on cooking extended for at least five more years. There was no reason to assume that more years and more money would achieve any better results. At Raytheon, a company with a reputation for cost control and accountability, a flagrant boondoggle was running up bills and sullying the ledgers.

Robert Decareau, one of the food technologists who worked on the microwave project throughout the 1950s (in a food laboratory dedicated specifically to microwave cooking), fingered the culprit. "It is extremely doubtful," Decareau wrote, "if the microwave oven business came even close to breaking even during those first ten to fifteen years. Certainly, it would not have survived to give birth to the tremendous consumer microwave oven market that exists today if it were not for someone with vision and faith in the potential of microwave cooking. That someone was Charles Francis Adams."[7]

The record shows that Adams, as an executive vice-president and eventually as chairman of Raytheon, carried out a series of actions—all of them costly and several of them risky—that might all be justifiable as reasonable corporate moves if taken separately. But combined, these actions fell together to support Raytheon's most unconscionable speculation, the microwave oven.

The early moves, including the establishment of the Raytheon Food Laboratory and the hiring of a team of Ph.D. scientists to develop microwave cooking techniques, are obvious offspring of the magnetron development effort. Similarly obvious are the licensing agreements with Tappan and Litton. But in the 1960s, Adams included an obscure Japanese firm, New Japan Radio, among a series of international acquisitions.

Since the NJRC acquisition about 1961, Raytheon has consistently owned one-third of the Japanese firm but has done almost nothing in partnership with NJRC. Few people at Raytheon even know that New Japan Radio is still a part of their company. The

---

7. John M. Osepchuk, "A History of Microwave Heating Applications," *IEEE Transactions on Microwave Theory and Techniques*, September 1984, page 1208.

only thing that NJRC ever did for Raytheon, apparently, was when Keishi Ogura made Charlie Adams a brand-new power tube. Then when acquisitions were in Raytheon's plans in 1964, somehow Adams and Phillips got an appliance company in Iowa onto the list of candidates.

Lurking constantly beneath his actions and in the back of Adams' mind was a tireless desire for—even an obsession with— the microwave oven. Every time he entered his kitchen at home, the latest prototype stared at him accusingly. And each one, in turn, seemed to say to him, "I'm too big, too expensive, too heavy, too strange, too dangerous. Stop me before I spend again!"

But Charlie Adams ignored even the nagging voice of an over-weight prototype. He stuck with it. It's certainly true that if the stages of a breakthrough are like the passage of a baton in a relay, then the baton was passed from Percy Spencer's concept to Keishi Ogura's development to George Foerstner's market campaign en route to the finish line. But the man who carried the baton in the long, long stretches between passes was Adams. His reason might have been the same sort of intuition that infected Spencer, Ogura, and Foerstner. At each passage there was an intuitive flash: Spencer and Palmer Derby warming their hands in a wave guide and saying to each other, almost at once, "Hey, there might be something here!" Then Ogura, holding the Raytheon magnetron in his hands, turning it over and over and seeing the things that could be changed, *must* be changed. And then Foerstner, looking at Raytheon's behemoth Radarange oven and, in an instant, seeing a whole new metaphor, the air conditioner!

If Adams shared an intuition with these three colleagues, it was something less palpable than what they felt. The action he took to respond to his sense that "there was a place somewhere" for microwave cooking wasn't as direct. He said, "It was my feeling that somehow or other this kind of cooking was going to break out some day. Don't say I'm the great genius who saw where it was going to end up, because that's not true. But I knew that some day, if we kept trying, it would eventually break through."

To say that Charles Adams was emotionally attached to micro-wave ovens perhaps sounds ridiculous, but it seems to be true. There was a hint of the real source of his emotion in his description of Bud Haagensen, a man whom almost no one else at Raytheon remembers. Adams was moved by the genius Haagensen applied to the invention of the microwave oven door and he was delighted by the rumpled style in which Haagensen did it. Adams describes Spencer with similar affection. "The way Percy Spencer's mind worked is an interesting thing," said Adams. "He had a mind that allowed him to hold an extraordinary array of associations of phenomena and relate them to each other. My analysis of him is as a great inventor. You couldn't help loving him."

And when Adams encountered George Foerstner, he sensed that finally he had found someone with the right style to carry the faith to its consummation. Perhaps more than anyone else at Raytheon, Adams possessed a (well-concealed) streak of adventure. A member of one of the great, historic New England families, Adams left a cushy post provided for him by blood and training at the brokerage firm of Paine, Webber, Jackson, and Curtis. Coming to Raytheon was an adventure for him, and because of that, he has always viewed Raytheon through a tinted lens. To most observers, Raytheon is a bastion of ivory-tower technocrats, favored by the feds and feasting on the government's boundless largesse. But to Charles Adams, Raytheon is a creative nest that blends straightforward men of sound business principles with a few unconventional personalities. "This company wouldn't be what it is, and that's true of a lot of companies, without a certain number of eccentric geniuses," Adams said.

Adams' dilemma has always been to convey this inventive force, Raytheon's hidden strain of adventure, to a wider audience. When the "eccentric geniuses" had succeeded in the company—as when Raytheon devised its transistor radio and its excellent television receiver—the company bungled the product in the marketplace. In Adams' eyes, the best chance for the world to know about Percy Spencer, Bud Haagensen, Bill Brown, John Osepchuk, and the Raytheon knack for nurturing eccentric genius was to make the microwave oven succeed. This could be their message to the world.

Adams is not an egoist. He is a man who, by birth and temperament, is engagingly comfortable with himself. If he had seen the microwave oven as a personal crusade, he probably would have recognized its hopelessness by the end of the 1960s. He would have been embarrassed by his own obstinacy, come to his managerial senses, and killed the thing. He never would have taken it to the point of acquiring overseas interests and venturing into an Iowa religious community. But Adams wasn't doing it for himself. Percy Spencer was his friend and his hero. For Adams, Spencer embodied the very best of what Raytheon stands for as a community of people. It was easy for Adams to persist in the microwave oven project, beyond reason and with untiring emotion—he was doing it for his old friend.

This isn't as crazy as it sounds, or as unusual. In another breakthrough, when JVC was struggling to compete with bigger companies like Sony to develop the first home-use video cassette recorder (VCR), project leaders Yuma Shiraishi and Shizuo Takano showed their machine to the patriarch of their parent company, a venerable and imposing man named Konosuke Matsushita. When Matsushita had seen their machine, he told Shiraishi and Takano they had made a "wonderful" thing, and he placed his cheek against it, unself-consciously, affectionately. It was an embrace that encompassed not just a machine but the two men who had poured years of their lives into making that machine.

Matsushita, months later, was approached by a business friend, Akio Morita, the chairman of Sony—whose own VCR was in bitter competition with the device created by Takano and Shiraishi. Morita asked that Matsushita order a halt to the JVC effort. With that request by Morita, Matsushita faced a number of implications. If he consented, his subsidiary company, JVC, would have to follow his command meekly, although they would certainly resent his meddling. His own company would go unscathed—by switching from JVC to Sony, it would continue to be a major participant in the VCR market. And if he refused Morita, he would certainly have to cope for years with the resentment of a very powerful colleague and competitor.[8]

However tough the decision might seem, it's unlikely that Konosuke Matsushita even hesitated before he refused Morita's request. He had committed not only his company's honor but his personal embrace to the work of Shiraishi and Takano. At another time and place, Charles Adams, like Matsushita, had taken an emotional step that could not be reversed. He had embraced the microwave oven project and, in doing so, had embraced the people in his company whom he most admired, whose talents he most cherished.

Today, after a remarkably long and twisted path, the microwave oven is one of the most pervasive products in the world, acknowledged as a technological marvel, a middle-class icon, and a commercial breakthrough. To make it this far, the product needed a

---

8. As reported by Lee Smith, "Sony Battles Back," *Fortune,* April 15, 1985, page 31.

series of advocates, experts, and tinkerers who picked it up and advanced it at critical moments. At the turning point in its existence, it needed an inventor who, in a single coherent perception, could sort through the knowledge and errors of a decade of research. It needed a great deal of creativity, corporate commitment, persistence, and luck.

But holding together all these elements that made the modern microwave oven possible was a tenuous strand of emotion—kept unbroken by Charlie Adams. What it needed most of all was an act of love.

9 Toyota: The Supermarket for Cars

Throughout the long generation of abundance that Americans enjoyed after World War II, warnings by experts that the earth's resources might eventually be depleted fell on deaf ears. There seemed to be plenty of everything. The shock of shortages did not come home to Americans until it permanently affected the most beloved, cursed, and indulged necessity of the consumer society, the family car. When oil started drying up in the 1970s, and all those cars began gasping for sustenance, and drivers found themselves simmering angrily in two-hour gas lines, people's perceptions of the world were changed irreversibly.

There were many greater implications for the world economy that stemmed from the oil embargo imposed on the industrial world in 1974 and 1978 by OPEC. But none was more dramatic than the fact that Americans swiftly lost faith in Detroit and began to look curiously toward foreign automobile makers who could transport people comfortably and economically in a four-cylinder roller skate that went forty miles or more before it dipped into its second gallon of fuel. Suddenly Japan, the best nation at making little cars, became a magnet for American drivers' attention.

In the mid-1970s, Japan, not the United States, became the leading nation in the export of automobiles. By 1983, Japanese auto manufacture exceeded 11.1 million cars, compared to 9.2 million made and sold by the U.S. makers.

American automakers belatedly awoke to a reality they had been ignoring for three decades. They weren't just getting whipped on the basis of price by these little cars from Japan; they were getting beaten by Japanese engineers, Japanese production technology, and Japanese quality. The American automobile had slipped to the status of second-rate, and the message was coming through to the American car makers from the most embarrassing source: American drivers. The speed with which the U.S. automobile companies sought out Japanese know-how on the building of small cars had the sweaty scent of panic. In their rush to learn something, anything, the Americans suddenly studying the Japanese understood one thing clearly: Toyota Motor Corporation, located in a bustling company town called Toyota-Shi (Toyota City), not far from Nagoya, had transformed the automobile industry. And the Toyota Production System might be not only one of the greatest breakthroughs of the 1970s, but also the hardest to understand.

The Toyota Production System is an interplay of production concepts that, taken separately, are simple and revolutionary. Taken together, these concepts are inextricable from the personal commitment and efficiency of each member of the Toyota work force. The Toyota Production System, under the leadership of one man, a former machinist and union member named Taiichi Ohno, took thirty years to develop to its current level of productivity. The exceptional efficiency of the Toyota Production System can be measured simply, powerfully, in dollars:

- The average Japanese automobile today, even though wages in America and Japan are approaching parity, costs only two-thirds as much to make as the average American automobile.
- The cost for the average Japanese automobile, shipped across the Pacific Ocean into the United States, with all duties, international taxes, and transportation expenses added to its base price, is still $1300 less than the same cost for the average American car driven from Detroit on the back of an eighteen-wheeler.

And today, notwithstanding Detroit's recent efforts to reverse this perception, many, if not most, Americans believe that the less expensive Japanese import is not merely a better deal but a much better car. In fact, it was quality more than price that drove automakers first in Japan, then in Detroit, to begin trying to figure out why Toyota's system was so effective. Most manufacturers found ways to hurry their versions of smaller, more fuel-efficient cars into production. Toyota's fellow Japanese carmakers had been doing it almost as long as Toyota. But no one could do it nearly as well as Toyota. The sudden influx of competitors studying the Toyota Production System struck Toyota's leaders with a triumphant sense of irony.

Fujio Cho, general manager of Toyota's Transportation Administration Office today, who worked in auto plants for much of his career in the company, recalled that Toyota was traditionally an oddball among Japan's carmakers. Toyota-Shi, a rural village far from Japan's larger industrial centers, stamped the Toyota people as bumpkins unable to understand modern production technology. "We were regarded as black sheep," said Cho, "even among scholars and academicians—the experts on production management. They thought we were doing something very strange. Our actual manner of production was very different from the ways everyone else was doing it."

To a significant extent, Toyota was doing things backward from the standard approach to auto manufacturing. One of the most imitated features of the Toyota Production System is called "just-in-time," and, said Ohno, it emerged literally when "we reversed our thinking and considered the production process in terms of backward flow." "Just-in-time" and a system called *kanban* are the two most broadly studied and discussed pieces of the Toyota Production System. Each is simple.

Just-in-time is a concept that eradicates the idea of inventory in a manufacturing plant. Parts are not kept in warehouses waiting to be moved to the production line. In essence, the production line itself is all the storage that exists in a Toyota plant. In order to realize just-in-time production, each production process on the line receives the parts it needs in the necessary quantity at exactly the right time from the preceding station on the production line. This seems to make sense, and it seems—to the outside observer—to be the way a production line ought to run, ideally. But turning the ideal into reality is something that took more than fifty years of automotive history and a quaint group of production revolutionaries at Toyota.

A key to the realization of this revolution was *kanban,* an "information-carrying device," actually a colored paper card that travels the line with the actual parts and indicates such details as where the parts should go, how many there are, and what time they must arrive at their next destination. *Kanban* circulation times are adjusted as the cards travel, according to the number of parts being used. Thus, if parts are being depleted more slowly, the *kanban* card tells the people on the production line to delay ordering replacement parts. And if parts are going fast, *kanban* is the automatic, nontechnological device that alerts the production crew to call for more parts at just the right time. Toyota has installed *kanban* not only in its own plants, but in the plants run by its outside parts suppliers, literally infiltrating this parade of colored cards throughout the Aichi prefecture of Japan.

Kanban limits the buildup of inventory provided from outside suppliers and eliminates any buildup of partly finished products between stations on the production line. Almost empty of any waiting stacks of half-built parts, a Toyota production line has an empty look, but it is fiendishly efficient.

In most automobile manufacturing plants, Ohno explained, "You don't want workers or machines to be idle, so you keep on producing parts whether you need them in the assembly stage or not. But if you do that in the just-in-time system, there is no place to stack them. If the workers have the materials to make parts but no place to stack them, they have to stop producing. When that happens the supervisor knows he has too many people working on that production stage, and the workers realize there are more people on the job than necessary."

In this brief explanation Ohno implies one of the most complex results of using just-in-time. While solving one defect in a manufacturing process, the system exposes a host of additional defects. It can, in fact, reveal a network of problems—waste of money, waste of time, waste of people.

Nevertheless, because of the outward simplicity of just-in-time and *kanban,* these things began to spring up in auto plants all over the world, along with a third Toyota idea called "quality circles." In fact, quality circles were most thoroughly described in the 1950s by an American named Edward Deming, who celebrated Toyota very early as a prime example. A "quality circle," in simple terms, is a group of workers who discuss ways to do their work better and make better cars. Quality circles work at Toyota because management does (more than 90 percent of the time) what the workers tell them to do.

Still, no company that faithfully imitated just-in-time, *kanban,* and quality circles did it nearly as well as Toyota. In many cases, other companies' quality circles were simply mechanisms set up to pacify workers. With all three concepts, other companies mimicked Toyota without understanding the ideas that bred and nurtured the unique web of people and automation that makes the Toyota Production System. To try to duplicate Toyota's attainment by installing just-in-time and *kanban* is like trying to visualize *Swan Lake* by reading Tchaikovsky's score; it is notes without music, dance without dancers.

To grasp even something as ostensibly simple as just-in-time, it is crucial to know its origins. The story, by now, is a blend of legend and fact, but the basic facts remain true.

The founder of Toyota Motor Works was Kiichiro Toyoda, the son of one of Japan's great inventors and industrial heroes, Sakichi Toyoda.

In 1935, two years before the first Toyota car was produced, Kiichiro Toyoda compared the automobile assembly line to an American supermarket. He noticed that in an American market, great quantities of food—much of it perishable—are gathered. It can't be stored on site, because the store doesn't have space and can't afford the cost of storage, and because much of the food would spoil in storage. So, as shelves empty in the store, the staff notes the need for more supplies; the supplier is informed and the bread or hams or fresh peaches arrive "just in time." If this system could somehow be translated to auto production, Kiichiro thought, the elimination of waste, the elimination of parts warehouses, and the greater coordination of all production stages could reduce costs dramatically. It would give the company that made it work a significant competitive advantage.

Kiichiro's concept was sound; it was intriguing. But it would be twenty years—two years after Kiichiro Toyoda's death—before Toyota Motor Works could even begin to practice this "supermarket system" of operation.

"Nineteen thirty-five—that's when the principle was introduced," said Taiichi Ohno. "No one really believed that it would be implemented."

The supermarket in Kiichiro Toyoda's vision was a key analogy in the development of the Toyota Production System. But that first notion of just-in-time couldn't stand alone. It had to be connected, with a series of separate, apparently unrelated ideas. The person at Toyota who gathered the threads and spun them together was Taiichi Ohno. Indeed, the eventual key to Toyota's emergence in the 1970s as a great company was not that Kiichiro Toyoda associated supermarkets and automobiles, but that he *shared* this odd notion with Ohno.

The Toyota Production System is no system at all. It is a philosophy, formed by Kiichiro Toyoda, Taiichi Ohno, and a network of Toyota leaders who adopted the ideas of Toyoda and Ohno. The Toyota Production System is just a jumble of flow charts and technocracy—until one comes to some understanding of Ohno, who poured his heart into the expression of this philosophy. Among Toyota people of every corporate rank, Ohno is known by the reverent title *sensei*. (The Japanese word *sensei* can be translated literally as teacher and master, but it is far more difficult to translate emotionally.)

It was in the 1940s that Taiichi Ohno became deeply impressed by Kiichiro Toyoda's supermarket analogy. That was when Toyoda, the company founder, was battling to bring his eight-year old company back to life after the devastation of World War II. Ohno was then a young engineer. Toyoda was an admired figure at his company because he was an unpretentious meddler who knew his people, talked with them, helped them. One day, for example, Kiichiro Toyoda was walking through the plant when he came upon a worker scratching his head and muttering that his grinding machine would not run. Kiichiro looked at the man, then rolled up his own sleeves and plunged his hands into the oil pan. He came up with two handfuls of sludge. Throwing the sludge on the floor, he said, "How can you expect to do your job without getting your hands dirty?"

Toyoda perceived in Ohno the intellect not just to understand his vaguely articulated supermarket analogy, but the will to expand it, form it into a system, and fit it into the Toyota organization. In confiding in Ohno, Toyoda had intentionally ignited an inspiration that couldn't be stifled. He had touched the heart of a compulsive teacher.

Taiichi Ohno was an engineer by profession. His career had begun at the oldest of the Toyoda family's companies, Toyoda Spinning and Weaving Company, Ltd.—founded by Kiichiro's father, Sakichi Toyoda. But, occupation notwithstanding, Ohno was a *teacher* by inclination, by vocation. In hearing from Kiichiro that supermarket analogy and in hearing from Kiichiro that dream of a production system unlike any other system in the world, Ohno obtained two necessities vital to the satisfaction of a teacher's passion. First, Kiichiro gave Ohno a subject to teach that would demand the complete intellect of the teacher. It would demand that Ohno learn constantly, even as he was dispensing knowledge. Second, Kiichiro gave Ohno a subject that would lead his pupils constantly to the limits of their potential and into the excitement of new discovery every day. Kiichiro had given Ohno a realm of learning that would never find peace.

Ohno believed the Toyota organization would support his progress wherever it might lead. Sakichi Toyoda, the entrepreneur of fourteen companies that now comprise the Toyota Group, had led his employees from the drudgery of the Industrial Revolution, at the turn of the twentieth century, by reasserting the greater value of human beings over machines. As important as the invention of his most revolutionary machine, the automatic loom, Sakichi Toyoda incorporated his faith in the worker into the atmosphere of Toyoda Automatic Loom Works. He expected more from workers than they often expected from themselves. He established the Toyota tradition of finding the best minds in the workforce and keeping them as long as possible "on the shop floor," where they could examine the way things are done and think of ways to make them better. He insisted that people can meet challenges that at first glance clearly appear impossible. But those people must have a catalyst, a leader—a teacher!—to show them the depth of their own inner strength.

Takumi Mishima, now general counselor of Toyota's Production Control Department, expressed in a few words the effect of Taiichi Ohno, the catalyst, who arrived at work every day, early, armed with Sakichi Toyoda's demanding legacy. "We were frightened," said Mishima, "because we were afraid we weren't living up to his expectations."

Taiichi Ohno is a perplexing figure at Toyota. Toyota is a company where, as with most Japanese firms, the "homogeneity" of the Japanese people is professed as the source of the company's "spirit of teamwork." Yet Ohno has no place in any philosophy of sameness. In a voice that rumbles and growls above everyone else, his remarks are bold, straightforward. His ego bespeaks a man who knows most of the answers and is impatient with the rest of the crowd for not getting around to the questions more quickly. His word for himself is *rebel*. He laughs with none of the reserve that marks the humor of the people around him; he seems to take pride in being the one guy in the room who knows a good joke when he hears one. Unlike many Japanese men who profess total devotion to their work, at the expense of their families, Ohno says he's glad to get away from the job and spend time close to his family. He draws a sharp distinction between Toyota's time and his own time.

Yet clearly, for thirty years of his life, the Toyota Production System was never far from Taiichi Ohno's mind. It became his obsession; it has become his legacy to Toyota Motor Works. He created an army of company executives who call themselves "Ohno's Apostles." To know about Taiichi Ohno is to know why the Toyota Production System has become the standard of automobile production for the 1980s and beyond.

Before Ohno, the various pieces of the Toyota Production System, such as the idea of just-in-time, existed separately at Toyota. These concepts had emerged at different times, in different places within the growing group of family-owned companies, and they had no discernible interrelationship. Ohno, in a progressive series of connections, fit them into a whole. In even making these connections, Ohno was violating an iron-clad law of modern manufacturing—that the more of a thing you manufacture, the lower each unit will cost. "It's a wrong notion to believe that mass production will guarantee you less cost. That was true in the 1960s, in those days, when there was a high demand," said Ohno. "But that notion has become a myth that no longer applies in the 1980s. Now production capacity exceeds demand. For some reason, many people in the world still believe in this myth and they will still take for granted that if they increase mass production they can reduce costs."

Fujio Cho called Ohno the "interpreter." Ohno was the man who seemed to see ahead to a change in the very basis of manufacturing. Already in the 1950s, Taiichi Ohno was saying to his colleagues at Toyota that, in the future, auto companies would be unable to dictate to car buyers a limited range of models and body styles and then gear their production schedules to that self-imposed system of supply and demand. Ohno foresaw the need to eliminate the production schedule entirely and produce cars according to customer preferences, even though some models, colors, and optional features would be demanded by relatively small numbers of customers.

"We cannot be dependent upon a production schedule to produce autos," Ohno said. "It's very important to have an extremely flexible system so that we can manufacture certain models regardless of which models sell the most." For the next twenty years, such thinking was sheer heresy in automobile production circles. Ohno looked within Toyota to find the elements necessary to prepare the company for the great change to come. But Ohno's active role in developing the Toyota Production System began as early as 1955, a decade after Kiichiro Toyoda had introduced him to the supermarket metaphor.

Before Ohno became *sensei,* Toyota had to experience its deepest, most shattering crisis. In 1949 Japan's economy had still not emerged from the postwar recession; goods and materials of all kinds were in short supply, inflation was rampant, and people in the cities were forced to trade their clothing and home furnishings for rice or potatoes just to keep themselves alive. When the Japanese government tightened money in 1949 to reduce inflation, Toyota management started to run out of operating cash. Inventories grew, salaries were cut, and finally, for Japan, the unthinkable happened. First, rank-and-file Toyota workers were laid off. Then the workers went on strike. In essence, what happened was that, after a half-century of "family," Toyota management and its workers had broken trust with each other.

For Kiichiro Toyoda, the crisis was crushing and irreconcilable. His dream lay broken at his feet. The loss of the dream occurred in a few weeks, but it was a dream that had grown over a period of decades. Kiichiro's dream was born in the angry determination of his father. One of the company's most inspiring stories is about Sakichi Toyoda, in 1890, visiting day after day the Exhibition for the Promotion of Japanese Industry. Sakichi Toyoda was there every day for weeks, and whenever a new machine was demonstrated he pushed his way to the front of the crowd. Some of the exhibitors eventually noticed this young man, obviously poor and countrified, annoying the more prosperous visitors. Someone finally told him to leave and not come back. Sakichi responded with anger, saying, "You're a Japanese, aren't you? These machines are all made outside Japan. Doesn't that mean anything to you? I'm proud of being Japanese, and I'm going to invent better machines and I'm going to make them in Japan!"

Sakichi Toyoda did what he had promised. He invented a new automatic loom and changed forever the face of the Japanese fabric industry. In the 1930s, Sakichi told son Kiichiro to accomplish in the auto industry what he had accomplished in the textile industry. In the shambles of a postwar Japan, Kiichiro only had been further inspired when General Douglas MacArthur, commander of the United States Occupation Forces, stated flatly that the Japanese lacked the ability to mass-produce good cars; MacArthur (and a majority of Japanese economists) told the Japanese car makers to leave that job up to Ford, General Motors, and Chrysler.

Before the labor troubles began at Toyota, said Cho, "Kiichiro Toyoda had a great dream. He had established already the first private automobile company in Japan. He told everyone that if we cannot catch up to the United States in three years, we probably will not survive."

When the crash of 1949 happened, the three-year goal was lost and the dream seemed on the brink of death. "When we had to lay off many of our employees," recalled Tokio Horigome, general manager of Toyota's Research and Information Office, "Kiichiro Toyoda took the blame. He resigned from the company. He said he would not let so many employees retire from the company unless he did the same."

For two months after the strike began, Toyota Motor Works lay idle and on the verge of bankruptcy. "The wild wheat was growing in the factory," said Horigome. When the strike was eventually settled, the workers came back bitter at management, alienated from them.

Management combed the ranks of workers in search of the extremists and agitators whom they blamed for wrecking their happy home. Kiichiro Toyoda fell ill, and though he was asked back to the leadership of his company, he never regained his health. He died before Taiichi Ohno devised the Toyota Production System.

Regardless of where the blame lay for the crisis in 1949, what management and labor truly felt was a sense of shared failure. Toyota had lost touch with the roots sunk by Sakichi Toyoda.

Ohno's vision of Sakichi Toyoda is that of a man whose heart was touched, when he was still young, by the brutal toil required of workers who produced textiles on industrial looms. "He used to see his mother work on the loom," said Ohno, "and he wondered how he could make that work better for people." When in 1897 Sakichi Toyoda invented and patented the automatic loom, he accomplished that goal and two others. First, he included in the automatic loom a device designed to stop the machine automatically whenever the weft thread broke or ran out. Additionally, he made a machine that could not produce a defective product, a machine that noticed its own mistakes and could stop itself before the product had a chance to go bad.

Taiichi Ohno was greatly influenced by the concept incorporated in the automatic loom. "I feel strongly that the word *work* refers to the production of perfect goods only," said Ohno. "If a machine is not producing perfect goods, it is not 'working.' In the Toyota way of thinking, mechanisms for stopping production of defective goods must be fitted into automatic machines."

In the very infancy of automation, Sakichi Toyoda had made the rare observation that automatic machines can be broken without seeming broken and can go on making bad things indefinitely without anyone noticing the problem. Born before the twentieth century, the idea at Toyota that counteracts this flaw in automation is called *jidoka*. Perhaps more important to the Toyota Production System than just-in-time, *kanban,* or quality circles is *jidoka*. To Ohno, *jidoka* is important because it demands so much from each worker, each Ohno's pupil, on the assembly floor. Because it requires workers to respond decisively with each automatic stoppage of any of dozens of auto assembly machines, at Toyota *jidoka* assumes a respect for the worker's intelligence. At the time of crisis in the mid-1950s, it revived the Toyota tradition of putting bright people on the shop floor in the middle of the action to keep the line moving.

In Japanese, *jidoka* can be translated straightforwardly as "automation." But at Toyota, *jidoka* means much more. It implies faith in the worker, as a human being and as a thinker. "What is the difference about human beings?" asked Cho. "How can we differentiate a human being and an animal? Man can *think*. He has brains. Then we thought we should respect those capabilities in human beings, promote their creativity. Good products, good thoughts, good ideas. It was a tradition, for the Toyota Production System, to think together, put all our wisdom together to improve the company, the product."

As a result of the labor strike at Toyota, management and labor had ceased to deal with each other as people and reduced each other to their jobs, their titles, their functions. So Ohno redefined *jidoka* to express Toyota tradition. He used his new concept of *jidoka* as a means of restoring the dignity of the rank-and-file worker. The first problem Ohno faced when Toyota management gave him an ambiguous mandate to improve production methods was to deal with the array of automatic machines. These were machines produced by other companies, mostly American, and they were supposedly "ready-made" to produce cars.

Fujio Cho recalled Ohno's thoughts about the new wave of production automation. "When management first decided to buy automated machines," said Fujio Cho, "they thought they would be able to replace people. Instead of using three people, the machines would work by themselves. But, in reality, they realized they still needed people to avoid defective items."

Management's solution was to park one person beside each machine. That person would watch the machine until it broke down, and then tell someone. Ohno regarded this as a pretty stupid way to use people on the assembly floor.

"Mr. Ohno, our *sensei,* asked us to think together, to find a way to add Toyota intelligence to these machines," said Cho.

"Left on their own, machines continue to produce items even though a problem has occurred," said Ohno. "So they produce defective items. To solve that, we installed a very simple sensor. This little simple thing saves many defects."

The "sensor" was an analog to the same device Sakichi Toyoda had installed as a basic part in his automatic loom almost sixty years before. Everyone at Toyota had forgotten or taken for granted Sakichi's self-regulating principle of automation—everyone, that is, except Ohno. "Mr. Ohno—we call him 'Father' or 'Poppa' Ohno—he wore a very serious face as he told us to do it. Otherwise we would not have even thought about it," said Fujio Cho.

This simple change, at first in one machine, set off a series of reactions, all of them incorporated slowly and meticulously over years into the Toyota assembly process. "Under most automation systems, the machine will keep making defective items, because it is a machine," explained Horigome. "It cannot distinguish. But *jidoka* is to teach the machine to do it by itself. In other words, it gives the machine a human intelligence so that the machine will know what it is supposed to do." *Jidoka* meant, for instance, that every worker would be involved in regulating automatic machines. One of the first technological steps in the establishment of *jidoka* was to invent and install sensors on production machines. It did not happen on all the machines at once. But gradually, over time, each production machine was given the ability to sense its own disorders. When the sensors recognized a malfunction in the machine, a light attached to the machine began to glow, and the machine stopped itself. Because the sensor anticipated breakdowns, the machine could be repaired *before* it broke.

As more and more sensor lights appeared on machines in a single production line, the managers who hurried from problem to problem became more and more pressured. Ohno responded with a new system called *andon*—a central "switchboard" connected with every machine. A manager monitoring problems in production could tell at a glance by looking at the *andon* board where a problem was happening. For Taiichi Ohno, *andon* was the fulfillment of a goal—to reduce by dramatic proportions the number of employees assigned to solve production problems. Because of the efficiency of the *andon* system, one manager assigned to the "improvement staff" on the production floor was able to cover the same ground once covered by ten people.

"There was an attitude change," recalled Fujio Cho. "Before *andon,* the improvement staff came in to work, and they didn't want to know about any problems. With *andon,* the improvement staff was able to collect information and gather complaints about problems before they actually happened. They collected everybody's troubles and corrected them. People stopped worrying about who was to blame for a problem, and the feeling of unity between the production workers and the improvement staff managers grew."

Andon meant, in fact, that the Toyota improvement staff manager and, to a lesser extent, the production worker had to be multifunctional. He must eventually learn every machine and every station on the assembly line, or he could not respond to the full range of expectations that *jidoka* implied. And it meant that each worker would, almost instinctively, begin to see ways to make the system, the interplay of machines and people, work better. It meant he would be virtually unable to resist telling someone else his ideas for making it work better.

It meant that each Toyota production worker had to keep *learning* from the day he began his career until the day he retired.

Jidoka, as Taiichi Ohno quietly fit its elements together at Toyota, had one fundamental tenet, a requirement that made it work. Ohno's perception was that, in order to react to every problem or opportunity as soon as it emerged, each worker has to be able to *see* everything operating. Ohno stripped all the sheet metal away from machines; he redesigned machines so that every moving part was visible. "Mr. Ohno said if a production line cannot be understood with your own eyes, then it's not a good production line," explained Cho. "You should be able to tell and see everything with your own eyes."

This "never trust a machine" philosophy, stated first in Sakichi's loom, is part of official company policy. This remark was made by the chairman of the board, Eiji Toyoda: "Society has reached the point where one can push a button and be immediately deluged with technical and managerial information. This is all very convenient, of course, but if one is not careful there is a danger of losing the ability to think. We must remember that in the end it is the individual human being who must solve the problem. Today, just as in the days when tools were pencils, paper, abacus, and ruler, the powers of observation and insight are still what count. When one prepares to tune a car engine or adjust a carburetor, I think that, before hooking up the oscilloscope or some other instrument, one should first look closely at the engine in its entirety and at the car itself. After first looking closely at the whole, then one should determine what must be done to each part."

With *jidoka,* Taiichi Ohno made sure that it wasn't just managers who had the privilege of using their heads. Ohno created a system of employee suggestions, since institutionalized as "quality circles." He perpetuated Toyota's "low technology" approach to manufacturing; he refused to allow the concealment of needed information inside machines and computers. He wanted all workers to learn every function. He gave every worker the responsibility to halt the entire production line whenever the worker saw a problem, small or large, that could become worse if not corrected immediately.

"In the United States [and other nations], stopping a production line is something wrong—evil!" said Ohno. "The Japanese approach is the other way around. *Jidoka* encourages people to stop the line when there is any trouble. If you don't stop the line when there is trouble, you are doing the wrong thing."

A visit to a Toyota line today—at Takaoka, for example—is a profoundly disappointing experience. It lacks the grandeur of great industry. Automobiles in various stages of assembly weave along a serpentine conveyor. There are many cars in process, many workers. But there is no sense of magnitude here, no glistening engines of industrial might. Areas on either side of the production line are relatively clear, because inventory buildups are forbidden here. Machinery is stark, stripped down, visible. Some sections of the line are almost unpeopled; one worker roams a wide area, observing the *andon* lights of a number of robotized production stages. Other areas contain a series of workers bustling through four or five assembly functions as cars inch by.

But each of these work stations has a sort of stylistic flair. Most stages are carpeted. The floor rises and falls along the line, allowing each worker the most comfortable position for each task. Workbenches are scrubbed and neat; each tool, once used, goes back to exactly the same spot, often right next to the flower vase or the picture of the family. It is a *quiet* assembly line, perhaps because each machine is only turned on for as long as it's needed, then it is shut off again. The Japanese imperative—"eliminate waste"—applies here to energy, movement, noise, space, even to bosses wandering around giving orders.

And the line does stop, repeatedly. Red lights go on, a bell sounds. There is a pause of perhaps ten seconds, perhaps as long as thirty seconds—and then it moves again. Regarded in most factories as subversion, these perpetual line stoppages at Toyota, these brave little acts of *jidoka,* seem terribly, disappointingly trivial. And they seem to accelerate the pace.

Andon, the system of warning lights and bells, means that a worker is free, as Cho noted, "to do other things." This is called, *"ijo kanri,"* the control and management of only the emergency. It was, of course, Ohno's belief that the "other things" workers would do would be to think about ways to make the system work better.

One of Ohno's pupils recalled a familiar Ohno tactic. At the beginning of the workday, Ohno appeared at a particular section of the assembly line, and he would stay there. He observed all day, pacing, watching, but never speaking. All day, he didn't say a word. But the improvement staff responsible for that production area was concerned. They understood something was wrong. "Poppa Ohno" had seen some way to do this job better. "All day, we wondered what it could be. We looked at everything. We whispered to each other. We studied every movement, because we knew if we didn't find it that day, he would come back in the morning and start screaming at us. He gave you one day; that was all!"

"When we see him nearby," said Horigome, "we start to sweat."

Even under Ohno, this sense of worker involvement, this vigilance for improvement did not occur immediately. The Toyota Production System was truly an evolution, almost twenty years in the making. Ohno had, at the beginning, no more authority than the average *kacho,* or section manager. In 1955 he was not yet regarded as senior management. He did his first experiments with the idea of *jidoka* and just-in-time inside the machine shop, with the experimental assembly of automobile transmissions.

"I gave the authority to myself and was a self-appointed manager," said Ohno. "I wasn't really self-appointed, of course. I didn't have the authority. I did it on my own responsibility, and I was ready to take the blame if it failed. For some reason, I'm still alive."

When Ohno's experiment worked in the machine shop, his system took its first big step. His transmission assembly process was installed on the regular assembly line. Then he started to restructure other sections of the line to work the same way. His pupils began to multiply.

"What I recall is that he would come to the plant, to the floor, and he would personally instruct the workers as to what to do," said Mishima. "We had then six thousand to eight thousand workers on the assembly line of Toyota. I thought it was remarkable that Mr. Ohno met all the shop floor people one by one."

Ohno recalled, "I was wearing more and more hats. I would be in charge of the final assembly line as well as the rough shop, the machine shop. When you have an idea, you have to have the people on the floor try it . . . to prove it can be worked out, before it can be further developed. So you really have to be very close between the shop and the assembly line."

Piece by piece, Ohno's ideas prevailed. Insidiously, Ohno's "authority" superseded other authorities who *thought* they ran the manufacturing process. Machines were changed to fit Ohno's specifications; management, unable to understand this drastically transformed environment, had to become pupils of Ohno in order to understand their own factory. Ohno had applied to this creation not so much a vision of how a perfect assembly line should appear, but a set of principles of how people should work together and treat one another in order to manufacture things. Ohno conformed to no plan or blueprint. As Godfrey Hounsfield applied a "mechanic's imperative" to inventing the CT scanner at EMI, Taiichi Ohno applied it to the reinvention of the assembly line. He introduced elements to it in a progressive, logical sequence, threw away those that didn't fit, worked with only the materials that were easily at hand and affordable—he made adjustments as the need arose.

The most telling example of this principle in application can be seen in the company's production through much of the 1950s. Replacement parts for assembly machines, all of them manufactured overseas, were not available to Japanese car makers. At Toyota, this meant that, in order to stay in production, the company had to repair what was already there. Ohno simply told people they could not let any machine reach a point of failure. Workers began to watch for subtleties, to seek the root causes of problems. A sensor light might flicker on, indicating that something was wrong with a production machine. "Why is that light on?" Ohno would ask. "Well," someone would reply, "maybe there is a defective part in the machine." "How do we find that defective part?" Ohno would ask. And this question would send the improvement staff poring over the machines for symptoms—until they found, perhaps, a seepage of oil, ever so slight.

"Explain the oil leak," Ohno insisted. The improvement staff finally discovered that the seams in the oil pipes were loose. "Why are the seams loose?" Ohno demanded to know. The answer came back that the machine's vibration made the seams weaken. "Stop the vibration," Ohno would say. It can't be stopped, would be the reply. "Then," Ohno would say, "how can we protect that point from vibration?" And the answer emerged! The problem part had been secured to the machine at two points. Secure it at *four* points and it will not come loose.

"We said you should really find out the exact cause of a breakdown," explained Cho. "If it takes time to do that, eventually you are able to *transfer* the time. *Jidoka,* on one end, means an effort to avoid the recurrence of this type of breakdown."

For a manager who perceives his responsibility as the "big picture," for whom stability and a hierarchy of authority is vital, the Toyota production line of the 1950s and 1960s had all the characteristics of the day room at an asylum. The constant atmosphere of shortages and deprivation, the attention paid to trivial matters like replacing two screws with four screws, the perpetual cycle of setting things up, then tearing them apart and setting them up all over again, would have been madness to a conventional manager. For Ohno, however, this was the perfect teaching environment. As things went along, everyone learned. And Ohno had to stay a step ahead of the class all the time. If he couldn't, if he faltered even once, he was not a worthy *sensei*.

Perhaps Ohno's greatest challenge with the Toyota Production System was implementing the elements of just-in-time and *kanban*—because these required the cooperation of outside suppliers. Ohno had two advantages. One was simple. All the suppliers to Toyota Motor Works are located close to Toyota City, in the prefecture of Aichi, and many are members of the Toyota "family" of companies. Ohno's visits to these companies, to teach and preach his system, became frequent. The other advantage Ohno had was psychological. All these companies shared with Toyota the trauma of near failure and deprivation that had gripped Japanese business after the defeat in World War II. There was, therefore, a fundamental logic in Ohno's explanation of working "just-in-time."

Inventory, he told the suppliers, is simply the institutionalization of waste and inefficiency. If you pile up parts before assembly, and if you pile up partly assembled products between each stage of assembly, then you never have to improve the quality of the production line itself. You can allow things to break, and even with prolonged periods of failure, you can keep putting out products from the accumulation of partly built things. Furthermore, Ohno explained, if you accumulate extra cars at the end of the assembly line, some will never get sold—they will go to waste.

In the 1950s and 1960s, most experts were talking about "mathematically optimal inventory control," matching the amounts of stored material with the anticipated average duration of breakdowns in production. Ohno was talking about "no inventory," "no breakdowns," and "just-in-time." You can make the assembly line work as fast as people are buying Toyota cars, he said, and you don't *have* to work any faster than that. If you can work at the right speed, you don't need to stack up parts in expensive warehouses and you don't need to park extra finished cars in expensive parking lots. The opposite realization, of course, is that you can't afford to make Toyota cars more slowly than people are buying them. You can't afford for the assembly line to break down. Ever!

But here was Ohno's triumph. With *jidoka,* the assembly line *never* breaks down. It never has broken down, because, rather than consisting of machines operating automatically, it consists of people and machines working together intelligently.

Ohno emphasized that the effectiveness of the Toyota Production System goes to the very definition of the worker himself. The word *rodosha* (laborer) is forbidden in Toyota. People are called *gino-in,* or "skilled persons." In each of these skilled persons there is an ingrained awareness not only of his own task on the assembly line but of how that task blends into the one before it and the next step beyond it. Ultimately, each *gino-in* knows all the tasks that go into a finished car, and he has a sense of the whole process. He must know this because he is equally responsible along with every other worker for sensing changes in the flow that might become problems if left unnoticed. There is a harmony, created by Ohno, that can only be attained when people understand each other's jobs as well as they understand their own jobs.

"Mr. Ohno says that a person should not think that he has done his job if he has just done what he is told," said Mishima. "We should always try to think ahead, and only that way can we make improvements."

"Mr. Ohno says" is a phrase that seems tattooed on the tongues of hundreds of people at Toyota. For thirty years, he was the spirit and essence of the Toyota Production System. The system became as individual as a style of painting that is visualized within a single, gifted artist and then conveyed through patient instruction to a group of disciples. As the *sensei,* "Poppa Ohno" was omnipresent at the constantly changing production lines at Toyota. He was an unfathomable presence to those who worked for him, sometimes seemingly on the verge of explosion, other times apparently about to embrace his "sons." People became dependent on Ohno for approval, partly because they believed he was interested in each of them. "One generation of us claims to be the students, the apostles of Mr. Ohno," said Cho. "That group of people are the core of the Toyota Production System."

As important as it is to know *what* Ohno taught people, the emergence of the Toyota Production System, as a *faith,* happened because of *how* Ohno taught. Ohno, the teacher, achieved his remarkable, gentle dominion over this mass of diverse individuals through a teaching method that is almost as old as mankind but never very popular. As demonstrated in his silent scrutiny over those nervous workers, his teaching contained a minimum of direct explanation. He taught by inference and inquiry. He expected his pupils to figure things out by clues and hints, by thinking. Ohno's approach could be frustrating. In another culture his "pupils" might have rejected him as an unreasonable eccentric who expected people to be mind readers. But Ohno's style has an ancient tradition in Japan, although it appears to be dying as Japanese education systems grow more Westernized. Today his teaching style is primarily associated with traditional arts and crafts in Japan—painting, dance, martial arts, sumo, pottery. One of Ohno's "apostles" compared Ohno to Musashi, the great archetypal *samurai* invented by one of Japan's greatest writers, Eiji Yoshikawa.

But Ohno's method precedes even the feudal hero Musashi. Two legendary teachers in Western culture taught through inquiry and parables—Socrates, who interrogated his pupils to near distraction, and Jesus Christ, who preached in fables and symbols. Both glorified the tradition of the teacher who hints at answers and demands perception from his followers. There is another parallel, modern and Japanese.

In the early 1970s, a young Tokyo potter named Takashi Oyama, who was both exceptionally talented and fanatically devoted to his art, wished more than anything else to study pottery in the potters' village of Mashiko, in Tochigi prefecture, under Shoji Hamada. Hamada is one of the great Japanese potters of the last century, so distinctive in style and so admired both in Japan and throughout the world that a museum was dedicated to his art while he was still living. Since his death, that museum has expanded to include his home and his pottery works in Mashiko. Hamada is credited with bridging the immense gulf between the traditional pottery styles of old Japan and the bold modernism of Western art, without an inch of surrender in either direction. He brought an ancient and beautiful art form into a new context, without sacrifice, and he has conveyed a fresh vision to Japanese artists and potters.

It was Oyama's passion to study under Hamada. But when Oyama graduated from secondary school in Tokyo, Hamada was more than seventy years old and had not taken any new students for years. Oyama nevertheless went to Mashiko, determined to impress Hamada with his talent and his dedication. Hamada abruptly told the young man that, regardless of his talent, he was too late; Hamada was too old for another pupil. Oyama, crestfallen at first, refused to be easily discouraged. He found a room in Mashiko and returned daily to Hamada's pottery works, pleading for reconsideration but only, in time, receiving permission to linger in the pottery works, touching nothing, not disturbing anyone, holding his tongue and his curiosity. Oyama came every day for six months, scratching out a living in odd hours in order to enjoy the privilege of Hamada's imperious, unresponsive presence. After six months, Hamada "rewarded" Oyama's persistence by agreeing to let him knead the raw clay to be used later by the potters. Oyama would receive no pay.

Kneading clay is grueling, dreary work. One massages mounds of leaden, uncooperative clay for hours, working out air bubbles that would otherwise burst in the heat of the kiln and destroy the potter's work. Typically, Oyama's work was only noticed when it failed and an art work was lost in the kiln.

Oyama, penniless and patient, spent more than a year kneading and watching. His silent vigil at Hamada's pottery works grew to eighteen months before, at last, Hamada approached Oyama and invited him to take a seat at the potter's wheel and begin to practice his beloved art under the guidance of its greatest *sensei*. But when Hamada "taught" Oyama, he said nothing; he explained nothing. Hamada had been observing the young Oyama for eighteen months; he knew Oyama had absorbed all that he had seen and heard, so when Oyama finally sat to touch and form the clay, he was an artist blessed already with a mature technique and insight. Today, in a village of 350 potters, Oyama is a *sensei* in his own right, honored as Hamada's last pupil and friend. He displays his work annually at exhibitions in Tokyo, Kyoto, and Kobe and is growing in international esteem. A true disciple of Hamada, he demurs his own talent and confesses that he has so much more to learn before he can rest.

Ohno taught the Toyota Production System in the style of Hamada. If Detroit or Nissan have difficulty adopting the Toyota Production System, it is because they lack the *sensei* to whom people are so devoted that they will in every moment of their work probe to determine the meaning of his gestures and inferences, study him to understand what he expects of them, wrack their brains to see what it is he sees.

Fujio Cho recalled an incident in which he tried to please Ohno. Cho was on the improvement staff for a section of the Toyota production line. He was concerned that his section's productivity was low. He couldn't determine the reason for the problem merely by watching the work so, although he was a manager of the operation, threw himself into manual labor on a section of the assembly line. For eight hours, Cho operated a stamping machine, working with unstinting energy and concentration. His results exceeded the section's production average—the normal rate of production on the stamping machine was less than 240 an hour; Cho had produced at a rate of 250 an hour.

Ohno heard of this incident and called Cho into his office. "Mr. Ohno told me that I seemed to have improved the efficiency of production by producing two hundred and fifty parts an hour. But, said Mr. Ohno, if I, as an inexperienced person, could do two hundred and fifty an hour, wasn't it reasonable to expect skilled workers to do two hundred and eighty an hour? 'Don't you think so?' asked Mr. Ohno. I said yes.

" 'But then,' Mr. Ohno said, 'if you think so, you're forcing the workers to work harder without making any real improvement in the production line. Our mission is to increase efficiency and produce more *rationally*—by streamlining, not by mere hard work!' "

Ohno gave Cho a book entitled *Respect for Humanity* and instructed him to read it carefully. "I read the book ten times," said Cho. Then he returned to Ohno's office. He was asked to return each day for four days to discuss the ideas in *Respect for Humanity*.

"Eventually," said Cho, "I realized that what I did was in contradiction to respect for humanity. I was an amateur, unaccustomed to how it feels to do that kind of work every day. Mr. Ohno said, 'That's a terrible thing to do—to make people work harder and faster for no good reason.' "

Cho was deeply chastised, but in private. However, the story does not end there. Cho noted that Ohno never praised people directly. "He feels that if you praise too much, that will be the end of improvement. Although he will not praise you directly, he will convey his goodwill to you through other people," said Cho. In the case of Cho, the praise came when Ohno was conducting tours for Toyota board members visiting the production facilities. "We have a member of our improvement staff named Cho," Ohno told one group of board members. "Cho is a manager, not an engineer. But since it was hard for him, from that vantage point, to understand how improvements in machines bring about improvements in production, Cho one day spent all day operating machines. That will and devotion to understand is necessary for everyone who wants to improve the Toyota Production System." Ohno's praise for Cho spread quickly throughout the Toyota family. It was a recognition as public as Cho's chastisement had been confidential.

Takumi Mishima had a similar episode of inquiry and revelation. During a difficult period of experimentation on a new assembly line in the early 1970s, Mishima was its foreman. When a finished automobile tested out as defective, it would be parked in a cramped area at the end of the assembly line, then returned later to the line for repair. Occasionally the number of defective cars would exceed the space available and one or two would be parked outdoors. One day the keys of one of the cars parked outdoors disappeared. They couldn't be found anywhere. Mishima had to replace the key cylinder in the car before he could move the car back inside for repair.

A few weeks later the same thing happened. But this time the keys were replaced by a note from Ohno. He had taken the keys, and to get them, the foreman must come to Ohno's "office"—which was little more than a glass enclosure next to the assembly line.

"Mr. Ohno told me not to leave cars there," recalled Mishima. "I promised him I would not do this again, and I thought that was the end of the story. But he wouldn't let me go. He said, 'Wait a moment,' and he held up to me another key, which was the key to the car on which we had already changed the key cylinder. 'What about this car?' And I said, 'Well, it's gone now.' He said, 'I don't care. Bring back that car. Here are the keys.' And I explained that the car is no longer in Toyota City. And to that he said, 'Bring back that car!' And we kept on like that. I think that through that discussion, what he was trying to tell me was that he wasn't concerned about that car. It was a question of having produced so many defective cars. He wanted a factory that could avoid, completely, the recurrence of production of defective cars. It was a very tough argument, back and forth. I finally said, 'Well, I will take a day off tomorrow; we'll cover our tracks to Kyushu.' And only when I said that, he said, 'That's all right. Never mind that car. You can go.' "

Ohno's "lesson" to Mishima consisted solely of shouting, "Bring back that car," and it didn't end until Mishima had divined the complex of feelings and principles that lay beneath that rude insistence.

Yoshiki Iwata, who is now general manager of the Production Improvement Department of Toyoda Gosei, noted that Ohno had an array of techniques for rallying people close together. "In front of people, he would scold me, and I was embarrassed," said Iwata. "But all my colleagues, who had also been scolded by Mr. Ohno, would sympathize. The next morning, when we met, we would concentrate on solving the problem and I would be saved from another scolding."

Almost always, after such an incident, the scolded person a few weeks or months later would find himself "hosting" a series of visitors from other areas of the production line—all sent by Ohno, all told that Iwata had come up with a clever solution to a difficult problem and they could learn much from him.

As indirect as Ohno's teaching was, and as indirect his praise, it never waned or faltered, and it carried an emotion that was almost palpable. The apostles of Mr. Ohno are an emotional group of people. Each lesson of Ohno reinforced the last and each conquered challenge expanded the team's sense of what could be done. Ohno had an intuitive grasp of how far he could push. Sometimes the distance was astonishing.

"We weren't sure if we were good enough. We tried to think of more things we could do, but we weren't sure what we were doing was enough," said Mishima. "It was not enough just to complete the first step, but he told us we were required to think ahead and be prepared. He was strict, with love. He made the workers feel that he cared for us."

The most dramatic example was the development at Toyota of what has come to be called Single Minute Exchange of Dies (SMED). The dies in question are huge stamping machines that, in one resounding motion, shape metal into whole sections of car chassis. Well into the 1970s, one of the basic tenets of auto manufacture was that a single production line has to make identical cars for long stretches of time, because the exchange of dies was a process of disassembly, reassembly, adjustment, and fine-tuning that took as long as sixteen hours. During that time, production was at a standstill.

"But then," said Cho, "Mr. Ohno began to insist that the

flexible production demands of the future require very fast die exchange." Thus began the great quest. For a frantic period of six months, the apostles of Mr. Ohno tirelessly studied ways to take all the labor of die exchange away from the stamping line, creating "modular" dies that could be restructured and adjusted *outside* the machine and then simply fitted into the machine, similar to the way a film cartridge fits into a camera. There was a moment of great triumph at Toyota when the team had cut their die exchange time from three hours to less than ten minutes. Ohno's only response was, "Well, we can probably do it faster!"

And they cut the time again, to five minutes—and again, to three minutes. And still, Ohno wasn't satisfied. Today, Toyota exchanges dies in a little more than sixty seconds; and Ohno with a cold twinkle in his eye, says, "If we can do it in a minute, we can do it in thirty seconds."

No one today at Toyota disagrees with that expectation; they know Ohno does not deal in fantasies. Though Taiichi Ohno has yet to draw up a plan or submit a proposal for anything, the people of the company have come to believe in his vision and hearken to his words. That was not always so. In the 1950s he simply had to proceed, without permission, with only an ambiguous blessing from the late Kiichiro Toyoda. For years, his blend of ideas—elimination of waste, respect for humanity, *jidoka, kanban,* just-in-time—made sense only to him. The only way it was expressed or justified was in people's efforts and in the increasing quality of the Toyota automobile. For years, the Toyota Production System grew because Taiichi Ohno didn't bother to discuss the issue with the boss.

"No matter how knowledgeable or concerned the management is, unless you have the support of the workers, it won't work. I thought it would be more important, more urgent, to have the people in the shop understand it and implement it," explained Ohno. "The workers would not necessarily understand what they are doing theoretically. They might not know what they are doing; they would just give it a try. After they've given it a try and succeeded, they would develop understanding. As they try, they gain confidence and see the visible results."

This remarkable description by Ohno explains vividly why the Toyota Production System attained productivity and quality—and variety—unimagined in other world outposts of the auto industry. This is the last piece that explains the strength of the Toyota

Production System. This is not *what* Ohno taught; it is not *how* he taught. This is *why* he taught.

It was never Ohno's foremost goal to make better cars. Teachers don't make products. Ohno's goal was to make better people. The cars were the vehicle to reach that goal. The Toyota Production System was Ohno's tenacious statement of "how life should be," ever-learning, ever-growing, ever directed toward fresh attainment.

Not more, but better! This is a concept that receives lip service from senior management everywhere; it is easily—and often—compromised. But in Taiichi Ohno the spirit of compromise had no room.

The system he created was an expression of his beliefs. When he began his creation, there was—it must be stressed—no need for a system that so intricately focused on quality, on the elimination of waste, and on the interplay of every element of the production line: people with machines, machines with machines, people with people, sections with sections with other sections, pieces with the whole. In that era, with demand for cars vastly greater than production capacity, numbers were the only established goal and almost any system was good enough. But for the individual, for the *sensei,* to say "good enough" is impossible. The vision of that one man was focused not on things but on people. And thus, from its birth, the Toyota Production System was governed, not by a market, but by pride!

"I worked so hard for Mr. Ohno because he was a very inspiring, wonderful person. But that's not the only reason," explained Cho. "He demonstrated that what he gave us was intended for our greater happiness. He was very fair. He tried to show that we are not doing this for his sake but for our own sake."

Like Dick Duke creating "an organization in which the people were the focus," Ohno focused on making the process better in order to get the very best from each person. Ohno might have been just as satisfied improving the process of textile manufacture at Toyoda Gosei (which is his job now, in what he slyly calls "retirement") or even lawn-spraying. As long as he could *teach,* advancing the *science* rather than the business, Ohno was heeding his own calling.

Ohno's sense of mission eventually pervaded everywhere in

Toyota. His presence lingers today, teaching, berating, peering over people's shoulders—the spirit of Toyota. People absorbed the presence of Taiichi Ohno. They began to teach themselves after the same fashion in which they had learned from their *sensei*. Learning and inquiry have become a way of life. Each person, to some imperfect degree, became an Ohno.

Because Ohno haunts Toyota, the system works, and people continue to depict the Toyota Production System as "still incomplete. We're still building the system."

"Because the expectations of customers change constantly, our production system has to change all the time," said Toyota President Shoichiro Toyoda. So Toyota continues to look for things to fix. In 1984, Toyota received 2.15 million suggestions for improvements in the production system from employees, and the company implemented 96 percent of those suggestions.

Today, even though it is possible to study the Toyota Production System and reproduce all its features, it is something that cannot be copied. Technologies and concepts are insufficient to the task. When observers look upon Ohno's system, they see a variety of automobiles produced to match the level of consumer demand and produced with such meticulous quality that *recall* is an almost unknown word at Toyota.

But, in fact, to understand *why* the Toyota Production System is so revolutionary and so uncannily effective, it is better to observe the transformation of a person, a *gino-in* such as Takumi Mishima. Beginning many years ago as a rank-and-file assembler, Mishima discovered and realized his personal potential by working within the Toyota Production System. Today he is a senior executive, a leader within the company. He is one of the apostles of Ohno and explains the value of the system not by presenting balance sheets and frequency-of-repair records, but by telling the story of the stolen car keys. Mishima, risen from the most ordinary circumstances, is today a proud man—and a success—through the vigilance and faith of Taiichi Ohno. The Toyota Production System, like Mishima, stands above its peers today because of the relentlessness and insight of a *sensei* who never said "good enough" to the people who make it work.

A General Motors executive, commenting on Detroit's struggle to catch up with the productivity of Toyota, made this remark:

"The Japanese are a very simple people. They believe in, and constantly strive for, perfection."

He was almost right. But Ohno shrugs at the notion of "perfection." Perfection is an *end,* a sort of death. He doesn't believe people ever can be finished with the goal of finding greater things deeper within themselves. More accurately, what the *sensei* in Japan seeks is not perfection, but harmony. Repeatedly, Shoichiro Toyoda, the company's current leader, depicts the Toyota Production System as "harmony and communication."

When Ohno took the keys from Mishima's defective cars and then kept insisting "Bring back that car!" he didn't settle for a resolution between the two men that henceforth they would stop making defective cars and would be "perfect" from that day on. Ohno would have heard such a promise as lip service to an impossible dream. Instead, he abruptly ended the long argument when Mishima said, "Okay, I'll go to Kyushu and find that car."

Then Ohno knew that Mishima shared with him, at last, the sense of urgency that he felt about the shipment of a defective product containing the work and pride of Toyota workers. The two men had attained *harmony;* they felt the same feeling. They would never reach perfection, but they would move toward it hand in hand. That striving for harmony—expressed in hours of Ohno's silent, unnerving stare and in his bursts of shouting—was Ohno's highest objective as *sensei.* His final testament—a blend that includes *jidoka,* "respect for humanity," just-in-time, *kanban,* a network of machines that literally tell their troubles to people—was finally *more* than harmony. The Toyota Production System became a symphony that—when people grew quiet enough to listen—changed the very rhythms of industry.

10 A Teacher of Competitive Response

Foot trouble and athletes have been associated with each other, inseparably, from the time of Achilles' infamous heel to the time of Jack Lambert, the Pittsburgh Steelers' All-Pro linebacker who was felled by "turf toe" in 1985. For most of that span—some 3200 years—very little was done to improve the shoes that go on athletes' feet. That situation started to change between the 1920s and 1948, with the birth in Germany of two companies, Adidas and Puma, who specialized in shoes for athletes. But the situation for athletes was still far from ideal. Adidas and Puma, both run by the Dassler family of Germany, were large and distant and—because they had little competition—often unresponsive to athletes' requests for design changes. Moreover, through the 1950s, there were no companies, not even Adidas and Puma, that made a comfortable running shoe for the *jogger*.

As pervasive as they seem to be today, there were no joggers at all in the mid-1950s. Jogging in shoes that were available in those days hurt too much for the average person to do. That painful fact might prevail today if not for one stubborn, glowering, and controversial man in Eugene, Oregon—the head coach of the University of Oregon track and field team. His name was Bill Bowerman and he invented the modern-day running shoe. More specifically, he fashioned with his own hands the first of those ubiquitous, comfy staples of popular footwear called Nikes—seen everywhere today from Wall Street to Big Sur.

Mostly because of Bowerman, today's athletic shoes are so well designed and so varied that they have the power to visibly transform an athlete's performance. They are so comfortable and attractive that they are an accepted item of daily wear. When actor Jimmy Stewart appeared on "The Tonight Show" dressed in evening wear and a pair of Nike's Cortez running shoes, he was the object not of amazement, but of envy. And today's athletic shoes are so intrinsic to the affluent cultures of the Western world that they have given birth to a myriad of commercial offspring, ranging from running bras and nylon sweatsuits to the New York City Marathon. Sneakers, once the province of jocks and little boys in striped T-shirts, have covered the distance from Madison Square Garden to Park Avenue.

Bill Bowerman by 1985 was the co-founder of a billion-dollar company, Nike, Inc., and an honored member of the National Track and Field Hall of Fame. But in 1952, he was a third-year college track coach at the University of Oregon. He was working to build a winning program at Oregon, and he was looking for every advantage he could find against the glamor teams of his college conference, the Pacific Eight—teams like UCLA and Southern California, whose athletes trained in fancier facilities and sunnier climes.

Like every track coach before him, Bowerman was fascinated with feet. As a former football player, track athlete, mountain soldier in World War II, and high school track coach in Medford, Oregon, Bowerman had seen more jocks with sore feet than he wanted to remember. He knew that all these athletes were not hypochondriacs. He knew that the shoes many athletes wore weren't very good. Shoes pretty much designed the same way went on every athlete, even though different sports required dramatically different movements and placed vastly different types of stress on the athlete's foot.

Bowerman theorized about different uses requiring different designs. He thought that even a basic single-design shoe could have a sole that was lighter and provided much better support, stability, and traction to the athlete's foot than was available.

In response to this problem, Bowerman meticulously drew his own designs for a better shoe and repeatedly sent them to leading American sporting goods companies. They all turned Bowerman down, indicating that they were happy with their shoes and were not about to take a chance on making something that might be too

expensive to sell. We don't tell you how to coach, they told
Bowerman, so don't tell us how to make shoes. The same message
came to Bowerman from other makers of athletic shoes.

That series of rejections brought Bowerman face to face with a
test of his own philosophy. Since his high school coaching days,
Bowerman had come more and more to describe himself to his
athletes not as a track coach, but as a "teacher of competitive
response." He had taught his athletes to value competition not so
much for its prizes and victories as for its intellectual and spiritual
demands. Bowerman's athletes came to regard each athletic contest as a problem. If you won, there was no problem, but if you lost,
the result was more interesting: You had obtained information that
would help you solve the problem the next time it emerged.

Sometimes, the competitive response to defeat in a one-mile
race was simply a matter of physical conditioning—become
stronger and you will win the next time. But more often, the
response required a complex of information—better race tactics,
more knowledge of the opposition, better equipment. Bowerman
taught his athletes that their resources to win the race were almost
limitless if they applied themselves to knowing and exploiting those
resources fully. Bowerman's track teams had exceptional self-
esteem; they believed in their own ability to summon up the
resources within themselves, not only as athletes but as people.

Bowerman's athletes absorbed a measure of his own intensity.
Bill Bowerman is a man who in every aspect seems to be *more* than
he really is. Not an exceptionally tall man, he seems taller. Not a
muscular man, he seems, at a glance, broader than he really is.
Lanky in his physical appearance, he seems archetypally lanky. His
jaw is set, his manner is reserved, his gaze is penetrating. But
beneath these manifestations of the hard-bitten frontiersman, Bowerman sends forth the unseen welcome of a person who is at heart a
teacher. There is a response in Bowerman that instinctively tests
the person he meets, but once the test results are satisfactory,
instruction commences without delay.

To the disciplines of track and field, Bowerman was a natural.
Track is a team sport in which members work and compete, for the
most part, in isolation from each other. Their greatest bond to each
other is their teacher—his management of their training, his jug-
gling of personnel to create winning combinations in a track meet,
his common beliefs instilled in each of them. Unlike most every

other team sport, the track and field athlete often relates to, and depends upon, his coach more than on any teammate. It is common to find in teams of track athletes and cross-country runners an almost mystical symbiosis, which embraces all the team members and flows obviously and directly from the coach. They seem a separate group from the mainstream of their peers and inseparable from each other.

Bowerman, through the force of his will, created that burning solidarity among the Oregon trackmen. He had long understood that it was this level of emotion that could make the difference in competition, because differences in physical advantage were too often very small. Track and field is a series of events of intuitive simplicity. These are events more dependent upon the body itself, without the aid of devices or rules, than most modern sports. Look at a group of athletes competing in a particular event, and you see an exceptional sameness of appearance. Milers look alike. Pole vaulters all seem formed in the same mold. This is because they are specialists—working as individuals in the cause of the team. Because of this equality, differences between competitors are measurable in small increments and subtle advantages. A coach who teaches competitive response has a responsibility to discover those subtle advantages and use them.

In shoes, Bowerman saw something that was not even subtle. Shoes could be a great deal better, if only someone would make them the way he knew they should be made! But no one would. Bowerman realized the competitive response he would have given to one of his athletes who came to him with this problem: "If you can't find someone to do it for you, the only answer is to learn to do it yourself."

So, Bill Bowerman became a shoemaker. He acquired the skill by trial and error at first. Going to a shoe repairman only taught him the basic vocabulary of shoemaking. After following that cobbler's instructions and ruining a lot of leather, Bowerman went back. The cobbler had not expected to see Bowerman again, but there he was. So he sent him to an expert, a bootmaker who lived outside Eugene, Oregon, and made custom boots for lumberjacks. The bootmaker taught Bowerman that the "lasts," or patterns, for shoe soles and uppers don't have to be fancy or durable. He told Bowerman that lasts could be made from old grocery bags and that he could keep drawing and redrawing, cutting and shaping, until he got the best design. From that insight, and a series of return trips to the bootmaker, Bowerman quickly progressed from grocery bags to leather.

That year, Bowerman designed his first pair of track shoes, for a middle-distance runner named Kenny Moore. Today that first pair of "Nikes" looks fragile and ragged at the edges—but also sleek, light, and purposeful. This was a shoe that would do its job.

Bowerman, who summoned from himself a new talent as shoemaker and technologist, began to outfit more and more of his athletes with his own custom-made shoes. Each pair was an experiment, but each got better. And each suited its use *and its user* like a glove. "A good racing shoe," says Bowerman frequently, "should be built to last the distance and then self-destruct."

To Bowerman's athletes, those shoes were the tangible embodiment of the competitive response. Bill's "guys" won races— wearing those funny-looking handmade shoes—because their coach had found a way to solve a problem that every other coach simply had accepted.

Most of Bowerman's athletes graduated from the University of Oregon and transferred the values embodied in their coach's competitive persistence to other pursuits in life. But one of them, Philip Knight, a middling-good miler who had grown into a superior athlete under Bowerman's fatherly teaching, saw in those custom shoes not just an example, but an industry. Because they solved persistent problems that had plagued runners, Bowerman's designs were better than any shoe being manufactured at the time. Knight believed athletes would embrace these new shoes if he could only find a manufacturer willing to make them. But who?

The American sporting goods companies were not interested. The established companies did not have to listen to the customer. Regardless of whether the customer was happy, he had only the existing sneakers to choose from.

According to legend, the first articulation of what would eventually become Nike, Inc., was a graduate school paper written by Knight while he was studying for his MBA at Stanford University. He suggested that an American company could open new markets for athletic shoes by "sourcing" the products overseas (buying finished goods and importing them), in Japan, then distributing them aggressively in the United States through direct contact with athletes and athletic teams. The key, Knight wrote, was that these must be shoes of a superior design. Knight's concept was more than theoretical. In Bowerman's shoes, he already had the potential technology; all he needed was two companies—a Japanese manufacturer and a United States distributor. To this problem, Knight applied the Bowerman principle of competitive response: If you can't find someone else, do it yourself.

On a postgraduate trip around the world, Knight decided to explore the possibilities for sourcing athletic shoes in Asia. One day in 1962 he called on Onitsuka Tiger, at that time Japan's best manufacturer of athletic shoes. He was only there to ask questions—or so he thought. At that time, very little business information crossed the Pacific Ocean. Onitsuka and Knight were equally mysterious to each other. Knight, however, conveyed an air of authenticity to the Japanese. His athleticism, his youth, and his urgent manner certainly made him seem like the typical American marketing representative, the sort of go-getter Japanese executives frequently read about in popular magazines and books.

Unexpectedly presented by the Tiger people with an opportunity to begin a business relationship on the spot, Knight realized that he didn't even have a *name* for the company he was supposed to be representing. It came to him instinctively. "Blue Ribbon Sports, Inc.," Knight told the Tiger people. Spontaneously, Knight offered a simple arrangement. Tiger would ship their shoes to Blue Ribbon Sports, which would be the sole distributor of the shoes in the United States.

With little hesitancy, Onitsuka said yes. For them, this was a golden opportunity—to be the first in the American marketplace. They set a nominal fee for exclusive Tiger rights in the United States. For $1000, BRS (Blue Ribbon Sports) would be Tiger's sole distributor in the United States. With that unexpected promise, Knight hurried back to America desperately in need of two things, a thousand bucks and a company.

The company came together over Bowerman's kitchen table in Eugene. Knight told Bowerman his idea, and Bowerman responded warmly. Knight was young but he wasn't crazy. Both men knew that if they were successful marketing Tigers in America, Onitsuka would probably agree to manufacture Bowerman's unusual shoe designs. And Bowerman had already begun to see beyond the needs of the track athlete to the needs of people who enjoyed running just for health and exercise. More and more Bowerman had come to believe that running was a terrible failure as a popular sport in America because the shoes were so bad.

Also participating in the kitchen table discussion was John Jaqua, Bowerman's next-door neighbor and attorney. Jaqua told them what they had to do to make a corporation. Bowerman and Knight, in a fairly simple and swift series of actions, became Blue Ribbon Sports, Inc., split the $1000 expense of buying from Tiger the exclusive right to distribute Tiger-made shoes in the United States, and then sent one of Bowerman's designs to Tiger.

What happened to Bowerman next was rather wonderful. Over the subsequent months, Onitsuka Tiger transformed their production facility to accommodate the Bowerman design and developed mass-production methods for this shoe. And by early 1963, less than a year after Knight had sat in an office suite in Japan talking to a group of strangers about a nonexistent company, a shipment of 200 mass-produced Bowerman shoes arrived in Oregon.

In the ensuing seven years, the distinctive nature of BRS, Inc., later to become Nike, began to take form.

Blue Ribbon Sports was, in those first few years, a flimsy enterprise. Both heads of the company worked part-time. Bowerman continued as coach of Oregon's track team for eight more years, winning National Collegiate Athletic Association (NCAA) championships in 1964, 1965, and 1970, and becoming, in 1972, history's most controversial Olympic track and field coach.

Bowerman overshadowed his athletes during much of the 1972 Munich Olympics by criticizing the structure of the International Olympic Committee and the facilities provided Olympians by the German government—including security. His complaints were tragically vindicated by the death of eleven Israeli athletes, killed by a Palestinian terrorist group that breached Olympic Village security. After the tragedy, Bowerman continued his onslaught of criticism, boycotting the memorial service for the athletes and calling the members of the International Olympic Committee "people using a tragedy to heighten their own sense of immortality."

Knight was less public than his partner, but no less busy. He worked as an accountant at firms in Eugene and Portland and even as an accounting professor for a while at Portland State University. The style of operation for BRS, Inc. was a sort of blueprint for chaos. Tiger wouldn't send shoes until BRS sent money, so the company was always in the hole, waiting months to sell products that they had already paid for. In essence, the more they sold, the more they owed. Also, shoes didn't always arrive from Japan as quickly as Onitsuka promised. Sometimes demand exceeded supply, and when Tiger made choices on which market to serve first, it invariably favored its domestic distributors over Knight and Bowerman on the other side of the ocean.

To sell their shoes, Knight and the small sales force that he developed worked out of the backs of cars. At first, this method was a matter of necessity—Knight couldn't afford to rent a store. But even after Nike had stores, the mobility of Nike people—the need to reach the people who used the shoes—became a company prerequisite.

Jeff Johnson is recognized as the first employee of Nike. He had been a part-time salesman for Nike's arch-rival, Adidas. But in 1965, then twenty-three years old, he switched to BRS, Inc. His reason for switching is the refrain that keeps emerging as people describe the competition that has raged between Nike and Adidas for twenty years. As an athlete who had competed against Knight and Bowerman, Johnson knew them as people who understood the athlete. Though they were small and their product lacked Adidas's packaging sophistication, Johnson felt more comfortable with BRS because they were close to the people who wore the shoes—BRS *were* the people who wore the shoes! As Knight said, "The company and the consumer were the same thing."

Johnson spent his days as a social worker in Los Angeles and his evenings and weekends as a shoe salesman for BRS. His retail store was his house; his office was his car. "I believed in Knight," Johnson said. "I knew I could sell those shoes, and I knew exactly how I was going to do it."

A couple of years later, Geoff Hollister became the BRS sales representative for the entire state of Oregon, because he was on Bowerman's track team and he wasn't fast enough to deserve an athletic scholarship. "Bowerman had sirloin runners and hamburger runners. I was hamburger," said Hollister. "Because of that, he gave me a job on weekends working in a mill. That led up to the grand opportunity to get to sell shoes at two bucks a pair. I got expenses out of that. They gave me the state of Oregon, so I'd just hop in my car and, between taking a whole [academic course] load, running for Bill, having a duodenal ulcer, I would sell shoes."

Eventually, BRS sales representatives Johnson and Hollister perceived the need for some sort of retail outlet. Too often, they had to arrange to meet the star quarterback of a nearby high school football team to outfit him with a pair of BRS Tigers. If traffic held up Hollister's van or a cheerleader lured the quarterback to the malt shop, the chance was missed and it was difficult to reschedule. Hollister became the proprietor of one of the first three BRS stores. His store was in Eugene; Johnson's was in Los Angeles; a warehouse sprang up in Wellesley, Massachusetts, behind a local mortuary, and Nike people used the warehouse and their cars as a retail outlet.

The Eugene retail outlet, founded in 1968, cost the company $75 a month rent ($25 more than the rent for the corporate headquarters, which shared a building in southeast Portland with a tavern called The Pink Bucket). Hollister painted the Eugene store with a combination of green paints he had taken from his parents' basement. Every time the garbage collectors came through the neighborhood, Hollister discovered he had to dust off his entire stock. "When the garbage trucks would go down the alley, if the sun was shining through your stockroom, you could see the dust coming through the walls. It wasn't a real stable place."

In Wellesley, the rent was $200 a month, which would have seemed exorbitant—but Knight "subtracted $100 from the guy's salary and let him live there." BRS's East Coast sales representatives were also able to put out a classier package from that store in back of the mortuary. BRS got shoes from Tiger without shoe boxes, and normally BRS people just handed out shoes in plastic bags. But in Wellesley, they noticed BRS's athletic shoes fit nicely into the embalming fluid boxes discarded by the mortuary. All they had to do was tape over the original labels. "They really looked nice," someone said.

These retail outlets were haphazard and crude in 1968. Although they had increased in number five years later, they remained a minor element in Nike sales and in the Nike mystique, which grew inexorably among the cognoscenti of the running world. Nelson Farris, a track athlete from Long Beach, who joined Nike on impulse in 1972 because he "liked these shoes," described the phenomenon that BRS initiated because the company couldn't afford to be more formal. "We were the right people with the right product at the right place and the right time with the right attitude. The reason we made such inroads against Adidas and the others was that by going around to sell those high schools in those days, and selling shoes to coaches and athletes, we brought to them the personal touch that wasn't there. We made friends. Our friends bought our product, and the stuff was neat-looking and light and cushy. It felt good. They gave us feedback. We worked our buns off to deliver."

The idea of "authenticity" recurs almost obsessively among the "older guys" at Nike. As the 1960s turned into the 1970s, BRS, then Nike, emerged more and more as the authentic shoe company serving jocks in the running sports. Even though other lines of shoes were complete—serving every sport—they also were rigid. If there was a flaw in a court shoe, it stayed in the shoe, because other companies had no one in touch with the athletes who were troubled by that flaw. Other products were developed in laboratories, not on playing fields. Other distributors stayed in their offices, talked on the telephone, wore suits, drank at lunch, and got fat—at least this was the impression shared by most athletes. The established companies were out of touch.

"Every aspect of the athletic shoe business was open and waiting, because there were only two substantial companies that were running the place—Puma and Adidas. It was just waiting to happen. I think what happened is that those companies didn't take us seriously. They didn't think running was going to happen in America. And *we* believed it *was* going to happen—with a passion! Because of that, we started going, and once we were going, you couldn't stop us," said Farris.

"We had an authentic presence. There was a lot of distance running happening all around, in small pockets. When our guys would go out, they didn't look like salesmen. All of our guys were skinny. They were all runners or had some running background, and they knew what they were talking about. So if our guy went to a road racer or a coach and talked about shin splints or something, he knew what he was talking about. It wasn't a fraud. It was an honest authenticity. We were accepted into the running community instantly."

That acceptance was vital in those days. When Johnson, Farris, or Hollister put on a coaching clinic or road race or gave away free shoes to whole teams of high school athletes, they helped to make up for the fact that BRS was not making the high-quality shoe that Knight and Bowerman might have envisioned. The company, in the early days, was at the mercy of Onitsuka Tiger, which took greater and greater advantage of their wildcat distributor in America. Sometimes sales were so good in Japan that Tiger factory "seconds" were shipped to Oregon.

Hollister and longtime Nike financial officer Del Hayes (who left

Price Waterhouse to work for Knight, his former employee) recalled a typical BRS crisis. "One year we got our load of basketball shoes," Hollister recalled. "There was a heat-activated glue for the soles and they forgot to run their shoes through the heat activator. These shoes would last a couple of weeks, and then they'd fall apart. I remember I replaced one team's shoes in North Eugene three or four times. I just had to keep going back and giving them a new set of basketball shoes; they were the defending state champions. We lost a lot of money. Yet we were able to sell basketball shoes to the same people in the future."

"We didn't jack them around," Hollister added. "We just replaced the shoes straight up."

But even though product failures were expensive and embarrassing, and the whole marketing scheme had the aspect of a Girl Scout Cookies sales campaign, three forces were emerging to guide BRS toward its eventual breakthrough. Two of them were inspired by Bowerman.

First, the shoe technology in Bowerman's basement laboratory was growing more sophisticated and more oriented toward a market beyond athletic specialties. Second, the competitive response, spawned by Bowerman's intensity, was taking over among the BRS workers, turning what had started out as a hopeful pastime into a crusade. "Those guys went out into the field like believers in the true faith," said Mary Marckx, Nike's public information manager.

Third, Knight's background as a Bowerman disciple and his experience as a gifted financial manager and cost accountant were a vital management combination. Knight proved to be a leader with an intuitive grasp of when people should be left alone and when they needed to be reined in. Rob Strasser, leader of Nike's new product development group, expresses a common feeling in Nike about Philip Knight. "He taught me the competitive response. He's just a leader, a great competitor. He has vision and faith. He inspires loyalty in a lot of people. I'd follow the son-of-a-bitch anywhere."

But even great leadership needs a good product. Without first infusing the BRS product with technological integrity, early employees like Hollister concede that the company would have remained little more than a minor participant in the specialty market of competition shoes for serious athletes. "Our product, at the beginning, really was not that great," said Hollister. "But I think we listened real well. We had come up from a background of using the other products. Our competition had a twenty-year head start on us. We'd worn all of their shoes, and we'd hurt, we had injuries. Bowerman was coming up with some neat ideas. He was taking mid-sole material and putting softer material up against our foot. He was experimenting with nylon uppers, and that was a lot more comfortable than leather. He began with a few small little things, and as you look back you don't think they're all that innovative, but back then they were pretty revolutionary."

The changes in the products spun out from a constant, animated cycle of communication. At the center was Bowerman. One of his dreams was to expand the sport of running to the average person, as an avenue to fitness, health, and well-being. Running, or jogging, is a logical method of lifetime conditioning, and the world itself—its streets and pathways—is the playing field.

But people didn't run, especially in the United States. "You forget what it was like back then," said Knight. "But it was a little strange. You'd go out and run in the streets, and women coming home from shopping would scream and run into the house. They thought you were weird."

One of the ironies of Bowerman's job of popularizing running is that most people didn't realize how uncomfortable most sneakers always were. From childhood, people tended to believe that sneakers are the most comfortable shoes, that we gave them up in adulthood because of social convention. Grown-ups didn't wear kids' shoes! Bowerman saw something else—that these things weren't comfortable at all except for children, who have no discernible muscles, and athletes, whose muscles are exceptionally developed. For average adults, traditional sneakers were an assault on the muscles of the leg. People who spent their workdays in shoes with heels and mid-sole supports gave up those supports when they put on sneakers and went out running. Their feet started to hurt; their legs hurt; they got shin splints, leg cramps, back pain, damaged knees, twisted ankles. "We had to design a shoe to fit the unfit adult," said Bowerman, "because they couldn't exercise in any existing shoe and enjoy it."

In 1966 Bowerman designed an all-purpose running shoe called the Cortez, with a heel wedge and a mid-sole support. It was the first technological advance in the general purpose sneaker since the 1920s. The Cortez made it possible for the unfit adult to run without pain. From the Cortez on, Bowerman kept blending athletes' advice and complaints with his own vision of good shoes. By the mid-1970s, when Nike was still a small shoe company, four elements had become basic in athletic shoes. Bowerman had introduced them all. There had been, in his mind, a whole—an elegantly composed concept—almost as long as he had been a coach and teacher. But it had taken him more than twenty years to gather the resources and technical skills to synthesize them into one shoe.

Virtually every running shoe now sold for the "unfit adult" has these elements: (1) the heel wedge—for heel support and protection against shock; (2) the cushioned mid-sole—to soften the impact of running; (3) the waffle sole (first developed when Bowerman poured synthetic rubber into Mrs. Bowerman's waffle iron)—which provides better traction with less sole weight; and (4) the nylon upper—light and more "breathable" than the old canvas or leather uppers.

With these changes in that old, old shoe, Bowerman provided the superior product that Philip Knight's quixotic enterprise needed to survive beyond the stage of nervous energy and novelty. As important was another evolution, a mounting sense of that true faith among the BRS crusaders. The resourcefulness of many of the early employees who had been Bowerman's athletes came partly from their ingrained competitive response, and also from their sense of sharing ordeal and triumph. There were a lot of things that reminded BRS people of being back on the team, gutting out a third-place finish in order to get one point for the team.

"This sounds a little corny but I think it's true," said Hollister. "Along with collaboration, back in those early days, you had some very definite feelings about the people you were working with, because you were going through this thing and it was a struggle. It wasn't pretty at times, and it was hard. You can look back now and say, yeah, it was a great success. But back then, at certain stages, I don't know that we considered ourselves successful. But somebody went out and won a small battle and they came back. You really had a feeling—I have to call it *love*—for other people in the company who might have been doing totally different things than you were doing."

Another element in that competitive response, which deepened the faith, was a growing animosity toward other athletic shoe companies, especially the giant Adidas. The Blue Ribbon team found out early that being an overwhelming underdog had advantages that touched both the retailers and distributors, as well as the athletes. Kenya Palmer, a long-time Nike employee, recalled, "The dealers we worked with were really mad and angry at our chief competitor for a number of reasons, but primarily because they had been forced to buy the product that company wanted them to buy at the price that company determined. When we came in we listened to our dealers and we really had the same relationship with them we had with our jocks. We were good to them. We were willing to take more of a risk than our chief competitor was at that time, and we built some real loyalties."

"We were extremely welcome with the athletes," recalled Hollister. "There were a lot of people who were really excited about us being competitive with Adidas."

Adidas, in essence, was part of the glue that bonded the Nike people into an eventually victorious team. Every team needs an opponent; Adidas was the perfect opponent for the "early guys" at Nike.

But in 1971 it was *not* Adidas who walked into John Jaqua's office and literally closed down Blue Ribbon Sports in one sudden announcement. One autumn day in 1971 in Eugene, five representatives of Onitsuka Tiger, led by an international sales manager named Katami Shogi, marched into Jaqua's office and announced that Tiger had cut off supplies to BRS.

Tiger had given Knight and Bowerman an indication of what was coming earlier, when they proposed a takeover of Blue Ribbon Sports by Onitsuka. Blue Ribbon had surprised Tiger by approaching $2 million in revenues by 1971. As long as it was only the manufacturer, Tiger earned a relatively small fraction of that growing BRS revenue. The temptation to get it all became too much to bear. Tiger made a rather unattractive offer to BRS to buy 51 percent of the company's assets and control two of the five seats on the board of directors, and to let Knight and Bowerman stay on the payroll. When Knight resisted the takeover, the cutoff of supplies came very quickly, and it was total. However, Jaqua was the only one present on that autumn day in 1971 who really understood the crisis.

"I don't think they [Knight and Bowerman] realized the finality of what Katami had done in the office," recalled Jaqua. "I think they thought the source would slowly dry up and give them time to reorganize and resource and refinance. But what was going to happen was that there would be an absolute ban on any shoes to us, and I'm convinced that Tiger's own distributorships had already been set up."

In fact, as revealed later, in the inevitable court case, Tiger had established a separate distribution organization in the United States. Katami was ready, as soon as Blue Ribbon had been disposed of, to switch shipments of Bowerman-designed Tiger shoes to other United States retailers without a break in the flow of products. It was a good plan. With Tiger in control of supplies and no other source available, Tiger could win the war even if it lost the initial legal skirmishes. "For a small company like this to have a hiatus in its distribution would have been fatal," said Jaqua. "That's why I told Knight to fly to Japan right away. It was either float or die right there."

Within twenty-four hours of Katami's bombshell, Knight was on a plane to Japan. Jaqua had begun to file the necessary legal papers to prevent Onitsuka Tiger from taking over Bowerman's precious designs and patents. He had told his brother-in-law, Charles Robinson, an international banker who eventually became a member of Nike's board of directors, to meet Knight as he was getting off the airplane in Tokyo.

With Robinson guiding him through new vistas of international trade, Knight accomplished in thirty days what should have taken eighteen months. Robinson introduced Knight to the leadership of Nissho-Iwai, a large Japanese trading company. Nissho agreed to serve as the financial middleman between Blue Ribbon Sports and their Japanese shoe manufacturer. But, of course, BRS no longer had a Japanese shoe manufacturer. Nissho provided introductions for Knight to two manufacturers. When these companies agreed to make the shoes, Knight produced copies of Bowerman's designs and offered to stay right there in Japan to help get the shoes into production.

Spurred by Nissho-Iwai's influence and Knight's persistent presence, the new Japanese shoe suppliers had products off the production line in weeks. A month after Katami's bombshell, Knight was on a jet flying back to the United States. Below him in the cargo hold were several boxes of shoes, ready to go to all his distributors in America. Jaqua was astounded at how fast Knight was able to switch manufacturers and keep the products flowing. Bowerman was amazed at how fast Jaqua had sized up the threat to the company's existence. "Chuck Robinson, through John Jaqua, saved our bacon," said Bowerman. "John Jaqua was almost a seer.

If he hadn't told Buck to get over to Japan right away, we were out of business."

"The trouble with Knight and Bowerman," Jaqua recalled with an affectionate shrug, "is they just trusted everybody. They're not the kind of people who would do that to anybody, so I don't think that either of them envisioned the infighting that could take place."

By keeping open the lines of distribution, even with just a few boxes of shoes, Knight broke Tiger's back before the preliminary court actions began. The victory in court was relatively easy for the American company, and Tiger virtually disappeared from the United States shoe market. They had tried to kill the goose that laid the golden eggs and succeeded only in making the goose self-sufficient.

By the end of 1971, Blue Ribbon had been renamed Nike, Inc., its name coined by Jeff Johnson after the Greek goddess of victory. Under the new name, in the next two years, the strength of Nike shifted from Bowerman's inventiveness to Knight's organization. Bowerman continued to devise shoes, but by the early 1970s, it became important to achieve a national market recognition for this new product.

While Bowerman was pouring rubber into his waffle iron, Knight was developing something called a "Futures Program" for his distributors. This program allowed people selling Nike to predict a certain level of sales of Nike shoes and finance that amount. The program allowed these distributors to have shoes made according to orders they received rather than be forced to keep a large and costly inventory of finished shoes. The Futures Program was a riskier way of operating than those followed by the established shoe companies, but it served the fragile solvency of Nike's peripatetic part-time distributors better.

Nike also benefitted enormously from its aggressive efforts to associate Nike footwear with celebrity athletes. The first of these, in 1973, was a "local hero," Oregon distance runner and world record holder Steve Prefontaine; then in the same year, tennis star Ilie Nastase and Boston Marathon winner Jon Anderson became Nike promoters. In 1974 the honor roll added Wimbledon and U.S. Tennis Opens titlist Jimmy Connors.

In 1975 Rob Strasser, Nike's overweight, non-athletic, and charmingly abrasive new marketing leader, changed the face of professional basketball by giving a handful of National Basketball

Association players—among them Elvin Hayes, Paul Westphal, John Drew, and Phil Chenier—$2000 a year plus a share of royalties to wear Nikes. By 1981, Nike had 65 percent of NBA players under contract to wear its shoes. Within several years, the "shoe wars" among different competitors like Nike, Adidas, Converse, and Pony had become an epidemic in pro sports. Every NBA player had a shoe contract by 1984, with the biggest stars' contracts approaching $1 million. By then, many consumers, weary of "logo-watching," had ceased to care which shoe their heroes wore. Strasser's little "NBA Pro Club," of twenty original "guys" collecting two grand to wear Nikes had turned into a monster.

By 1985 Nike also had become a monster, although a friendly one. Revenues were nudging $1 billion per annum. The company had grown more than hundredfold in ten years. But most of Nike's growth did not happen until after 1977. To credit the public's desire to dress up like their favorite basketball player or Charlie's Angel is a very small part of the explanation for Nike's immense growth. After Nike had survived the Onitsuka Tiger takeover try, there was a sense, a hope, among this bunch of guys interested in the same thing that the company could grow to as big as $10–20 million a year. It was a reasonable expectation.

A story from 1967, told by Robert Woodell, another old Bowerman jock, who eventually replaced Knight as CEO during a one-year sabbatical in 1984, describes the level of success Knight perceived. Quoted in a study by the Harvard Business School, Woodell said, "I remember the night I was at Knight's place on New Year's Eve. He and Penny [Knight] and I were drinking mai tais. We had added up the sales and realized we just sold a million dollars in the last twelve months. Big deal. So we had another drink to that. We were sitting there, just marveling at a million dollars and how big that was. I said, 'Imagine that. Someday we are going to be a $10 million company.' Knight looked at me and said, 'Do you realize how big $10 million is?' And I said, 'Yeah, but I think we can make it.' "

Jaqua, who "uncled" Nike while Bowerman fathered it, said of Knight, "I think he thought he'd have a national distribution company and he was going to try to distribute more shoes than anybody else. But I don't think he envisioned anything more than a $5 or $6 million company. He felt he could at least penetrate that market if he could find somebody who had innovative ideas, and that they not only could siphon off some of the market, but also enhance what the market was. He thought he could make a comfortable living. He wasn't going to have to teach."

Competing intelligently against the bigger shoe companies, Nike might have advanced even beyond the $10–20 million that seemed, in the early 1970s, beyond Knight's wildest dreams. How much farther Nike could have climbed—in a normal atmosphere—is hard to judge.

By the second half of the 1970s, the United States was in the midst of a phenomenon that has been described as the "Me Decade," an era in which a rising generation of young Americans, wealthier and better educated than any generation in history, became possessed by an almost religious self-absorption. It was an era in which conformity and rebellion seemed insolubly confused, in which conservation of resources and conspicuous consumption became the weirdest of bedfellows. Young people began expressing themselves in new forms that were intentionally self-centered, unsullied by the stain of institutions. Among the trends that took hold most tenaciously was the so-called "fitness movement."

With the sudden emergence of that fitness movement, a scruffy, idiosyncratic, anti-Establishment shoe company was in the position to be the touchstone for a generation. Suddenly, an old, wiry collection of "serious runners" found themselves in the middle of a crowd of scowling strangers in electric-blue nylon designer ensembles. Very often, the place where the old runners encountered this crowd was a run sponsored by a Nike retail store.

By the mid- to late 1970s, Nike was everywhere real runners were. Nike people had established a network of retail stores, and each store was responsible for sponsoring one run, ranging in distance from two miles to a twenty-six-mile marathon. Store proprietors, like Hollister, in Eugene, and Nelson Farris, in Long Beach, had for years beaten the boondocks in station wagons, conducting clinics for high school coaches and teams. They had repeatedly stood in the cold mist of Northwest winters, listening to groups of gaunt distance runners complain about things like lateral stability, knee hyperextension, shin splints, and untethered Dobermans.

Now, besides the "old guys" whom they'd been seeing for years, they were listening patiently to a growing host of dilettantes and amateurs. "Like bicycle riders or skiers, runners searched out the best stuff," said Farris. "That's why we had this BRS store in Culver City [California]. People would ride fifty miles to that store—or further—to go buy a pair of Nike shoes, because that was, first of all, a store that was authentic. These guys who were in there knew what they were talking about. Then the guys who were the real runners would go back and run the race, and all the putzers [amateurs] who were there would see them in Nikes. The concern with health and good food and all that was starting to happen. And we were there—the guys with the good stuff."

Hollister added, "We were concerned about the serious guy, and the serious guys bought our product. People started looking around at this guy who was running road races and looked fit. He had these shoes on his feet. A lot of people wanted to follow his example." Suddenly, the Nike work ethic had come into confluence not only with the broadening product need, but with the psychic need. When the fitness movement struck America in the second half of the 1970s, Nike was the best-prepared shoe company to take advantage.

Of course, one of the elements of Nike's preparedness was a matter of lucky location. Nike was a company well established in California, the source of many trends in American physical culture. When Farris mentions Culver City, he refers to the town that has the best claim to being the birthplace of the fitness movement. It was in Culver City that Nike held one of its first public product promotions—at the then-unknown Western Hemisphere Marathon (and it was in Culver City where—at the Mr. America pageant in 1970—Arthur Jones demonstrated the first Nautilus machine). Having a strong distribution base in California was a matter of lucky geography for Nike, Inc., and it might be that Nike's rise just happened to coincide historically with the fitness movement, a rising tide that lifted all boats. But this explanation disregards how low Nike was in 1976 compared to how high it got by 1985.

In 1976 Nike's business totaled less than $29 million. By comparison, their top competitor, Adidas, had about $2 billion in revenue.

Farris recalled, "In the 1976 Olympics, we sent nine promo people back there [Montreal] to learn and take care of the handful of guys who had our products. Adidas had three hundred people— an entire wing of the hotel. It was just overwhelming power and prestige—absolutely overwhelming." While Nike spent $75,000 on that Olympics, Adidas's promotional expenses were estimated at

$6–9 million. In that Olympics, Adidas fielded a host of medal winners. Nike's only potential medal winner, marathoner Frank Shorter, at the very last minute, in the very last day of the Olympics, in a sudden onset of superstition—*changed his shoes.* In stunned silence, Nike people watched a Nike Olympian, on national television for more than two hours, run the Olympic marathon in somebody else's shoes. "I sat there in the living room in front of the TV," said Knight, "and I wouldn't allow Penny to turn any lights on. The whole evening!"

"After that happened, I went to my in-laws' farm in Illinois," recalled Hollister, "and I stayed in bed for eight or nine days." However crushing such disappointments, Nike had never really depended on celebrity endorsements or Olympic medals (Nike's first Olympic medal was in Moscow in 1980). The basics were in the grass roots, serving the people who made up the loyal core of the running movement. From that "basic" approach, Athletics West, the first company-sponsored running club, sprang up the year after the 1976 Olympics. Even as Knight and Hollister were slowly recovering from the Shorter debacle, Nike was becoming, as Strasser noted, "the shoe made famous by word-of-foot advertising."

Farris's "putzers" were seeking, among the experienced runners, among experts in fitness, the most *authentic* products. They were looking for new names; they were believers in craftsmanship. They were in need of salesmen who could counsel them toward fitness. Nike's focus on serving the needs of the runner, Bowerman's constant tinkering improvement of the basic shoe, the company's obsession with comfort in running shoes—suddenly all these factors appeared to the fitness-conscious consumer public not merely as product features but as "values."

Nike emanated a sense of caring. Nikes were a product you not only wore in comfort, they were something people could buy and display as symbolic of their fitness, their individuality, even their resistance to the big business establishment that had brought the world to such a sorry pass.

"By being involved with athletes at the grass roots, we had an invitation to the party in virtually all sports," said Strasser. "We belonged and people recognized us as belonging."

And Strasser added, "At the top, with Phil Knight, we have values. These days, winning and losing is not a popular way to term values, but that's what we like to do—but not only *winning,* or winning at any cost, but just trying to be excellent."

Nike's values, expressed in the ever-improving quality of their products and in the way they treated people, eventually coincided—and this was the lucky moment for Nike—with a time when millions of people were looking for something with a dash of integrity in the things they touched every day. Nike exuded a wholesomeness that struck a responsive chord.

As the 1980s began, that resounding chord rang in for Nike, at last, an era of spectacular revenue (and expenditure), and an era in which the corporation expanded into new facilities, new production sites, new countries (including China), and new product development methods. Nike became a far more structured corporation.

It's difficult to look at the Nike, Inc., of today and see any vestige of its origins. At the beginning, among a tenuous linkage of part-time workers, people with a grab bag of college degrees ranging from English to art, Knight had been the rare exception with a business degree. They were people who, for the most part, were more interested in life's pastimes—sports and games—than in its serious pursuits. Hollister called them "park bench material." Neither these people nor their commercial centers, in oddly scattered locations like Eugene, Santa Monica, and Wellesley, seemed to have the makings of a long-term enterprise.

But the outward appearance of Knight's "old guys"—and what he has insisted on more and more in his "new guys"—is as deceptive as the inscrutable stoicism in Bill Bowerman's gaze. Formed in the competitive crucible of Bowerman's tutelage and inspired by the confidence of Bowerman's foremost disciple, Knight, Nike people never were isolated in their work, no matter how far they were from corporate headquarters. Like old trackmen, they were instinctively conscious of the value of each individual's effort to the success of the whole team.

Bowerman acted—often *in absentia*—as a presence that touched everyone in the early years at Nike. "They were all loyal to Bowerman because he was kind of a godfather to them," said John Jaqua. "And he is a man some people think is a little extreme, because he has a very, very set code, a moral code with which he has been totally consistent. So he doesn't bend for expediency when some people think he should. But that's what made him a great person in the eyes of people who worked for him, ran for him. Bowerman is one of the few geniuses I've met."

"Bill Bowerman was involved from the beginning and there is

no question. He was so competitive," said Hollister. "I don't know how he did it, but he really taught you that competing was very important. If you didn't go out and compete, you shouldn't be playing the game. It rubbed off. It was more from example than talking about it. It's something that kind of happened. We wanted to *win*. We covered some distance in a very short period of time. A lot of that had to do with our competitiveness."

"If you had to say in one word what made Nike happen, it's really 'Bowerman,' " said Knight. "Here was a whole bunch of guys who grew up under one system, who came to work here with a common view of how the world works."

"It was like what we're doing is right, and it's going to make a better world," added Mary Marckx, Nike's public information manager.

In the stoic gaze of Bill Bowerman, there was a look of certain survival. Like Bowerman, the people who built BRS, and then Nike, rarely if ever contemplated total defeat. As Hayes noted, no one ever worried about having to do it *all* by himself. Bowerman conveyed to Knight and a few others, and Knight conveyed (perhaps more gently) to many more that a shared commitment requires a balance of outstanding individual performance and a simultaneous willingness to contribute that performance to the efforts of a heterogeneous and unequally talented group. Bowerman taught that a shared commitment returns to each individual more than he puts into it, even if one individual's contribution is a lot bigger than everybody else's. By beating every other team in the country repeatedly, Bowerman proved to his teams that this could be true. Knight, in turn, showed his people at Nike (most of whom believed it anyway) that this could be done even in business. To most of the rest of us, this notion of excellence without ego remains a fairy tale. Even most athletes don't live up to it.

Ned Frederick, a researcher who has been associated with Nike since 1978, adds, "If your ambition is to be *someone,* you're going to have to go somewhere else, because you don't succeed at Nike by climbing the ladder. I don't think there is a ladder. There are just a bunch of jobs out there that need to get done. Your satisfaction is the approval of your peers and that sense of a job well done, not the big promotion with the raise, and not the sign on the door, and not the bigger office and all that. In one way or another, I think four simple principles explain how people feel about Nike. When we're feeling good, it's because we feel a part of it, feel we are getting a fair deal, have a way to keep score, and get a chance to show our stuff."

In 1983 and 1984, the fairy tale—probably to the delight of realists everywhere—was on the skids at Nike. Returning after his year's sabbatical, Knight found a company that had begun to hire people the way most American companies hire people—fitting the person's qualifications to the job. The team had broken up, and a business had taken its place.

Del Hayes, ironically one of the few Knight old guys from an established corporation—Price Waterhouse—was most emphatic in his complaints to Knight about the changed atmosphere at Nike— "people sitting around worrying about their career paths, titles, and job descriptions."

"I've learned [at Nike] that I hate big business," said Hayes. "And when you start pushing on a billion dollars you start to become a big business. But I think that in the last twelve months, in spite of the numbers, we've tended to become a little bit smaller, to revert a little bit to some of the old practices—which in spite of everything else, were fairly successful. You never go back to when there were fifty people on the payroll. But I think that some of the principles that were embraced during that time, you can still embrace."

Knight's response to Hayes's complaints included moves to impose a tight discipline on company finances to phase out some of the wild expenditures on entertainment and celebrity shoe contracts and to bring the product development group under more control. His main focus was on personnel. He had a discordant team, and he moved aggressively to get rid of people who wanted to do the same thing all the time, who didn't enjoy arguing, who couldn't tell jokes and got dressed up for work and expected their secretaries to have *The Wall Street Journal* on their desks every day at 9 A.M. sharp. Like Kozo Ohsone setting up the Walkman team and then letting it run itself, and like Dick Duke creating a brilliant service organization from people whose sole common qualification was a zealous belief in hard work, Knight applied to Nike's recovery the simple principle that once you've got the right people on your side, you're probably going to make out all right.

"I want to work with people whom I want to work with," Knight said. "We grew so fast that we brought a lot of people in, and some of them aren't as much fun to work with as the old guys, and as we regroup, we go back to the old guard and the new guys who have worked well together—regardless of their talents. I've grown increasingly respectful of the Japanese style of managing businesses. You major in the *business;* you don't major in the discipline. And you work toward a common goal. It sounds simple, but I think it's almost an educational process."

People at Nike, explained Hayes, for a while stopped measuring their success in terms of each other and started measuring it in terms of the outside world's images of success. Nike faltered until Knight, who is thoroughly unimpressed with how the world perceives his success, returned to reimpose his image of how Nike people should behave. He reminded them that it matters less what you do in your job or the way you go about getting it done than how you feel about the people you do it with. If people value each other more than they value themselves, the organization tends to find a way.

Nelson Farris, looking back on a sixteen-year Nike roller coaster ride, assessed his feelings about the experience. "I listen to all the people who have jobs, and I know two-thirds of them don't like what they do—and that's a stunning amount. There are so many people who have shitty jobs. It's hard for us to believe—sticking with a job that's bad that you really don't like.

"The thing that has been most exciting about being part of this deal has been putting yourself in a place where you like to do what you're doing, to be able to go home and have laughs about your job. We were a bunch of people with individual achievements and team victories. It was a place and time to do your best stuff and have a lot of fun. We could never duplicate that. They were the best of times."

11 | Nautilus: The Unfinished Breakthrough

I n an atmosphere dominated by dozens of nearly naked men dressed only in strips of Day-Glo bikini, their musculature enormous, rippling, tanned, shaved, and buttered to a wet-marble sheen, the problem of diverting people's attention would seem to be overwhelming. But at the Mr. America Contest of 1970, in the Culver City (California) Auditorium, the most attention-getting individual poking up from that sea of glistening glutes and pulsating pecs was a short, balding man in his fifties, fully dressed in baggy clothes and standing in front of a big blue steel machine. The machine, affectionately called the "Blue Monster" by Arthur Jones, its proud inventor, was large and complicated enough to be mistaken for something used to crush automobiles.

In a deep, rasping voice, accompanied by a patronizing scowl, Jones explained—patiently—to anyone who ventured near that this machine was a revolution in exercise physiology, the first exercise machine ever devised with an understanding of the way the human body uses and increases muscle.

Most of the people who paused to listen to this ardent man ended up smiling nervously, nodding and backing away from him carefully. His pitch was provocative but not very believable. The majority of people attending Mr. America in 1970 were lifelong devotees of the craft of bodybuilding—a grim, slavish procedure that has often been described as sculpture from the inside out. It is something that requires men (and women) to sacrifice normal jobs

260

and sex lives, to submit religiously to exhausting, mind-numbing repetitive weightlifting routines for four to six hours a day—without relief—in dark, dingy gyms. It is the pursuit of ultimate beauty through an endless cycle of brutish, petty agonies.

But here was Arthur Jones, talking about great strength and bigger muscles almost overnight. He was insisting that by applying resistance efficiently, consistently, and variably, his machine could outperform barbells and the other free weights traditional to body-building by twofold, threefold, tenfold! He could turn a year's work into a matter of weeks!

> *Quotations from Arthur:* "I am not the best exercise physiologist in the world. I am the *only* exercise physiologist in the world."

Few of those people knew Arthur Jones. Few of them knew his uncanny tendency to make apparently outrageous claims and back them up with performance. Few of them knew how Arthur Jones could be seized by an obsession that drove him, and everyone near him, relentlessly, endlessly, sleeplessly for days, months, years, decades. If they had known, they would have realized that Jones was telling the truth. Within the Blue Monster was contained almost forty years of irritation, ego, study, and grinding labor. Used properly, the Arthur Jones exercise machine would do what the man said—build muscle on the human frame faster, more evenly, more effectively than any bodybuilder or athlete had ever dreamed possible.

The Blue Monster, a four-station, multi-exercise behemoth that required the help of two other people for anyone to use it, was not the ultimate exercise machine. But it was the father of ten advanced single-station machines called Nautilus, each focused on one complete human muscular movement.

Within the decade of the 1970s, Nautilus became the linchpin of the fitness movement. *Nautilus,* a word once associated only with seashells, Jules Verne, and nuclear submarines, became a shibboleth in the heavily publicized world of professional athletics. For a brief, crucial period in the late 1970s, Nautilus machines—every one of them designed personally by Arthur Jones—became the preferred training aid of the professional athlete. One trained with Nautilus to get bigger and stronger, hit more home runs, hit golf balls farther, serve more aces, tackle more quarterbacks, and slam down more gorilla dunks. Within a few years, Nautilus had become, as Arthur Jones had promised those skeptical crowds in the

Culver City Auditorium, the ultimate exercise machine, and by 1978 word of its wonders suddenly spread everywhere through the medium of television and the giddiness of TV sports announcers. By 1980 anyone who professed to be involved in physical training or muscular development, weightlifting, aerobics, rehabilitation, natural foods, or yoga was certain to encounter eventually the question: "Do you do Nautilus?"

By the early 1980s, with the fitness movement in full swing, no image of fitness was more prevalent than that of a bronzed woman in a yellow satin leotard, drawing together the chromed, padded arms of a Nautilus chest machine. Frequently that chest belonged to Terri Jones, Arthur's fifth wife, whom he found in a teen beauty contest when she was fifteen, married when she was seventeen, and turned into "the Nautilus Woman."

No economic measure of the magnitude of the interplay between the Nautilus craze and the fitness movement is possible, because Arthur Jones for more than fifteen years has refused to release to the public any figures for his still privately held company. There also are no figures that indicate on a national scale the revenues for health clubs, fitness spas, reducing salons, racquetball clubs, aerobics centers, and other outposts of the fitness movement where Nautilus machines are mandatory items of furniture, either for serious use or merely for the sake of interior decoration. However, some measure of the magnitude of the fitness industry lies in estimates of sales of fitness products (excluding Nautilus and most other exercise machines, and all forms of workout clubs) of about $1.5 billion in 1984. The best guesses about peak annual sales for Nautilus Sports Medical Industries range between $200 and $400 million. Conservative estimates of the number of Nautilus machines currently in circulation in the United States—and virtually all of them in good working condition, because Arthur builds things to *last*—range upward fom 500,000. Roughly, *there is a Nautilus machine for every 450 people in America.*

The impact of the explosion can readily be seen in its effects on Arthur Jones. In 1970, in order to get the Blue Monster from the porch of an unpainted bungalow in the pine-and-palm barrens of Lake Helen, Florida, Jones had to borrow money to rent a car and a trailer to haul the thing to California. He had been unemployed for more than a year and was living mainly on money borrowed from his sister and from odd jobs that his (fourth) wife, Liza, and son

Gary could scrounge up in the depressed central Florida employment market.

By 1985 things really had changed. Arthur Jones was the proprietor of a vastly expanded Nautilus headquarters in Lake Helen, the most remarkable feature of which is a $70 million television studio and stage large and elaborate enough to rival most, if not all, network facilities in New York and Hollywood. Jones makes repeated visits, almost on a weekly basis, to his two Nautilus manufacturing plants in Virginia and Texas. He has fled the bungalow in Lake Helen to become the proud sahib of "Jumbo Lair," a 600-acre estate in Ocala, Florida, large enough to accommodate a 7550-foot landing strip and jetport, where Jones keeps his two Boeing 707 jets and a few smaller aircraft. Jumbo Lair gets its name from the herd of sixty-three baby elephants that Jones once airlifted from Zimbabwe to save from a government herd-thinning program. The airlift was filmed and shown by ABC on its prime-time news magazine, "20/20." Among the other exotica harbored at the Jones estate are three rhinoceroses, 150 rattlesnakes, 300 alligators, 400 crocodiles, and a gorilla (all of which, his wife, Terri, notes, are more dear to Jones than all the people he knows).

Arthur and Terri have been guests on such television shows as "The Tonight Show," "Lifestyles of the Rich and Famous," and "America Talks Back." In 1985 Terri entertained but refused requests to take off her clothes for photographers from *Playboy* magazine. Arthur Jones has amused and delighted millions of television viewers with a gruff flamboyance that resembles nothing more than a profane cartoon character.

> *Quotations from Arthur* (to "America Talks Back" host Stanley Siegal): "Is there sex between us? You're damn right! She's my wife! What the hell else would I have her for? . . . Would you like to have a sexual contest? We could have ten or twelve starlets here."

Nautilus machines changed Jones's life, from isolation and privation to conspicuous luxury. But his private style has remained unaltered. The driven hard-sell inventor of Culver City in 1970— rather than the blustering talk-show guest of 1985—is the real Jones. By the time Jones presented a working Blue Monster to the best bodybuilders in the world, he had pondered, built, destroyed, rebuilt, and revised the problem of exercise machines for most of his life.

His first attempt was a pullover machine he assembled at a YMCA in Tulsa, Oklahoma, in 1948. He built the machine after achieving what he regarded as inadequate results lifting free weights. He had begun lifting weights in the first place because he wanted to be bigger. Arthur Jones is a perpetually wary person. His rumpled array of clothes always includes a clearly exposed .45-caliber pistol. His security force at Jumbo Lair is large and humorless in demeanor. His Lake Helen headquarters used to contain an enclosure filled with live crocodiles. Jones is the sort of man who would like—if life were fair—to fend off people merely by his appearance. But his short stature and a build that, beneath his clothes, is deceptively small preclude his realizing that ideal. And so, Jones began in the 1930s to lift weights and build muscles. He was one of millions of teenage boys for whom physical strength was a way to wrestle the ambiguities of life into submission. But Jones brought a unique intellect to the practice of weight training.

He is intellectually as anomalous as a human being can be. By ninth grade he had abandoned formal education forever, disappointing parents who were both physicians.

> *Quotations from Arthur:* "All that school was ever capable of doing was weeding out the incompetents. . . . We learn, when we learn, only from experience, and then we learn only from our mistakes. Our successes only serve to reinforce our superstitions."

Despite his refusal to "be educated," Jones dedicated his life fanatically to understanding things, to a constant regime of learning—not just how to do things, but how they work and why they work. He has evolved into an instinctively pedagogic man, a teacher who is both contemptuous of his "pupils' " ignorance and unable to resist the urge to teach them things anyway.

> *Quotations from Arthur:* "As an instructor you put people into a situation where they can make mistakes and blunder around and then eventually you decide that this guy is so incompetent that he is never going to learn, and then you wash him out. Well, you, the instructor, have learned. He hasn't. He can't. Or won't. . . . If the guy blunders through that and learns, then you put him over his head a little further, and if he blunders through that, you throw him in even deeper water. And then you add the waves. And then you add the wind. And then you add the cold. And then you add the sharks. And at some level, he'll fail. Well, now you know his level—but in the meantime, he's learned from the experience."

His speaking style, which was on display in front of the "Blue Monster" in Culver City, is the lecture method. He bristles at questions that interrupt his cascade of words. His mind is a churning, bright cauldron of thoughts, not always under control but compellingly articulate. He converses in measured phrases, as though he expects people to be taking notes and composing outlines from his words. His descriptions convey a sense of imagery unique to the creative mind. He inspires.

"With Arthur," said Inge Cook, a young woman who has labored as a photographer, machine-scraper, elephant caretaker, and all-purpose assistant for Jones for twenty years, "I found myself. Before I started to work for Arthur Jones, I didn't think of myself as a person. I didn't think about why I would do something, why I felt the way I felt about this, that, or the other. That's what I learned after I started working for Arthur. He would ask, 'Why? What do you think about that? How do you feel about that?' He made me stop and think. How do I feel? What do I think? I feel I grew up. I became a person."

Asking 'Why?' has been a lifelong pastime for Arthur Jones. When he was a teenager lifting barbells and he didn't get as big as he thought he should be, he was annoyed—but he also started to wonder why. He could not rest until he knew the reasons for this problem, and then the solution.

"As soon as I picked one [barbell] up, I began to suspect that there was something wrong with the tool," recalled Jones, "because it produced very good results in some portions of your anatomy and much lesser results in some other areas. Then, I assumed that by training with different weights, by training more, by training harder, by doing more exercises, different exercises or more repetitions or faster repetitions, at some point I would achieve the good result everywhere."

But, as with all weightlifters, the barbells had strengthened Arthur Jones in some places wonderfully and in other places negligibly. "Therefore, I suspected something was wrong. Initially, I didn't blame it on the tool. Initially, I blamed it on a lack of knowledge. So I sought out the 'experts.' "

The experts to whom Jones harkened were a handful of dedicated power lifters who labored in gritty isolation in small pockets throughout the United States—in cellars, gyms, YMCAs. Jones asked how to get uniform results by the proper manipulation of the barbell. But he found out that they had come to accept the inconsistency of muscle development as a fact of life, an unalterable condition of human travail.

"I found out they didn't know," said Jones. "Oh, they believed they knew. They had opinions. They had answers, except the answers didn't work. . . . It was obvious to me they didn't know what they were talking about."

Jones wasn't just perplexed. He was angry. These were men who were supposed to be receptacles of the highest knowledge in their field, capable not only of showing him how to do it better, but of telling him the reasons why that's a better way. He found men who not only did not know, they had never bothered to ask. They were neither as bright nor as curious as he was, and they possessed an expertise based not on superior technique or higher intellect, but on a congenital predisposition toward big muscles. In Arthur Jones's view of life, these so-called experts were frauds.

An issue of curiosity had become, for Jones, a matter of truth. People who do not understand how something works should not, he believed, be telling people how to do it. He determined then to collect everything he needed to know to understand why lifting weights builds muscles and how it could be done better. "What motivates me?" Jones asked rhetorically. "To the degree that I can answer that question satisfactorily, all I can say is curiosity. I didn't set out to achieve financial glory or fame or adulation. I was simply curious. It aroused my curiosity. I investigated it and found that maybe a lot of people had opinions about it, but they didn't really know what they were talking about. So I set out to try to solve the problem myself."

At the very beginning, Jones focused his efforts on the "tool," the barbell, but he also started to learn the sciences—physics, physiology, kinesiology—that would reveal to him the "why" that lay beneath the "how" he had begun relentlessly and tirelessly to seek. At that point in his life, Jones never thought that in the end his rational barbell would become a commercial product leading to a successful business and decent living for himself.

But like many breakthrough creators, Jones was primarily driven by an "I'll show 'em" attitude. Dick Duke prevailed in the founding of ChemLawn Corporation partly because of his desire to demonstrate his exceptional worth to the leading citizens of Troy, Ohio. Sir James Black proceeded tenaciously to hunt for the first known H_2 compounds and the ultimate discovery of Tagamet in the face of expert research—by people just as smart as he was—that "proved" he wouldn't be able to find a thing. Even George Foerstner of Amana Refrigeration took an inordinate pleasure in standing at a head table in Boston and proving that a Midwestern appliance salesman could teach "that Harvard crowd" a thing or two about microwave radiation. Each of these men felt, for some reason, a sense of exclusion from a self-appointed elite, and they spent years and spectacular energy to prove themselves through a creative attainment so clear and so truthful that even the elite must pay tribute. In a number of breakthroughs, this emotion emerges as a powerful driving force, more intense because it is deeply personal. There is no gratification sweeter than the last laugh.

> *Quotations from Arthur:* "I tried various things. Then I started modifying the barbell, the tool. It was obvious to me, for one thing, that you're stronger in some positions than you are in some other positions. Now, if you are three times as strong in one position as you are in another (and that's not unusual) in a movement, how much weight can you use? Obviously, the most you can use is that which you can manage in your weakest position. Well, that's going to be a third of what you could handle in another position. So you are stimulating yourself only in the weakest position. Obviously then, the weight has got to vary during the movement. During the late 1930s, I added chains to barbells, so that the bottom of the chain was on the floor, and as you lifted the barbell more and more of the chain would lift, thereby adding weight."

With that intuitive addition of chains to barbells, at that time an unheard-of innovation, Jones was on his way to the Blue Monster. "Step by step," said Jones, "I became aware of the problems. Step by step, I solved them."

But more than thirty years intervened. For most of that time, Jones was too busy with other challenges to concentrate fully on the creation of the ultimate exercise machine. The details of Jones's biography remain murky, mainly because he prefers it that way. He refuses still to reveal his age. But among the certain details of his past are the experience of personal hardship during the Depression, made worse by the fact that he had virtually disowned his own family. From the beginning, Jones embarked on a life of fanatical romanticism. He insisted, to his own misery, on doing almost everything by himself; his religion was self-sufficiency, and he carried into every enterprise a passion for doing everything the hard way.

In 1939 Jones took up flying, barging into a haphazard flight school somewhere in the West and proving, inevitably, to be a brilliant, tenacious student. His interest in flying had a practical basis.

Quotations from Arthur: "An airplane is a tool, a means of getting from A to B without spending your life en route. I'd tried walking and hitchhiking and riding freight trains and crawling through the mud, and I didn't like those methods of transportation all that much. I wanted something better."

Within a year Jones was making a living as a pilot, and his livelihood through two decades of alternating affluence and destitution came largely from airplanes. He built up businesses flying people from A to B in South America and importing animals and fish to the United States from South America and Africa. He holds the dubious distinction of being the first man to capture live adult crocodiles. This was a typical Arthur Jones attainment. Nobody in the world needed live adult crocodiles; you could go through your life without hearing anyone ask for one. And even in the "crocodile market," such as it was, every buyer had always been happy to accept juvenile crocodiles, which are lots easier and less dangerous to catch, and raise them to adulthood. But somewhere along the line, Arthur heard from someone that *no one* had ever caught a live adult crocodile.

That was all he needed to know. Within a few months, he was crating up live adult crocodiles by the dozen, skipping them into Louisiana, setting up his own crocodile farm, and finding the occasional crocodile buyer in various places in the United States.

Besides the crocodiles and airplanes, there were also four teenage wives and Arthur claims several tours as a mercenary soldier fighting left-wing forces in the Third World.

Quotations from Arthur: "Politically, I'm sixty-four thousand miles to the right of Attila the Hun."

By the mid-1950s Jones yearned to have one of his wild animal captures on film. When he couldn't find a wildlife cameraman on whom he could rely, Jones took up filmmaking. He became good enough to make a handsome living as a producer of television shows that featured the killing and/or capture of exotic beasts. The most successful of Jones's productions was a series called "Wild Cargo."

Jones was in Rhodesia in 1968, making wildlife films. The features of his life there contained many elements that remain in his life today in Ocala. He had an "aging" wife, Liza, wife number four, by then already past her twentieth birthday. There was around him a small but intensely loyal entourage of people. Included in the Jones colony was a herd of pet elephants, several airplanes, a helicopter, lots of film equipment, a few crocodiles, some snakes, lots of automatic weapons, and—yes—an exercise machine. Arthur Jones had assembled around him the basics of life.

Then Shangri-La caved in. Aware of his political leanings, the newborn government of Zimbabwe (formerly Rhodesia) declared Arthur Jones *persona non grata* and preferred that he get out of the country by sundown. When Jones left Rhodesia/Zimbabwe he had to leave everything behind but Liza and Inge Cook, who had joined the entourage when her previous employer ran out of money and fled home to Germany. The next stop for Jones and the two women was Lake Helen, in his wife's home state of Florida.

> *Quotations from Arthur:* "I was not run out of Rhodesia. They didn't have a big enough army to do it and they weren't stupid enough to try."

Jones was flat broke. He had no income, he had no job. But Arthur Jones never looked for jobs. Instead, he borrowed $2500 from his sister, sent Liza and Inge out to forage for spare change, and found himself at last with the leisure to bring together thirty years of thinking about the ultimate exercise machine.

> *Quotations from Arthur:* "In Africa, I had built an exercise machine. One night, about two-fifteen in the morning, I had an idea for a component to be added to the existing exercise machine. I called one of my employees and told him at two-fifteen in the morning to get a piece of paper and a pencil. And I drew it over the phone: 'Go to the upper left-hand corner of the page; now go four inches to the right. Now come down the page two inches. Now make a dot. Now go six inches down the page further and make another dot. Now join those two dots with a straight line,' and so on. At about three o'clock, I completed the conversation. I told him to immediately make those components, assemble them, and bring them to my house later on this

morning, and install this component on the existing exercise machine. Then, it didn't work at all. It failed. But it failed in such a dramatic fashion that I knew why it failed and I also knew what it would take to redesign the entire machine so it would not fail. Because I suddenly *understood the problem.*"

The problem Jones had understood was a matter of physics. When a person lifts a weight, the combination of gravity and the variations in leverage in the human body create wide disparities in the weight's resistance, and thus in its benefits to the weightlifter. In Africa, in his moment of vision at 2:15 A.M. Jones finally conceived a more effective mechanical way to replicate his crude chains-on-barbells idea. He had perceived a way to make resistance *vary* according to the strength available at each point in the curve of a muscular movement.

"I'd been working on the problem since the 1930s and was near to the end of the 1960s and I hadn't really defined the problem yet, and understood it," said Jones. "The problem was the fact that a barbell is a unidirectional tool. It provides resistance in one direction—straight down. But man is a rotational animal. You do not move in straight lines, you rotate. Even if you move your hand in a straight line, that is the consequence of three rotations—around the shoulder axis, the elbow axis, and the wrist axis."

In Lake Helen, within weeks of his move from Rhodesia, Jones was assembling a junk pile of necessities for the construction of his machine. Contained in what he began to assemble were many concepts that by themselves were not profound or revolutionary. To a physicist, they were high school material, but combined and applied to the improvement of human strength, they formed an exceptional synthesis.

Jones created a machine that uses the human body as the leading technology in weight training. Until Arthur Jones's discovery, the barbell had always been the leading technology. The person responded to what the weights could do, which was to move in straight lines—following the dictates of gravity. When weightlifters refer to "free weights," it is an instructive phrase, because while the weights are free, the weightlifter is a captive of their limitations. Arthur Jones studied and fretted over the physics of the body and the weights long enough to devise a machine that no longer moves in straight lines. Jones forced the resistance to rotate on the axis of the human body. Jones freed the body and made captive both the weights and the forces of gravity.

The pulley that Jones eventually created is not round, like most pulleys. It is more accurately a *cam,* a wheel that has been stretched and bent. The familiar forms in nature often applied to describe this shape are the bean and the kidney. But a more appealing natural organism also contains this shape, the beautiful mollusk called the chambered nautilus. In 1972, Jones changed the name of his company from Arthur Jones Productions to Nautilus Sports Medical Industries, in tribute to the form that was at the heart of his invention and would be the foundation of his fortune.

The uneven surface of the Nautilus cam conforms to the variations in strength in virtually all human muscular movements. For example, at the moment that the arm is strongest, it is forced by the cam to lift the weight in the Nautilus machine the longest distance; it encounters greater resistance. As the arm reaches a weaker position in its complete range of movement, the cam demands a shorter pull, less resistance but resistance that nevertheless taxes the muscle at this point in the movement to its limit.

The result is dramatic. The body, a rotating machine, encounters measured, almost intelligent resistance from the Nautilus, another rotating machine, and draws from that resistance the maximum benefit to achieve growth. This is simple; it makes sense. Everyone who has spent any time lifting weights has eventually understood, intuitively, the wide variation in the resistance of the weights and has sensed that the variations are a result of a rotating body fighting the linear opposition of gravity. But no one, before Arthur Jones, ever effectively applied that intuition to the creation of a tool that might improve the quality of the rotational movement to make the body uniformly stronger.

Variable resistance, with all its implications, was only one aspect Jones synthesized into his Lake Helen contraptions. He also designed a device that increases the body's flexibility by extending resistance through the complete range of each physical movement. *He made a machine that stretches as it strengthens,* which free weights do not do.

Paul Katz, a many-faceted entrepreneur who met Jones in 1970 and shortly thereafter became one of the first proprietors of a Nautilus fitness center, expressed the impact of the Nautilus machine's ability to aid flexibility. "I thought, This is a great idea," said Katz. "This guy is a genius. He's got the full range of motion. He's got flexibility, which every single athlete needs, more so than strength. If this gives you full range of motion, I said, this guy *did it*. This guy revolutionized the whole field!"

Jones made a machine in which improvement would be measurable. He made a machine that could be infinitely adjusted upward according to improvements in strength or maintained at a constant level. The user could get perpetually bigger and stronger or settle at a happy medium. He or she would be in control. Jones created a machine that, because its model is the human body and not weights, will not cause injury as long as it is properly used. He made a machine so efficient that it works with incredible speed, especially at the early stages of use, when typically weak muscle groups have so much to gain. In fact, it has always been Jones's contention, supported by a series of studies conducted under his supervision, that the maximum use of a Nautilus machine is thirty minutes every forty-eight hours.

Clay Steffee, another twenty-year employee of Jones, explained, "You'd train maybe thirty minutes a day three times a week. But it is a brutally hard workout if it's done properly. It takes you a couple of months to build up to the point where you can stand that thirty minutes of training. But that's all you do. And that makes it a lot more popular, because a lot larger percentage of the people can afford thirty minutes a day three times a week. Not everybody can afford six hours a day six days a week. [A Nautilus machine is] a device that enables you to get very good results in very little time."

To a bodybuilder, Jones's notion constitutes unthinkable lunacy. To make muscle the "old-fashioned way," you had to earn it—by putting in four to six hours a day, repeating identical lifts hundreds and hundreds of times, increasing the weights eventually to gigantic levels. But Jones was saying it didn't matter how long you lifted a weight; it didn't even matter how *much* the weight was. The important thing was to lift it until you couldn't get it up again—to the point of failure—and then quit.

Jones operates on a simple perception of physiology. He believes that the body grows muscle not as a response to work, but as a response to overload. If the existing muscle is capable of doing the work, no matter how long or how hard, then it doesn't have to grow. But if the muscle experiences a shocking burst of work in which it fails, then the body will eventually respond, in a period of forty-eight hours, by enlarging muscle cells.

> *Quotations from Arthur:* "Exercise is not capable of producing anything of value. It stimulates. Exercise can pull a muscle; it can break a bone. It can cause exhaustion; it can cause all kinds of problems. Those are not things that you want. The body will respond if it is being stimulated. Exercise provides the stimulation. Then if other physiological factors are right, you will grow. Stimulus comes from overload. No overload, no stimulus. No stimulus, no results."

Among the implications that Jones has not fully exploited is that the Nautilus machine can be used to build muscle *or* to provide aerobic stimulation by working short of the "point of failure." It has proved, on the rare occasions when it has been used for that purpose, an amazing tool to help athletes prevent and recover from muscular injuries, to help disabled and injured people attain swift rehabilitation. It represents a potential miracle for the recovery of stroke victims. Its market embraces athletes, athletic trainers, physicians, physical and rehabilitation therapists, dancers, and all people for whom overall fitness is important to the quality of their lives. In the Nautilus machine, as a result of that thirty years of churning the problem over and over in his head, Arthur Jones created a device that incorporates most of the results that can be obtained from sensibly exercising muscles. The Nautilus cam and Jones's theories of resistance are so thorough and efficient that virtually all exercise technology, from this point, must begin with Arthur Jones. In the area of exercise technology, he achieved the kind of advance made over the period that human flight progressed from arm-flapping to the Concorde.

However, the suffering that Jones endured during the genesis of his first machine at the bungalow in Lake Helen was something that would have crushed a less tenacious person. Into that suffering he drew Liza and Inge and his son, Gary. Exiled from Zimbabwe and stranded in Lake Helen in 1968, Jones began making plywood models of exercise machines. More often than not, he designed these by making crude drawings on scraps of paper as he paced through the house during sleepless nights. It is a design method that he has never modified, and design is a function that he never has surrendered to any employee of his.

Inge Cook recalled, "He would go to a fast food place; he would sit there and mull things over. He would get out a pencil and on all the paper napkins—he would go through half a dozen or so—he would start doodling, fiddling around what comes into his mind. That's how he developed the machine. He would drop his napkins the next morning: 'This came in my head. See what you can do with it.' But he was always—and is—the only person who actually developed the machine."

Eventually Jones's designs were ready for a steel prototype. He had very little money, and the equipment he had for this task amounted to a few hand tools, two women, and his son. Jones found the welding equipment and working space he needed at a welding shop in nearby DeLand, Florida—where he also met the man he would eventually hire as a prototype developer, Don Stevens.

The hours he worked to create his machines were strange, but they suited a man too nervous to sleep. "I went in there after they were closed in the evening and rented the use of the space and the tools to build these things," recalled Jones. "They didn't build them for me. I went down to the DeLand Metal Works every night, worked all night until opening in the morning and, if I wasn't in the way, sometimes during the day. And on weekends. From Friday evening I worked straight until Monday morning."

In the daytime, Jones would rest and Inge would labor on the porch of the bungalow in Lake Helen, filing and sanding down Arthur's ragged welds. Inge Cook, more than Jones, expressed the isolation of those penniless days of dispiriting work under "this strange man, walking around in dirty pants, unshaven, unkempt, speaking in four-letter words . . ." and welding his improbable machine.

"The worst thing was the beginning, living on borrowed money and no guarantee at all that this would ever come to a success," Cook recalled. "We were working so hard. And for myself personally, I had to figure at that time a number 14 blouse size and a number 8 skirt size. Because of the work I was doing, my arms were that big. My back was that big—which made me a bit unhappy. I make my own clothes, so I was aware of this—working that hard physically, outdoors, in the summer, hot and humid, sweat dripping in my eyes and salt itching all over. I painted at first in the open air with the wind blowing the sand on my freshly wet paint, making a mess of things. It took quite a while, several months, before I got a covered shed to paint in. And then it was a tin enclosure, which was very hot."

The result was the Blue Monster and the trip to Culver City, which became a pilgrimage to survival for Jones and his strange entourage. They held no expectations of wealth or triumph, just a faint hope that they could build these painful machines and make a living at it. Curiously, the least promising market for Jones's machine was among those "so-called experts" in the tight-knit bodybuilding world. Although the ignorance of these people had spurred Jones's original quest, they remain stubbornly unconvinced even today that Nautilus is superior to free weights. In a way, the bodybuilders are right. Their goal is "bigness," just as Jones's goal had been when he was a teenager. As long as bigness is more important to bodybuilders than flexibility, and as long as illegal dosages of anabolic steroids, testosterone, and human growth hormone are part of the formula for bigness, then Nautilus machines will be a minor aid in the bodybuilder's regimen.

Nevertheless, the element that secured Arthur Jones's future in Culver City in 1970 was the desperate curiosity of the typical bodybuilder. So hungry is he for a competitive edge, in a sport judged by almost invisible subtleties in muscular conformation, that he will try anything once. Jones's Blue Monster and his several days of standing in front of it, haranguing people tirelessly, stirred eager interest at the Mr. America Contest. Jones actually got an order from a man who wanted the machine.

A more important ripple of interest came from a man named Perry Rader, editor of a muscle magazine called *Iron Man*. Delighted by the articulate controversiality of Arthur Jones, Rader cut a deal in which Jones would get free advertising in *Iron Man* if he would agree to write a series of unpaid articles describing his theories of exercise technology.

That agreement with *Iron Man* was a more critical moment in the future of Nautilus than Jones could have realized then. Jones might have been a good salesman and theorist, but he had neither the patience nor the experience to market a product. In the next five years, Jones repeatedly had to struggle to gain a substantial following among bodybuilders. One of the greatest triumphs of his life was when he took a young bodybuilder named Casey Viator as his protegé in 1970, trained him intensely on several of his very first machines, and one year after introducing the Blue Monster, saw

Viator win the Mr. America title. It was a hollow victory in the long run; bodybuilders still couldn't be convinced. And Mr. America titles mean nothing to the real world.

Far more significant was that, through *Iron Man* and a grapevine that extended from the bodybuilding community into other forms of weight training, word about Jones's exceptional devices slowly spread. Football teams started to call. Among the first callers was Don Shula, coach of the National Football League's Miami Dolphins. In the first year after Culver City, Jones made twice as many machines as he expected, perhaps as many as 200, and obtained the vital assurance that he would make a living with these things. All of those first machines were assembled, welded, ground, filed, and painted by hand.

While the tin building in Lake Helen buzzed with production, James Flanagan, one of Jones's new employees, took several machines home and set them up in his garage in Orlando for his own workouts. Flanagan met Paul Katz, then a real estate developer and later a Nautilus entrepreneur, while they both were jogging in a park. Katz, a burly man who played handball as a pastime, had just completed participation in a lengthy handball tournament and was suffering the usual painful aftermath, a stiff back.

Flanagan led Katz gently to his garage full of Nautilus machines. Within minutes Flanagan had loosened Katz's back and relieved the pain on a back machine that might have been one of the first Nautiluses ever manufactured. Like Jones, Katz was a lifelong student of exercise physiology who constantly sought intelligent ways to exercise more effectively and more safely. "That day," said Katz, "when I saw Jim's setup in the garage, I said, 'This is for every *average* man and woman on the street.' I said this tool could fit everybody. I knew that, under supervision, no one could ever get hurt on this stuff. You couldn't tear muscles. Jim started getting a lot of people coming into his garage. It started as just a little neighborhood thing. He said to me, 'What do you think if I open up a center? Do you think it will go?' and I said, 'Of course it will go.' "

It is almost certain that Flanagan's Orlando Nautilus center, equipped with machines that were barely out of the prototype stage, was the first Nautilus training center. By 1971 and 1972 similar centers were beginning to spring up spontaneously in other places, first in California. This is because something else happened among bodybuilders when Jones began to sell his first machines. It didn't take a great leap of imagination for a bodybuilder to figure out the advantages of opening a Nautilus center. Because Jones's machines cost relatively little and he applied no additional financial burdens, such as license fees to use the Nautilus name or franchise costs, it was remarkably inexpensive to equip a gym with a complete array of ten Nautilus machines—as little as $33,000. A bodybuilder could open a Nautilus center, serve serious athletes in a number of sports, spend his days in the gym, and make a comfortable living for himself. These Nautilus entrepreneurs were frequently still devoted to free weights and most had never learned (Jones was literally the only person who knew) how to "properly" use a Nautilus machine. But they provided enough service—a full battery of machines, showers, and towels in clean, carpeted surroundings—to make users feel comfortable and welcome.

By chance rather than by design, the market had been primed for the fitness explosion. Nautilus was "authentic"—after the fashion of Nike footwear—having emerged gradually, almost unintentionally from the ranks of committed athletes. And Nautilus was a shortcut to fitness, requiring significantly less time and none of the gritty masochism of bodybuilding and weightlifting.

Until Flanagan and Katz, in conversation in Orlando and with other people in other places, identified carpets and nice showers as necessary accessories to the Nautilus machines, gyms generally had been dingy and unattractive. The Nautilus atmosphere allowed sociability to blend with conditioning. Indeed, as much as Arthur Jones's technology, it was the cleanness and brightness of Nautilus centers that sold weight conditioning to the huge audience of fitness-conscious people who seemed to spring from the woodwork in the late 1970s. Most of the time, these people were not using the equipment to more than a small fraction of its potential. Like a neighborhood tavern, the fitness center turned out to be a nice place to drop in, meet people, and work off a day's tensions. The Nautilus machine became the new social lubricant and moved weightlifting from the boiler room to the living room.

This happened regardless of Arthur Jones. It happened almost in spite of Arthur Jones. Although Jones was far too bright not to perceive the fitness and medical potential in his machine, he exploited it only halfheartedly. When celebrity athletes began to endorse Nautilus training enthusiastically on television, it was not because Jones had contacted them. Jones's association with celebrity endorsements was a consequence of Nautilus's success, not a cause. Jones accidentally overcame an absence of marketing because Nautilus sold itself. The technology was so thorough and so compelling that those who found it couldn't help but talk about it.

Jones had done four things that inventors must do.

First, he had followed Edison's dictum that the whole thing must be envisioned, its problems and its solutions blended into a single image, before the work begins.

Second, as Yuma Shiraishi was also required to do before the VCR triumphed at JVC, he had to have the insight and courage to scrap all previous assumptions and "go back to scratch." As Jones himself said, "The fact that something has been done in a particular way is no proof that that's a good way to do it. In fact, the result that you are producing may be in spite of what you are doing."

Third, like Godfrey Hounsfield with the invention of the CT scanner, as the inventor he took on the job of mechanic, making seat-of-the-pants adjustments with available materials to solve the hitches and minor problems that occurred along the course of development. "I've used a drafting board," Jones remarked, "but I've learned that's not necessary in the early stages. You can use a drafting board until you're blue in the face. Build the son of a bitch. Strap it on your ass, run down the runway, and see if it will fly. And if it will, then make the improvements."

Fourth, as Paolo Galli had done in the development of Montedison/Mitsui's revolutionary polypropylene catalyst (see chapter 12), he had penetrated the basic science of how things work in order to have any hope of making them work better.

Jones made a brilliant technical breakthrough because all these ingredients were present in his concept. Indeed, like Sir James Black, Jones succeeded in the discovery of something with more applications than he foresaw. Jones also broke through significantly by always staying on top of the explosive demand that pushed production of Nautilus for more than seven years. Though Nautilus Sports Medical Industries operated with only the Lake Helen facility until 1980, the longest delay any buyer had to tolerate between order and delivery was three months. And the quality of the machines was never an issue. Today, Nautilus's new machines face some of their stiffest competition from used Nautiluses that won't even begin to wear out for another ten years.

But the most significant breakthrough in the Nautilus story is one that has yet to happen. The Nautilus machine is an invention whose potential benefits barely have been touched. It is today, in the vast majority of its installations, a misused and misunderstood machine. Besides inventing the machine, Jones developed a series of routines for its use—one for building muscle, another for increasing cardiovascular fitness.

Some of the varied potential for Nautilus use was shown in a study done jointly by Nautilus and the United States Military Academy at West Point. In a comparison of two groups of Army football players—one group using Nautilus training and the other free weights—differences in strength and flexibility improvement were extraordinary. The Nautilus group, in six weeks, increased physical strength by an average of 60 percent, while the non-Nautilus group improved less than 20 percent. The Nautilus group had an 11 percent improvement in its two-mile run, the other group a 2.55 percent improvement. The Nautilus group increased its vertical jumping ability by 6.5 percent, the other group 1.4 percent. While the controlled group did not improve its flexibility measurements by more than 1.3 percent in any of three categories, the Nautilus group had improvements ranging from 5.6 percent to 11.6 percent.

Paul Katz, who grew from his Nautilus introduction in Orlando to eventually serve for several years as strength coach for the National Football League's New England Patriots, made some discoveries not anticipated by Jones. As noted, he found that he was able to relieve some muscle injuries almost instantly by using the Nautilus machine, and he was able to prevent the occurrence of pulled muscles among the football players for the duration of his service with the Patriots. He discovered uses for the Nautilus machine, including a stirring aerobic routine, as a result of his constant exposure to the equipment. But, Katz asserts, it is not an easy technology to understand, and the available books on Nautilus training simply do not provide the information necessary to use a Nautilus machine to its full potential. Katz believes that few people, especially those in such specialties as rehabilitation, neurology, orthopedics, and gerontology, have had enough Nautilus exposure even to begin to understand the machine's capacity. The deceptive popularity of Jones's machines, because of their mandatory presence at health clubs, has made their effective implementation, to use a common business phrase, a mile wide and an inch deep.

Paul Katz today is out of the Nautilus business largely because he tried to use the machines properly. "My Nautilus center closed down because Arthur Jones was selling equipment to people across the street from me, nineteen-year-old kids just out of high school who didn't know the first thing about using the equipment," said Katz. "They didn't know their ass from their elbow about Nautilus. But they got their equipment on a 5 percent–down deal with a leasing company. Then they went out, sold $80–90,000 worth of memberships at $100 or so, then went out of business. Then the leasing company came back, resold the equipment to somebody else, and the cycle went on. In the meantime, I'm competing against these guys. I'm asking for three times as much money, I'm making people go to a doctor for a physical before they can sign up, I'm putting them through a killer of a routine—for a half hour, forty-five minutes, three times a week. In order to use this equipment right, it's like dancing. You have to maintain your discipline, your form. Once you break form, you're not doing yourself any good."

Katz's disciplined approach to Nautilus use, complete with individual instruction and personal programs adapted to each user, was what Jones had envisioned from the early days. It represented a less lucrative, longer-term approach to Nautilus. It meant the creation of a service industry that would parallel and augment the manufacture of the equipment itself. But the flood of popularity that struck Arthur Jones never motivated him to create a long-term service network. And it might have been too hard for him ever to rely on other people to help him create such a structure.

Quotations from Arthur: "I've spent millions of dollars trying to educate people, and I've found that it's impossible."

"Would he have made more?" asked Katz. "I believe he would have made more and I believe he would have taken a lot more people with him to make a hell of a lot more. But his ego became inflated. He got into the circus business. You see, he started out as a street person. He's a tough, tough son of a gun. He just barreled ahead. And then he saw all this stuff coming in. He could have been a giant among giants. He could have been another Einstein."

Katz also describes business potential in terms of compassion, which seems odd. Yet for Nautilus that simply meant the ability of someone in the organization to perceive what the equipment could do for all sorts of people who needed it, then helping those people learn to understand and use the equipment. "He should have had a training program for these people," said Katz. "And these people could have paid for the training program."

"My problem," Jones says to that, "is not lack of compassion. My compassion is what has gotten me into trouble all my life. I've gotten kicked in the head every time . . . and who the hell would want to be as *dumb* as Einstein?"

For Arthur Jones the idea of needing help or helping others is a sign not of business perception, but of weakness.

> *Quotations from Arthur:* "I could write you on three or four pages an exact formula which would make you a millionaire in three or four years, from scratch, with no resources to start with. One, two, three. Follow this pattern. Do not deviate from it. Don't change it. Don't modify it. Don't add to it. Don't leave anything out. But you wouldn't follow it. You'd change it—because you're stupid, because you're opinionated, because you're lazy, because you have prejudices and biases and an empty head, not an open mind. So, there would be parts of it [the formula] you like, and you'd concentrate on those. Some you wouldn't, so you'd manage to rationalize to yourself that those were unimportant. For whatever reason, you'd change it. You would not follow the instructions, and you'd fail, and you'd blame it on me."

Jones also regards people as fundamentally felonious, attracted to men of his exceptional gifts and wealth in order to steal it. This sense of perpetual threat in the human universe comes not just from Jones, but from everyone around him.

His wife, Terri, explained this. "Sometimes I get a view like he has—kind of a cynical, hard view about people. But I've been exposed to a lot of dishonesty, a lot of theft—which I hate—a lot of people trying to take advantage of you because you've got something they all want, and they all want to steal it! And I've seen this over and over again. Very few people are honest. You've got to spend so much time babysitting, motivating, watching things so that they don't steal. That's the thing that I hate so much—that we hate so much—everybody wants to steal from you."

Quotations from Arthur: "Try to kill me. Give me the opportunity to kill you, and that makes me feel good. Because then I know we have communicated!"

Harry Lafconski, Jones's camera operator for the last twelve years, stresses the insistence of Jones on absolute loyalty—a loyalty he refused to acknowledge in Lafconski until the latter had worked through a four-year personal probation. "I remember him being very jittery when he first started Nautilus," recalled Lafconski. "I can now understand why. It was because of people trying to steal his ideas. He had something he knew was going to work. He had the fortitude. He had the confidence. He had the drive. He had everything going for him. I'm not trying to say he stepped on people—the only people he stepped on were the people that were trying to do him in. And he knew it, that they were trying to steal his ideas. The minute you try to step on him, the minute you try to steal his ideas—and not being honest about it . . . and being disloyal. You'd do the same thing, wouldn't you? You'd do the same thing if you had that idea, because it was an idea that created a multi-million dollar industry."

Under the constraint of such profound mistrust, it is almost impossible for Jones to allow any aspect of his business to develop outside his personal control or that of one of a tiny handful of loyalists. Jones promised some fitness center proprietors the latest generation of computerized Nautilus machines by 1977, but they were not available until 1985—largely because Jones insisted on conducting every phase of design, literally making all the design modifications himself. His best designers were people who could reproduce perfectly a Jones napkin drawing. His prototype maker for years was Don Stevens. "I understand there are people who will take advantage of people," said Stevens. "I appreciate Arthur's feelings about what he wants done, and I understand it's hard to get people to do something exactly the way you want them to do it."

"Arthur developed the idea," recalled Lafconski. "He'd sit down sometimes for hours and days at a time and work on a particular project. Then he would delegate that project to a person he had confidence in and say, 'Do it exactly the way I have it here. Then when you do it that way, bring it back to me, so I can look at it, and then I'll revise it and I'll give it back to you.' And it would go back and forth like that. As far as the idea itself, he was it."

"Depending on other people—that's a very difficult thing for him to do," said his wife, "because he's done everything in the past himself. He would sweep out the office. He would design the equipment. He would answer the phone. He would open the mail. It's really difficult for him now to extend the responsibility. He won't allow anyone to open his mail. Right now, if you go into our kitchen, we have stacks of mail on our kitchen table and counters. I can't do anything in the kitchen because there's mail everywhere. He won't allow a secretary to open his mail. He wants to do it himself, because she may make the wrong decision or throw something away that's important."

As much as anyone who ever has attained a commercial product breakthrough, Arthur Jones has done it by creating a company in his own image. In the formative years of Nautilus, that image was an extraordinary reflection of technical ingenuity and unstinting hard work. His ability to express his concepts in a real product and to instill in others that passion for hard work opened the doors to a huge, unexpected market. But at the point where the needs of a broad range of consumers, including sick and disabled people, have become the key to the company's future, the image of Arthur Jones is a hindrance to the final breakthrough.

"He's the guy who just got off the boat—and he did it the hard way," explained Katz. "And it's got to be his way. And he's got to make his kids work hard, so his kids will make their kids work hard. That's what he does with all his people. He makes them work hard."

There is a comparison to Richard L. Duke, founder of ChemLawn Corporation. Like Jones, it was important for Duke to "show 'em," to demonstrate his aptitude to a world that had underestimated him. But Duke fought the world's unfair underestimate of his talent because, more than anything else, he wanted to be involved with people, to help them and to lead them. He perceived his business as a dialogue, as something that's better because it's shared. To Jones, on the other hand, the act of sharing is an invitation to theft.

"He's better with a small group of people," explained Clay Steffee. "He can take a small group of people and just accomplish enormous things. As far as picking people to manage different areas of the business, he doesn't seem to have been as successful in getting people to work, between him and a larger mass of employees. I don't think that's been so much the fault of the people he's picked as it has been the style of management he uses."

While Dick Duke enjoyed the experience of passing the baton on to his disciples and seeing them expand the ChemLawn phenomenon and find new ways to take care of customers, Jones went in an opposite direction—growing more uneasy as more people entered his sphere of influence. He watched them all the more closely. The size of his organization became an ordeal, because it created more room for people to fail him, to steal from him. "He says he would love to have a business right now where he could do it all himself," said Terri Jones. "Go back to the old days, when he used to do television shows. He did it all. He was the cameraman. He was the producer. He was in the film—with one little kid acting as a go-fer, doing whatever he said. And the people today just create so many problems for us. But you have to deal with them. That's what makes him want to give up. I think he feels like he's digging holes and being creative and other people are pushing the sand back in."

> *Quotations from Arthur:* "I would like to be in a business all to myself. But the problems I've had have not been from *not* trusting people. Every single problem I've had has come from trusting people. There's nothing in the world that would please me more than to have someone else to turn everything over to. But every time I have ever turned any aspect of it over to anyone else, they have utterly destroyed it. And damn quick."

In gathering around himself the trappings of opulence, Jones finally has the financial resources to support, in grand style, creatures he trusts more than people—elephants and crocodiles. "He loves the animals," said Terri. "The crocodiles are his life. Every day he asks what the big crocodile ate, before he asks for weekly balances on his sales."

"He could have snowballed and snowballed and snowballed in the years to come," said Katz. "I can see it. But he took the short money. He took the power. He took that ego trip."

In fact, the chance might still exist for Nautilus to transform itself from a company that only makes machines—ever more complicated, ever more costly, ever more specialized—to a company that responds both to the marvelous potential of its unique basic technology and to the needs of those people whom the technology can help. As Nautilus grows bigger, there are pockets of divergent thinking within the company. And even in Arthur Jones there is a hint of compassion that emerges occasionally, in spite of his rugged philosophy. It emerges in his urge to teach, to improve those people closest to him.

"I think that he had faith in me," said Don Stevens. "He gave me an opportunity to express myself, use some ideas I had. He gave me an opportunity I never had. Very seldom do people reach a situation where they're satisfied about the work they do and get rewarded, too, and feel good about both of them. Arthur Jones gave me that."

Today the future of Nautilus, like Arthur Jones's age and income and much of his past, remains a mystery. Gathered in Lake Helen are the seeds of even greater accomplishment. But if it's true that trust is the force that passes the baton and drives the breakthrough, then the ultimate triumph is still waiting for Nautilus. The baton is lying around the kitchen at Jumbo Lair, waiting for Arthur Jones to notice it and share it with others, waiting for him to return from feeding the crocodiles.

12 | Dreams Deferred

talo Trapasso's life led him to an opportunity that few people ever have. He fulfilled a dream that had been born in his childhood and lost before he was a man.

Trapasso's dream was to be a research chemist who finds an answer no one ever knew before. His dream was to spend his life hunting for solutions to mysteries that elude the notice of all but a handful of exceptional detectives. But his dream, born in his youth in the 1950s, went unrealized for more than twenty years, until 1975.

In Japan, thousands of miles east of Trapasso's home in Italy, another youthful dream was approaching belated fruition, also in a man advanced in age, a man like Trapasso, toughened by the harshness of his circumstances and the resistance of employers. Yasuji Torii and Italo Trapasso had many things in common, even as far back as the early 1950s, when both their countries faced reconstruction after the devastating defeat of World War II. Each man was an idealist who believed in the miracle potential of chemistry. Each man waged a battle with his company and won a victory for himself—for all scientists who worked in the quiet diligence of corporate laboratories. While both men were still dreaming and deferring their dearest hopes, they met and became friends, sharing the kinship and uncertainty of dreamers in an unromantic industrial world. Partly because of their friendship, each man created an unforeseen commercial triumph for his organization. Trapasso's battle and victory came in the 1970s at Montedison SpA., Italy's largest chemical concern. Torii's battle came earlier, in the 1950s and 1960s, with Mitsui Petrochemical, his lifelong employer.

The thing that eventually turned Trapasso and Torii from friends to business partners, in 1975, was a substance called polypropylene, known to almost no one by name but to almost everyone by its presence everywhere in modern life.

In its manufactured forms, polypropylene is a nondescript, colorless plastic. More accurately, polypropylene is a *polymer,* a plastic so stable and flexible that it adapts to thousands of uses, so valuable to manufacturers that it proliferates worldwide at a rate of 14 billion pounds a year. It can be found, though hardly any of us looks for it, in automobiles (interior and exterior parts), in clothes and carpets, in upholstery and furniture, in the sterile disposable items used in hospitals, in coating films for packages, in computers and television sets, in pipes, in pump housings and gears, and in a hundred other humdrum things that smooth the flow of our daily routine.

However, neither Trapasso nor Torii invented polypropylene. That was done in 1954 by an Italian Nobel Prize–winning chemist named Giulio Natta. Natta discovered the process for polymerizing polypropylene ("a completely unknown and unimagined substance"!)[1] that year at the Milan Polytechnic Institute, and thus added powerful impetus to the modern era of plastics. His discovery became a manufacturing process when it was adapted by the new research laboratories of Italy's biggest chemical company, Montecatini (which merged with the giant Italian utility company Edison in 1966 to become Montedison). The new Montecatini research center that went to work in 1954, adapting Professor Natta's polypropylene discovery, was located south of the company's Milan headquarters, in the small industrial city of Ferrara.

Though polypropylene was a breakthrough worthy of the Nobel Prize in the late 1950s, over the years it gradually lost its luster. For it to become a breakthrough again twenty years later would require the wits and courage of Italo Trapasso and Yasuji Torii and the

1. *Structural Order in Polymers,* Ciardelli and Ginsti, editors, Oxford and New York: Pergamon Press, 1981. "Polypropylene: A Quarter of a Century of Increasingly Successful Development," by P. Galli, page 63.

brilliance of a handful of researchers working for each of them. Working on the same chemical process thousands of miles apart, Trapasso's people and Torii's people slowly came together. In a way, the magnetism that drew together the kindred spirits of Trapasso and Torii was irresistible.

Still, for the Japanese researchers working under Torii at Mitsui Petrochemical Industries and the Italian researchers working at Montedison to weave together a new polypropylene breakthrough in 1975 required a seemingly impossible journey across time and geography. A Chinese proverb says, "The journey of a thousand miles begins with a single step." Strangely enough, in this case that first step was not taken by either Torii or Trapasso and not in Italy or Japan. It was taken in Germany in 1953 by a chemist named Karl Ziegler.

Until Ziegler began to work on them, plastics were, by modern standards, crude and brittle, laden with impurities. A material called polystyrene was the best of them, and it was restricted to uses that entailed bearing very little weight and enduring very little physical stress. When Ziegler discovered a new, far more flexible substance called *polyethylene,* chemists in every industrial nation responded with exultation and an explosion of research.

What Ziegler had realized was that, in the chemical soup that reacts together to synthesize polymers, certain metallic compounds—actually metallic *salts*—aid the process and often encourage the formation of polymer molecules, which, under very high magnification under a microscope, appear as clusters of chemical "pearls." Ziegler's breakthrough came when he created a "catalyst system" upon which the pearls were able to form chains.

Although this laboratory process could not be easily converted to an industrial process, Ziegler had made a breathtaking scientific advance. He had coaxed molecules to gather together with similar molecules in a chemical reaction that separated them from the substances that surrounded them. He had prompted these molecules to form something new and useful from a lot of things that were old and not very useful.

Independent of any further development, polyethylene became far more important than Ziegler might have realized. Today it is a pervasive substance in every society. It is the ingredient in food wraps, garbage bags, thousands of children's toys, food containers, furniture—in everything from badminton nets to gasoline filters. It is a durable, flexible, ubiquitous material, easy to make, melt, mold, and manufacture.

And it is the forebear of polypropylene.

First, Professor Giulio Natta, in Milan, used Ziegler's discovery as a launching point for the remarkable discovery of polypropylene, an even more promising substance. What Natta achieved has been described by chemists as the equivalent of training pearls to make themselves, without oysters—and then getting the pearls to string themselves obediently together.

Following Natta's discovery, he was hired by Montecatini. There he led the Ferrara research team in an equally impressive scientific accomplishment, turning polypropylene into an industry within three years—by 1957.

In those same days of the early 1950s, Italo Trapasso, an aspiring chemist, enviously watched all the excitement that Ziegler and Natta had started. Trapasso had been preparing for this kind of excitement himself since he was a little boy. He had built his own laboratory when he was fourteen years old, working as a tutor through his school days to get the money to equip the laboratory. Throughout secondary school and university days, it was his habit to tutor until after nine or ten at night, then hurry home to his laboratory to run chemistry experiments into the night and early morning, oblivious of time or fatigue. He loved chemistry devoutly. As a student at the University of Genoa, he focused more and more on polymers and began to blend his study in chemistry with a philosophical concept that Gottfried Leibniz had called *monady*—the idea that all the processes of life are simple and comprehensible, if only they can be divined by man. Trapasso believed that knowing the processes as deeply as possible through exhaustive study is the key to changing and harnessing the process of chemistry.

"I consider study one of the biggest satisfactions in my life," said Trapasso. "I used to practice research in polymers at the university, in polystyrene. I expected to continue studying, all my life. It was my dream to be a chemist in polymer research."

He was made a graduate assistant at the University of Genoa, and his dreamed-of life of research seemed at hand when the university offered him a permanent position as a teacher and researcher in polymer science. It was an exceptional honor. But, on the same day that he learned of his university appointment, Trapasso was ordered into the army for his required military service.

The teaching post would not wait. It went to someone else. Italo Trapasso saw his dream abruptly stifled. When he finished his military service years later, he was a stranger at the university. There were no opportunities and he had scant credentials to do research.

Trapasso had missed out on his dream, but he refused to feel sorry for himself. He kept himself informed on polymer research breakthroughs as he muscled his way through an impressive career as a manager in the Italian chemicals industry. Trapasso was probably the only high business executive in Italy at that time whose greatest personal heroes were Karl Ziegler, Giulio Natta, and a former coal chemical engineer in Japan named Yasuji Torii.

While Karl Ziegler and Giulio Natta were creating new polymers in European laboratories, Torii was laying his foundation in polymer research as a chemical engineer in the Japanese coal industry. He was one of a handful of engineers in the large Mitsui group of companies who insisted that in order to bounce back from World War II the company had to diversify—Mitsui had to expand from coal science into petroleum-based chemical processes. When the Mitsui Group spun off a new company called Mitsui Petrochemical Industries (MPC) to pursue that direction in 1955, Torii was the engineer put in charge of the new company's research efforts. He was then already in middle age. He had patiently toiled through the step-by-step promotion process common in Japanese companies, and he had carefully nurtured his energy. Like Trapasso, Yasuji Torii was passionate about research. He was sure the company that committed itself to understanding the basic processes of science could bypass its competitors.

The founder of MPC was a Mitsui Mining Company executive named Takeshi Ishida. Ishida's first act as president of the new company was to convince the Mitsui Group to buy a process for synthesizing "higher alcohols" from patent holders in Germany. But when Ishida got to Germany, he forgot about higher alcohols. Instead, he encountered the excitement over Karl Ziegler's polyethylene discovery. Ishida recognized immediately that, if Ziegler's concept could be translated into an industrial process for manufacturing large amounts of this versatile new plastic, it would be far more valuable to Mitsui than a process for higher alcohols. But buying the polyethylene process from Ziegler was a major risk. At that time, it was only a laboratory discovery. Ziegler had neither an industrial process nor any interest in helping a company develop such a process.

"Ziegler said it was not his responsibility to establish know-how for commercialization," Torii recalled. "That was the responsibility of private enterprise. . . . Mr. Ishida, my president, who had faith in the capability of the Japanese people, believed that though MPC had acquired only the patent, we could develop a manufacturing technology."

Ishida was right. Under his and Torii's guidance, Mitsui had an industrial process for polyethylene within a year. But while they were vigorously promoting the production of high-density polyethylene and the development of its applications, Ishida and Torii saw a flock of Japanese companies hastening to Montecatini in quest of Professor Natta's polypropylene discovery.

Two things kept MPC from following the other Japanese supplicants. One was pride. Ishida had not enjoyed traveling to a fellow defeated nation to beg technology from an autocratic German. Both he and Torii knew that Japan's recovery must eventually grow from creating its own technologies, rather than buying them from other countries. Also, by 1955, the Japanese Ministry of International Trade and Industry (MITI) was enforcing the same philosophy. To save foreign currency, MITI began strictly limiting Japanese companies' acquisitions of foreign technology. Already in possession of one European polymerization process, MPC was unlikely to receive MITI's permission to buy another.

Torii had another idea. He suggested to Ishida that MPC could make a polypropylene discovery similar to Natta's by discovering a catalyst system based on Ziegler's polyethylene catalyst. Ishida said no. He had good reason to refuse. Natta had made an epochal discovery in catalysis to convert a simple gas, propylene, into polypropylene. It was absurd to believe MPC's researchers could duplicate that feat from a different angle without infringing on the Montecatini patent.

But Torii believed polypropylene to be an even more promising material than polyethylene, crucial to the success of MPC and the prestige of Japanese research. So he shrugged at President Ishida's refusal and told his researchers to go ahead. Yasuji Torii persisted in his polypropylene research and kept asking Ishida if it was okay to do it. President Ishida kept on saying no.

After five years of research at MPC's Ziegler Research Center in

Iwakuni, near Hiroshima, it looked as though Ishida had been right. Torii's researchers were spinning their wheels. They had devised a polypropylene process, but they would have had real trouble differentiating it from Natta's process if it were challenged as a patent infringement. They needed a more dramatic difference, and they seemed unable to find one.

Torii quietly relented in his resistance to buying a foreign process and, in 1960, went to Milan to seek patent rights to the Natta catalyst. He was entirely on his own. Not even Ishida knew of his trip to Milan. But Montecatini refused Torii. They already had enough licensees, they told him. In fact, four Japanese companies had been licensed by Montecatini to make polypropylene by the Natta process. Once he was refused, the choice was simple: Torii could either abandon the polypropylene research and admit that President Ishida was right, or he could find another way to do it.

The choice was even simpler than that. If Torii were to give up, he would have to listen to President Ishida saying to him, "I told you so." For Torii, even the thought of such a thing was an insufferable annoyance. Yasuji Torii is a man whose strength, both physical and spiritual, is evident in his eyes, gestures, even in the way he stands. A career in the coal chemical industry had given him a healthy perspective on the meaning of danger. He had crawled through and survived enough dark pits in the earth so that the prospect of "losing face" in a well-lit office building held few terrors for him. So, unafraid of that potential loss of face to his beloved rival, President Ishida, Torii stubbornly rededicated his team to the polypropylene discovery. The difficulty of the challenge was, in a way, greater than Natta's. Natta had found the most accessible route. Torii had to find an alternative route, less apparent, that would not cross in any way the path laid out by Natta.

Torii's quest for a polypropylene catalyst was complicated in another way. His duties at MPC didn't allow him to focus all his attention on the cloister of chemical research in Iwakuni. While sparring with President Ishida and driving his researchers toward a new polypropylene process, he was also serving in a more mundane role, as technical director of MPC's manufacturing plant in Iwakuni. That job took him in 1959 to Grangemouth, Scotland, where he sought a license from a British company for a process to develop chemicals called cumenphenols.

There, Torii met another man seeking a cumenphenol license, an Italian named Italo Trapasso.

The relationship that developed between the two men was that of a talented young student, Trapasso, learning under the guidance of a great *maestro,* Yasuji Torii. In the course of the next five years, they took turns visiting each other's chemical plants. More important, they became friends. They shared each other's hospitality and each other's troubles. Each knew what it was to dream of scientific discovery but to see the dream forestalled by practical considerations of career and duty. They both believed in the simplicity of natural processes and in man's ability to understand those processes. "We shared knowledge; we shared trust," said Trapasso.

Both Trapasso and Torii loved research more than anything, far more than the management of chemical plants. But in the early 1960s, Torii could share with Trapasso little of the knowledge that was emerging slowly from his researchers' work on a polypropylene process in Iwakuni. And Trapasso was then still a sort of manager and, in a sense, in exile from research. Both men might have dreamed of working hand in hand toward a discovery, as scientists and friends, but realizing the dream was unlikely. The closest they would ever come, probably, was to talk about it in the wee hours of the morning over a pitcher of *sake.*

Not long after Torii went to Milan to buy Natta's polypropylene process, his research group broke through, discovering a titanium-based polypropylene catalyst that could be patented separately and licensed to manufacturers without worrying about Montecatini's patent. Finally, in 1965, Torii was able to go triumphantly to Ishida and tell him that MPC could make its own polypropylene and need not seek permission to do so from any other company anywhere in the world.

"Mr. Ishida thought about it very carefully, and he said, 'I shall not oppose MPC manufacturing polypropylene any longer,' " said Torii. The battle of wits between President Ishida and Torii, his most valued manager, was over. They had both won. Torii believes that Ishida's opposition was intended from the outset not to *stop* MPC research, but to motivate it.

"Our researchers were disappointed with management when MPC did not have anything while all our competitors had obtained polypropylene patent licenses from Montecatini," said Torii. "But Mr. Ishida had a firm belief that, if this challenge were left to MPC researchers alone, eventually the researchers would succeed in developing a catalyst of our own.

"Now," added Torii, "Mr. Ishida is probably smiling in the deepness of his grave."

While the period from 1960 through 1965 was an era of great ferment in MPC's research group, it was a time of gradual decline in research at Montecatini. Even though the legendary Giulio Natta had become head of research at the Ferrara Research Center, and even though he shared with Karl Ziegler the 1963 Nobel Prize in Chemistry, Montecatini's researchers made no new discoveries. The worst thing that happened in that period was that Professor Natta, in 1960, declared polypropylene research complete. The Ferrara Research Center ceased in its efforts to further refine Montecatini's patented polypropylene process, while other companies continued trying to make it better. And the other companies succeeded. Manufacturers licensed to use the Montecatini polypropylene process devised ways to make purer polypropylene at less cost, using less energy. Eventually, most of the polypropylene makers in the world were using a "second-generation" process, while Montecatini remained stuck in the first generation.

The best thing that happened to the Ferrara Research Center in that period was the arrival of a brilliant, handsome young chemist named Paolo Galli, in 1961. Galli came to Ferrara after winning a national competition among doctoral graduates in industrial chemistry. Though he was still a young man, he established himself with extraordinary rapidity in several avenues of research in Ferrara and became one of the Research Center's leaders.

But beneath his successes, Paolo Galli was a frustrated individual. One of the reasons he had joined Montecatini with such eagerness was the company's Nobel Prize reputation in polypropylene research. But when he arrived, he found the polypropylene process gathering dust on Montecatini's shelf. He found a research group that was entering what he calls "the Dark Age"—they were simply working on product improvement. Galli and his small group of researchers yearned to explore the very nature of things and to make discoveries, but mostly, all they did was *talk* about discovery.

"The Dark Age" (1965–1975) bridges the merger of Montecatini and Edison into Montedison. The consistent feature of this period, regardless of the leadership, was that the talent of the Ferrara Research Center was being misused. This Dark Age was occupied with less fertile realms of polymer research. Ethylenepropylene (EP) rubber was a favorite product for Montecatini, and the Ferrara group made substantial advances in this area, led by Galli. In another area of mundane product improvement work, Galli distinguished himself dramatically, leading a small group that discovered a better form of synthetic paper made from the chemicals that also serve as the base for polyethylene and polypropylene. Galli's reputation as a versatile, talented, and engaging professional grew.

Paolo Galli is a man with the looks and demeanor of an Italian matinee idol. Impeccably dressed, ingenuously warm and hospitable, he is equally comfortable expressing himself in English and Italian, whether using technical/chemical jargon or business buzz words. His outward suavity conceals in Galli what is more visible in Trapasso—both men have been seduced by the lust for discovery. They tremble with a hunger to understand not just the shape and form of what they see, but the secrets in what they cannot see—the wondrous things that lurk and brood behind, beneath, and within the dreary outer shell of appearance. Both enjoy the labor of examination more than the thrill of promotion or the triumph of a whopping profit margin. Galli's passion shows through in his favorite pastime. He roams the bottom of the Mediterranean in scuba gear, hunting for remnants of ancient civilizations. Even in relaxation, his urge for discovery consumes him.

For Galli, the Dark Age was a maddening standstill. "By the end of the 1960s, Montedison was one of the last-place companies in the production of polypropylene," said Galli. "We lost completely our leadership. America and most Japanese companies, continuing their research, became the best producers in the world."

The period of 1965–1975 was a black one for all at Montedison. The company was a ward of the Italian government, top-heavy with executives appointed by political allies and often inexperienced in the industries they were chosen to direct. Remarking on the Dark Age, one business historian called the Montedison of the 1960s and 1970s "little more than a bloated political football, run by political appointees and dedicated more to the furtherance of state social policies than to profitable operations."[2]

The real life of the company revolved around small groups of people, sometimes individuals, who had the initiative to forge a course of action that served both their own personal goals and

2. Quoted from *International Management* magazine, January 1984.

helped the giant company. As Professor Galli and Trapasso swiftly learned, the aggressiveness of a few individuals tended to confuse the leadership of the "Dark Age of Montedison." The top management of the company often opposed the aggressive actions of the committed few but then often spent months—or years—contemplating what to *do* about any rebellion.

Polypropylene and the undiscovered secrets of its synthesis were more important than the projects assigned to the Ferrara researchers by headquarters in Milan, but Galli and his researchers were prohibited from working on polypropylene. A team of researchers was assembled and ready but standing idle because company management had no awareness of the talent available in Ferrara. Galli was emerging as the leader of this group, which included Adolfo Mayer, a meticulous researcher whose attention to detail was driven by emotion; Camillo Barbe, a key man in the synthesis of the new polypropylene catalyst; and Tonino Simonazzi, a *maestro* in his own right at assaying and testing new laboratory results for the polypropylene catalyst. Galli had the right people. He had a World Series team, but the owners had taken away all his baseballs. As the corporation's budget faltered in the 1960s, the Ferrara Research Center became a bottom-line concern and the company's dedication to research weakened even further.

Montecatini's merger with Edison in 1966 resulted in an even greater threat to the survival of the Ferrara Research Center.

When the agreements had been signed and the details of merger had been ironed out, it rapidly became clear that the Edison people dominated the new management of Montedison. Montecatini had been a company proud of its accomplishments and reputation in original industrial research and development. Edison, on the other hand, had established a corporate practice of minimizing its own research and development costs by buying technologies from other sources. When the Edison clique emerged on top after the merger, the implications for the Ferrara Research Center were dire. Paolo Galli, as clearly as any member of that research group, realized that every day was going to bring a fresh battle to keep top management in Milan from pulling the plug.

"The managers of Edison who became managers of Montedison did not trust research. They were against the people of Montecatini," said Galli, "and there was the strong tendency in all the people of Edison to eliminate [us], to keep only Edison people in management."

In such a negative atmosphere, any scientific breakthrough should have been impossible. Montedison should have collapsed upon itself under its own massive weight and the pressure of its internal conflict, as it nearly did. But hardship only seemed to fire the imagination and steel the determination of the research team in Ferrara. In the midst of the confusion, Galli waged an ill-equipped little guerrilla war to fight off the phase-out of Ferrara. He accomplished heroic things with his group. They created scientific achievements that forced Montedison to keep Ferrara alive, and Galli managed to hold off catastrophe until the eleventh-hour arrival of his saviour, Italo Trapasso.

In 1967, shortly after the merger, Paolo Galli began to exhibit an uncanny knack for turning rebukes into opportunities. The new Montedison management announced its decision to *buy* a second-generation version of Karl Ziegler's process for synthesizing polyethylene. They planned to negotiate with Phillips Petroleum in the United States. Galli was appalled. Here was the greatest polymer research company in the world ignoring its own polymer research laboratory.

Galli knew that if he allowed Montedison management to bypass its own researchers in this fashion, Ferrara was as good as closed. Galli recalled, "Our commercial sales department asked for immediate entrance into the field of polyethylene and they said that we don't like to lose time researching. . . . We want to enter the market and to avoid losing time, we will *buy* the know-how."

But if there was money to buy the technology, there was also money to do research. Montedison's first post-merger profit margin was an impressive 9 percent. Galli knew that the negotiations to buy a polyethylene process from Phillips would be long and expensive. He played his ace in the hole. This is the company of Giulio Natta, Italy's greatest researcher, he told his bosses. Let us try to develop our own polyethylene catalyst while you are courting Phillips. Why settle for buying a second-generation process when you have the forces who can develop a *third*-generation process? he asked. Give me a year, he told them, and we can do it!

Galli and his men entered a race against time, against the plans of their own management.

The Ferrara research group had another adversary in their race to a new polyethylene catalyst. The adversary was in Japan. Polyethylene was, after all, the special strength of the researchers at Mitsui Petrochemical Industries. They worked in a research facility in Iwakuni that was named in honor of the father of polyethylene, Karl Ziegler. And in Iwakuni, researchers had already begun looking for a *third-generation* polyethylene. The leader of the Mitsui research team was a brilliant young polymer chemist named Norio Kashiwa, but the spirit that guided them was the passionate elder statesman of MPC research, Yasuji Torii. The researchers in Iwakuni faced little resistance from their management. Research Director Tsutomu Tanaka had brought Kashiwa to Mitsui with a mandate to keep the company on the forefront of research in polymerization catalysis. So while in Japan Kashiwa and his team were launched lovingly into the mainstream of corporate aspirations, Galli and his team in Italy, though seeking the same result, were swimming against the corporate current.

By the time Galli's year was almost up, very early in 1968, he had created a dilemma for Montedison's leaders. Ferrara's polyethylene work had already shown dramatic progress, too much to call it quits. Besides that, Galli and Adolfo Mayer had gone ahead and spent lots of money equipping laboratories and building a pilot plant to scale the anticipated catalyst from laboratory to mass production. Galli had made the investment too big to abandon.

Montedison responded with indecision. Management issued no order to Galli to cease and desist, but neither did they offer any encouragement. The implicit threat that Ferrara might be cut off at any time remained in the air.

A reprieve of sorts came along in mid-1968, and it permitted the Ferrara research group to intensify its efforts greatly. All of the management group went on vacation for two months in July and August. "We were all alone at last," said Galli. "So we had the opportunity of working for two months very quietly. The holiday of management gave us the freedom we needed. In those two months, we found the catalyst!"

Left to their own devices in the summer of 1968, the researchers of Ferrara made the greatest advance in polymer catalysis since Professor Natta's discovery of polypropylene in 1954. The discovery of a new catalyst for polyethylene not only made Montedison an important licensor and supplier of polyethylene to the world market, it saved the tarnished escutcheon of the Ferrara Research Center, keeping it alive for at least another eight years, and created the scientific basis for the Montedison/Mitsui polypropylene discoveries of 1975. The Dark Age was far from over at Ferrara, but Galli and his men were burning a defiant light.

In little more than a year in Ferrara, a handful of chemists had made the crucial breakthrough. Plastics technology had been pushed into a new era of greater purity, efficiency, durability, and environmental consciousness.

The polyethylene discovery at the Ferrara Research Center, under the leadership of Paolo Galli, struck the Western chemical industries dramatically. As quickly as they could, European and American manufacturers were studying the new Montedison process and adapting their operations to incorporate it. But meanwhile, in the East, within weeks of the Ferrara breakthrough, there was an almost identical breakthrough at Mitsui Petrochemical. Working under Norio Kashiwa, MPC's research team at Iwakuni also devised a new high-yield catalyst for polyethylene.

Galli and Kashiwa had never met. They didn't know each other's names; they'd never read each other's papers. They knew little of each other's companies. Yet they had each led a team to the same discovery, starting almost simultaneously, finishing in a virtual dead heat. Adding to the coincidence was the fact that their work in polyethylene catalysis was the first new science in that polymer since Ziegler's discovery in 1953. There had been a lull of more than a decade, and then simultaneous bursts of activity, thousands of miles apart in two very different cultures.

The Ferrara and Iwakuni discoveries were so similar that they could not, in the long run, be patented separately. A clash between Montedison and Mitsui was inevitable—as soon as each found out what the other had done.

But meanwhile, in Milan, Montedison's leaders first had to deal with the fact that a division they didn't really want had engineered the greatest breakthrough in polymer science in the decade.

Their considered response, slow in coming, was to form new plans for the elimination of Galli and his research organization. This polyethylene discovery was probably just a fluke. Certainly, Galli couldn't keep it up, and if he tried to keep it up, his work would be too costly for the company to support over the long term.

But Galli was also making plans. He took as much advantage as possible of his short-term reprieve and pushed Montedison into the next level of research, a *polypropylene* catalyst based on the same principle.

    Galli and his researchers knew that they had opened the door to a family of catalysts that could change the nature of polymer science and the billion-dollar industries that relied on it. In the 1950s, both Natta and Ziegler had found a way to "make pearls without oysters." Every oyster needs an "irritant," usually a grain of sand, around which it can build its pearl. For the creation of polypropylene molecules from a sort of propylene soup, Ziegler and Natta discovered that the best irritant, or catalyst, was a metallic salt, titanium chloride, $TiCl_3$ (the Japanese call it "tickle-three"). When they used a titanium chloride catalyst, it was as though Ziegler and Natta were pouring many grains of sand into the water of an oyster bed and suddenly finding the water to be filled with strings of pearls (better known to science as "stereospecific polymers").

    But there was a problem with this little miracle. For the better part of twenty years, petrochemical manufacturers had to solve the problem of getting all those "grains of sand" back out of the water. Once it made its pearls, the titanium chloride became a pollutant. Because of this, manufacturers of polyethylene and polypropylene had to put the polymer through a series of solvents to remove the waste, a process that was both time-consuming and expensive.

    What Galli in Italy and Kashiwa in Japan discovered in 1967–1968 was a way to polymerize polyethylene with "hollow grains of sand," empty irritants. They realized that another metallic salt, magnesium chloride, could work as a partner with titanium. They discovered they could create molecules of catalyst—or grains of sand—that were made up of titanium chloride on the outside but magnesium chloride on the inside.

    What a change this was! Suddenly, the amount of $TiCl_3$ available to pollute the polymer was reduced by 90 percent. The need to purify the polymer had disappeared because so little of the new catalyst was required, and the magnesium chloride was so benign it could be left in the product. Both the magnesium chloride and the small proportion of titanium chloride could now blend undetectably into the polymer.

    To shift analogies momentarily, it was as though the scientists had found a way to replace golf balls with Ping-Pong balls. The chemical reaction of the polymer only needed to use the surface of the ball; it never had any use for what was inside. Take the cover off a million golf balls and you are left with a warehouse full of rubber bands and cork. Take the covers off a million Ping-Pong balls and all that remains is air. This is what happened when the scientists of Montedison and Mitsui, working separately, added magnesium chloride to their traditional mixture of titanium chloride and ethylene.

When the two companies realized they had both done the same thing and were both trying to license the same basic catalyst under two different patents, the inevitable lawsuit followed. The patent battle that began in 1968 wasn't settled until 1982, in Montedison's favor. The lawsuit was good reason for the two companies not to see eye-to-eye in the 1970s. But research leaders at both companies understood they had found something special when they discovered a "catalyst support" for polyethylene. Galli in Ferrara and Kashiwa in Iwakuni both saw vividly that the magic bullet that made a polyethylene molecule of remarkable uniformity and clarity would also—eventually—do the same thing for polypropylene. And if they could do it with polypropylene, a much more important polymer, the impact on industry would be staggering!

"The polyethylene discovery became a flag in our hand. We could say we've demonstrated to management that we are able to discover in a short time, a few years, a new catalyst and a new revolutionary process," said Galli. "By that time, polypropylene had become a very interesting market . . . so we said, 'We have strengthened the technology of polyethylene, which can be adapted. Please give us some time—one, two years—and you will have a possibility of a new process and a new product.' "

In selecting polypropylene as the next project for Ferrara research, Galli was pointing in the most logical direction for the new Ziegler-Natta magnesium chloride catalysts. But he was also pointing toward one of his company's crying needs. By the late 1960s, polypropylene was still one of the key polymers in the manufacture of hundreds of products, but it was a material also starting to decline in popularity because of the wastefulness of its synthesis. Shortages of petroleum were beginning to loom, and a supply crisis could be disastrous to companies that were already making only minimum profits on polypropylene. Montedison, for one, was making tons of polypropylene but very little profit on it.

By the early 1970s, when Galli tried to convince his company to return to its most important discovery, the Montedison manufacturing process was outdated. Every other polypropylene company in the world had a better, faster second-generation process. In embarrassment, Galli sent representatives to Japan to buy from one of his company's licensees, Mitsubishi, a second-generation process for polypropylene. For a proud Paolo Galli, the irony of that acquisition was cruel. The laboratory that had taught the world about polypropylene was forced to buy notes from one of its students.

Through Galli's efforts, the Ferrara Research Center, at least for a while, enjoyed a rejuvenated reputation. It was working on a process that Montedison needed very much, so plans to close the research facility had to wait for a while.

But not long! Research dragged on longer than two years. In the meantime, management support for Ferrara Research collapsed entirely. Montedison management grew concerned that Ferrara might be developing another breakthrough. If that happened, they might never be able to close down the place. Management's solution was to shift official approval for new research projects—including the new catalyst for polypropylene—to Montedison's Donegani Research Center in Novara, Italy. Ferrara was left with odds and ends.

"We ignored their orders," said Galli. "We just continued to work."

In 1972 Ferrara completely lost its budget and was placed under a general research budget. Galli got no money at all earmarked for polypropylene research and was told again to work just on manufacturing problems specified by the company. He and his group were expected to report to plant management, an even worse organizational condition for creative researchers.

But they never stopped, and they never ceased to believe in their work. They became aware that they were being watched ever more closely by Milan. "The Edison people were very narrowminded. They understood nothing and controlled everything," said Galli. "We took our research into the closet. We were very excited, but we had to pretend we were working on plants. By 1975 we had succeeded in isolating a high-yield catalyst using magnesium chloride. We did it on our own, with no big boss in Milano showing any interest. In fact, they were against us. We were working in a black corner."

The isolation of that polypropylene catalyst was a dramatic

breakthrough for Galli and his team. But an even more important breakthrough had just occurred in—of all places—Milan! The Montedison leadership had named Italo Trapasso to head the company's new Plastics Division. Included in Trapasso's new division was the laboratory in Ferrara.

At last Italo Trapasso had his own laboratory again. The dream so long deferred was restored to this man who loved study, who believed in research more passionately than anything else in his life.

But to Ferrara's researchers, the news was just another pronouncement from the accountants in Milan. Nothing in Trapasso's past nor in his demeanor suggested to Galli that this man could be Ferrara's liberator.

Trapasso is short, beetle-browed, and earthy. He looks neither the scientist nor the academic. His career after his army service had been a series of bootstrap efforts to build chemical manufacturing facilities, and recruit work forces to fill them, throughout Italy. He had performed so successfully in this capacity for such companies as Mobil, Monsanto, and Edison that he could literally thumb his nose and walk out whenever he felt management leaning too hard on his creative style. He was a man used to standing in the sun, shouting orders and trading insults with the men driving heavy machinery. He was a man comfortable among engineers, mechanics, and foremen.

Nevertheless, Trapasso's populist credentials probably didn't impress Galli and his group. Trapasso had been a member in good standing of the Edison management structure for years. Galli's people had learned through experience that if someone was from Edison, he was the enemy.

But Italo Trapasso was nobody's company man. And, whatever his experience in life, in his heart he was a chemist. Trapasso embraced the dilapidated research complex in Ferrara like a father would a living son who had been given up for dead in a war.

Surveying for the first time the Ferrara Research Center, Trapasso did not notice the decay of the Montedison factory complex that surrounded the research center like a soiled scarf. Trapasso saw only a laboratory, the repository of his dreams. In that lab he saw—immediately—a group of scientists who could, with his support, restore Montedison's tarnished reputation in scientific inquiry. Though corporate leadership had failed to see the importance of the group's discovery of the polyethylene process in 1968,

Trapasso recognized it as historic. He immediately began a sweeping series of changes in the structure of his division, moving people, battling with Milan, and embracing the stunned researchers in Ferrara, calling them "family," telling them he *trusted* them to come up with great discoveries. "I want to develop things," said Trapasso. "I'm not a clerical man. I don't like people who don't trust workers."

In talking over this situation, Trapasso found himself balanced between a threat and a triumph. If he paused even briefly, other laboratories in other companies would take from Montedison the secret and the glory of its great scientific breakthrough. But if he seized the moment, he might become the inspiration for a true discovery—a new and entirely different generation of polypropylene.

"When I arrived, the research laboratory was reporting to the plant manager [of the Ferrara manufacturing facility]. Can you imagine? The man responsible for research was reporting to a plant manager who was busy following other kinds of things. Not technology! Not research!" said Trapasso. "My task was to get top management to change its idea of research. I spent nine hours explaining that I wanted the Ferrara Research Center independent, to create again the Ferrara Research Center as a true research laboratory."

Within less than a year of his arrival, Trapasso restructured his division so that he had separate deputy general managers in charge of plant operations, engineering, technology, and research. Galli was made the deputy general manager of research.

"Dr. Trapasso saved us," said Galli. "He was the only Edison executive I knew who had scientific training and vision. We made the discoveries. He made an industry. He is a saint!"

"I attacked very strongly the Montedison reluctance to support research," recalled Trapasso. "There are no limits to research . . . I had full confidence in my people [at Ferrara]. I would have signed a blank check and given it to them."

Trapasso acted with a speed and decisiveness that was shocking in the deliberate world of Montedison management. When he applied his knowledge of chemistry, he realized that Galli and his team already had a new high-yield catalyst. If Ferrara had one, he knew that Mitsui, their Japanese arch-rival, might be almost as close, perhaps even ahead of Ferrara.

* * *

While he restructured his Plastics Divison and Montedison management worried about what might be happening in Japan, Trapasso fulfilled another of his dreams. In the summer of 1975, Italo Trapasso got in touch with the man he calls "maestro," Yasuji Torii.

Suddenly, these two men, who years earlier had sat up through a dozen nights drinking and talking earnestly like two university students obsessed with the dream of discovery, were coming together. They had waited patiently. Finally they seized their chance to design, hand-in-hand, their great experiment. And Trapasso and Torii were ready for the chance. Not only did they have the same goal, but each man had, in his research laboratory, a team of the world's best polymer scientists.

Trapasso told Torii it was time for the brilliant researchers working in Ferrara under Paolo Galli and in Iwakuni under Norio Kashiwa to start working in unison toward the same goal. Trapasso suggested a joint research venture to Yasuji Torii. It did not take long for Torii and his colleagues at Mitsui Petrochemical to decide whether they ought to team up with the Italian research group. They had admired and watched attentively the brilliant advances that had been made in Ferrara since the mid-1960s. Yasuji Torii knew that his company and Trapasso's were in a race to synthesize a manufacturable high-yield polypropylene catalyst. Like Montedison's leaders, Torii did not relish the prospect of another long patent suit. And Torii had a classically Japanese view of the competitive situation: He knew that the ultimate discovery of a high-yield catalyst would transform an industry and generate spectacular wealth for the company or companies that made the discovery. In that light, Torii knew there would be "enough to go around."

Torii called Trapasso back and told him that a deal was possible. Negotiations followed very quickly, and in August 1975 Mitsui and Montedison signed an agreement that combined their research knowledge and precluded the possibility of another court battle over patent rights.

The results of the Mitsui/Montedison marriage came amazingly fast. On its own, each laboratory had made huge strides in adapting the polyethylene discovery into a high-yield catalyst for polypropylene. When they shared their notes and repeated each others' experiments, it was relatively easy to repair each other's minor miscalculations. If they had had to undertake this refinement process independently, Galli and Kashiwa agree, the emergence of the catalyst would have taken years. Instead it took three months. "If MPC had not decided to cooperate with Montedison, eventually the company by itself would have succeeded, but it would have taken a much longer time," said Kashiwa. "Even at the time the agreement was executed, neither MPC nor Montedison figured that such speed would be possible."

In November 1975, in Ferrara and Iwakuni, researchers saw, in the images recorded by an electron microscope, long, perfect strings of pearls, so pure and uniform that they could go directly into use, without purification. Since these were pearls to be used as building blocks—as part of crystallized solids—their uniformity was also important. They had to fit together without lumps, distortion, or flaws. But that was no problem! These polypropylene molecules were the most flawless strings of pearls any chemist had ever seen.

These remarkable pearls emerged through the efforts of both laboratories on an almost identical timetable, even though there were vast differences in the environment in which they existed. While Mitsui researchers had followed a smooth course of constant scientific inquiry and development, the Ferrara group had faced an almost constant series of halts, threats, and misdirections.

With polyethylene and then with polypropylene, the research team at Mitsui had started sooner than the Montedison group. The Mitsui researchers worked under a mandate issued by senior management and under the benevolent leadership of Torii and Research Director Tsutomu Tanaka. Yasuji Torii's triumphant duel of wills with President Ishida between 1955 and 1965 had established fundamental research as a necessity at Mitsui. The corporation believed in its research team and indulged it with praise and money. Research is a religion at Mitsui. By contrast, by 1966 at Montedison, fundamental research had become heresy, and it remained so throughout Ferrara's greatest burst of creativity.

The paradox of successful research as virtual heresy is not limited to the discovery of a high-yield catalyst for polypropylene. In many of the stories included in this book, it was true that the company that began its inventive efforts from a disadvantage, or from the position of the underdog, emerged at the end more swiftly with a better solution. This was true of JVC, whose video cassette recorder research team faced both the resistance of their company and the technological and market head start enjoyed by Sony, their main competitor. In the development of the Post-it Note Pad at 3M, Arthur Fry began the successful development of the breakthrough product by simply rejecting all previous developments and breaking down the product to its beginning elements.

It appears that the Italian researchers at Montedison kept pace with their more affluent Japanese cousins because they shared with the Iwakuni team a belief in *basic* science. But they also prevailed because, although they lacked organizational support, they made up the difference in emotional involvement. They cared passionately about the project and about each other.

"Galli said to us that our success would come in dedicating our research to basic physical chemistry—not kitchen chemistry," said colleague Camillo Barbe, who co-authored the scientific papers with Galli. "When you understand, you can make changes in a rational way."

"When you have an experimental, practical problem, you don't try to solve it practically," said Galli. "You theorize. First you understand what are the basic phenomena. You interpret, look for mathematical laws, and then go to the solution. Not trial and error, but interpretation! That is absolutely the key. . . . You must have a deep knowledge of theoretical phenomena."

But Galli also kept one eye focused ahead—on the next steps to be taken, beyond laboratory results. At the beginning of the polypropylene research in 1970, Galli emphasized the importance of turning laboratory results into industrial process. In a way, by looking ahead to the dilemma of manufacturing, Galli turned Montedison's worst disadvantage into an advantage. He knew that in 1970, Mitsui already had sophisticated second-generation manufacturing facilities in Japan making both polypropylene and polyethylene. Montedison was dramatically behind Mitsui in production technology of this sort. As problem-solvers, the Montedison group thus had an ironic advantage over their friends in Iwakuni. *They had a bigger problem.*

As a result, the Ferrara research team did what Thomas Edison would have advised. They halted, assembled all the details of the problem, and outlined a series of goals that covered virtually every contingency. Four necessary goals that Galli listed for Ferrara's proposed high-yield catalyst seemed to deal solely with characteristics of the catalyst itself: (1) high activity, (2) excellent stereospecificity, (3) good molecular weight distribution, and (4) superior and unique polymer morphology. These goals were defined and attained as the result of a systematic scientific approach based on physical chemistry studies carried out during the darkest period of the Dark Age, "when we were completely abandoned," said Galli. But as they developed these goals, the Ferrara team matched each one with its effect on pilot plant testing, full manufacturing scale-up, marketing advantage, sales appeal, and advantages for manufacturers who would eventually buy—or not buy—a license to use the Montedison process.

Mitsui, whose laboratory goals were logically similar to those devised independently at Ferrara, had an excellent research plan. But, under the gun, Galli and his group had added to that a number of subtleties, many more pieces of the problem. With more to worry about, they thought more broadly and more imaginatively.

Nevertheless, Ferrara's well-formed plan would have failed without Mitsui. Montedison money for Ferrara—even for the relentless Trapasso—ran out in early 1977. Montedison leadership would not spend the needed money to convert one of its industrial plants to mass-produce polypropylene by a process that had never been used industrially. "We needed in a short time the attainment of a catalyst and we developed the catalyst here in Ferrara and tested it in our pilot plant," recalled Galli. "At the same time, Mitsui reached the same result in their pilot plant, and immediately they brought their catalyst from pilot plant to industrial plant, because they had much more advanced industrial polypropylene technology."

What Mitsui did was to modify its own manufacturing equipment, essentially bypassing many of the purification stages built into the old catalyst process. Within months, Mitsui's factory had synthesized tons of a polypropylene that was cleaner and simpler than the chemical world could have imagined a few years earlier. Trapasso cheered Mitsui's success at the industrial level. It was an accomplishment that would have been impossible at Montedison for years.

With proof of the feasibility of the new process, Trapasso began a dramatic push to establish a dominant world presence for the new polypropylene. The first step was the $4 million conversion of an old Montedison first-generation polypropylene plant in Brindisi, Italy. The changeover in Brindisi was costly and risky, but it was within Montedison's means. Even if this promising new polypropylene was a failure, the company could absorb a risk that involved the conversion of one aging chemical plant in Italy.

The second step, if Montedison took it and stumbled, could have caused irreparable damage. Trapasso told the directors of Montedison that one manufacturing plant was not enough. "We had to expand our presence in polypropylene in the biggest potential market, in the United States," said Trapasso. "We had to decide to build a new plant there, and we had to decide then, in 1977."

The ideal site was in LaPorte, Texas, which was close to a plant that produced propylene. Trapasso insisted that Montedison acquire the site in LaPorte and begin building immediately.

The decision to go ahead with the U.S. plant was complicated by lingering doubts in the scientific community as to whether the new catalyst really was new at all. Montedison was still the only company with even so much as a pilot plant dedicated to the new polypropylene. (Mitsui did not complete a manufacturing plant until 1984.) Trapasso had driven Montedison forward so fast into industrial development that at last he was left almost alone, standing on a plant site in Texas, waiting for the world to catch up to him.

"When the decision came whether to build a new plant to make this high-yield catalyst in Texas, it followed my recommendation that we had to have at least two plants for manufacture," Trapasso remembered. "But many people were against it. Only the ex-chairman [Eugenio Cefis] of ENI [the giant conglomerate of Italian companies of which Montedison was a member] was willing to back me up. Even some of the senior Montedison research people said that this catalyst was a common catalyst."

Eventually the corporate leaders at Montedison deferred a decision, leaving the go-ahead on a multi-million-dollar overseas manufacturing plant to an impetuous division head who had charged through life with a chip on his shoulder. "Cefis said to me, 'Trapasso, you decide.' And I decided, we go ahead. . . . And I did not sleep for two years."

Given even a hesitant go-ahead, Trapasso stormed through the Brindisi conversion in less than a year and had the first new polypropylene on the market in 1978. And then it became clear to everyone in the scientific and manufacturing communities that this clean, simple, cheap, and remarkably versatile polypropylene was nothing like the old stuff.

The product that began to flow from Montedison's plants in Brindisi and LaPorte looked drab. Mostly, polypropylene leaves the chemical factory as little white pellets of plastic "foam." To a nonchemist it looks like the stuff used as packing material to keep fragile items from being broken in shipping parcels. But to manufacturers, this polypropylene—lighter, stronger, cleaner, and cheaper than any they had ever seen—opened worlds of opportunity. Every major petrochemical company in the world began to search feverishly for new ways to use it. This material was so adaptable that it could be molded, extruded, stretched, bent, and manipulated unlike any previous polymer.

The manufacturers began to find new applications within months, and that parade of applications has led to an infusion of polypropylene into everyday life that is as pervasive as it is invisible. It's virtually impossible to move in any direction in a modern house or automobile without touching or being surrounded by polypropylene. If the building you are in is less than five years old, it is likely that there is polypropylene above you (in the roofing material), below you (in the carpeting), around you (in the upholstery and support webbing of chairs and sofas and in the pipes and the electrical system). It is part of the mattress and box spring. It is the agitator in the washing machine and the plastic fixtures inside the dishwasher. It is in the refrigerator in your kitchen, both in the shelves and in the food containers that house your mayonnaise, barbecue sauce, milk, butter, and chocolate syrup.

Polypropylene might be in your underwear and your ski outfit, and it is certainly in your baby's disposable diapers. If your car is new, its bumpers, floor, dashboard, and most of its plastic interior trim are all polypropylene. The outer casing for every video tape cassette is made of high-impact polypropylene, and polypropylene is the reason why cassettes don't cost more than they do. Because the collaboration of scientists at Ferrara and Iwakuni produced a substance more flexible and easier to make than any previous form of plastic, it is inevitable that every day more polypropylene will move unseen into every person's environment. Things will be lighter in weight, stronger, more durable, and safer to use.

All this came about so quickly because, by the end of 1979,

Montedison had converted to the new catalyst at a product plant in Belgium and was already near the completion of Trapasso's daring venture in LaPorte.

The ending was happy for Montedison. A strategy that was born in Paolo Galli's elegant matrix of goals in 1970 was carried resolutely forth on the chip-strewn shoulders of Italo Trapasso. The world learned of the new polypropylene mainly because Trapasso goaded Montedison into making an awful lot of it—in Italy, in Belgium, and in America.

The happy ending became easier, however, not just because of Trapasso's rugged individualism. In 1977 Montedison stepped from its Dark Ages to its Renaissance with the appointment of a new vice-president for finance named Mario Schimberni. Over the next seven years, Montedison learned to focus its business. Schimberni became president and chairman of the board in 1980, and he led the company's efforts to divest itself of a plethora of competing interests within its sprawling network of businesses. He began aggressively to weed out of Montedison the layers of management that had grown into the body of the company like a rampant fungus. This was not an easy task. Things were terrible, financially, until 1984, when Montedison finally broke even. In 1985 the company made a significant profit and convinced a long-skeptical business community that the Italian giant would no longer ignore its most promising projects, like those of the research group in Ferrara.

In summer 1984 Schimberni said, "The biggest problems are in the past. Montedison has a new structure. We have selected our business portfolio; we have clear strategic goals. We know who we are. We are a diversified company with strengths in primary chemicals, specialty chemicals, energy, and services. . . . We know where we want to go. . . . Our management is now innovative, flexible, open-minded, and accepts the challenge of change."

By 1986 the most impressive demonstration that Montedison management had finally changed for the better was the return of Italo Trapasso, who not long after he had brought the LaPorte, Texas, chemical plant into production had grown frustrated with company bureaucracy and quit.

He stayed away for several years.

In 1983 Montedison formed a new company called Himont, Inc., in partnership with Hercules, Inc., of Wilmington, Delaware—the acknowledged world leader in polypropylene production by the (now obsolete) second-generation process. Himont, the new company, was staggeringly successful, showing first-year revenues of $600 million and earnings of $73 million. Unlike Montecatini in 1956, Montedison kept a tight reign on its patent rights. By 1991, Montedison and Mitsui estimate, almost three-quarters of the polypropylene manufactured in the world will be under their joint patent.

Today, the Ferrara Research Center (which has been renamed in honor of Professor Giulio Natta), under the direction of Adolfo Mayer and the scientific leadership of Camillo Barbe and Tonino Simonazzi, continues to refine the process of polymer catalysis, to seek what Trapasso, after Leibniz, calls *monady*. "The chemical industry is not the steel industry. It has all the ingredients to *create*," said Trapasso. "By its very structure, nature is composed of single elements. . . . I feel that all chemical processes will be simplified!" When he made that statement, Trapasso was in his new office at Himont, Inc., headquarters in Delaware.

The formation of Himont gave Montedison the opportunity to call Trapasso back into the company, and Trapasso came willingly, encouraged by Montedison's new respect for research. His return was welcomed warmly by Galli, who has become vice-president of Technology at Himont, working side-by-side with Trapasso in Delaware. In his new position, Trapasso today is a more tranquil man than he has ever been. Looking back on the discovery of the high-yield polypropylene catalyst, he conveys an ambivalent blend of pride and modesty.

"I must be honest. I had not too much time. Because I work in the Italian system, I had to implement the good people," said Trapasso. "My work experience allowed me to understand who were the right people. If you do not have the best people doing research, you are not doing research."

Trapasso's emphasis on having the right people is, in one sense, his way of shaking a fist at the Italian system. But it is also a compelling insight into what happened in Ferrara during the search for new polypropylene. "All I did," said Trapasso, "was to recognize the merit of the people, all the Ferrara people. I was a kind of servant of them. I was their assistant."

Trapasso believes that a manager's most important supervisory function is in choosing the best people to do the job. Once that's been done, his foremost value is in protecting these people from meddling by senior management. In fact, Trapasso directed all of his energy, all his aggressiveness, not at the research center, but at his superiors. It was his bosses whom Trapasso "managed." He left the Ferrara Research Center to its own devices. To him they were *family*. "In research," he said, "you don't need a boss or an executive. Research is so much satisfaction that it is *enough*."

Trapasso uses the word *enough* as though it means "everything."

By itself, Trapasso's ideal of research possesses a fragile estheticism. Simonazzi called the research team at Ferrara, struggling through their Dark Age, "a very little group that tried to maintain something living." Trapasso, in his ideal picture of life, would have been one of that very little group all along. But he had compromised with life.

Perhaps Trapasso always felt that he would get another chance. Perhaps that is why when at last his path crossed that of the researchers he so admired and so envied, he became immediately what Galli and his group needed to complete their scientific odyssey. Trapasso supplied the muscle to thrust discovery from its womb. Trapasso knew that it's good to be a researcher but even better when the world knows what you have discovered. And to make sure of that, what you have got to do—what Italo Trapasso did—is sell it.

Trapasso didn't rest until he had raised the Montedison/Mitsui catalyst discovery to a mature product that had captured the attention of the world.

"Would it have survived without me?" Trapasso wondered.

And then he answered his own question with a shrug and a smile.

"Probably not."

13 Federal Express: The Knights on the Last White Horse

I f a majority of American companies had always followed the no-waste principles instilled at Toyota Motor Works by Taiichi Ohno, it is likely that the breakthrough of an air freight company called Federal Express would never have happened.

In Japan in the 1970s, Toyota redefined the automobile industry, because Taiichi Ohno created a system that allowed no breakdowns, no surprises, and impeccable timing. In the United States in the 1970s, Federal Express redefined the air freight industry because its founder, Frederick W. Smith, based his business on the expectation that American companies would break down incessantly, unexpectedly, and at the worst possible moment.

Founded in 1971, when Frederick Smith was only twenty-seven years old, Federal Express was at first based on a speculative relationship with the United States Federal Reserve Bank. Like so many other things that Smith tried in the ensuing four years, that deal with the Federal Reserve fell through and left the company on the brink of catastrophe. Between 1971 and 1975, Smith fell $30 million in debt, was indicted for defrauding a bank, got sued by his own family, saw his investors replace him as commander of his company with an Air Force general, then got it back again nine months later.

Through a special kinship shared by Smith with a loyal corps of executives, pilots, and rank-and-file couriers, Federal Express survived crisis upon crisis with a sort of John Wayne spit-in-their-eye bravado—and Federal Express became the standard for air freight operations for the future.

Federal Express in 1983 exceeded the $1 billion mark in annual revenue. The phrase "Hello, Federal!" has become a permanent feature of American parlance. To say "Hello, Federal!" today means that you can get a crucial machine part, a parcel, or a paper delivered right away—even if you were negligent until the eleventh hour! Speedy nationwide delivery of packages—which was un-thinkable in 1970—was synonymous ten years later with the name Federal Express.

In a decade, American businesses elevated Federal Express to the level of a necessity—along with such staples of corporate operations as the computer, the photocopier, and the telephone. Fred Smith has offered many retrospective analyses of the aston-ishing success of the Federal Express idea. He cites most often the emergence of high technology industries that require safe delivery of tiny but critical electronic components or tiny vials of perishable biotechnological specimens on extremely short notice.

"In the past," Smith explained, "if you ran a big factory and a lathe broke down, you always had a couple of very good craftsmen in the shop who went in there and welded it back together and did whatever was necessary to solve the problem. In the case of those first-generation industries, the cost of production delays wasn't all that significant, but in the 1960s electronic machines started to become prevalent. When that machine broke down, there was no way they were going to extract the data base out of the inside of that IBM 360 computer. It wasn't on tablets anyplace. It was *in there* and it was locked and you couldn't get at it. There was no way some craftsman was going to go to the DuPont plant and carefully mix the stuff that produced the new chemicals—you were just out of business. The people who supplied these new electronic ma-chines had a terrible logistics problem in providing timely repair and parts replacement because the country had become—by the mid-sixties—a national market."

Logical as this explanation is, it just isn't enough. It doesn't explain why printers, jewelers, architects, and wholesalers of plumbing fixtures depend on Federal Express for daily economic survival. If it built its success on high tech and biotech, Federal Express would have become only a modest commercial success. The simple fact is that when Federal Express's remarkable "Super

Hub" sorting complex in the Memphis (Tennessee) International Airport topped the 400,000-packages-per-night plateau in early 1985, barely one in ten of those parcels contained electronics and precious biotech specimens.

Most of the stuff was mail. It was plain, ordinary, garden-variety business mail. It was paper, the stuff that computers were supposed to make obsolete by about 1985. High technology might have inspired Federal Express, but paper is what made it a roaring success.

Federal Express was, and is today, a triumph of Parkinson's Law, a demonstration that "work expands to fill the time available for its completion." America once wrapped up its important business documents two or three days in advance of deadlines because two or three days was the time it would take an air freight service (Emery or United Parcel Service or even the much-maligned United States Postal Service) using commercial airline flights to get the document to the eager client. Federal made it possible to put off work until the last minute and still get it there on time—overnight! Absolutely, positively overnight!

Arthur Bass, who was Smith's chief operating officer at Federal from 1976 to 1978 and one of the devoted handful who kept the company alive through its first four preposterous years, explained, "Before Federal Express came into the business, everybody was satisfied with what you would call the 'as-soon-as-possible.' It's an art form. When Federal Express changed that perception to 'overnight,' Federal Express in itself became the time machine."

In the second half of the 1970s, businesses in America started paying $10 and more per envelope to send a one-page letter 800 miles from Hartford to Memphis in order to be sure it would arrive 100 miles south in Manhattan by noon. If this was madness, it was madness that worked. And if the client didn't know he was shipping from Hartford to Manhattan via Memphis, he was better off not knowing.

Like so many breakthroughs, Federal Express boiled irrepressibly within an individual, Fred Smith, who grew more sure of his idea the more "experts" told him it was silly. Like other breakthroughs, Federal Express faced a huge crisis early in its existence but emerged intact because its originator was able to combine a clear vision of his goals with a flexible response to obstacles he would not see until they suddenly appeared. Most important, the

Federal Express breakthrough, like so many others, happened because the originator, Fred Smith, rallied around him a force of individuals who found in themselves a wellspring of talent that had lain fallow through a lifetime of more ordinary attainments. There was emotion at Federal, and it still fairly bristles from Federal at the hint of a doubt, a challenge, or an outsider's skeptical glance.

Tucker Taylor, a former Navy pilot who looks and talks like the all-American boy from Yale, was one of Federal Express's leaders in the early years. Smith assigned Taylor in 1974 to the task of keeping happy a sporadically paid and overworked labor force. He tried to explain why everyone felt so good when things were so bad in those days. "One of the things that kept all of the employees' morale so high," Taylor said, "was the fact that Federal Express was losing money. I mean there was an awful lot of this 'we're all in the trenches together' feeling. We prided ourselves on being like the Viet Cong, not really knowing what the words *convertible debenture* really meant and wearing cheap suits and talking about the investment bankers like they were the 'jackals of Wall Street,' and that kind of stuff. We were going to make something work without playing the game!"

Arthur Bass added, "It was a crusade! It was my chance to prove everything I knew about business in an environment that would allow it to happen."

The crusading spirit was not just a feeling that touched the leadership of Federal Express. It spread, with equal passion and equal propriety, among even the package handlers in the gaudy orange and purple courier vans that became the company trademark. The egalitarianism that existed at Federal Express was—more perhaps than any of his corporate strategies and financial triumphs—the creation of Fred Smith. He made people believe that he felt the same thing that they felt and vice versa.

For Fred Smith to achieve this rampant kinship among the people of his company seems inconsistent with his roots. Fred Smith's father, James Frederick Smith, built a multimillion-dollar fortune running bus lines throughout the southern states. He left to Fred and his half-sister, Fredette, and Laura Ann, his adopted sister, each an inheritance in excess of $3 million, partly in the form of stock in a family holding company, Frederick Smith Enterprise Company, which was then worth more than $15 million. Fred went to the best schools and then to Yale University without a worry about the price of tuition. He was a student of exceptional ability, a popular, handsome, gifted young man, schooled in the manners of the Old South. Tucker Taylor, who was at Yale a couple of years behind Smith, said, "He's the guy you hated worst when you were in college. Not only does he have an IQ that's twice yours, he stays up late and studies."

While he was at Yale, Fred Smith began to use his exceptional intellect to synthesize a number of ideas and interests that had shaped his life. The idea that most captivated him was articulated in a junior-year paper submitted to a business professor and returned with a mediocre grade. The concept, the teacher told Smith, was interesting and well-formed, but in order to earn better than a "C," the idea must be feasible. Fred Smith had failed to convince the professor that his imaginary enterprise could exist in the real world.

The concept that Smith devised, at the age of twenty, was (absolutely, positively) overnight delivery. The best part of this idea—according to the teacher—was his logistic theory for a "hub-and-spokes" air freight system. Smith suggested that a freight forwarding company could draw a circle around, for instance, Detroit's airport. The airport would act as a "hub." A number of truck routes would be the "spokes." All day, little trucks would scurry around inside that circle, gathering parcels from businesses that wanted the packages sent quickly some place else in the United States.

At the end of the business day, all spokes would lead to one airplane waiting at the airport. The truck drivers and pilot, all working at furious speed, would empty the trucks and fill the airplane with the little packages. Once loaded, the plane would fly off to a bigger hub somewhere in the center of America—Memphis would be a perfect spot! Airplane routes to Memphis, from Detroit, Chicago, Los Angeles, New York, Miami, Houston, etc., would be the big spokes. In Memphis, all the planes would land and be emptied. Then all the packages would be sorted and the planes loaded again, and the Detroit plane would have only Detroit parcels, the New York plane only New York parcels, etc. Then the planes would simply go back to where they came from, and when they landed, those nimble little trucks would be waiting at the airport. Even before the sun was up, the Detroit fleet of trucks would again be scurrying about inside that circle, delivering the packages and gathering another batch of them for delivery the next day.

That's it; that's all there was. It was as simple as could be. Keep doing that—every day—said Smith, and you could make a lot of money! The idea was not even new, and Smith made this clear to his doubting professor. "American Airlines tried to set up a hub-and-spokes system for air freight in 1948 in Topeka, Kansas," said Smith. "The Indian Postal Service operated this way from the end of World War II on. The French Aero Postal, that's the way they operated. The only way to ship something from anyplace in the United States to any other place was to gather them all into a central point, clear them at a clearinghouse, and ship them back to the various locations where they were destined. And I recognzied the solution by observing simply the way the banking industry operated, where they send all their cancelled checks into a central location, swap them around and send them back."

But Fred Smith's skeptics, beginning with his professor at Yale, explained in response that, even though banks and other organizations have used the hub-and-spokes system, nobody ever tried to do it *overnight*. With the American Airlines experiment and the banking system as precedent, the big freight forwarders in the United States—such as United Parcel Service (UPS), Emery Air Freight, and even the United States Postal Service—obviously had thought of Smith's idea before Smith, and they had rejected it. The cost of all those airplanes, all those trucks, all those pilots and couriers, and the hub facility itself all would be enormously expensive. And none of the big freight forwarders had ever *heard* of any customers who wanted *overnight* delivery. Nobody expected it; nobody ever asked for it.

Still, Fred Smith knew that if people had overnight delivery they would like overnight delivery, and they would begin to *depend* on overnight delivery. He insisted that the proliferation of high tech industries would make overnight delivery increasingly desirable. He said people, regardless of where they were in America in the 1970s, expected instant and sophisticated services. He said, "Look, if I get only 1 percent of the current air freight market, I can support this service."

Notwithstanding Fred Smith's certainty of his idea, two things certainly would keep the idea from working. For one, in order to start, this overnight delivery thing had to be a *national* service on the very first day. The network, which would cost tens of millions of dollars to build, had to be in place at the outset. Even though he was a millionaire, Fred Smith didn't have that much money. Even if he got all his sisters' money, he wouldn't have enough money. Simply put, in order to start Federal Express, Fred Smith would need the largest infusion of venture capital in history. He would need the help of a team of investors of enormous wealth and influence, none of whom at that point had ever heard of him, and if they had any idea what he was thinking, they would think he was nuts.

And if that didn't make it totally impossible, one other thing was missing. As a Yale graduate, at age twenty-one, Fred Smith wasn't good enough to pull this thing off. He was bright, confident, charming, even courageous, but he still had few of the personal tools necessary to pull together and motivate an enterprise composed of diverse and socially incompatible human beings.

The key that would activate Fred Smith's concept did not, could not, emerge until he had gone through one more life experience.

That experience was the Vietnam War. The missing element, which emerged from within Fred Smith to become the burning ember of his energy from that experience forward, was *leadership*. Fred Smith calls himself a manager because he can balance books, explain tactics, and formulate strategy, but he created Federal Express—he gave it life and constantly renewing hope—because he loved people, because the one thing a leader must do is to make people believe he cares more for them than he does for himself and the bottom line. Fred Smith would have come to this understanding eventually over years, because he always cared for people. But in Vietnam, everything was desperate, accelerated. The deep idealism within Smith's nature was baptized by fire.

Smith joined the United States forces in Vietnam in 1966, almost immediately after graduation. "I had a typical Southerner's viewpoint of the military," said Smith. "I knew I had to go."

Smith's choice to go to Vietnam was almost devoid of political interest. He simply regarded military service as a matter of every man's duty. There was in Smith—as in Richard L. Duke, the founder of ChemLawn Corporation—a sense of responsibility for other people, which marked him as different from other people. Both men felt that, because they had gifts that others lacked, they must use their gifts on other people's behalf. Tucker Taylor expressed Smith's unusual blend: "Fred Smith is an admixture of two traits. One is egomania, the other one, though, is this tremendously overblown sense of responsibility—I say overblown to a fault," said Taylor. "That's a conflict in the man. Fred Smith has a sense of responsibility to whatever he embraces."

Smith served two tours of duty in Vietnam, first as a company commander in India Company and K Company of the Third Battalion, Fifth Regiment of the 1st Marine Division, then as a forward air controller, spotter, and reconnaissance flyer in the bloody and tragic I CORPS area south of the Demilitarized Zone in Quang Tri province. Upon his discharge in 1969, Captain Smith was the recipient of six medals for bravery, including a Silver Star and two Purple Hearts. He was lucky to be alive. But what he had gained in Vietnam was an outlook that could not have emerged without that searing experience.

In a television portrait of Fred Smith, commentator Bill Moyers suggested that the creation of Federal Express was Smith's effort to atone for the "sins" that he—or perhaps America—committed in Vietnam. But Smith went to war as a matter of personal duty. He did not judge the merits of the particular war, and he is guiltless about his participation in Vietnam. But he did return home with the desire to fix something that he thought was wrong. Smith had gained in the war a sense of how wasted were the efforts and abilities of those soldiers to whom he grew so close. He saw not merely lives that were wasted in sudden death, but lives that would be wasted in the future because the "managerial class" who hired these working-class men would expect so little of them—and receive so little in return. In Vietnam, Fred Smith discovered the intelligence and character of men he might once have described as "average."

"Most of the folks who run companies, or large organizations, are very snobbish, and they really do look down on the people who are working on the factory floor," said Fred Smith. "They have a disdain for the average person, and even though that person may be the one who is making them zillions of dollars, they just don't like him."

In Vietnam, in the face of death, Fred Smith learned the two emotional foundations of leadership. The war itself was overwhelming to him and to everyone else. Smith was stripped of his individuality in a way that shrank his ego. He fell under the control of forces that would not acknowledge that he was different from anyone else. For the first time in his life, the institutions that surrounded him regarded him as a nonentity and he realized their power to crush him without remorse. From this crash course in humility, Smith learned that powerless people demand only one thing from life and their fellow man: *respect*.

Also in Vietnam, Smith learned that the only imperative of leadership is to take care of your men. The only goal worth pursuing, in war or in peace, is to get all your people to a better place, a safer place, from where they are now. You do not lead people into danger unless you can lead them out again, into safety.

In Vietnam Fred Smith not only *discovered* that "people are more than they seem." He turned that discovery into a mission. He was determined that the "average people" he got to know would be the builders, the mainstay, the crusaders of his crazy idea for an overnight delivery. He was going to put them in planes and in trucks, set them loose and trust them to the very end.

After his discharge and until 1972, Fred Smith ran a family-owned business called Arkansas Aviation Sales, Inc.; he bought and sold used corporate jets. But this was merely a means for him to establish himself in the airplane business, creating contacts, capital, and resources to fulfill his goal: learning how people could move things fast on trucks and airplanes.

In June 1971 Smith crystallized this goal by spinning off from Arkansas Aviation a new corporation called Federal Express. Almost immediately, he lost his first customer. The United States Federal Reserve had been interested in contracting with one company to transfer its cancelled checks among the many branch banks in the United States; then the branch banks killed the idea. Even as it began, Federal Express had its future cancelled. But Fred Smith barely flinched. He moved quickly to a new strategy.

Since the day his idea had first been dismissed at Yale, Smith had understood that the people to whom he had to sell his air freight service was the group of people least likely to believe in him. They were not the shippers and secretaries who would eventually depend on Federal Express, but banks and corporations in need of tax write-offs, who would finance him. He knew that these were conservative people, unwilling to part with a penny unless they saw proof on paper that his idea would make a profit in the end.

Fred Smith's first stroke of inventive ingenuity was to hire not one, but *two* market research companies to test the waters for overnight delivery. He contacted both companies in December 1971. Both were in New York City: A. T. Kearney, Inc., an old respected firm steeped in the culture of Wall Street, with an account executive named Roger Frock leading the Federal Express research in the first few months of 1972; and Aerospace Advance Planning Group (AAPG), which consisted entirely of three men—Tucker Taylor, Arthur Bass, and Vincent P. Fagan. They, like Smith, were insecure aviators in the used plane business.

The AAPG trio had met Smith a few months before, in Little Rock, Arkansas. "Because of our mutual understanding of airplanes and the corporate airplane business, we ended up down there making a presentation on something to Fred Smith. It had to do with airplanes. And when the presentation was over, he described this *dumb* idea about buying a bunch of corporate Falcons, cutting big doors in the sides, and flying them all over the place and meeting at Little Rock, Arkansas. I mean, it really sounded to me like a banana's idea," recalled Tucker Taylor. "He asked us to take a look at that idea, and could he hire us as consultants? It was a crazy idea, but he had money. So Art Bass, Vince, and I sat down and decided, 'I suppose we can talk this guy out of this, but why should we? He is going to pay us while we are doing it.' We started the research on the concept, and as it turned out, that became the means to help him raise the money."

During the first months of 1972, Smith traveled frequently from Little Rock to New York, usually accompanied by his close aide, Irby Tedder, and three Arkansas attorneys. He would visit his investment counselor, White, Weld & Company, then A. T. Kearney, and then AAPG for discussions and updates on the research.

Taylor was amused, even then, when he realized Smith had hired two companies to conduct the same research. Both research companies were surprised when the research turned out in Smith's favor. The more shippers, freight handlers, and managers the researchers contacted, the more they heard the same response. "Sure, I would use a service like that, but I will believe it when I see it."

The basic conclusion was that Fred Smith needed to invest, up front, about $20 million, and for that investment he could eventually attain what Taylor called "a nice little business. He could make some money. But it would never be anything big."

Almost everything the researchers had said turned out to be wrong. That $20 million grew into $72 million. Federal Express would indeed eventually become big; Smith claims today that he always knew the cost of the enterprise and the eventual size of the enterprise. Whether he did or not, he got his money's worth out of his market research. A. T. Kearney and AAPG had said, in writing, for investors to read, what Fred Smith already knew—that there was a market waiting for overnight delivery and that the business could make money.

Frock, quoted by Arthur Robert Sigafoos in his Federal Express history, *Absolutely, Positively Overnight,* explained the fascination that captured him when he met Smith and eventually led him to relocate in Memphis and commit his future to the risk and unlikelihood of Smith's company. "These fellows would come up from Little Rock. Fred often didn't bother to introduce them to me by name, so I didn't know who they were," recalled Frock. "There was a mystery to it all. And there was this urgency to it all."

Fred Smith's urgency might have been part of his nature. It might have been something he cultivated in Vietnam, where a stationary object was an easy target. Certainly, it was real. Smith had to broaden his financial base very quickly. He was depending too much already on family money, funds obtained through the Frederick Smith Enterprise Company, the corporation partly owned outright by Smith and his sisters, and partly owned by trusts that held the stocks for them. All that Federal Express owned, thanks to loans from the Enterprise Company and the National Bank of Commerce of Memphis, were two used French-built Dassault Falcon corporate jets. Smith could not have proceeded very far into 1972 without the "numbers" to convince bankers he wasn't a crackpot.

But more than numbers, Fred Smith needed people. At the beginning Fred Smith had a perception that has also been expressed, in another breakthrough story, by Kozo Ohsone, production manager of Sony's Walkman team: The personnel choices one makes at the beginning of a project are basic. Nothing is more important.

Smith didn't expect to find the right people in the established companies, and he didn't want to. "Fred did want innovators," said Taylor, "and he did want people without any preconceived notions, and he did want people who were a little bit wild. But also, it is a good thing that is what he wanted, because if he had wanted someone from Emery, he couldn't have gotten him."

In Vietnam, Smith had come to value flexibility of intellect. He had seen men die because commanders could not or would not deviate from a plan even in the face of the unexpected. And he had seen common soldiers respond spontaneously to a crisis, guiding groups of men away from a threat that had emerged only seconds before. Smith wanted people like that, alert and resourceful, indifferent toward structured planning, and able always to move forward with only the tools they had in their hands and minds. Smith knew that when Federal Express was in the throes of crisis, he would not be available to scout the terrain and lead the way through all the operational details. He was going to depend on other people for that, and he needed the right people more than money, more than airplanes.

"Fred has a very clear view of the future," said Bass. "And he has a single-mindedness. He uses a lot of brain power to manipulate things and make them work, to accomplish his ends. He is not a tactician. Fortunately, he surrounded himself with doers who did not give a damn, who were not inhibited by worrying about anything except simply, 'Let's get this job done.' "

"I've always subscribed to the Bear Bryant school of football," Smith explained. "I mean, I have never seen very many successful endeavors where somebody goes out and hires a great resume, where it turns out well, because that person, to build that resume, knows all the reasons you can't do something. So it has always been my experience that you are a lot better off trying to grow your own. You go out and get a kid who can run like hell, and you make him an end or a halfback. It was the same thing with Art, Vince, and Tucker, those guys. They had a philosophy of life, they weren't afraid to make a decision, they understood the game, they liked this proposition. They just fit."

Smith's technique for getting qualified people like Roger Frock to come to Little Rock was a mixture of showmanship and boyish enthusiasm. "Fred gave me an oral commitment. He said that if Federal Express succeeded, I would get stock," said Frock. "There was nothing written and I didn't expect anything written. I took a big pay cut going down to Little Rock from New York, but I was thirty-five, and I wanted to take the plunge in a risk venture."

In 1974 Smith added perhaps the most unlikely of the group, Peter Willmott, who served years in the madhouse of Federal Express bookkeeping as the company's chief financial officer. Willmott came to Federal from International Telephone & Telegraph (ITT), perhaps America's most conservative company. He admits that the culture shock almost killed him, but the excitement that followed the shock was the greatest of his life. Now chairman of Carson, Pirie & Scott in Chicago, Willmott—like all the former members of the Federal Express inner circle—yearns, without gratification, to recapture that Federal feeling.

"The four years we were trying to set up some sort of financial structure—any structure—was the longest and shortest time of my life," said Willmott. "It was a very emotional, very profound experience. I can't describe it; no one can understand it unless they felt it."

To complement his unusual hand-picked management team, Smith also went out and found people who could fly airplanes and fix airplanes, people who could drive trucks and fix trucks. "I am not sure of the ingredients that make a good cake, but the one that fell off the shelf was a good one. This assemblage of creative talent at the outset is what distinguished Federal Express from many contemporary companies," said Bass. "We were the last of the gunslingers."

By 1973, the spirit of Federal Express had been born. The people were in place. There was a camaraderie among pilots, drivers, and executives that reminded one of the spirit displayed by multi-ethnic bomber crews in movies about World War II. The team had been assembled and the team spirit was strong. Then, and only then, did Fred Smith take off his flak jacket, don his pinstripe suit, and begin to romance the "jackals of Wall Street."

The research reports from AAPG and A. T. Kearney that emerged in the spring of 1972 were the first elements in a fund-raising campaign that culminated in November 1973 in a $52 million venture capital investment in Federal Express, the biggest that had ever been made.

The dynamics of that eighteen months of financial dealing by Smith are almost impossible to reconstruct or understand. From May 1972 through the Big Deal in November 1973, Smith's company did nothing but lose a fortune. Any sensible investor examining the company's operations should have seen almost nothing to hope for in the future. Indeed, the company could have folded, on "opening night," March 12, 1973, when airplanes for the first time flew into Memphis from all over the eastern United States—with a total of *six* packages.

After that first night fiasco, it was a month before Federal flew again, and the package count on April 17—186 packages—was hardly more encouraging. The company might well have folded at the end of April 1973, when the end-of-fiscal-year report showed an accumulated loss of $4.4 million.

The company should have folded when—in order to keep the cash flow going—Fred Smith authorized documents that secured for Federal Express a $2 million loan from Union Bank of Little Rock. In early 1973 he pledged his own shares of the privately held Frederick Smith Enterprise Company to the bank. In order to make the transfer legal and acceptable to the bank, he signed the name of his attorney, Bobby Cox. Given the familial atmosphere of the Enterprise Company and its burgeoning offspring, Federal Express, Smith felt this authorization to be a routine matter—even for a sum as large as $2 million.

"When I made the loan, the bank needed a take-out, since the Enterprise company was not listed on the stock exchange," said Smith. "I went down and simply dictated a resolution of the board of directors, which would permit the company to buy into my shares." Since Smith was one of the Enterprise Company's five directors and its president, and since a similar buy-back provision had been used by other family members, he felt this was an acceptable practice.

"Then I made a very bad mistake," Smith said, "which was characteristic of the loose, familial way we ran the company. I signed my lawyer's name."

The company should have folded in September of 1973, when a series of multi-million dollar loans, secured by using those promising AAPG and A. T. Kearney reports, fell due and then fell into default. In September 1973, a memo to employees, signed by Fred Smith, read, in part, "With the most profound regret, we would like to request from each of you that you do not cash or deposit your payroll check until next Monday, September 17, at the very earliest. Naturally, for those of you whose sustenance depends on immediate use of these funds, please feel free to do so. For those of you who can do so, it would be greatly appreciated that you hold these checks until we can announce to you that the intermediate funds have been received and that a final closing date has been set within the next ten working days. As you know, we have made every effort to see that every payroll has been made, and were it not for circumstances completely beyond our control, we would not be asking for a sacrifice such as this."

Part of the reason Federal Express survived all this catastrophe—and more besides—was that, as Taylor noted, Fred Smith was just so charming. In the gray world of bankers and investment counselors, this aviator, this Southern gentleman from Little Rock via Quang Tri, was a peacock—or perhaps the better term is *chameleon*.

"He's got a high degree of charisma when he wants to," said Taylor. "He's a little bit like Zelig [famed supersalesman Fred Zelig]; Fred Smith can be what Fred Smith has to be. When he's talking to New York bankers, back in those days raising money, he could sound like he just fell off the turnip wagon from Little Rock. He'd talk with a southern accent—'Gee, I'm just so naive and if you guys could just help me on this thing and gee, I'm just a good old boy.' Or, he could just go gong! and be David Rockefeller. And he's got a very good sense of *when* he is supposed to do *what* he is supposed to do."

But Federal kept surviving because of another exceptional thing about Fred Smith. While everyone in the business world around him was behaving like a general, Smith was moving like a platoon leader. While his investors were invariably thoughtful and deliberate, Smith's movements were sudden and impulsive. After the positive market reports in the spring of 1972, Smith escalated a series of loans from banks in Little Rock and Memphis. They were exceptionally large loans for those banks, but they were based on the Smith family's standing in those communities, the solvency of the family's Enterprise Company, and the proven positive market outlook for Smith's new company. These loans allowed Smith to buy, rather than lease, from Pan American World Airways almost all the used Dassault jets available in the United States—thirty-three of them. The cost for the planes was $56.1 million, a bargain. But Smith would not have the money in his hands when Pan Am came to collect in 1973 and 1974. Seduced by Fred Smith's charm, the banks went into this thing as deep as he was.

By July 1973 Federal Express was one of those exciting little entrepreneurial outfits with a case of raving schizophrenia. Even as the president of the company was jetting off to Chicago to meet with the legendary chairman of General Dynamics, Colonel Henry Crown, to toss around figures like $16 million, the folks back in Memphis were eking out their payrolls by ignoring their couriers' expense vouchers and their withholding tax payments to the Internal Revenue Service (which is the small business equivalent to Russian roulette). In Chicago, the good news Fred Smith got from the General Dynamics board of directors was that the giant company would back up, for a while, a $23.7 million loan package for Federal Express. This wasn't such good news, really, because the loans would start falling due very heavily in September, and Smith knew he would not have the cash to pay them back then.

Even this much help did not come without conditions. Smith noted that Colonel Henry Crown, of General Dynamics, then in his mid-eighties, was uneasy with committing money to a company run by a whippersnapper still two or three years shy of thirty. "To Colonel Crown," recalled Smith, "a guy that was twenty-seven, twenty-eight years old was barely out of the crib."

Crown insisted that Smith, at least for the sake of appearances, find an older executive to serve as chief executive officer of Federal Express for a period of time. Smith agreed to that condition and began seeking the right person to share his management of Federal Express.

In the meantime, the bad news from General Dynamics was awful. General Dynamics also had been considering purchase of a controlling interest in Federal Express for $16 million. That would have put the company in the black and given Fred Smith the time and money he needed to prove overnight delivery could succeed beyond anyone's wildest dreams. When General Dynamics said no to buying into Federal Express, Fred Smith had to go back to the payroll ordeals, the clamor of impatient creditors, and the legal disputes with his family in Memphis without any real hope that the company would survive. He was as close to despair as a pathological optimist could be. "I went to the airport to go back to Memphis," Smith said in an "NBC News" interview, "and saw on the TWA schedule a flight to Las Vegas. I won $27,000, starting with just a couple of hundred, and sent it back to Memphis. The $27,000 wasn't decisive, but it was an omen that things would get better."

Smith had never really gambled before and has not gambled—at least with cards and dice—since that day. But the encouragement of that strange moment of luck protected him from discouragement and sent him exploring another option. The next option became his relationship with a company called New Court Securities, based in New York and funded by the Rothschild banking dynasty in Europe. Two New Court executives, Charles Lea and Richard Stowe, had learned about Federal Express through White, Weld & Company.

Lea concluded by July 1973 that Federal Express might indeed be able to live up to Smith's wild prediction of volume and revenue. Lea, Stowe, and Henry W. Meers, of White, Weld & Company, began to work with Smith on a financial package to save Federal from default and collapse before Christmas. When September came around, there were then just a lot of couriers holding their paychecks. By then, the Smith family Enterprise Company was on the hook for $7.9 million. The Chase Manhattan Bank had $24 million in outstanding loans to Federal Express. One bank in Little Rock—which had a loan ceiling of $2 million—was into Federal Express for $9 million.

Fred Smith smiles at the memory of that 1973 crisis. It is the smile of a platoon leader who has outflanked and cornered a superior, better equipped enemy force. "In the first couple of years of operation, we lost a total of $29 million. But we learned a very important principle," said Smith. "Don't ever borrow a little bit of money, because when you borrow a little bit of money, you have a serious creditor if you run short. If you borrow a lot of money, you have a partner when you get into trouble."

In October 1973, with foreclosure threats a daily litany at Federal Express, New Court Securities assembled a galaxy of investors in New York City. Among the eventual participants in the Federal Express venture were Prudential Insurance, Allstate Insurance, General Dynamics, the Heizer Corporation, Citicorp, the Bank of America, and the First National Bank of Chicago. After five and a half hours of negotiations, Smith emerged with $52 million in financial backing. Federal Express could now afford to lose money for years—which it did.

In fact, even with all those partners and all that money, things got worse before they got better. By March 1974 relations within the Smith family had deteriorated. An attorney working for Fred Smith's two sisters, Fredette and Laura, advised them to disavow his actions in pledging his shares and, believing Federal Express would not be successful, to attempt to bankrupt it and recoup much of the investment through tax refunds. That lawyer wrote letters to the federal attorneys in Little Rock and Memphis, and the result was an indictment against Fred Smith for exceeding his legal authority as president of the Frederick Smith Enterprise Company.

Smith was not officially charged with fraud until the following January, but the possibility of the company's founder and leader going to jail did not comfort Smith's investors, or the Federal Express board of directors.

In June 1974, the chairmanship of Federal Express was turned over to a retired Air Force general named Howell Estes, in accord with Smith's agreement with Colonel Crown, of General Dynamics. The transfer of power proved to be a trauma for many people at the infant company, and it was more of a trial for Smith than he had anticipated. For the first time since Vietnam, Fred Smith the platoon leader was answering to a general again.

To many at Federal Express, the courtly and authoritarian Estes was a terrible shock. Tucker Taylor, who had to report directly to the general, almost abandoned the company on the spot. "What the company needed in that period was Mao Tse-tung, and they gave us Metternich," said Taylor. "He made pompous announcements like a general does. He was the only one who had a parking place with his name on it. We were all driving Volkswagens, and Fred Smith was parking eight blocks away and walking in the rain, and here was this reserved parking space."

Tucker Taylor might have been the leader of the anti-Estes resistance, and he might have left the company if he hadn't, very early after Estes' arrival, got a reading from Smith of what the future held in store. "I went into Fred Smith's office and said, 'I'm not going to ask you anything except but one question: If it comes down to a fight between you and General Estes, who's gonna win?' And Fred Smith said, 'I will.' And I never talked to him about it again."

As resistant as the Federal Express work force was to the presence of Estes, Smith bore the change with relative calm. Drawing an analogy to a different pair of contrasting commanders, Smith recalled, "It was Ho Chi Minh versus Bismarck."

Fred Smith gave Estes respect and kept his distance. But he also saw that Estes' devotion to rigid lines of command was inconsistent with the trust and freedom Federal Express people had come to expect. Estes and the people working for Estes drifted farther and farther apart. The company developed a dual leadership, with people paying lip service to Estes' orders but checking with Fred Smith before taking action.

When the eventual power play between the general and the

guerrilla happened in February, only eight months later, Estes resigned, and Fred Smith was reinstated as chief executive officer. The board also started to search for a new CEO to replace Smith, but it was a search that no one really took seriously.

At the end of 1975, a federal jury exonerated Smith of illegally authorizing his own loan documents, ruling that he had acted basically for the best interests of a company that was largely under his personal control. The decision of the court came rather quickly. Both of Smith's sisters had had second thoughts about prosecuting their brother, and they refused to testify against him. Bobby Cox, the attorney whose signature Fred Smith had borrowed, told the judge that the nature of the company and his relationship with Smith were such that he had signed Smith's income tax forms for him.

"It was like trying to prosecute somebody for borrowing the family car," said John Patterson, one of the former brothers-in-law, in his testimony.

Throughout the long personal ordeal, which lasted from 1974 through 1975, Smith retained his composure. He insists today, almost angrily, that the crises of litigation and finance are fearful only for those who have never faced the sort of terror Smith faced in Vietnam. "You ought to get into a goddamn firefight and see what it's like," said Smith. "Nothing of the things that happened to me in those two years were particularly traumatic at all, considering where I've been. If you want to get the hell scared out of you, you get out some night and have about two thousand guys trying to overrun you. That's scary!"

Smith, who styles himself today as a manager, regrets that he loses his composure and talks about "firefights" and swarms of Viet Cong. Yet the strength of Federal Express through the desperate period from 1973 through mid-1975 was that, as Taylor noted, "We were all in this together." The company was composed of gunslingers, daredevils, and barnstormers. They were largely a hand-to-mouth group, involved in the creation of a company without much regard to risk and not much concern about the future. Smith's troubles with investors, with his sisters, and with the incongruous presence of General Estes all strengthened the kinship he shared with his work force.

"The most fun I had was when the pressure was the most," recalled Taylor. "I mean, all that stuff when Fred Smith was going to resign and the things with the board of directors. When the pressure was on, I thought that was wonderful. The fact that the company didn't have any money wasn't really important—this was the great experiment! We were going to prove it can be done anyway."

Foreclosure was a reality that threatened everybody, the boss as well as the working stiff, and when everybody had to deal with it, it didn't seem so awful. As Taylor pointed out, everybody at Federal was an entrepreneur, one man's idea about starting a new office in a strange place was as good as anybody else's. "For the first three years, we didn't know what we were doing," said Taylor. "Really. Literally. We didn't have any data about the market. So when you opened a station in Miami, you found the best kid you could; you gave him a map of Miami and told him to call you if he had any problems."

Individual style became a sacred item in those early days at Federal. Once a courier set out on his rounds, he was as independent as any Pony Express rider galloping toward the sun. Each driver was expected to pick up all of his packages on time and get them to the airport any way he could; nobody ever asked questions as long as the driver made it through. There are stories of couriers so committed to their mission that they pawned their watches to buy gasoline.

As bad as finances got, though, Fred Smith insisted that the law of the platoon must prevail. Nobody got laid off at Federal. Smith's loyalty to his people came back to him in equal measure. "Federal Express never laid anybody off," said Taylor. "One of our convictions in this thing was that, even if the sheriff was about to take the airplane, we never laid anybody off. What we would do, we would take pilots and put them in the hub and make them station managers when we would open a new station. We had pilots all over the place. Then as the company grew, we would take them back and put them on the line [flying airplanes]."

As crazy as Federal Express people like to be, they were neat. Like Dick Duke at ChemLawn putting his lawn care specialists in uniforms and teaching them manners, Fred Smith, from the first day, emphasized that the image of air freight—at Federal—must be changed from shabby to professional. "The public isn't too impressed when they have to deal with a gruff, sloppily dressed character chomping on a stale cigar in some seedy shed near an airport or on the back of some loading dock," Smith once said. "If the opportunities were going to be fully exploited, the public image had to be changed."

Arthur Bass was one of the keepers of the image. "The company's schedule was good. Its reliability was good. The people were clean and knowledgeable and well shaven, and every truck was washed every day," explained Bass. "Woe betide he who didn't have the truck washed, because that was our logo—this was even when we didn't have enough money to do a lot of things. I couldn't tell you the number of times I got on the phone and somebody said, 'We don't have enough money. We can't wash trucks.' And I said, 'You're telling me we can't afford water? Is that what I am hearing?' "

No one at Federal, not even Smith, ever had run a service company. There was no instruction manual. But caring about each other, taking care of each other, was an ethic that pervaded their work. The customers were infected also with the "Federal feeling."

"We found that in a start-up company in a service business, people are important because customers respond to people," recalled Taylor. "One example: Every quarter we would ask one-fourth of our customers what they liked about Federal Express. These questionnaires would come back with little notes inscribed on the side like, 'Say hello to Ginny in Wichita for me.' It finally occurred to us after looking at enough of those things that customers were giving their packages to people, not Federal Express. I mean, they could really give a shit about the airplanes, but they knew Ginny had never let them down.

"The number of people who called me during the early days to say, 'We think your company is just as screwed-up as [the competition]. I wanted to tell you that because I don't have the heart to tell your courier, because that kid is busting his ass out here for you, and we are going to be sure that you still get the packages. But if you ever screw up again, that's going to be it.' The kids had built this unbelievable feeling in the company," Bass recalled.

After 1975 the sheer chaos began to subside a little. By the beginning of 1976 the hub in Memphis was handling thousands of packages smoothly every night, and the fleet of Falcons was often flying fully loaded. The fear of foreclosure began to fade. But, in the great scheme of things, Federal Express was still a tiny air freight company. Two things worked against Federal to keep the company small—public recognition and federal regulation. In 1978 two breakthroughs occurred to overcome these problems.

Between 1976 and 1978 Fred Smith spent most of his life in Washington, D.C., learning legislative and regulatory intricacies in the nation's capital. His mission was to eliminate weight limits for irregular-route air freight carriers. These laws, which allowed carriers to move freight over any route they chose but under severe weight limits, dated back forty years to the beginning of commercial aviation. As long as weight limits existed, the biggest plane Federal could fly was a Falcon, with a payload of about 6,000 pounds.

By late 1977 Federal Express had as many as five Falcons flying in formation on some of their heaviest routes. The image was wonderfully romantic, but it also demonstrated graphically the limits to company growth, especially with the dramatic rise in fuel prices that followed Federal's launch. If Federal Express, as Smith wanted, were free to buy and fly bigger airplanes, the older freight forwarders—"biggies" like Emery who used cargo space on commercial airlines—would lose freight, money, customers. The battle lines in Washington were very clear. Fred Smith had two advantages over his competition. One was his tenacity. The other was the administration of President Jimmy Carter, which was strongly in favor of deregulating the air freight industry.

"The people who make decisions in Washington, which is only lately becoming known to a lot of people, are not the senators and the congressmen, but the staffers," said Smith. "So because of our age and inclination and money and prestige, we lobbied the staff. We knew we had right on our side, and the forces of history. A question that remained was, 'How do we topple the big guys?' "

The struggle to topple the big guys might have ended in 1976, with the passage of an amendment called the "Federal Express Bill." By the fall of 1976 Smith, having done his homework and learned the ropes, had obtained considerable support in both houses of Congress for a special dispensation on payload limits for Federal Express. Then that was killed by California Congressman Glenn Anderson, who buried it in the House Subcommittee on Aviation. Anderson, eventually a friend of Federal Express, refused to support what he felt was "preferential treatment" for Federal Express. Smith was disappointed but undeterred. He responded with another Vietnam analogy. "If you keep working at it, in the last analysis, you win," said Smith. "We're like the old Ho Chi Minh. They've got to kill us one hundred times. All we have to do is kill them once."

In 1977 Congressman Anderson introduced the bill for complete reform of air freight, covering such issues as freedom of entry, weight limits, pricing, and scheduling. The infighting, between a group of upstart carriers, led by Smith, and a powerful lobby of older, bigger freight forwarders and regular route air carriers, continued to the last minute. But in the aviation world of the 1970s, the forty-year-old restrictions made little sense. This was obvious to the administration and to the Congress. The deregulation of air freight was favored so overwhelmingly in both houses of Congress that it passed by voice vote in October 1977.

The impact on the future of Federal Express was epochal. Within six weeks, Smith had begun to change the Federal fleet over from Falcons to Boeing 727s—each with ten times the payload of a Falcon. Today many of Federal's fleet are DC-10s with a payload of more than 120,000 pounds each.

Robert Sigafoos, Federal Express historian, drily expressed the impact of deregulation on Federal: "Without the freedom provided by air cargo deregulation, Federal Express would have faced a flattening of its growth curve within a year or two, and it probably would have remained a small, moderately profitable air transportation company. But the growth limitations imposed by continued reliance on the Falcon fleet would have negated continued interest by the investors and the lenders. Talented staff and technical people would have abandoned the company in droves. But with deregulation, Smith and his bright, entrepreneurially oriented colleagues were given new motivation to try to take Federal Express to unprecedented heights in the air cargo industry."

Tucker Taylor was one of the leaders of Federal Express, along with Smith, Bass, and others, who knew that if the company seized the opportunity presented by Smith's success in Washington, it could become immense. "When Jimmy Carter signed the Air Cargo Deregulation Act, I knew then it was not a matter of whether or not I would get rich, but how rich," said Taylor. "And not how well Federal Express is going to succeed, but how big the success was going to be—we owned the market."

*　　*　　*

Taylor was right. Federal Express did own the market. But they could have lost the market without one more major step. The last key was for people to know about Federal Express, to know its name as well as UPS and better than Emery.

In 1976 Vincent Fagan, the talented and caustic marketing man from AAPG, began working feverishly on that major step. His partners in this effort were a couple of New York advertising men named Carl Ally and Amil Gargano. Ally and Gargano took a while to understand the unconventionality of Federal Express. Like many observers, at first all they could see was the technology—the airplanes and the hub system. While they were learning, Federal began using television in a revolutionary way. Air freight didn't normally advertise on television but, even though Federal was still poor, Smith and Fagan agreed that the gap between Federal and the "biggies" required a little daring.

The ad campaign focused on "the difference" between Federal and their competition. The print ads, all that the company could afford at first, emphasized that Federal Express was the only freight forwarder to fly its own airplanes. An ensuing campaign used a survey, conducted by Opinion Research Corporation, that showed Federal overnight packages arriving before noon at twice the success rate of the next fastest company, Emery. The reason for the difference was simple. Federal was flying its own fleet, while Emery still depended on commercial airline flights to move their customers' parcels. Federal's slogan became, "Twice as good as the best in the business."

That was a breakthrough for Federal, because it got real attention from shippers and it irritated the arch-rival, Emery. Emery eventually followed Federal into overnight delivery in 1977, when Federal was still flying Falcons and Federal employees were still running scared in the shadow of their huge and dominant competitors. "Emery Express brought fear into the hearts of a lot of the employees of Federal Express," said Bass. "I would literally go around telling this story, which we used in pamphlets, papers, and everything else—the bear and the alligator analogy. In a fight between a bear and an alligator, the winner is not determined by the skill of the combatant as much as by the terrain. In 1975, if Emery had really caught on to what we were doing, they could have pulled us out of the swamp and killed us. In 1977 they jumped in the swamp. And it was a whole different battle."

When, in 1978, it was time for Federal Express to undertake a fresh advertising initiative, to hit television hard in the wake of deregulation, Ally and Gargano and their staff focused attention first on Smith's hub-and-spokes concept and the great frantic melee that occurred every night at the hub in Memphis. There, packages poured from airplanes and flew along a multi-story racetrack of conveyor belts, while hot rod cargo trucks and forklifts buzzed down long concrete alleys. The hub was hypnotic already then. The super hub, today, has twenty-three miles of conveyors on 600 acres of land beside the Memphis International Airport; with almost 3,000 employees handling 400,000 packages in less than two and one-half hours, it is a kind of mechanical Fantasyland.

Fagan had to fight with Ally and Gargano. "Everybody thought that the hub was so unique that it should be our story," recalled Bass. "Fagan had to convince everybody that that was not our story. All that people cared about was that it *got there*—all they wanted was to know it had to be in Boston tomorrow. If somebody really convinced them that it was going from Worcester to Memphis to Boston, because we were so proud of our system, we would be killing ourselves."

Fagan had found out something else. Smith had had an intuition years before that people *wanted* overnight delivery. Now, in the late 1970s, Fagan had an intuition of *why* they wanted it. He found a researcher in California who asked a lot of questions and verified what Fagan had known all along. "People didn't care about speed, and didn't care about price," said Bass. "What they really cared about was peace of mind. The agency wouldn't accept it, and Fagan had to take the president of the advertising agency out to California to the guy who did the research . . . and sit down and tell him, 'Now listen to what this guy is telling you!' "

The result, finally, was a series of television ads that became part of American cultural history. If any one of those ads could be said to sum up the difference Federal Express aimed to communicate, it was one depicting a hairy, small businessman standing in a store that specialized in electric light bulb sales. He is on the phone to "Dingbat Air Freight," insisting, "If those bulbs aren't here tomorrow morning, I am out of business!" The next scene in the abrupt two-scene commercial shows the Dingbat Air Freight courier arriving "two days later" and looking in dismay at a closed door front. True to the nightmare, across the front of the store is a sign that reads, "OUT OF BUSINESS."

Beginning with those early, shockingly successful vignettes, all the Federal Express television ads—even today—have focused entirely on the individual who will get in trouble if the package doesn't arrive on time. There was, from the first day of Federal Express, a kinship between the boss and the rank-and-file. Fred Smith had given his company a working-class bias and this resulted in working-class commercials. But the charm of the Federal Express commercials was that the "working-class" people who identified with the people in the television spot went all the way up the management ladder to the outskirts of corporate power. Fagan had uncovered the fear and injustice that people feel when they have to take the blame for somebody's screw-up.

"Hello, Federal!" spoken again and again, thousands of times to millions of viewers in those funny, irreverent, unforgettable commercials, became a punch line and an alibi. It even implied a certain defiance of authority. In one commercial, a series of self-important executives parade into a corporation shipping room, handing packages to a harried clerk, insisting that he send the packages overnight via Federal's various competitors. They threaten him with loss of his job if he fails. After all the packages are stacked beside him, the clerk picks up the phone, an impish, confident smile playing across his features, and he says only, "Hello-o-o, Federal!"

Fagan, who died in 1982, said at the time, "We put everyday people into these ads so that they could see themselves and all the forces aligned against them."

"Everybody's got a problem moving something in an organization. It doesn't just happen on the shipping dock," explained Taylor. "But the farther you move down in an organization, the more the needs become personal, as opposed to corporate. The chairman of the board of a company, all he cares about is the bottom line. But you go down to the secretary's assistant, and all he or she gives a shit about is his own well-being. He doesn't care about the bottom line. And that's where that 'Hello, Federal!' thing came in. The whole issue there is moving down an organization and saying, 'Forget what this thing is going to do for your company. This is going to make *your life* easier.' And the sales proposition for using Federal Express is not that the package will get there overnight, because that person doesn't really give a shit whether it gets there overnight or not. The issue is, if you send it Federal Express, who can get mad at you? You've done the best you can. You spent the most money you can—which is all right, it's not your money you are spending—so I think the breakthrough is when Federal Express figured out what they were really selling is peace of mind."

Sigafoos summed up the importance of Fagan's intuition, and those inventive Ally and Gargano vignettes: "Advertising, especially the comic situational commercial, created a market where none previously existed, a market whose dimensions have been beyond the wildest dreams of the air transportation industry. Federal knew it had a good product. It knew it had the stamina and the ability to deliver. It knew it had the legal, financial, and entrepreneurial talent, but even so, it was Federal's innovative advertising which propelled the company forward to become the unchallenged market leader."

Since Federal's commercials began to captivate people in the late 1970s, Federal Express has barely hesitated in its growth. Today Smith points to the future of the company as being linked with space-age communications technology. Federal Express's telefax service, called ZapMail, is emerging slowly from a number of technological hitches, but it remains positioned to become the next "time machine," moving paper overnight to same-day delivery.

Whatever the future for Federal, Fred Smith's legend is clearly safe. If anything bothers Fred Smith, it is the fact that there is a legend at all.

Fred Smith is uncomfortable with his image as a hero of industry, a genius of strategic management, and a one-man show. Smith wisely aimed, at the beginning, at finding the right people to help him, because he could not do it alone. He explains—often to the deaf ears of business writers—that his greatest attainments throughout Federal's long, hard times were to give each of his employees a mission, to challenge the employee without overwhelming him, and to conceal from everyone else how overwhelmed he himself sometimes felt.

Smith began the Federal Express breakthrough as Dick Duke at ChemLawn, Taiichi Ohno at Toyota, and Philip Knight at Nike, and others began theirs. He was a guide and a teacher, articulating a vision more clearly to others than he could truly see for himself. He set things in motion and stepped back. "People will rise to the occasion if you give them a chance, whether it's a delivery guy or Tucker Taylor designing a new telephone system or Vince Fagan coming up with a new advertising campaign or Art Bass coming up with a new system control network," said Smith. "Give people the challenge and they've got the basic intelligence and outlook to do it. They will rise to the occasion."

The enormous energy that poured from Federal Express from the very first day was built not so much on what Fred Smith could do—which was exceptional—but what he *couldn't* do. From the outset Smith, with absolute trust, committed ordinary people to extraordinary responsibility. He expected from them decisions that touched the very survival of the company. And Smith never looked back. He had seen people like this make wise survival decisions under fire in Vietnam. Like Taiichi Ohno at Toyota, Fred Smith—more than anything else, more than financial success—wanted his people to be better, to become the very best they could be. And because he had learned in Vietnam to depend on other people, he understood that trust is the thing you give first. "Federal Express is a creature of Vietnam. I don't think I would have done anything like this [without that experience]; I don't think I would have had the same perspective about money," said Smith in his interviews with Bill Moyers.

"The biggest thing was the fact that I had gotten a lot of people to work for me, and I felt a tremendous responsibility. There was no way I was going to let that thing go down the tube, if I could possibly help it. I had gotten all these people who believed in me and I just couldn't turn back."

In a way, Federal Express came about not through the vision of Fred Smith, but through the thankless heroism of the grunts in India and K Company. With Federal Express, in spirit, Fred Smith gave those comrades in arms almost everything Smith hadn't been able to give them in Vietnam—a purpose, a worthy job, a chance to grow, a sense of dignity, respect, and hope. He also wishes he could give them the credit. Fred Smith wishes he could surrender to his workers all the recognition that inevitably has fallen to him. However, what the troops understand better than Smith is that his recognition is their triumph. He made possible feelings that they never would have known without Federal Express. For so many people who experienced the birth of Federal, there was something worth fighting for, something to believe in, and something that was fun.

"The word *grandeur* once occurred to me," said Art Bass. "At Federal Express, we delivered on the promise—I don't mean for customers. I mean we brought together people who were proud of what they were doing, people who had very few other opportunities in their whole lives to be proud of anything. We all remembered the story of the knight on the white horse who went off to fight the dragon, and he never knew whether he was going to get any support when he met the dragon. The knight was on his own. Well, that's the way we all felt, whether we were in a truck or in a plane or in the hub. You were all alone out there, but everybody was depending on you. You had to come through.''

14 The Message for Managers

reativity is an elusive quarry, even for those who can afford to fund a big hunting party. In exploring sixteen companies to understand the evolution of twelve of the most significant commercial breakthroughs of the past twenty years, we have found no company that succeeded in developing an "environment for creativity." We have found no "corporate culture" that is more felicitous to breakthroughs than any other culture. Indeed, in the company most often praised for an environment supportive of "innovation," 3M Corporation, we saw in action a corporate culture that, over a period of five years, appeared at times to discourage and stifle the Post-it Note Pads, the most pervasive office product breakthrough since Scotch Tape.

That might seem like bad news for senior managers who want creativity in their companies and want to know the way to foster its emergence. But the good news is that creativity is more prevalent and more hardy than most people imagine. The evidence of these breakthroughs is that new, extraordinary ideas can emerge from any environment. In this series of stories, we have found breakthroughs that grew from rich soil, but also from barren soil, rocky soil, and no soil at all. Breakthroughs have come from creative teams that were ignored by their organizations, supported only belatedly by their organizations, misunderstood by their organizations, even assaulted by their organizations. Breakthroughs can emerge just as readily from no organization at all.

As a manager, as an organization, you can get a breakthrough whether you deserve it or not.

343

The reason for this is that breakthroughs are children not of the milieu, but of the mind. A breakthrough, because it is something new, something *unheard of* before, transcends the culture and the environment from which it springs. A breakthrough is so often oblivious to its surroundings because it comes first from an individual and then from a group of people who have been changed, torn from their surroundings, by that individual. Breakthroughs are not organizational creations, although afterward they are eagerly claimed by organizations. They are more like works of art than works of commerce. Teams of people who accomplish breakthroughs behave more like disciples emerging from the tutelage of a great painter than like the graduates of a prestigious management curriculum.

On the other hand, organizations, through good personnel practices and some fairly traditional incentives, can foster research and development that is genuinely innovative. The 3M model is an example. For decades 3M has provided periodic injections of money and constant encouragement to its researchers to enhance and adapt its existing product line. Steady, incremental improvements in old products have resulted in better new products. A process of evolution from the first crude cellophane tape to Scotch Tape to Magic Transparent Tape is just one example of 3M innovating effectively within its limitations. For people at 3M, there is no break in the progression of a product line, there is no relaxation of the focus on making their products and technologies incrementally better. But ironically, this is the reason that the Post-it breakthrough almost died at 3M. Spencer Silver's unique adhesive, with no discernible application, required not a step forward, but a leap to an entirely different plane of consciousness. It was a concept beyond innovation.

Innovation, as we came to understand it in our breakthroughs research, is the art of doing the same thing you are doing now but doing it better. A *breakthrough* is the act of doing something so different that it cannot be compared to any existing practices or perceptions. Breakthroughs, whether in commercial enterprise, science, or politics, are moments in history. Innovations are events behind the scenes that set the stage for history.

Raytheon Company, for example, failed in the marketplace with its Radarange microwave oven because for them the oven was an incremental adaptation based on the heat generated by the magnetron power tube used for radar. At Amana Refrigeration, George

Foerstner realized the importance of *seeing* the microwave oven as an entirely new invention. He had no understanding or reverence for the power tube. His sympathy was not with the generations of technicians who had painstakingly refined the microwave oven for almost twenty years. He cared only for the housewife who would tolerate no technology in her household more complicated than a toaster or an air conditioner. Foerstner's vision—seeing the microwave oven as a personal tool, rather than as a technology—was a leap beyond the steps of innovation that had both sustained and doomed the Radarange at Raytheon.

The examples of Spencer Silver and Yuma Shiraishi and so many of the breakthroughs people chronicled in these stories underscore the fact that the breakthrough leap is something that comes from individual people, not from organizations, and not from anything the organization does to those people. These individuals are not motivated by a specially designed environment or by techniques of management. The Silvers and Hounsfields and James Blacks are people deeply, individually driven, and they are—for some reason—instinctively unresponsive to the exhortations of executives. If, as a manager, you make the development of breakthroughs a corporate mission and begin to pontificate on your strategies to attain this objective, the creative people in your organization will immediately recognize you as the worst sort of pompous ass and will retire to their recreation rooms and garages to work on their ideas as far as possible from the cheerleading scrutiny of Big Brother and the holding company.

This may seem a dispiriting message for managers. If management cannot build an environment conducive to creative ferment, what is the point in examining breakthroughs? It's mostly a matter of luck, hoping that the right people in your organization happen to be thinking of the right things at the right time!

But there are in fact, management actions that have fostered breakthroughs. They happened at Montedison, Toyota, Raytheon, and several other of the breakthrough companies in this book. However, these actions fall more accurately in the realm of "responsiveness" rather than under the heading of "management." Commercial breakthroughs do not happen in a single explosive moment but proceed through a series of events—of smaller breakthroughs in concept, in technologies, in emotion, in organization, in the marketplace. There are no general rules for what happens. But it is clear that, as a breakthrough concept forms into something that consumers eventually will buy, there are both moments when traditional management can be terribly destructive and moments when responsive people in traditional management roles can save the concept from destroying itself.

When Robert Dee repeatedly "gave in" on the continued development of Tagamet at Smith Kline & French (SK&F), when Geoffrey Nicholson took up the cause of Post-it notes at 3M, when Italo Trapasso at Montedison became the savior of the new catalyst for polypropylene, it was an instance of a responsive manager accelerating a breakthrough that would have been in deep jeopardy without him. Each of these managers, in order to support the creative work that had already occurred, had to change the environment within the organization. And yet, before these managers were even aware of the potential breakthrough, the people who thought of the new idea in the first place, already had changed the environment dramatically.

The pattern is clear. Invariably, in a breakthrough, long before management has any idea of what's happening "down there," people start changing the system. They do it by themselves and they do it according to their own very specific vision. They do it because the normal flow of activity in an established organization allows neither the time nor flexibility to accomplish something really new; schedules are preset, personnel are preassigned, budgets are pre-established. For most creative people, the diversion of organizational flow is a matter of necessity, it is survival. These are people who learn the system mostly for the purpose of finding its weaknesses, perverting it for their own purposes. They find gaps in schedules, slush funds in budgets, and personnel who have interests compatible to theirs. They build benevolent conspiracies. They succeed because no environment, no matter how rigid it seems, is immutable.

These conspiracies are usually—and *best*—kept safely out of sight of management. A breakthrough concept, often only vaguely formed in the mind of an inventor like Godfrey Hounsfield, Percy Spencer, or Fred Smith, has a short life expectancy in an established structure where people, in order to move up, must constantly prove they are smarter than other people—where the easiest way to accomplish that is to attack ideas that are unfamiliar and unproven. Deviant notions are the cannon fodder of corporate ladder-climbing. As Smith said, a great corporate resume is usually assembled by someone who "knows all the reasons you *can't* do something."

Fortunately, organizational resistance to a new idea will not kill an idea if it is good and its originator believes in it. The worst it can do is uproot the idea and send it elsewhere seeking congenial soil—witness Sir James Black taking the idea for Tagamet from the unresponsive establishment at ICI to the Welwyn Research Institute, where an absentee landlord (SK&F) would not immediately subject his concept to analysis and watch him like a hawk.

The most important reason for original breakthrough people to conceal their actions from management is that they almost invariably have an idea that cannot be justified in terms of its potential market. The concept is something new, something no consumer has ever bought. And if no one has ever bought it, how do you know anybody is *going to buy it?* Creative forces within structured organizations eventually discover the Catch-22 of new product marketing: People can't buy it until we sell it, but we don't dare sell it until somebody has bought it.

This tautology has spawned one of the most popular myths of innovation lore: that new things are almost always created because the market is ready; the market cries out, and the innovator listens. This "market pull" theory applies nicely to the incremental innovation so well sustained at companies such as 3M. Everything new that you're going to make is similar to something old that you already make; and since people bought the old thing, they will be sure to buy the new thing, because it's better than the old thing.

However, almost always, a breakthrough does not *join* a market—*it gives birth to a market.* With no comparison to a *status quo,* a breakthrough cannot grow from a market perception. It grows, rather, from an itch.

The source of each breakthrough concept is a problem—an itch that its possessor cannot easily scratch. Breakthroughs are problems that certain people—someone, an individual—cannot shake. For thirty years Arthur Jones pondered the ultimate exercise machine, because he wasn't happy with his muscles. For forty years, Taiichi Ohno of Toyota sought harmony between human beings and automation, because he valued people more than the machines that seemed on the verge of defining life in their own image. For fifty years, Kenjiro Takayanagi pondered the passivity of television, because he wanted people to be free to make their own programs. Each breakthrough is finally, easily traceable to one human being, to one unscratchable itch, because nothing less than the irritation of a tireless, sleepless mind can sustain the pursuit of incomparable solution.

Always, the solution to the problem has little in common with the established order of things—whether that established order is Spencer Silver's 3M Corporation, or Richard L. Duke's scoffing community of Troy, Ohio. If people like Duke had taken the Establishment seriously—shared its ideals, values, and objectives unquestioningly—they would have perceived the folly of their ways; they would have acceded to the "wisdom" of the majority and squelched their search to scratch the itch. But the definition of a breakthrough person is that he does not take the Establishment seriously. For its own greater good, or what he perceives as its greater good, he begins insidiously to guide the organization in a different direction, toward the solution of a problem the organization is not particularly concerned about.

Inexorably, the stubborn, itchy, tenacious individual begins to force the system to respond to his needs. His conspiracy surfaces.

Finally the first distress of a breakthrough is experienced by the organization. The concept may already be years old, but there are no outward signs of this concept, of the conspiracy, until, from the point of view of the Establishment, things start to go wrong.

EMI, which was supposed to be a record company, found itself developing some sort of radiology machine, because Godfrey Hounsfield—this seemingly absentminded and compliant researcher—committed the company to an alliance with the British Department of Health and Human Services (DHHS).

Things start to go wrong.

Montedison, a conglomerate that had tacitly decided to phase out its research and development operations, found itself pumping money into a new polymer research program, because Paolo Galli, glib and brilliant and handsome, had challenged management to a race. "I can invent new technology faster than you can *buy* it. Just give me one year," he said "and a little money for test tubes . . . and other things."

Things start to go wrong.

SK&F agreed to support for a while the search for a new pharmaceutical response to gastric acid secretions, mainly because there was this compound that could be found "by Christmas." Two years and millions of dollars later, the guy who mentioned Christmas in the first place, James Black, was still working on that vaguely defined compound and he had lots of people involved in it with him. SK&F in Philadelphia said, "Okay, that's enough. Cut it out." And William Duncan, the manager of the project in England, said, "Okay, right away," and two more years later, James Black was still spending millions and he was still chasing that elusive compound.

The power of the organization to control its destiny is often dwarfed by the resourceful individual's power to rewrite the organization's destiny. Often, by the time the Establishment—and this can be a community like Troy, Ohio, or a coterie of experts like Arthur Jones's bodybuilding rivals—recognizes the behavior of the breakthrough individual as deviant from the norm, his project has assumed a dramatic momentum. SK&F, Montedison, EMI, and Fred Smith's throng of Federal Express investors had already been drawn into enormous financial risks by the time they realized what was going on. Without its knowledge, the saboteur took the organization *beyond the point of no return.*

When this happens, the organization finds itself wondering where this guy came from. It is a question born in crisis and frustration at the moment that the individual's "problem" becomes a problem for the organization. But in retrospect, when breakthroughs are studied, it is a question raised with longing. How does *our* organization find one of these special creative people? There is a myth among students of innovation that companies can go out searching for a certain creative type of person, a maverick who can shake an organization into thinking new thoughts and fathering innovations.

Almost always, the breakthrough person is not an outsider. Indeed, the best people at twisting the system to their own objectives are people who know the system through long experience. Perhaps the most benign example of this truth is Kozo Ohsone, the conservative production manager at Sony Corporation, who at first opposed the development of Walkman I because he thought—like a good doubting manager—that it would not sell. But when he was given the task of assembling a team for Walkman II, he knew he needed a variety of talents that did not fit the normal functions and demands of the organization. At once, he knew where to find his band of mavericks. Ohsone could not have imagined going outside

Sony for this talent; an outsider—no matter how gifted—wouldn't have known where to begin. Ohsone needed people who knew their way around.

By the time the Establishment discovers a breakthrough concept rumbling in its bowels, its originator has already found a way, searched out over time, to express the problem. If he has not reached this point, there is no breakthrough. There is not even a concept. If the problem can't be shared, it can't survive.

The sharing can only occur when the originator of the breakthrough concept makes an intuitive leap. He stops perceiving his problems in familiar terms and compares it to something outside the realm of the familiar, outside the terminology of his salaried profession. One of the characteristics of breakthroughs is the eclecticism of the people who discover, examine, and articulate the problem. "Specialization," as Arthur Jones so often intones, "is for insects." The breakthrough individual connects two unrelated planes of thought, relates them, and states the problem in a new way.

Hence, Godfrey Hounsfield intuitively compared pattern recognition to radiology, not to mathematics or alphabets, and envisioned the right way to take pictures inside the human body.

At Toyota, Taiichi Ohno's instinctive perception for the ideal automotive assembly was not the automobile technology of Henry Ford, but the automatic looms of Sakichi Toyoda. Federal Express's forebear was not UPS, but Vietnam; and Nautilus overcame the bondage of chains and pulleys when Arthur Jones envisioned seashells.

John Wright encountered the ChemLawn breakthrough while loading sod onto a pickup truck with Paul Duke and his talkative son, Dick. The designer of Walkman, Mitsuro Ida, said the bathroom is one of his favorite places to mull new ideas. And Arthur Jones found the key to the Nautilus machine in the midst of a bout of insomnia. Often intuition is so intensely personal that it cannot break through except within the one person who saw the problem first and then struggled with it ceaselessly. Edison's caveat holds true for all workable inventions, for all breakthroughs. A new concept cannot proceed toward its realization as a product of the mind and hand until "all parts of the system [are] constructed to reference to all other parts." The creator cannot begin until he perceives the whole in its finished form. He need not perceive in one blinding flash all the solutions to all the problems along the way, but he must foresee the problems and he must harbor, in his mind's eye, a vision of his triumph.

One of the most frequently repeated characterizations of break-through originators, communicated as we conducted this research, is contained in statements like these: "He could see what was going to happen before it happened. He was always a few steps ahead of everybody else." It's a description that was volunteered, often redundantly, in separate interviews—about Kenjiro Takayanagi, the "grand old man" of JVC; Dick Duke at ChemLawn; Kozo Ohsone and Akio Morita at Sony; Godfrey Hounsfield at EMI; Percy Spencer at Raytheon; George Foerstner at Amana; Sir James Black at SK&F; Bill Bowerman at Nike; Arthur Jones at Nautilus; Taiichi Ohno at Toyota; and Fred Smith at Federal Express.

The vision to see ahead, the intuitive leap that gives birth to an elegant concept, is individual and rarely diagrammable. Sir James Black, who is not a chemist, had to convey in word pictures to the chemists who worked for him his vision of an H_2 compound. His vision was so clear and articulate, as it turned out, that the right compound was among the first six that the chemists formed from Black's description.

There is no more pure concept than Taiichi Ohno's vision of what became the Toyota Production System. He began with an image of life itself—with the belief that a well-lived life is one in which the experience of the past and the promise of the future are combined by human intelligence into a timeless whole, each experience capable of touching every other experience, with all the combinations leading toward an understanding, a vision of the future. To translate this "philosophy" to a factory that makes cars would seem an impossible, an almost absurd dream. Yet, because the vision was clear and so insistent within him, Ohno applied to its consummation a spirit, patience, and tenacity that was almost unearthly. And when the system was in place, it seemed to those people immersed in it—who would have thought it crazy if Ohno had ever *explained* it to them—the only way to do things.

Emotion is a key element in every breakthrough. Beginning with that itch and proceeding to an intellectual fascination, the problem becomes an emotional focus for the breakthrough individual. Sometimes, as with Spence Silver, that emotion is subdued and patient; but remember that subdued or not, Silver kept hammering relentlessly at 3M with his functionless adhesive for five years, every chance he got. More often, the emotion of the breakthrough individual is a raging cauldron—often driven by the urge to triumph over a doubting world, to "show 'em that I'm right and they're wrong."

The creator of the concept, when he finally reaches out for *help,* conveys his emotion, along with the expression of his concept, to other people. Sometimes the team that forms consists solely of a man and his family—as with Arthur Jones, initially hobbled in his breakthrough by not embracing enough people. Sometimes the team is an industrial research organization standing alone against the flow of the corporate mainstream, as with the Welwyn Research Institute and the Ferrara Research Center. Sometimes the team is a handful of new people thrown together by common interests and pure chance to form a new enterprise, as with ChemLawn, Federal Express, and Nike.

Always, the members of the team *feel* an affinity for this new idea. It is a concept that fits a gap in their knowledge that kept echoing, nagging at them; it answers a question that had always lurked, unspoken, in their minds: "Why can't things be like this?" Before anything else happens to drive a breakthrough, the emotion of the originator is the thing that passes first from one person to another. Technology development, resources and equipment, even understanding of the concept—all these things come later. The *feeling* is the baton.

Emotion, of course, is not enough. If what brings the breakthrough team together is emotion, what sustains their energy is a body of extraordinary knowledge, which they as a group possess. It is knowledge that separates them from other people, makes them special. The leaders who originated breakthroughs were able to convey them and give them fresh life through the formation of a deeply committed team. If the leader had not been able to articulate that concept vividly, it would have been trapped impotently in the seething prison of his mind.

Eventually, every breakthrough originator needed help. To get people to help him, he had to teach. Sometimes he was a great natural teacher, like Bill Bowerman or Taiichi Ohno. Sometimes he was a crusty, reluctant teacher, like James Black. But whatever this breakthrough teacher's style, his subject matter contained a hypnotic eloquence and a symmetry that was self-evident. And the voice of the master was irresistible.

The breakthrough leader conveys to his "apostles" not just knowledge, but values, a philosophy, a mission and—usually—*compassion* for the people with whom he pursues the goal. The apostles admire the leader because they are in it together—in conspiracy, in danger—and because he has worked intensely to share the knowledge that will help them all transcend the danger. Because of what they know, they have the unity and strength to get to a better place together.

When Shizuo Takano stood before his young engineers at JVC and asked them if they would "commit suicide" with him (see chapter 2), he already knew their response. He had taught them the rightness of their idea and had instilled in them the emotion of his commitment. But also he had demonstrated to them that JVC had designed a product more complete and more sophisticated than anyone else's. They believed they were *the best*. Takano was the second generation of this faith. He had received his mission from a mentor, Kenjiro Takayanagi, and from Takayanagi he had learned the skills of the *sensei*—when to teach, when to challenge, when to trust your pupils to teach themselves.

When breakthroughs happen, then, the core team is no larger than the handful of pupils who once followed Socrates. There can be no more members of the core team than the leader can know intimately. Because intimacy is important, there is, as Fred Smith noted, a "grow your own" characteristic on the team. That's why outsiders are rarely sought. Even John Powell, who arrived late at EMI to launch the CT scanner into a marketplace large beyond the inventor's wildest dreams, was never wholly embraced by Godfrey Hounsfield and his loyal handful of clinicians.

Once the team is formed, there is a difference between the team and the larger, established organization that never will be reconciled.

In Troy, Ohio, Richard L. Duke had a reputation and a role in the community. He believed himself far greater than the limits assigned to him by the conditioned perceptions of the community. Part of the mission he carried out when he created ChemLawn was to free his followers from the preconceptions of an establishment that saw them not as people, but as roles or functions.

Duke was a typical breakthroughs leader, expressing through the creation of his team a faith that people could attain far more than seemed possible. Dick Duke's apostles at ChemLawn still marvel at themselves, wondering how they could have risen from such humble beginnings to such triumph. Similarly, Philip Knight's jocks at Nike laughed at their own origins, referring to themselves as "park bench material." Breakthrough leaders, who are also teachers, believe, almost arrogantly, that any group of people they assemble will contain the innate talent to attain anything, to keep the baton moving, the emotion burning, to the end!

Though they begin in individual problem-solvers who rage against their itch until they invent a way to scratch it, commercial breakthroughs are not, in the end, individual attainments. James Black would still have had a great moment in science when he found the first faint H_2 antagonist at Welwyn Research Institute. But it was his team, staying in the lab after he had left, and SK&F, the corporation, that turned Tagamet into the biggest prescription drug of all time. Like the baton, breakthroughs pass from person to person. The emotion rejuvenates and assumes new shapes in different people who lend to the task different talents, different inclinations.

A breakthrough is like a work of art, formed in the artist's mind, sketched by the artist's hand, but often made by others. A prime example of the parallel between realizing an art work and a breakthrough is the creation of Henri Matisse's masterpiece "The Snail."

In 1953 the French painter was less than a year from his death. He had been ill, bed-ridden, and unable to work at an easel for five years. But, even at the age of eighty-four, the restless vision of his art was still active in his mind. He had been studying and sketching the form of a snail's shell. However, when he had formed the image of a painting, he could not stand up to paint it, he could not lift his arms to put brush to canvas. But Matisse had all that he needed to create his masterpiece; he placed his vision in the hands of his pupils.

"The Snail," one of Matisse's last paintings, was "constructed" at the Regina Hotel in Nice. Matisse painted large sheets of paper in bright colors. These he cut into panels and gave to his pupils. Then, directing his pupils from his bed, Matisse composed the immense montage that made up "The Snail." His pupils patiently moved the panels on the great canvas, conferred with him on the positioning of the panels and the harmony of colors, moved them again until Matisse was satisfied, marked the position of each panel when

Matisse was finally sure of its placement, and then—when "The Snail" was finished—made a meticulous tracing of the painting so that they could reproduce it perfectly if it met a mishap on its trip to Paris.

"The Snail," now in the collection of the Tate Gallery in London, is a rare example of a work of art whose concept and completion were achieved by different people sharing a single vision. The pupils of Matisse were sustained by their relationship—even in anonymity—to an exceptional mentor, by the changes that he instilled in their perceptions, in their careers.

The pupils of Taiichi Ohno, of Arthur Jones, and Fred Smith also became different. Their commitment to a special course has separated them irreversibly from other corporate citizens. The original team at Federal Express, the confederates of Fred Smith, all have departed the more orderly Federal Express of today; and they all convey a wistful hindsight, a yearning to return to those good old days. The "apostles of Mr. Ohno" at Toyota set themselves unconsciously apart from those who learned the Toyota Production System without knowing the *sensei* himself.

Clearly, the members of breakthrough teams in these stories were not just followers. They were assembled with the leader's expectation that they might have to carry on in his absence, and they frequently did. Something even deeper than the charisma of the mentor was the sustaining force that kept them striving toward the final breakthrough. The baton too often passed so far from the originator that his presence in the final breakthrough was barely evident. This was true at Nike, with Bill Bowerman hidden in the background while Philip Knight assumed the mantle and the burden of creating the masterpiece. This was true at Welwyn, when James Black changed laboratories. Percy Spencer had long before the final victory turned microwave ovens over to other baton carriers at Raytheon, and Spenser Silver, who devised the adhesive that made the Post-it Note Pad possible, was neither a teacher nor an entrepreneur.

The question then is, what do people continue to believe in if the mentor slips away?

In so many breakthroughs, even though the team members make a commitment to an individual, they quit needing the leader. The emotion becomes unquenchable; the baton is transferable. This does not happen because the team is committed to the concept itself above all. They believe in the concept, they enjoy it, and they foresee its greatness, but they don't seek ownership of the concept. They assign the triumph to the individual who gave it birth. These are people in whom humility is a giant strength. Their humility is a greater force than the ego of the teacher—because they are capable of handling the details that frustrate the teacher. Matisse couldn't tack up the squares of color. But his students, excited at being a part of greatness, did it lovingly, perfectly, passionately.

Humble though they are, these people don't keep pushing on, even in the absence of the leaders, because they love the company for which they work. These are people who have spent too much time bucking the Establishment to suddenly reverse their feelings and embrace the corporate functionaries and doubting traditionalists who have thrown so many obstacles into their path.

Their commitment, in the homestretch, is to each other. The key to sustaining the breakthrough, in almost every case, was *a sense of mutual responsibility*. The people grew near to each other as the project moved forward. They understood not only their own work and sacrifice, but that of everybody else. They valued each person's effort with equal intensity. The team became a team because they felt more deeply about each other than they felt about the concept, the company, even their mentor. Each person felt he would be letting down everyone else if he failed to do his part.

Hence, those passionate couriers at Federal Express. Hence, Henry Wendt's overstated anxiety about opening that desk drawer and carrying out a rationing plan for Tagamet.

It was because of this sense of mutual responsibility that ChemLawn's lawn care specialists never needed a supervisor to keep them working until the sun had gone down and the neighborhoods of Dayton and Columbus were dark. Mutual responsibility kept those lonesome Nike representatives speeding from field to field with cars full of shoes. Mutual responsibility explains the tirelessness of Kenji Sano and his Walkman II production crew. It explains that desperate door-to-door market test for Post-it Note Pads in Richmond by Joe Ramey and Geoff Nicholson. Ramey said that he went to Richmond not for the sake of making a breakthrough, but because he felt for the people who had worked so hard on Post-it notes. And compassion is why an entire roomful of young JVC engineers put their careers on the line for Shizuo Takano, Yuma Shiraishi, and the VHS format that had become their obsession.

In every breakthrough, the team carried on because of one another, because they cared more for one another than anything else.

If all these things that seem to characterize breakthroughs are true, then the message seems to be that in many cases the best thing that can happen to a new idea is that management doesn't notice it until it is too late for management to kill it. It seems true, in many cases, that the only role management can play without confusing the development of a new idea is to stand by and observe. Managers do not normally fit into the bumptious subculture that generates—without much discrimination—crackpot notions and brilliant breakthroughs.

But as defiant as many of these breakthroughs were, there were still true managers who handled the baton without dropping it—Kozo Ohsone, the production manager of Walkman II at Sony; the redoubtable Charles Adams, who nursed the microwave oven through fifteen profitless years at Raytheon.

None of these "breakthrough managers" sought or *fostered* innovation as a policy of practice. They were competent corporate citizens who did what good managers do. They kept the stated interests and agenda of the organization foremost in their responsibilities. Remember that Geoff Nicholson at 3M gave new life to the Post-it venture team within a company-sanctioned, fully funded research and development program; Nicholson was not a maverick setting up an innovation laboratory in the cellar. In fact, a manager who starts trying to stir up breakthroughs by hiring "unusual," "creative" people, setting off little cells of creative ferment and using the word *bootleg* a great deal, is more than likely to waste a lot of money, run around in circles, and discourage a lot of creative people who were there all the time but didn't get invited to the party.

People like Charles Adams and Kozo Ohsone, however, were more than just loyal to their organizations. They were students of their workers. Adams challenged Percy Spencer about the bizarre presence of Bud Haagensen, a porcupine in the Raytheon chicken coop. When Spencer replied, "He's worth it," Adams remembered henceforth to see people in terms other than their appearance and their job descriptions. Kozo Ohsone selected the Walkman team from a storehouse of individual personnel profiles that were stored in his memory; he *saved* all the impressions he had gathered over years of observation. He knew his people, and he understood knowing his people was as important as knowing his responsibilities to the company.

If there is an aspect of "breakthrough managers" like Ohsone or Adams or Henry Wendt that deviates from the conventional outlook of the organization, it is the measure of trust that they conveyed to their people. It was their willingness to trust, more than anything else, that made them worthy carriers of the baton.

None of the managers who became directly involved in breakthrough teams deviated from the corporation's goals until the team had established a direction different from the direction of the company. A few of those people who seemed to have managed breakthroughs—for example, William Duncan at SK&F—were team members from an early point in the project, and in their case, they simply *pretended* to foster the goals of the corporation while pouring their full energy into the conspiracy. But even in doing that—in changing the corporation's agenda—they acted on the company's behalf, like Duncan's presuming he was in a better position than the executives in Philadelphia to know what really was good for SK&F.

When successful breakthrough managers finally stepped in and involved themselves in a project that was already well advanced, their role was to serve as "sword and shield." They shielded the team, and fenced with the Establishment. Perhaps the most distinctive characteristic of these managers who helped breakthroughs was their humility. They employed their status within the company only when they dealt with senior management. Within the team, they were no better than anyone else. They became the pupils of the breakthrough mentor and served the project as humbly as everyone else. They didn't try to take possession of the idea, even though they had the power to do so. They knew that if they tried to pull rank, they might well kill the spirit of the team, and thus the possibility of a breakthrough.

Italo Trapasso stated the only effective philosophy for a breakthrough manager when he said, "I was kind of a servant to them. I was their assistant."

A manager can't *make* a new idea spring up within the organization. He cannot create the creative team. Like saboteurs, creative people hatch their own plots and form their own little cells. A manager can't control it; he can only help. This is why knowing your people enough to trust them is so important. Breakthroughs have no formula. It's possible, as we have done, to find the elements of intellect, inspiration, and emotion within an individual and a team that keep an unconventional idea alive and moving toward a potential breakthrough. But there isn't a process. You can't buy a *Field Guide to Native Breakthroughs* and wait for one to perch outside your laboratory window. Each breakthrough follows the pace, energy, enthusiasm, and work rhythms of the people involved, and it responds to the complexity of the problem that has come to obsess those people.

A manager who has come to know his people well can discern when they are just fooling around with an interesting notion and when they have seized upon an exceptional concept. And when a manager recognizes the moment—as Henry Wendt and Robert Dee did at SK&F, as Charles Adams did at Raytheon—then he changes his role from devil's advocate to advocate. It's time for the manager to stop spouting the Establishment's line and begin to change the Establishment to accommodate the emergence of the breakthrough.

Geoff Nicholson, at 3M, saw the moment and made himself into a vital "servant" of a breakthrough that had grown from the thankless diligence of Spence Silver and Arthur Fry. Italo Trapasso, at Montedison, was an impressive sword and shield. He shielded the Ferrara Research Center passionately and, using his sword, restructured an entire division so that it followed the lead created by the Research Center. In Paolo Galli, Trapasso even cultivated a successor to his position as wielder of sword and shield. Adams, at Raytheon, played sword and shield by exerting the influence invested in an executive vice-president to assure that the fragile lifelines to the microwave oven were never threatened. And when microwave oven development needed his sword, he extended it as far outward from Raytheon as Iowa and Japan.

John Powell wielded his sword to take the CT scanner breakthrough into a commercial arena unimagined by its inventor, shattering the humble parochialism of Godfrey Hounsfield, EMI, and the gang of doctors at DHSS. Robert Dee and Henry Wendt at SK&F did it spectacularly, rousing a sleeping organization into an international marketing battleship that then had to sit in the dock, hopefully waiting for its pharmaceutical ammo.

But let's face it. These were lucky people. A manager doesn't get many chances to play sword and shield to a commercial breakthrough. It's a responsibility for which most managers are neither trained nor inclined. This is one of the reasons why so many breakthroughs—at Nike, Nautilus, ChemLawn, and JVC—happened without the aid or intervention of any of the members of what Fred Smith calls the "managerial class." The sort of people who make breakthroughs are so driven, so abrasively self-sufficient that if you hesitate to help them, they'll just go right past you. And they'll find someone else to help. Or they'll say, "Never mind. I'll do it myself."

For every group of people or organization that experiences one, a breakthrough becomes the most exciting event of a lifetime. But even though it eventually spreads and expands to affect the entire organization, and becomes a pervasive element in society, remarkably few people are really involved in it at the beginning—when excitement is in the air and danger is a stimulant in the blood. For those who get the chance to be involved, the baton is only stretched out to them for an instant. If they drop it or refuse it, the race flies past them and never comes around to them again.

But perhaps the players who seize the chance and run the race are not so lucky either. The excitement of that one great race often leaves them with a lifetime of remembering "the best of times" or wondering if they will ever itch again.

In these stories, even when the thrill was gone, something lasting remained with those who lived through the experience of a commercial breakthrough. It is something more substantial than the wealth that enriches people beyond their brightest expectations, more significant than the social impact of a potpourri of pervasive products, services, and industrial processes such as emerged between 1960 and 1985.

For the people who spent the years of deep involvement that eventually brought them and a lot of hangers-on to the mother lode of a commercial breakthrough, the experience of a common feeling is almost universal. It is a feeling incongruous with corporations and with commerce. They were people, on their respective teams, who redefined the meaning of *responsibility*. For them, the definition of responsibility became not a matter of taking the blame, but taking care of each other.

This shouldn't be a revelation. It shouldn't be nostalgia for a privileged few. Taking care of each other shouldn't need a commercial breakthrough to make it worth the trouble.

Index

A

Abbink, Opal Duke. *See* Duke, Opal
Accent, 4
Adams, Charles F., 180–81, 186–89, 193, 196, 201, 203–7, 357, 358, 359
Adidas, 236, 243, 245, 248, 249, 252, 254–55
Acrospace Advance Planning Group (AAPG), 323, 324, 326, 327, 337
Agranulocytosis, 120–21, 122
Air Cargo Deregulation Act, 336
Allstate Insurance, 330
Ally, Carl, 337, 338
Amana Refrigeration, Inc., 6, 14, 180–81, 192–202, 267, 344–45
Ambrose, Dr. James, 159–61, 164–66, 171, 175–76
American Airlines, 319
Ampex Corporation, 25–26, 49
Anderson, Charles E., 25
Anderson, Glenn, 335–36
Anderson, Jon, 251
Andon, 220, 222
Antihistamine, 107

Archer-Daniels Midland, Inc. (ADM), 57, 58
Arkansas Aviation Sales, Inc., 322
Art of Creation, The, 18
Athletic footwear, 6, 236–59. *See also* Nike, Inc.
Athletics West, 255
Atkinson Morley's Hospital (Wimbledon, England), 160, 164, 166–68, 170, 172
Automobile industry, 208–35. *See also* Toyota Motor Works

B

Bank of America, 330
Barbe, Camillo, 296, 307, 312
Bartel, Dean L., 193n
Bass, Arthur, 316–17, 323, 325, 334, 336, 341
Beaming, 154–55
Bell Laboratories, 19, 132, 187
Benjamin, David, 6
Beta blockers, 103–4, 107–8
Betamax (Sony), 26, 28, 36–38, 39–40, 43, 45, 46, 48, 206